JAMES DEAN
THE MUTANT KING

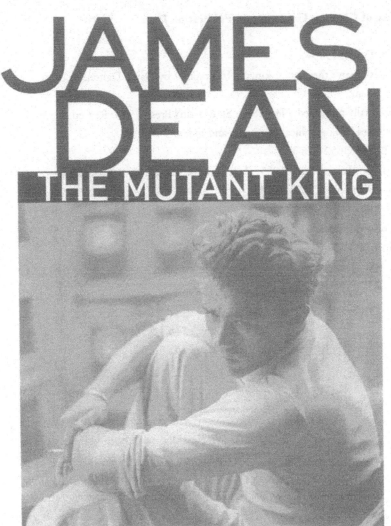

A BIOGRAPHY

David Dalton

CHICAGO REVIEW PRESS

An A Cappella Book

Library of Congress Cataloging-in-Publication Data

Dalton, David, 1945–
    James Dean : the mutant king : a biography / by David Dalton.
        p. cm.
    Originally published: New York : St. Martin's Press, 1983. Rev. ed.
    Includes bibliographical references and index.
    ISBN 1-55652-398-X
    1. Dean, James, 1931–1955. 2. Motion picture actors and actresses—United
States—Biography. I. Title.

PN2287.D33 D3 2001
791.43′028′092—dc21
[B]   2001035068

For B. A. M.

Cover design: Rattray Design
Cover photo: Roy Schatt
            TM/© 2001 James Dean, Inc. License authorized by CMG Worldwide,
            Indianapolis, Indiana, 46256 USA www.cmgww.com

FSC
Mixed Sources
Product group from well-managed
forests and other controlled sources
Cert no. SW-COC-002283
www.fsc.org

Contents

Acknowledgments

I am grateful to all the fans who wrote to me about Jimmy for this new edition: Bob Rees, Allen Abshier, David K. Bunton, Thomas Crown, Tom Fagan, Sharon Hauser, Elizabeth Milo, Larry F. Minor, and, for coordinating all this correspondence, Sylvia Bongiovanni.

I want to thank Antonia for her elliptical insights, Tina L'Hotsky, Valerie Boyd, Sylvia Price (for her scholarly advice), Steve Yaeger for the discography, and David Loehr—the dean of Deanology—for updating the bibliography.

To Carol Mann, my agent with the patience of Juno, to Bob Miller, my editor and inspiration, and to Diane Mancher who brought us all together, my unspeakable thanks. And not forgetting Sara Jones and Richard Sassin for resembling themselves so uncannily. Lastly—but first in my debt and affections—my collaborator and spirit guide, the tireless, winged Coco Pekelis of the keen eye and wry ruthless wit, the *primum mobile* of this new edition.

Introduction to revised edition

The violent psychodramatics of James Dean's performance in *East of Eden* still reverberate in those who worked with him. Twenty years after he played Aron to Jimmy's Cal, Dick Davalos seemed unable to shake off the effects of his contact with Jimmy. In 1973, after interviewing Davalos for *The Mutant King*, I casually walked him to his car. With terrifying suddenness he turned and shouted at the top of his voice: "YOU FINISHED?" You could hear the Japanese gardeners all along Mulholland Drive dropping their rakes and, stunned by his outburst, I wondered what I could have said to provoke such unfathomable rage. It was only later that I realized it was a *line* from *East of Eden*, and Davalos was still playing Aron; two decades later, he was still delivering that line with the same suppressed fury he'd unleashed on James Dean before Jimmy knocked him to the ground. What a blow that phantom dealt him!

There is something unnerving about the kind of force Jimmy could magnetize in his roles; not only do they seem "more real than real life," but they carry on an unconstrained life of their own, *especially* after death. This is, I suppose, just what ghosts are, and if James Dean is the Incubus Disincarnate of them all, a colossal CinemaScope spook, it is Jimmy's *own* terror that Davalos dreads. It's as Tacitus said of avenging spirits: "They terrify lest they should fear."

"Possession," says William Burroughs, "is the basic fear. There is nothing one fears more or is more ashamed of than not being oneself." And there *is* something absolutely hair-raising about the reckless manner in which Jimmy abandoned himself to the roles he played, embracing them all with the urgency and desperation of a lover in an autoerotic embrace. He took possession of them almost animistically, yet it was he who was to be haunted by *them*, never to be released from their jealous grasp.

James Dean's identification with his characters was total. The density of link between motivation and action was complete. And self-incorporation and implicit identification became precisely the criteria for the new star. Adolescents, like actors, haven't quite decided who to be (at least not who to be *forever*), and to "play" oneself, to put oneself on as an Other is the teenager's favorite form of recreation. Jimmy didn't only play himself, he played *us* as well.

As the exasperated child of self-deluded parents in *Rebel Without A Cause*, James Dean defined himself as the future constituent of a new community. Dissolving the myth of maturity in a solution of wishes and dreams, *Rebel* became a primary text in the creation of perpetual adolescence. By suggesting that teenagers can create their own surrogate family and, by extension, an adolescent society, *Rebel* set in motion the idea of a youth culture, and James Dean became *the* Totem of Teen—a rallying point for fans who can identify each other by their protective (and provocative) coloration: blue jeans, red jackets, boots, pentecostal hair, or just plain *attitude*.

In the United States alone, a year after his death, there were four million dues-paying members of the James Dean Memory Ring and other posthumous clubs devoted to him. Not an exclusive group, exactly, but the very size of his constituency was a statement in itself, and merged with rock 'n' roll for the next phase of the Teen Dream: it was okay to be a teenager, especially an alienated, vulnerable, potentially irruptive one. Teen was now the consummate state; the stigma of adolescence became its stigmata, a sign of grace. Jimmy insisted in every gesture on the unassailable desirability of the adolescent state. He had freed the slaves, and the pubescent beast was, for better or worse, unleashed on the world.

In the beginning was *East of Eden* and the teenage Cain it harbored in its widescreen bosom. By 1956, it was too late to speculate on whether it was a good idea or not. It just *was*, and no amount of moralizing would be able to do anything about it. The infinite suggestibility of James Dean's image baptised almost any adolescent pose as long as it exhibited, in some way, an allegiance to adolescent revolt, frustration, self-assertion, alienation, or any manner of torment brought on by the above. King Elvis literally took James Dean as his acting model (although one can hardly hold Jimmy responsible for *this*), paying homage, on bended knee, to Nick Ray, *Rebel*'s director, in the Warner Brothers canteen. *Elvis* liked to be called "the James Dean of rock 'n' roll"! Just as Frank Sinatra successfully (if ironically) based the sensitively nuanced macho of his acting style on Montgomery Clift, Elvis shamelessly attempts to duplicate a scene from *Rebel* (where

Jimmy confronts his father) in *King Creole*. The scriptwriters, Herbert Baker and Michael Vincente Gazzo, were specifically asked by the producer, Hal Wallis, to make their adaptation (from Harold Robbins's *A Stone for Danny Fisher*) as close to *Rebel* as possible, so that the parallel between Elvis and Dean would be unmistakable to young audiences.

Then there are his androgynous progeny—Mick Jagger, David Bowie, Jackie Curtis. Jimmy opened up a new range of permissable behavior for men. It was, Jimmy said so, all right to be sensitive. Or macho. Or both. And you could take yourself anywhere as James Dean. Which is more than you could say for Elvis or Brando, who were too unwieldy and theatrical to fit comfortably in your average suburban living room. Although he is often given the epithet "the first rock star," Jimmy's spastic bongomania and baseball mitt guitar playing during *Giant*—so awful that Chill Wills ended up smashing a guitar over his head!—could qualify him as the first punk star, on the basis of aggressive amateurism. There is a line of descent there, anyway, from James Dean, the John the Baptist of Pop, to that self-lacerating Monk of Punk, Sid Vicious. James Dean preceded rock 'n' roll, and may actually end up outliving it.

I stopped writing this book in the spring of 1974, but, bitten by the bug of biographomania and unrepentant idolatry—a chronic condition that Macauly called *Lues Boswelliana*—it has not stopped writing itself. James Dean's hypnotic image has grown in power in the nearly ten years since *The Mutant King* was first published, due in part, no doubt, to rather poor standards in the production of heroic mettle during the seventies.

More than any time since the fifties, James Dean now represents *the* coherent icon of our time. He is an American object whose nature is condensed energy, an objectification of attitudes simple and immediate enough to become a brand whose implicit value, like the Coke bottle, is reinforced through repetition.

In Tokyo today there are dozens of James Dean jigsaw puzzles and "quality" shopping bags with laminated photographs of *him*, some printed on denim, others like miniature sacks with rivet stitching, and most with some worshipful inscription, in solid-state instructioneze: "IT IS FACT JAMES DEAN PLAYED ROLES OF THREE." In these tote bags, Japanese punks reverently carry their fifties costumes and Chuck Berry tapes to the park on weekends.

Among the artifacts you can still find in France are a James Dean pencil case, and a James Dean piggy bank (very Cal Trask!) with a profile of Jimmy from *East of Eden* bearing the motto: "Only made three movies and lives on in our hearts forever."

In the eighties, Levi Strauss made a series of commercials using James Dean lookalikes. The cast and crew went down to Marfa, Texas (where *Giant* was filmed) to shoot the first commercial in front of the old Reata mansion facade, apparently not realizing it had crumbled long ago and had been hauled away in pieces by fans. Substituting a building that resembled it as closely as possible, one of the commercials features an actress wearing a cowboy hat and Levi jeans, with her boots up in an antique Rolls Royce convertible—imitating the classic James Dean pose in *Giant*. In France, Jimmy's image is so culturally associated with blue jeans that a huge billboard outside Paris uses only his *face* to advertise Levi jeans.

Then there are the real pieces of the true cross. "My prize Dean memorabilia," writes a member of the James Dean Memory Ring, "includes a chunk of plaster from the set of Reata used in *Giant*. Also I have one of the fence posts Dean walked past while 'marking off the land' in the same film."

This fetishism is echoed in Robert Altman's play and movie of the same name, *Come Back to the Five and Dime, Jimmy Dean, Jimmy Dean*, in which a fan (played by Sandy Dennis) treasures a fragment of gingerbread molding from the Reata mansion as a sacred memory of the part she played as an extra in the crowd scenes of *Giant*.

In 1977, on the twenty-second anniversary of his death, a memorial was dedicated to Jimmy a mile from the site of his fatal crash on Highway 46. The stainless steel monument surrounds a tree of heaven outside the Cholame, California post office, mirroring the bend in the road where Jimmy died. It was erected by a Tokyo businessman, Seito Ohnishi, who became a James Dean fan after seeing *East of Eden*.

When I first visited James Dean's hometown of Fairmount, Indiana in 1973, there were no postcards of Jimmy in the drugstore, no souvenir ashtrays, and no plaques in the high school auditorium. You could still get a memorial placemat—on request—from Dot's Restaurant and Party House, and there were still copies of the Fairmount *News* commemorative issue. But the townspeople seemed ill at ease talking about their most famous son. What was there to say, after all, anymore? Behind this was a Quaker suspicion of idolatry, fame, and fortune; a down-to-earth philosophy that seemed to them confirmed by Jimmy's fate. Jimmy had tried to be "better than" them, to transcend his background, but, in the end, it was to them he was returned. Sacrificing his life for his way of life was a gesture so extreme that it virtually negated his success for them.

In 1980 (twenty-five years after Jimmy had been laid to rest in Fairmount's Park Cemetery), his hometown, after a long hiatus, agreed to honor the Silver Anniversary of Jimmy's death with a four-day festival, which has now become an annual event. Fairmount's tribute to Jimmy included a rock lasso contest, church services, and a "Grand Old Opry" show featuring Elvis Presley's former drummer, D. J. Fontana. Lee Strasberg and Martin Sheen joined other celebrities on the memorial committee. Sheen, who paid his tribute to James Dean with the role of Charles Starkweather (who also modeled himself on Jimmy) in *Badlands*, donated a bronze plaque to the local high school, and dedicated a bronze star at the site of Jimmy's birthplace in nearby Marion. Sheen also spoke at Jimmy's grave: "Jim Dean and Elvis were the spokesmen for an entire generation. When I was in acting school in New York years ago, there was a saying that if Marlon Brando changed the way people acted, then James Dean changed the way people lived."

Sara Jones, the feisty agent in the punk movie *Smithereens!*, visited Fairmount's museum during last year's festival: "The museum is crowded with artifacts. They plan on moving to a house around the corner by next festival. Encased in glass are the black cowboy boots Jimmy wore in *Giant*. Glass cases surround many Dean artifacts, including trophies won in car races in Palm Springs in 1955, three first place and one second place. Under a photo of Jim in his favorite shirt, a white cotton polo with red stripes, is the actual shirt. There are photos of Jim—from his last visit home—at the Sweetheart Ball. Photos of his bedroom on the farm, high school team photos, his graduation picture, a photo of his mother, all are on display. Jimmy's bongo drum is there, and high school team shirts. There is also a signed plaster cast of the hand and footprints that Jim made as a child in the cement floor of the barn. Here is the life mask used in *Giant* to design his aging makeup. All personal objects from Fairmount's favorite son."

Only the most crystal images survive from incidents in Jimmy's childhood: a theater made from a cardboard box, with dolls as actors; Jimmy accompanying his mother's coffin on the train, slipping a note with a wish under her pillow in the funeral home—"the wishing game." Lacking the obligatory detail, these precarious images resemble motifs from folklore. They've become frozen, perhaps, because survivors have repeated the same stories so many times or because, for many, it's simply too personal a tale.

Jimmy's father, Winton, lives in constant terror of the Dean Cult. Relentlessly pursued by the ghost of his son, whenever fans or journalists discover his whereabouts, he simply packs up and leaves.

There are those who believe that Jimmy, having survived the crash, lives among us. The most ingenious theory came from Jackie Curtis, who believed that Andy Warhol *was* James Dean (this would account for the wig and the complexion). In the years following his death, Warner Brothers received thousands of letters addressed to a living James Dean. The star as mythical creature—substitute for saints, kings, heroes, gods even—is already a species of living dead.

Of course, I, too, believe James Dean lives. But where? For one horrible moment I thought I'd found out. And the choice would have been typical of Jimmy: a seedy, rundown hotel near Times Square. In 1973, I checked into the Iroquois Hotel on 45th Street (where Jimmy shared a room with Bill Bast in the summer of 1952) to get the feel of Jimmy's early days in New York. The desk clerk knew the number of the room James Dean had lived in: "802. That's the one they always ask for," he said. The hotel wasn't exactly booked up, so I took his word for it. One night I was sitting in the bathtub when the overhead light suddenly went out. I reached up to turn on the fluorescent light by the side of the medicine cabinet and got such an incredible jolt of electricity that I assumed *I* was dead. "Oh my God, it's him," I thought in that split second. "He's still living here!" Of course, having checked in permanently to the Hotel James Dean, I wouldn't be in any condition to tell anyone of his whereabouts or, for that matter, finish this book. Which, it later occurred to me, might have crossed Jimmy's mind, too. He always was a practical joker.

If James Dean was "a way of life" as much as he was a star, his violent way of death continues to provide the pretext for ghoulish teen introspection about life beyond the grave, communication with spirits, and, of course, about one's own very sad, if remote, demise. Just the sort of sentimental morbidity that teenagers, who can afford this sort of thing, have always found quite irresistible. But morbidity is only the first stage of the initiate. It's just a short step from unenlightened grief to a refusal to believe in the hero's death. The death of superhumans is always suspicious to the faithful, in any case, since they believe that their idols are immortal to begin with.

In 1978, Sylvia Bongiovanni co-founded We Remember Dean International (the only authentic James Dean fan club since the James Dean Memory Ring) which issues a monthly newsletter containing comments by fans, Dean memorabilia, where-to-find-its such as TV sound tracks, photocopied articles, drawings, cartoons, photographs, interviews, and such trivia as a "MINI-REBEL QUIZ: What was Judy's phone number?????"

Yet, despite pilgrimages, fan clubs, revered relics, biographies, and communications with the Departed Dean, we ultimately have to accept that we will never know Jimmy. The further we get from his time, the more frozen he becomes, the more impossible it becomes to extract him from his myth. More and more, we receive the myth of James Dean as the most complete, consumable story. Myths, as capsules of eternal forms, proceed into history in that most indelible state of all—the star state.

Stardom gave an indestructible aspect to "James Dean," but it was the deceptive ordinariness of his creation and the very casualness with which he adopted it that made him so believable and effective. There is an averageness, an almost statistical norm, a boy-next-doorness about his acausal delinquent, and almost as much of Tom Sawyer as there is of Cain. Jimmy spawned a collective individuality, a fashionable non-conformity that would in turn generate the trendy freaks of the sixties and the fantasmaphoric punks of the seventies. Demonstrating the syntax for a new sensibility, Jimmy codified and canonized a new teenage wardrobe, and he gave adolescence a face—his face.

A crystal clear code is beamed through James Dean in all his films, and no teenager could fail to grasp the unspoken: *there are others like you.*

James Dean is the multiphrenic father of us all, the Sphinx of Youth to whom every generation poses its riddles. What the "Lord of Forms," Osiris, said of himself (hieroglyphically speaking, of course) in *The Egyptian Book of the Dead* could be put in the mouth of James Dean without scratching out a glyph of it:

> *I am today. I am yesterday. I am tomorrow. Undergoing my repeated births I remain powerful and young.*

As the first youth hero and the last great Hollywood star, Jimmy resolved the paradoxes of American life for the first and last time it would be possible, and through his self-intoxicated narcissism made of himself a mirror in which any facet of America could find its reflection. The serial enigma of James Dean as star, anti-hero, and victim. Through the star state, he merged the Teen Dream of nonconformity with the American Dream of success. The contradictions inherent in these dreams (and in himself) only reinforced his myth and made him the prototype for the schizophrenic star system of the sixties. He made star status the only acceptable form of success, the only desirable form of adulthood. This method of aging without growing up found its ultimate incarnation in rock stars, a sort of unannointed royalty who rule by divine right.

The first to confront the paradox of pop, Jimmy was both a star *and* a convincing anti-establishment figure. Not only was Jimmy the first Teen Rebel and the prototype for the Rock Star, he was also the first Pop Star—the first person to be revered as being pop, the first Pop Person. Like the Rolling Stones' rose-pink-Cadillac philosophy, Jimmy managed to transcend the contradictions of an antisocial attitude and commercial success through stardom itself.

"Immortality," according to Freud, "is to be loved by many anonymous people." But immortality must have bodies, and James Dean's promiscuous identity—both on screen and off—was almost generic, and so universal that it made him a symbol for just about anything imaginable: Jett Rink redneck Deans, biker Deans, bongo-playing Deans, sensitive Deans in glasses, country Cal Trask look-alike Deans, *Fureur de Vivre* hustler Deans in Paris bars, punk Deans, leather queen Deans, and any number of shadings in between—all cloned from him and saying *Jimmy is me*. The original Beatles in Hamburg are five James Deans slouching against a wall. It is the Frankenstein Effect, a James Dean kit, create your own clone. Carrying him around in thousands of incorporations, each of his fans *is* James Dean. The pieces have been returned to those from whom they were borrowed.

"*One of those images of light, which conjurers evoke and cause to shine before us, in apparent tangibility, only at arm's length beyond our grasp; we make a step in advance, expecting to seize the illusion, but find it still precisely so far out of our reach.*"

Hawthorne, **The Marble Faun**

CHAPTER ONE

The Double World
1931–1940

Jimmy is born in a small Midwestern town;
the Deans move to California;
Jim's mother and her death;
he is sent back alone to Indiana.

J ames Byron Dean was born on February 8, 1931 in a small town in Indiana. He was delivered at home and given the first name of the attending physician, James Emmick, and his middle name, it is said, for the poet Lord Byron.

Jimmy was born under the influence of the planet Uranus, a symbol of light. Light is the nature of fire, mist, phosphorescent insects, lightning, crystals and the moon. It is also the medium of a star and the element into which James Dean transformed himself. On the screen, his presence shines with inexhaustible illumination through his eyes, his mouth, radiating in luminous traces like the firefly's glowing arc. "The poetry in a man's life," said Emerson, "is the light which shines on a man's hat and in a child's spoon. . ." As an actor, James Dean revealed the subtle light which rests so eloquently on everyone, and as we follow his sleight of hand, we wonder how it ever managed to be so elusive. Like everything intimate, remote and transforming, when all was nearly apparent, he disappeared, leaving only his iridescent traces. This was James Dean's magical capacity.

Marion, Indiana, where Jimmy was born, is an industrial town about fifty miles north of Indianapolis, and he lived there for four years until his parents moved to Santa Monica, California. Winton

Jimmy at four months old. *Age two and a half, with Aunt Ortense and Joan.*

and Mildred Dean were both native Indianans—Mildred (*nee* Wilson) from a Methodist family that Jimmy said was part Indian, and Winton a Quaker from a line of original settlers that could be traced back to the *Mayflower*.

The doctor's fee for delivering Jimmy was fifteen dollars, a little less than half the thirty-nine dollars originally paid to the Miami Indians for the entire city of Marion. Considering its present tawdry appearance, it seems appropriate that Marion should have been bought at a discount and that its major contribution to civilization is the invention of the paper plate. It is the typical disposable city.

Here in Marion, Jimmy lived for the first few years of his life in the Green Gables Apartments, a rambling building put up in the late twenties that might now pass as an antique in the rapidly dissolving fabric of the city. When Jimmy was almost three, his father quit his job as a dental technician at the Marion Veterans' Hospital, and the Deans moved to Fairmount, a small farming community about ten miles to the south, where they lived on Ortense (Winton's sister) and Marcus Winslow's farm in a small cottage along Back Creek, a meandering country stream that flowed through the property. Here Jimmy's father rather whimsically took to raising bullfrogs. Whether he was trying to "grow 'em with six legs," as told in an Indiana tall tale, is not known. It's hard to imagine much of a market for frogs' legs at the height of the Depression. In any case, the project was a disaster and Winton, Mildred and Jimmy returned to Marion.

Winton, then in his twenties, was a thin, dark-haired man with a somber air. He had never really been interested in carrying on the

A three-year-old's smile.   *A Yucca on tiptoes. Age five in Los Angeles.*

family's farming tradition and was more comfortable when he returned to the familiar routine of the hospital. However, a year later, in 1935, he was transferred to the Sawtelle Veterans' Hospital in Santa Monica, California. Mildred was reluctant to leave her family to start a new life, but conditions were hardly ideal in either Marion or Fairmount. They migrated west with the same kind of earnestness found at the beginning of a James M. Cain novel: ". . . Things were really tough . . . I moved to California . . . I walked down that shabby palm-lined street, 18 cents jingling in my worn gabardine suit . . ."

The Deans moved into a typical Southern California "cream-colored stucco igloo," the kind Jim Backus described with confectious humor in his book *Rocks on the Roof*: "It was twenty by thirty, but the walls were four feet thick. Sort of a miniature fortress from *Beau Geste*. Instead of windows, it had slits, obviously designed for the pouring of boiling oil on peddlers."

Mildred kept in touch with the folks back home, sending frequent photos of little Jimmy to Winton's parents in Fairmount. In a snapshot of him at five outside the Deans' home in Santa Monica, with his hair sleeked down and squinting at the sun in overalls and straw hat, he might as well be standing on the farm except for the Yucca which looks as if it had tiptoed up behind him and, like some thorny monster, waits fiendishly for him to turn around. For her birthday, he sent his grandmother a picture of himself and a chubby little girl with his note on the back that said, "My sweetheart." The little girl beams, but even then Jimmy's look seemed mildly ironic, almost cool, as if he is on the other side of the camera as well.

3

Jimmy was a sweet-looking child with features, his grandma used to say, "of a china doll, and the complexion of a ripe apple. Almost too dainty for a boy." He was sturdy looking in build, but delicate by constitution, often suffering from nosebleeds and internal bleeding which caused black and blue marks on his arms and legs. He was sensitive and probably influenced by his mother's interest in poetry and art. One writer ascribed the source of Jimmy's restlessness to the fact that his mother read the *Eumenides* to him. But it's hard to believe that the furies he heard within himself were really those avenging ladies of antiquity in their frozen draperies.

It's not known whether Mildred Dean had ever heard of Byron. "I don't think she knew who Lord Byron was a'tall," said Bing Traster, a long-time native of the town. "She recited poetry at church gatherings and such, but she never heard tell of Lord Byron. Jimmy Dean's dad had a chum who was named George Byron Fiest and that's how he came by that name." (Byron is a common enough name in farm country, getting appropriately pronounced B'arn farther south.) But in California his schoolmates thought it "queer" and, when they found out how sensitive he was about his middle name, teased him about it.

Mildred Dean created a little theater for Jimmy and herself, and on stages made of cardboard they invented plays, using dolls as actors. Through these childhood afternoons in Santa Monica they materialized many a daydream, fugue-like figures working through tenses from present to past to future, replacing the world around them with one of their own devising.

One of the most compelling stories about Jimmy's childhood is of the wishing game, a variant on that generous person the tooth fairy and a fantasy that was supposed to be his favorite. Before he went to sleep, Jimmy would put underneath his pillow a piece of paper with a wish written on it. Mildred would slip in while he was asleep, read the wish and, if possible, she would make it come true the next day.

Jimmy was almost nine and his mother not yet thirty when Mildred began to complain of severe pains in her chest. X-rays revealed that she had breast cancer and that it was already considerably advanced. In May of 1940, Winton wrote to his mother in Fairmount that Mildred was dying and asked her to come to California immediately. "I'll never forget the day the letter came telling us that

Mildred, who was so young and lovely, wouldn't get well," said Emma Dean in a *Photoplay* story, "The Boy I Loved." "I took the letter to our doctor and he judged I'd be in California about six to eight weeks. I was gone seven to the day, and when I brought Mildred's body back, Jimmy was with me. I'd said to Winton, I recall, 'Now, I want you to think this thing over carefully. If you see fit to let Jimmy come back to Fairmount, Ortense and Marcus would like to take him in. They'll raise him for you if you want.'"

"She was only twenty-nine," Winton Dean later told *Modern Screen*. "The doctors told me it was hopeless. How do you tell an eight-year-old boy his mother's going to die? I tried, but I just couldn't make it. Jim and I—we'd never had that closeness. And my Jim is a tough boy to understand."

Shortly before Mildred died, Winton told Jimmy that his mother was not going to come home again. "Jimmy said nothing—just looked at me," Winton recalled. "Even as a child he wasn't much to talk about his hurts."

After Mildred's death Winton considered returning to Fairmount, but moving would have worsened the already aggravated financial

"My sweetheart."

5

condition which his wife's illness had created. "I was deep in debt with doctors' bills, X-rays, radium treatments and everything else. I was alone without anyone to look after the boy when I was at work. I had to get my feet under me again." Winton had sold his car to pay for his wife's last operation and couldn't even afford to go to the funeral in Fairmount.

Sending Jimmy to live with his sister, Ortense, and her husband, Marcus, seemed like the best thing Winton could do. Winton's mother, Emma Dean, encouraged it: "Ortense and Marcus are a daughter and son-in-law any woman would be proud to own. They do their share in the community . . . both are wise and gentle and have a great gift for loving. Theirs is like a Quaker home should be. You never hear a harsh word. Best of all, they are happy as well as good—and that's what Jimmy needed most after the shock of losing his mother."

Little is known about the mother Jimmy lost when he was just nine years old. Since there has never been a published photograph, writers cannot even agree about her physical appearance and accounts of what she looked like differ: she has been variously described as

Jimmy incorporated the soft, liquid lines of his mother (with Natalie Wood in Rebel Without a Cause).

"dark and plump" or "slim and fair." But she was engraved in Jimmy—his androgynous features in their soft, liquid lines, incorporated her. You can see it most clearly when he is a child of eight or nine (as if sensitive to the coming separation, he was imprinting a memory of her on himself), and later as the languid young Jett Rink in *Giant*. Behind Jimmy's tough-kid facade always shone the face of his mother—a pure, unattainable figure. She "moves in my blood and whispers to me," Robert Louis Stevenson had written about this presence of his parent within him, "and sits efficient in the very knot and center of my being."

One can also see his mother's influence by noting the reverberations in his behavior, the concentric memories of her sunk within him. There are the telltale mother substitutes to whom he attached himself throughout his life: first Ortense Winslow, his aunt, whom he always called "Mom"; then Adeline Nall, his high school teacher, who introduced him to theater and nurtured his separateness; in college in Santa Monica there was Jean Owen, another drama coach; and in New York he found a mother figure in Jane Deacy, his agent. On the movie sets he found Julie Harris, Mercedes McCambridge and Elizabeth Taylor to play the role for him. Jimmy saw his mother in them, and they recognized the child in him.

Barbara Glenn, an actress Jimmy dated years later in New York, said, "Sure, we would sit around and talk about his mother and father and Ortense and Marcus, but the only person I could believe was really close to him as a person was his mother, who died. He never really had anybody, because at that point I think Jimmy lost everybody. It was such an irrevocable loss that it could never be filled.

"He said she had long black hair, that she was thin and very beautiful. He said that she was soft and very gentle and he felt very loved by her. In a strange way she was this fantasy creature even to him. He loved her very much and I don't know that he had not fantasized a lot about her.

"We talked about his mother a great deal when we first met. I don't know that it wasn't a resemblance to her that attracted Jimmy to me. He told me I looked like her—slim, long dark hair . . . At that time my hair was down to my waist.

"Jimmy had a terrible anger for his mother. *She died.* He was a nine-year-old child saying how can you leave me? When he talked about her, it wasn't a twenty-one- or twenty-two-year-old. It was a child and he was deserted. He'd loved her desperately. He'd loved her desperately and she left him. I think it had a profound effect on him. And he expressed it in terms of his art."

Jimmy was both Oedipus and Hamlet—the somnambulist stumbling into tragedy and the dreamer fighting his way out. Comfortably as these labels nestle into the folds of analysis ("All neurotics," said Dr. Freud, "are either Oedipus or Hamlet"), the terms will only lead to redundancy. It might be more revealing to say that Jimmy trusted profoundly in the efficacy of magical action, and whether it was a delusion or not, it became the source of his power. These beliefs began in his childhood and were the legacy of his mother.

Jimmy recalled the parts he played for his mother in an interview with Hedda Hopper. It is a catalogue he did not care to elaborate on. "When I was four or five my mother had me playing the violin—I was a blasted child prodigy. My family came to California and before it was over my mother had me tap-dancing. Not at the same time I was playing the violin. My mother died when I was eight and the violin was buried too."

Poor Mildred. Staked out by speculators and prey to the games of analysis, her image staggers and heaves, squeaking on the edge of silence beneath such gravity. Given the rampant Freudianism of the era, she has become through manipulation an imaginary being, as unlikely as an Indiana Isis or barnyard Bovary, the source of all Dean mysteries, the Great Mother of the world who dreamt her Little Prince into being in a land inhabited by oafs and farmers.

In a fictionalized biography of his life, *I, James Dean,* author T. T. Thomas melodramatically ascribed Jimmy's angst: "I, Jimmy Dean, never knew who I was or what I was . . . I was the hopes and dreams of my farm-girl mother, for when the years had broken her of any real hope for herself, she passed on to me the dusty dreaming of her youth. I never had a chance to be Jimmy Dean . . ."

And yet this story of the overly romantic mother who led her delicate child across the first threshold into the Double World is close to what Jimmy himself believed.

"My mother died on me when I was nine years old. What does she expect me to do? Do it all by myself?" Jimmy said later in a *Look* magazine interview.

Bill Bast, his roommate in college and later New York, said, "Does it really matter whether she read Byron or not? Jimmy believed she named him after Lord Byron and that's what counts.

"I get the feeling that she was a woman who tried to extricate him from the rural community they came from. Hell, I didn't know who Mrs. Dean was, but I picture a woman who was a romantic—she named her son, after all, Byron. She knew what she was doing. She made him take—I don't know—I think dancing lessons and music lessons. And you don't do this to a young boy without stigmatizing him. And a woman who is embracing those kinds of things wants to keep him aloof, away from certain kinds of situations.

"It's a highly protective kind of thing, demonstrative to the child of a special kind of love. Forget about what kind of neurotic compulsions that led *her* to do it, to the child it looked like he was really something special, *i.e.*, enormous ego, or, *little man dragging big balls along street*.

"So that's number one. You *start* with that. We're a special little darling. And then, we're very alien. The world around us is alien. We're not like all those others, you and Mommy. Closely knit? So what do you expect? Mommy leaves him in the lurch. So what's he gonna do now? Suddenly say, Mommy was wrong, I *am* like all the others, and use camphorated oil to shrink the overgrown testes? No, he's going to go on looking for his mother and nurturing the fantasies she taught him. And I don't care how literal she was, just giving him the name Byron—telling him what that was—was sufficient. It was good for starters."

It is in the charged spaces between fond mothers and spellbound sons that relations primitive and fantastic arise; shadowy images are sewn into the tissue of the unformed child and keep him always a wanderer in this unstable zone. He leaves the luminous darkness of childhood, part figment of a mother's wishes, a chimera of illusion and substance. These early experiences breed in such children a prolonged infancy which, though it hobbles them in common sense, gives in exchange a special, almost self-generated quality, envied and desired by others.

Jimmy traveled back to Indiana in 1940, unaware that he was orphaned. He had actually lost both his parents, for he would see his father only occasionally for the rest of his life. The world his mother left him was so compelling that her memory would accompany him always, and from this time on, Jimmy would look upon life with a

kind of irony.

Jimmy traveled with his grandmother on the same train that carried his mother's body back to Fairmount to be buried. In the apocryphal movie *The James Dean Story*, Stewart Stern, who wrote the script for *Rebel Without a Cause* and knew Jimmy well, tried to analyze a dead boy's thoughts about his dead mother, assuming Jimmy's nine-year-old's anxieties: "I was bad. She wouldn't have died on me if I hadn't been bad. She would have loved me and taken care of me. If she didn't love me nobody can. I was bad all my life."

At the funeral, Jimmy snipped off a lock of his mother's hair and for the first two weeks in his new home played the wishing game on his own.

Long ago a man named Johnny Appleseed
passed through our land and among the
thousands and thousands of seeds, there
was one separate and special seed—the
seed of the Golden Rain Tree. And over
the land high and low we searched for where
this one seed might take root and grow.
It flourishes right here in the middle of
our fair county . . . but where this
tree was planted nobody knows. They say
it can be found near Paradise Lake. Find
that tree, boy, and you'll learn the secret
of life itself and become the hero
of Raintree County.

—from Metro-Goldwyn-Mayer's *Raintree County*

CHAPTER TWO

The Omphalos of Normalcy
1940–1949

Growing up in Fairmount;
Uncle Marcus and Aunt Ortense Winslow;
life on the farm.

O ut of Nothing, Nothing can be created. This gloomy axiom had vexed the Western world until well into the eighteenth century when a leatherneck named Martin Boots first set foot in Indiana, a land so uncannily level, it was as if a Divine Hand had prepared it, sweeping all the untidy hills and hollows to the south and east. Boots' monikers marched briskly into Grant County, and following closely on his heels was an odd contingent of proper nouns—the Paynes, Noses, Ices, Inks, Doves, Scales, Woolens, Winslows, Wilsons and Deans. These Quakers were a people who, far from fleeing the terrors of the void, had actively sought out a land as next to Nothing as could be found on the earth's crust: a place pared down to the rind and as plain and unadorned as their own lives. And Nothing, in their severe philosophy, seemed almost too good for them.

Night, the sea, deserts and plains are screens for the projection of latent images, and on this land—formless, malleable and virgin as it was—they could create whatever they wished. The emptiness they found had a meaning as clear as a prairie dog's eye: Indiana was to be a blank page on whose surface *anything* could be written. They stretched their substance over the void, for ingenuity is the trait of a people who have had to invent not only their history, but their geography as well. It was their destiny to release, like the genie from his bottle, the huge storehouse of mankind's wishes and dreams. They had planted these millenial fantasies as they traveled westward, but like the seed of the Golden Rain Tree, there was only one spot where these ancient dreams would take root and grow—one special place where their inexhaustible energy would stream into the inner body of the world. This one place, as the professor in *Raintree County* pointed out, can be found in the middle of America in a deceptively normal town.

Fairmount, Indiana, the town that James Dean considered home, was that town. It is the fount of some archetypal images without which the very idea of America might dissolve—the birthplace of the hamburger, the car, the airplane and the ice-cream cone.

The hamburger was invented in Fairmount in 1885 by a man named Bill Dolman. Bill and his wife owned a rolling lunch wagon that did a pretty good business in Fairmount, especially when it was the horseracing season and folks from miles around flocked to the town's track. Once, when Bill's wife got sick, the doctor prescribed only smoked ham and cured meat as a diet, and Bill cooked patties made out of smoked ham ground very fine so it would be easy for her to digest. As his wife's health improved he began mixing the ham with beef for variety. A customer got a glimpse of what Bill was doing one day and asked if he could try one of the round, brown treats. By the time they appeared on Bill's regular menu, they were made out of all beef; but originally they were made of ham—hence the name *hamburgers*.

They say Fairmount's tinkerers were toying with an idea for a horseless carriage a few years before Ford's combustible engine. Orlie Scott, a nineteen-year-old-boy who inherited some money, backed an experiment that resulted in a car that could run quite well except for the fact that it didn't have brakes. The car's final resting place was a ditch at the end of a small hill on Fairmount Pike, not more than fifty feet from where James Dean is buried today.

And the idea for the airplane first came into a little boy's head in Fairmount, for the Wright family were natives of that town. The brothers left for the softer sand of Kitty Hawk for their experimental flights, but they returned to the old family farm often. On Orville's seventy-third birthday, he insisted on demonstrating how young he was by running up and down a "flight" of stairs. He died there of a heart attack.

Finally, one more primal American image before James Dean – the ice-cream cone. Ice cream was once a rare ambrosia, an unobtainable delight the majority could only dream of, until the cone made it parochial. It was another citizen of Fairmount, the unsung Cyrus Pemberton, who during the late 1880s first rolled a pancake into a conical shape, modeling it perhaps on Liberty's torch, and filled it with ice cream. This was the precursor of the waffle cone we know today, and by this simple Promethean act Pemberton stole a rare food from the palaces of princes and Sunday dinner tables and made it into something anyone could eat, anytime and anywhere.

Then there is James Dean, archetypal American boy, the Adolescent Incarnate whose invention was himself – typical and ideal – an image as American as Adam and as common as a Coke.

Fairmount is a plain town and plainness is a native virtue of Indiana. It means that by your roots you're pretty much tied to everybody else, you "grow up straight and strong" (as Alan Ladd advised Brandon de Wilde in *Shane*) and you don't pretend to be better or worse than your neighbors. Fairmount is a quiet, simple sort of place and, as writer Stewart Stern pointed out in that celluloid epitaph, *The James Dean Story*, "It's not just a quaint little town, but a useful town, used well and long by its people."

Fairmount, population 2700, lies forty miles north of Indianapolis and just four miles west of Route 69. At the intersection of Highway 22 and the Jonesboro Pike, a green and white sign reads "Downtown Fairmount" ("that's so's you won't miss the town altogether") and points into a nest of shady maples. Green arches in rhyming curves line both sides of North Main Street, making an almost ceremonial entrance to the town. Everything here breathes intimacy; you must reduce yourself in scale as you touch the threshold of the town, entering as you would enter through the eye of a photograph.

The matronly white of well-kept houses, warm reds and blues of rusted signs, school bus yellow and the bug green of lawns with regulation trim – so simple and primary in texture that the accumulated effect is a kind of poetry of the commonplace. A freckled paperboy just escaped from Norman Rockwell, who leans over to drink from an old water fountain that's been there since Jimmy was in town, and the green '49 Olds parked next to the Payne family's grocery store conspire to create a deception of timelessness. Shades and silences are interrupted only by tiny sounds—the whirring of bicycles, an occasional bird, the rattle in the distance of the old *CW & M* between Jonesboro and Fairmount or a children's parade which goes marching by the gossipy rows of clapboard houses.

The town, complete within one hundred fifty square blocks, has the familiarity of the miniature towns found alongside a child's railroad tracks. In the 1970s it's your average country town, with things almost the same as they were in 1949 when Jimmy left for California. Technology has tensed it, surrounded it, but only strengthened its resistance to change. Little deliberate attempt has been made at restoration except in the case of the Citizens Bank, a grand lady in elegant red and white dressing, with a fine golden cupola on her head. Her turret once served as a great secret place where Jimmy played hide-and-seek with his friends as a young boy.

It's a Quaker town, and a Quaker, as *Readers Digest* once defined him, "is not one to make pomp out of any circumstance," a people who "praise the zero in themselves" and who work at maintaining that still point. Maybe nothing will ever tip the scales of Fairmount, and if James Dean and the madness which followed in his wake

Payne's Grocery Store. The deception of timelessness lingers.

16

couldn't upset its balance, it's hard to conceive of anything that could.

If you had to answer the silly "Lady in a Box" in *Our Town* when she asks, "Is there any beauty or love of beauty in Grover's Corners?" you'd have to go along with good ol' Mr. Webb and say much the same about Fairmount too.

Mr. Webb: Well, ma'am, there ain't much—not in the sense you mean. Come to think of it, there's some girls that play the piano at High School Commencement; but they ain't happy about it. No ma'am, there isn't much culture; but maybe this is the place to tell you that we've got a lot of pleasure of a kind here: we like the sun comin' up over the mountain in the morning, and we all notice a good deal about the birds. We pay a lot of attention to them. And we watch the change of the seasons; yes, everybody knows about them. But those other things—you're right, ma'am—there ain't much—*Robinson Crusoe* and the Bible; and Handel's "Largo," we all know that; and Whistler's "Mother"—those are just about as far as we go.

Fairmount, Indiana is pretty much Grover's Corners, Vermont, *mutatis mutandis*, that is. Even the folks of Fairmount think so. *Our Town* was one of the first plays they chose to put on for the James Dean Memorial Foundation, and Jimmy's old friends and teachers took part in the production. The *Fairmount News* said what an excellent choice it was too; it had "something symbolic of the honesty, the sincerity and breadth of appreciation that characterized Jim in his relationships with others. This is a play of the American people at their finest in the fundamental aspects of life."

In short, Fairmount is the quintessence of the small town, as it was and as America will always dream of it. But it could just as well be Penny Lane or Llareggub Hill as Grover's Corners or James Whitcomb Riley's Zekesbury. It's the hometown that heroes and prodigal sons always return to, Gulliver to his Nottinghamshire village, Quixote to La Mancha, Odysseus to Ithaca. On a misty morning it could well be the streets of Monterey, where Jimmy prowled in the opening scenes of *East of Eden*. It has the perfect economy of a Warner Brothers' set—a back lot Anytown sandwiched squarely between Westerntown and Anytime, New York. It's so still it almost seems to be holding its breath, and so succulent in its plainness it seems ripe for the Universal monsters—the prehistoric lizards and atomic spiders who loved to prey on small towns in all those fifties horror movies.

A real-life outlaw, Jessie's brother Frank James, retired to Fair-

Main Street, Fairmount.

The Winslow farmhouse, where Jimmy grew up.

mount, and what was left of the Dalton Gang also hid out and settled in the town, guessing that the Kansas Rangers would never dream to look for them there. Bad guys don't always come from somewhere else though—the first train robbery ever pulled in the United States of America was perpetrated by a native Indiana gang, the Reno Boys, in 1886.

In 1940 Jimmy arrived at Marcus and Ortense Winslow's handsome fourteen-room house, sensibly built to conform to the matter-of-fact ideas of its original owners, Ansel and Ida Winslow. It stands overlooking three hundred acres of land on a small hill which rolls down into the meadowlands that lead eventually to town. Jimmy lived for the next nine years on his aunt and uncle's farm and was happy to be near his grandparents, Charlie and Emma Dean, who still worked the land they owned on the other side of Fairmount though they'd moved to a little pink house in town.

Fairmount had been founded on the banks of Back Creek, a thick green stream that runs through the Winslow farm. The countryside is rich with the textures of trees and flowers. In fact, it was the trees that convinced the first settlers to stay there. (The bigger the trees, the more "furtile" the soil, as any farmer will tell you.) Soldiers heading down the Mississenewa to "thrash out a bunch of Indians" made the first tracks; others coming east cut a trail for their cannons; and where the two paths crossed marked the site of the town.

Jimmy enjoyed the routine of farm life even though when he first arrived he was anemic. "I don't know whether I was looking for a greater source of life and expression . . . or for blood." His chores were milking, collecting eggs, feeding the stock and harvesting. Marcus ran the farm on his own, except for occasional help during busy times, so Jimmy was a big help to him. By the end of his first year with the Winslows he could drive the tractor. He found the runt of a litter of pigs, bottle-fed it to keep it alive, and it became his pet. When Jimmy and his dog, Tuck, ran across the farmyard, the little pig would be squealing and oinking behind them, trying to catch up.

To the Winslows' only child, Joan, who at fourteen was five years older than her cousin, Jimmy was "never one to sit still. Always had to be best at everything." In the summer he learned to swim by throwing himself into the creek backwards. He caught carp in the pond. Once he was swinging so successfully on the trapeze Marcus had rigged in

Jimmy arrived at the Winslows' at age nine.

the barn that he swung right into a pipe and broke his two front teeth.

"Getting healthy can be hazardous," Jimmy told Hedda Hopper, the columnist he cautiously grew friendly with later on in Hollywood. "You have to assume more responsibility. Now, this was a real farm I was on and I worked like crazy—as long as someone was watching me. The forty acres of oats was a huge stage and when the audience left I took a nap and things didn't get plowed or harrowed."

"Mostly we've been around Fairmount or Marion ever since the family first settled here," said Emma Dean. "Charlie and I live on Washington Street in Fairmount, but he still farms, as he always has done. Charlie's a great hand at having two or three things going at once. At various times he's been a stock buyer, run a livery stable, sold automobiles and raced a string of horses. We're not very rich, but we're not poor either. So long as I live, I'll have a porch to sit on, a rocking chair to rock in and a clock that strikes."

Jimmy's family went back to the deepest layer of American history. The Deans and Woolens begin with the roots of Grant County, and the Winslows go back even further—their ancestors came over on the *Mayflower*.

"You might say we're a close-knit family," said Emma Dean. "That's what comes from living in one place for so long. The first Deans came from around Lexington, Kentucky and settled in Grant County about 1815. My family, the Woolens, and Jimmy's mother's family, the Wilsons, got here about the same time."

Jimmy went out to his grandfather's farm whenever he could. He'd play with his dog, Tuck, and together they'd chase chickens, feed the cows or follow behind nurseryman Bing Traster, a huge tree of a man whose good-natured country humor is delivered with the deadpan expression of an old-time fiddler. Bing, now eighty, won a medal as the "World's Champion Liar," and the townsfolk don't see any contradiction in the fact that he's also the local historian. There's something incongruous about the huge appetites these stalwart old Quakers have for listening, as tireless as children, to improbable and fantastic tales mixed right in with stories of inventions and storms and visits by President Roosevelt.

This gift for wordy outpourings of spirit, humbug, mimicry and salvation is probably what Jimmy loved most about Bing, who would explore with him that Double World he lived in.

"You know how ice cream came to be invented, Jimmy?"

"No, how, Bing? Do you know? Were you there?" Jimmy might have innocently asked before he caught on that there was a story coming.

"'Course I was there . . . in fact, it happened right here on your Grandpa Dean's farm. Why, one day in August we was working, trying to get the cows in from the meadow, and it was so hot, why it was so hot the corn began to pop right off the stalk and the whole meadow was covered with big white drifts. And ol' Bessie was out in the middle of it and she didn't know what was goin' on . . . she thought it'd gone and snowed. She made her way through that corn shivering like it was the middle of winter, and by the time we got her to the barn all the milk in her udders was frozen and if you pulled on one, out came vanilla ice cream . . . pulled on the other, out came chocolate and so on and so forth."

From the time Indiana began to be settled it was a Land of the Tongue, where forensic stump orators, professors of phrenology, hog callers and vendors of Old Mohawk Indian Tonic tilted with preachers of hellfire and knights of the temperance league. It's a carry-over from old frontier traditions (beyond the civilized world anything can happen), and where boundaries meet, contradictions generally exist happily side by side. "Hoosiers" actually relish the absurdity of their state poet, James Whitcomb Riley, earning his bread as a snake oil salesman and blind sign-painter.

At one point the land became so outraged about being outdone by her progeny that she created a few improbable events herself. Fairmount's Trenton Rock was penetrated in April 1877, giving birth to "Jumbo," one of the largest natural gas wells ever mined. A few months later an accident caused it to catch fire, resulting in flames so high that they could be seen for forty miles around. The pressure of the well was so great that the flame itself stood some twenty feet above the ground. No one could figure out how to extinguish it, and while the firemen racked their brains, the train company put on special sightseeing cars so folks could come witness the phenomenon. Old-timers remember it burned so brightly that it was hard to tell day from night. Chickens didn't know when to roost and fell dead from exhaustion. And the trees, thinking it was spring, came into bloom in early winter.

Finally, the fire was put out by a hobo who came through town and showed them that dynamite would do the trick.

It was this joy of invention and absurdity of life which Jimmy loved and cultivated in himself. He was fond of telling tales and told a friend about a "goose necklace" he once made: "I remember one time when I found out that if you give a duck a piece of salt pork, it goes right through him in about ten seconds. So I got me some fishing line and tied a piece of pork to one end and fed it to a big drake. It passed on through and I gave it to another duck and then another, and before long I had the whole barnyard full of ducks all strung together like pearls on a string. You should have heard them quack."

The Depression brought hard times for the Winslows. They managed to hold on to their farm and struggled to pay off their debts. They treated Jimmy well, conscientiously making sure he got everything Joan did and more. Jimmy repaid them by patterning himself after Marcus in every way: he wore a tee shirt and blue jeans, slouched a bit and distrusted strangers, worked diligently at his job and even made his occasional forbidden cigarette a Camel.

Ortense became "Mom" and in her Quaker way raised Jimmy as if he were her own son. There's a delicate quality about her, suggesting perhaps some of the fragility of her sister-in-law, Mildred. She sits in her favorite rocking chair, her back to the light that streams through the huge Victorian windows that stretch the width of the living room. "They don't make curtains that big anymore," she'll tell you. "We have to order them special."

The house is spacious and light, its dark cherry-wood paneling polished to a high gleam so that a visitor feels as if inside a giant antique instrument—a huge piano or titanic cello—trying to tune the house's resonances and squeaky wooden surfaces to hear the hum of its echoes of the past.

Next to the front door is a TV topped by a bowl of artificial flowers and two framed photographs: one of Jimmy and one of Joan. A grand piano sits in isolation at the far end of the room. In the opposite corner, an electric Hammond organ.

"Jimmy inspired me to play," says Ortense. "He brought his bongos home the last time he came back, just after finishing *East of Eden*, and he used to peck at them all the time."

The living room's hardly changed since that last visit of Jimmy's, yet nothing looks old or worn. Perhaps like most country people, time is spent somewhere else—the kitchen table, the front porch.

In the bookcase at the foot of the stairs are the volumes Jimmy grew up with—*Boys and Girls in the Bible*, *Rover Boys* adventure books, a few versions of the Bible. At the top of the staircase is Jimmy's bedroom. When he expressed a liking for the sturdy old maple furniture in the room where Marcus and Ortense slept, especially the bed with its posts turning in polished spheres like little minarets, they put the furniture in his room and bought something else for themselves. On a shelf in his room are books visitors have sent or brought for the Winslows. On his small maple bureau are three publicity pictures. The room is compact and very wooden, like a ship's cabin built especially for a small boy.

Outside on the front lawn a swing, hanging from an old oak tree, moves slightly in the breeze. Jimmy's bike gathers dust in the cellar. Everything seems to be waiting for him to come back and awaken them. The trees slouch around the house. There's a purple iridescent globe near the house, peonies trim the porch and two pink flamingos stand on the well-kept lawn.

"He was a boy, like any other. Always chasing some kind of ball," says Marcus Winslow, a little warily. He can read a face with half a glance. Miraculously well-built for a man almost seventy, he still takes care of the farm by himself. Wearing blue jeans and a white tee shirt (Jimmy's favorite outfit), he won't let you take his picture. "I've said it until I'm sick of sayin' it," he says, taking off his Farmer's Co-Op cap and running a muscular hand through his hair. "Jimmy was just like any other kid who grew up in this town. He played baseball, went to Sunday Meeting at Back Creek Quaker Church and did his chores on the farm. Used to tag around after me opening gates so I wouldn't have to get off the tractor. And he loved to ride that little cycle of his through the meadow. After a bit, we let him take it to school."

For almost twenty years, two decades after Jimmy's death, people have come here year after year asking the same questions, and gone away hardly satisfied with Marcus' simple answers. A description of a childhood so devoid of incident has left some visitors with the suspicion that the Winslows were hiding something, or were simply not able to understand this enigma whom they had adopted as if he were a foundling left on earth's doorstep. Many times, insensitive reporters have deliberately twisted the facts to wring some romance out of the Winslows' quiet replies.

"Why, just last month," Marcus says with growing agitation, "a reporter came around here to ask some questions about Jimmy and the next thing you know I'm reading about it in the *Philadelphia Enquirer* and they got me killin' cats! Well, that's just a damn lie. I never killed a cat in my life. Do you even see any cats around here to kill? That writer just plain misquoted me. What I'd told him was that *I'm as busy as killin' cats.* That's an old sayin' I learnt a long time ago. So you see how things git turned around?"

Exasperated by the media's caricature of Marcus as a tee-shirted Rube and Ortense as a weepy keeper of the chapel ("squeezing a handkerchief embroidered with tiny violets she fights back the tears"), they still display a remarkable tolerance to the constant train

Jimmy's grandmother, Emma Dean.   *Jimmy's dresser.*

of visitors, the endless questions and cruel deceptions. (Under the guise of writing a story a fan took a precious album of baby pictures, swearing to return it, and was never seen again.)

Ortense talks softly and is less defensive about strangers and reporters than Marcus. You can see she feels compassion for those who make the pilgrimages in search of Jimmy. But what with the racial trouble in Marion, she has lately become a little wary about who she lets pass through the screen door on the porch. You'll probably never see the radiant sweetness of Ortense in her photographs, because her face taughtens in front of the camera making her look unnaturally severe; but in person she is friendly and sympathetic. Her kindness is returned by the many fans who come to visit and wind up writing to Marcus and Ortense frequently, sending them gifts of flowers, glassware and paintings. In the past they've occasionally put people up—like an old sailor named Lew Shanks, combination Merchant Marine and Buddhist priest, who meditated and slept in Jimmy's room, and burned incense and chanted at his grave. Campers have set up in their meadow, seventy cars pulling in on one busy weekend to ask for something of Jimmy's or beg to see where he slept. They're too polite and steeped in the good neighbor tradition not to talk with strangers who appear at their door, but their contacts with the outside world are reduced to minimal exchanges—a bit of talk about the weather, what's doing on the farm, where they've spent the four-week vacation they take once every eight years.

"We've just about quit givin' out any information at all," said Marcus, taking a break from feeding his stock. "It's the only way to stop those people from Hollywood and the rest of them from twisting everything around. Now they can believe what they want. They just don't want to hear that Jim was just an ordinary boy, 'cause you can't write it in a magazine or a newspaper like that. People just won't read it, so they've gotta put something in there to pep it up a bit. And, you know, that's where all the trouble starts. But like I told you, Jim was

Fairmount Grade School's basketball team. (Jimmy: middle of top row)

26

just like everyone else 'round here."

When Marcus and Jimmy's school friends say he was like everyone else, they are suggesting the creed of an elemental Christianity whose first article of faith is that the meek shall inherit the earth. Conversely, and our pride conceals this truth from us, *they* are as good as he was. He just happened to have a talent in him that made him go places.

If "nothin' in partikler" went into the making of his character here, then it must have been everything in general. But the details have long dissolved by now, lost in the fluid anonymity of time. Only an outsider, a sociologist or a linguist recording the bleak poetry of lunch counters would have found anything memorable enough in Jimmy's life here to set it down, and only a time traveler would have had the insight into the daily living to manipulate it into news or history.

As Emily in *Our Town* observed after she'd died and traveled back to one of her favorite memories:

It goes so fast. We don't have time to look at one another . . . I didn't realize. So all that was going on and we never noticed. Take me back—up the hill—to my grave. But first: Wait! One more look.

Good-by, Good-by world . . . Mama and Papa. Good-by to clocks ticking . . . and Mama's sunflowers. And food and coffee. And new-ironed dresses and hot baths . . . and sleeping and waking up. Oh earth, you're too wonderful for anybody to realize you!

The mystery of James Dean lies not in his abrupt end, but in his origins. Jimmy was as ordinary a boy as ever came out of Grant County, and his frequent trips home, his allusions to Indiana and reveries of the farm where he grew up are the indications he left behind, as if he subtly led us back here with his clues. The very opacity of Jimmy's life in Fairmount must persuade us that through his very lack of distinction he represents a typical outgrowth of an Indiana childhood. The sum and epitome of his region and town, from which he emerged after a long incubation.

"Nothing much happened to the boy while he was here with us," say his neighbors in Fairmount, where he lived between the ages of nine and eighteen, a good third of his natural life. They don't really mean Nothing, of course, "jest nothin' in partikler, nothin' to speak of." So to see Jimmy in his childhood, you have to look closely at his hometown, the farm and the people around him, because those special qualities which made Jimmy up, and which Jimmy tapped to make something of himself, are from the same vein of natural wit, diligence and love of invention that the inhabitants of Fairmount have drawn from the land since they first came here.

"The spirit of place is a great reality," said D. H. Lawrence. "Different places on the face of the earth have different effluences, different vibration, different chemical exhalation, different polarity, with different stars." It's a convention in the life stories of heroes to begin, after all, with an inventory of matters geological, historical, meteorological and genealogical. If a cloud is a map rolled up, then each individual is a seed on which the land imprints itself clearly, forcing him to reproduce its likeness. The seed may grow differently elsewhere, but it will always possess the characteristics of its region.

If the Midwest is the "middle" of this country, then where, you might ask, is *its* navel? Consider this case for Fairmount as the Omphalos of America.

In every United States Census from 1890–1940, the national center of population has been Indiana.

Twenty miles to the south of Fairmount is Muncie, the town chosen by sociologist Robert Lynd for his classic study of middle America, which resulted in a book called *Middletown*.

Twenty miles to the north of Fairmount is a town called Normal.

And if all this isn't convincing enough, the magnetic center of zero runs right through Fairmount (as well as through Dorothy's city of Oz in Kansas).

Fairmount, named in 1850 after a park in Philadelphia, was called by its original settlers AI, almost suggesting a geometric axis, a center, the Inexhaustible Point. With these factors Fairmount / AI could be considered the common denominator for everything in America, a sort of Edenic equation with a base so simple that it contains all forces and possibilities.

"The Midwest, the prairie country," said John Dewey, "has always been the center. It has formed the solid element in our diffuse national life and heterogeneous population. It has been the very middle in every sense of the word, and in every movement. Like every mean, it has held things together and given them unity and stability." This is perhaps why we have always drawn our heroes from the Prairie

Table—Gary Cooper, James Stewart, Thomas Edison, the Wright Brothers, F. Scott Fitzgerald, Marlon Brando, Montgomery Clift, moonman Neil Armstrong (his family was originally from Fairmount) and Abraham Lincoln. In *Planet of the Apes,* typical earthling Charlton Heston came from Fort Wayne, Indiana.

The unbounded possibility of wide open spaces somehow spawns heroes, as if it provided access to the order latent in the cosmos. It is within this still center that Jimmy Dean's dreams began and the dreams began to form him. After he left, wherever he went and whatever he did, Fairmount would always be the stable point to which he would return.

The nervous monotony of the
schoolroom inspires a sometimes unbearable
longing for something astonishing to
happen, and, as every boy's fundamental
desire is to do something
astonishing himself, as to be the centre
of all human interest and awe, it was
natural that Penrod should discover
in fancy the delightful secret of
self-levitation. In his mind he
extended his arms gracefully, at a
level with his shoulders, and delicately
paddled the air with his hands, which
at once caused him to be drawn up out
of his seat and elevated gently to a
position about midway between the floor
and the ceiling, where he came to an
equilibrium and floated; a sensation
not the less exquisite because of the
screams of his fellow pupils, appalled
by the miracle. Miss Spence herself
was amazed and frightened; but he
only smiled down carelessly upon her
when she commanded him to return to
earth; and then, when she climbed upon
a desk to pull him down, he quietly paddled
himself a little higher, leaving his
toes just out of her reach.

—from Booth Tarkington, *Penrod*

CHAPTER THREE

School Daze
1940–1949

Grade school; readings for the WCTU;
Jimmy's first motorcycle; high school dramatics,
sports and forensic competition;
Jimmy graduates and leaves for Hollywood.

N ot much had changed for school boys in rural Indiana between Penrod's day and the fall of 1940 when Jimmy began his school years in Fairmount. They might well have sat in the same classroom; for the Fairmount Elementary School is a sluggish, saurian structure from the Victorian age, with hinged wooden desks and high, rounded windows casting Gothic shadows on the flaking plaster walls, where South America, in the creamy liquid colors of Cram's Physical and Political Map, still waits like an enameled reptile for future Penrods and Deans.

It was a new school for Jimmy and the change seemed good to him. He had not been happy in Brentwood Public School in California. He was a poor student there and frequently got into fights, but with the transfer to Fairmount his grades and popularity improved. He made new friends and had an older "sister," Joan, the Winslows' daughter, to help him with his homework.

Jimmy and Penrod probably paddled through many of the same daydreams, drifting over their exercises in a world made up of half-understood thoughts and overheard conversations. Ideas awakened by the tides of listless afternoons would plunge them suddenly into exotic adventures: dreams of saving the world by committing daring crimes, desert escapes, foredoomed curses, tests of strength, reefs, stars, alligators and Arabs.

Jimmy's school days must have passed in much the same way as Penrod's, but there are some differences. Childhood is no longer such a comic matter as it was in Penrod's day, when antics of the young would only raise a knowing smile. The essential difference is that Penrod never materialized his phantoms, as far as we know; he simply continued to spin on his prankish orbit while Jimmy's little denizens grew fat on their daydreams, plodding season after season through their forest of neurons until they had established comfortable synaptic habits. They became healthy and solid as any good burgher, until at last they were ready to make their way in the outside world.

"He had the sweetest laugh as a little boy," his grade school teacher, India Nose, said, recalling Jimmy's high-pitched, contagious giggle. "I can hear him laughing to this day." The first years he was in Fairmount he seemed happy and was a good pupil, adapting to the "quiet" ways of the people around him. Still, his teachers noticed melancholy bouts. "He was sometimes moody, and often unexplainably stubborn," said Miss Nose. "He could be forgetful, too, as if he were lost in a daze. Sudden noises would startle him and questions in class seemed to interrupt some faraway thoughts." He was an imaginative child, the sole audience in his own planetarium, and The Voice seemed to call out, "I'm speaking to the boy inside."

How the sudden descent into his surrogate family affected him he wouldn't say. Only once in his arithmetic class did he break down and burst into tears. When asked what he was crying about, he replied, "I miss my mother."

Although he became the Adolescent Incarnate who spoke so totally for our unspoken causes, Jimmy's own youth passed with the same painful inhibitions so familiar to everyone his myth awakened. Jimmy was always considered an outsider in Fairmount, the "new boy" in town, facing some of that same painful scrutiny he encountered as Jim Stark in *Rebel*. Since he had come to live with his aunt and uncle, most of his classmates considered him some kind of orphan. How could he explain to the other fifth graders that it was only his mother who had died and that his father was still alive in some faraway place? He was a transplant, and though the Winslows treated him as a son, he was still Jimmy *Dean*—and they could never replace his deeply imbedded roots with their own.

Young Jimmy thus fulfills the first requirement of the myth-

ological figure, the orphan, the hero abducted and somehow separated from his parents, like Oedipus or Moses. Symbolically, this
figure—torn from his roots and a stranger in a new land—is a mutant,
a bridge between where he has come from and where he's going, yet
belonging to neither.

"I started teaching in Fairmount the same year Jim moved in with
the Winslows—1940. Kind of a coincidence," said Adeline Brookshire
Nall, Jimmy's high school teacher and first drama coach. "His teacher
at the time was India Nose, who was a very good friend of Jimmy's
mother; so I'd heard of the boy and seen him around. He was a
nine-year-old youngster. When we started the local theater at the high
school in 1940, we would bring the grade school students over to see
the dress rehearsal and charge them a dime. Well, the very first play I
did Jim was there. He'd see two good plays every year; so, you see, he
grew up with the theater."

Ortense Winslow first encouraged Jimmy to get up on the stage
when he was in the seventh grade by persuading him to do a reading
for the Women's Christian Temperance Union. "I felt a need to prove

As the "new boy" in Fairmount, Jimmy faced the same painful scrutiny Jim Stark encountered in Rebel.

33

myself and had the facility to do so," Jimmy told Hedda Hopper about the dramatic readings for the WCTU. "I was that tall, and instead of doing little poems I recited gory odes. This made me a straight little harpy in short pants. But I won all the medals the WCTU had to offer. I became pretty proficient and later I won the Indiana State dramatic contest reading 'The Madman.' The decision to act was never prompted. My whole life has been spent in dramatic display of expression."

His first reading at the WCTU won him a prize and encouraged him to continue to recite stories of vice and tragedy, and he looked forward to competing for the WCTU's highest award, the Pearl Medal. He was given a maudlin tract against John Barleycorn and his boozy crew, a wild diatribe called "Bars." (There's a double-entendre here somewhere, pleading to be released.)

In preparation, Mrs. Nall suggested he use a chair as a prop, so his little face could peep suggestively from between the rungs. He gripped the chair tightly with his tiny hands while he rehearsed his lines.

Bars! Bars! Iron bars! No matter which way I look I see them always before me! Long, menancing, iron bars that mock and sneer at me, even in my sleep. At times I think I hear them shout: "You killed a man! You killed a man!" Then I shout back at them: "I didn't! I didn't! I tell you, I didn't!" But did I? My God above, did I—I who as a boy could not bear to inflict pain on anyone?

From here on things just get worse and worse. So much worse, it seems almost unthinkable that anyone would have a nine-year-old child reading such hysterical Victorian humbug.

When the night of the reading finally came, it happened to be the same night of the junior high school track meet. Jimmy was torn between the two, but Ortense's insistence won. Just before his reading, the committee took Jimmy's "bars" away, since props weren't allowed, a technicality Mrs. Nall thought they would overlook. Jimmy began, faltered, gave up and stood there saying nothing until he was gently urged off the platform. "I was sure then of what I had known all along," Ortense said. "You couldn't make Jimmy Dean do things he didn't want to do."

John Potter, principal of Fairmount Junior High, said Jimmy was known as a troublemaker. "But kids like this are telling you, plain as

Adeline Nall, Jimmy's high school teacher and first drama coach.

day, that they want you to involve them in something," Mr. Potter explained while standing in the quiet, highly polished hallways. "It ain't a bad sign; it's a good sign. It's clear to me that he was a hyperactive child. Now that's not a sign of ignorance, mind you. But it is often a sign of greatness, and too often a busy high school teacher won't recognize a genius. They just don't understand a kid like that. But when you see the signs, boy, you've got to encourage them. I just don't think Jimmy's teachers recognized that."

Because he received little understanding from most of his teachers, Jimmy cloaked himself in apathy, developing a "cool" attitude toward studies, teachers, grades and the future. Misunderstanding led to apathy and apathy to restlessness, until everything was massed in a pre-quake state.

"Kids of Jim's age didn't think it was too 'hep' to be good in school," Mrs. Nall told us. "But he had this tremendous energy—joined every team the school had even though he was a little fella—and he was always busy with one club or another.

"It's true I gave Jim a lot of attention, but he asked for it. He couldn't do enough. If James Whitmore (an actor he studied with in California right after leaving Fairmount) hadn't told him to go to New York if he really wanted to make it, he would have had a whole other career. But he went there and he knew he had to make it fast. For Jim the time was propitious and he knew it."

His mother had wished him into being, the Winslows nurtured him and Mrs. Nall, like some helper from folklore, led him along his destined path; but it was James DeWeerd, pastor of Fairmount's Wesleyan Church, who swung open the gates. He had a magnetic personality and an earthy quality. He was cultured, worldly and eccentric—if ever a name was meant to mean something, it was his—loved a good joke and dabbled in the mystic regions. He'd come home from the Second World War a hero of sorts: a Silver Star for gallantry, a Purple Heart with Oakleaf Cluster and a chestful of scars from schrapnel. He was popular with the young boys in town and especially interesting to Jimmy.

"Jimmy was a parasitic type of person," said Al Terhune, editor of the *Fairmount News*. "He hung around DeWeerd a lot, picked up his mannerisms and absorbed whatever he could." Unlike most people Jimmy knew in Fairmount, DeWeerd had tested himself in the outside world; he was cosmopolitan and had been a friend of Winston Churchill, later attending his funeral on invitation from the Queen herself. Jimmy started to rely on him and, according to DeWeerd, confided his deepest secrets to him: "Jimmy poured out to me his belief that he must be evil, or his mother would not have died and his father wouldn't have sent him away."

Fairmount remembers DeWeerd as a minor-league Billy Graham, a volatile combination of actor and minister. In his sermons he was outspoken, witty and openly critical of Fairmount and its way of life. "The more things you know how to do and the more things you experience, the better off you'll be," he told Jimmy. At the home that he shared with his mother, DeWeerd introduced him to art, classical records and yoga (which DeWeerd practiced because of his wounds), talked of poets and philosophers and showed him home movies of bullfights in Mexico. The world which lay beyond the Jonesboro Pike with all its wonders and terrors began to beckon to Jimmy.

James DeWeerd appears in Jimmy's life like the wise old man in folk tales, the embodiment of the spirit world—"the weird"—a holy hobgoblin who arrived at that point in Jimmy's pubescence when he most needed a guide. DeWeerd had the insight, understanding and a certain sympathy for unformed ideas and ambitions that Jimmy so sorely needed but could not muster from his own resources.

One day Jim brought DeWeerd a faceless clay figure, four inches high, with the head and body slumped forward like a body escaping from form. "What is it?" he asked. Jimmy hunched his shoulders imitatively and said, "It's me. I call it 'Self.'"

DeWeerd delivered Jimmy from the conspiracy of littleness surrounding him. He encouraged his idea of separateness. "Everybody is the square root of zero," he used to tell him as they sat on wicker chairs on the pastor's porch. He introduced him to the Midwestern philosopher Elbert Hubbard. "Conformity is cowardice," this mad scribbler of moral precept had once said to his blotter. "It's better to die on the Horeb of isolation knowing you've been true to yourself, than to rot away in the mephitic alleys of the commonplace." Jimmy took it to heart.

DeWeerd also taught Jimmy how to drive and in his senior year took him to the Indianapolis 500, where he introduced him to Cannonball Baker, a famous ace of that time. On the way home the pastor and Jimmy talked of cars, speed, danger and the possibility of *sudden death.* "I taught Jimmy to believe in personal immortality. He had no fear of death because he believed as I do," said Dr. DeWeerd, "that death is merely control of mind over matter." *Personal immortality*—it's a typical draft from DeWeerd's Morality Trust, Inc. and it made Jimmy then and there a shareholder in The Great Beyond.

After Jim left for California in 1949, DeWeerd corresponded with him almost daily, always enclosing some pompous proverb or busybody saying which he encouraged Jim to memorize—thereby improving his memory as it elevated his spirit. There's something delightfully incongruous about Jimmy hoarding up these mental crackers to be let off as the occasion arose. Like the ardent apprentice he was, Jim in turn would inflict them on friends like Bill Bast at UCLA.

"'You're running so fast, it's all passing you by,' Jim would tell me," Bill said.

"Hard as I tried, I could not learn from his brief explanation what he meant to do to remedy the condition. I would go away and mull over what he had said, then return to him for another word of explanation.

"'People,' he would say. 'You've got to give and receive.'

"Again I would struggle through a few days, trying desperately to divine what he meant. Again I would return for more words of wisdom.

"'You've got to bounce the ball,' he would advise.

"Over a period of weeks I developed a nervous reaction to the thoughts he was trying to put into my head."

Whether these maxims helped Jimmy or DeWeerd to become more spiritual is not known. "Spiritual? I don't understand what you mean," Bing Traster, a member of DeWeerd's congregation, said. "You mean, did he talk with the dead, stuff like that? I never heard of it. But I always felt that if anybody could talk with the dead he could.

"Well, I don't want to use the wrong word," continued Traster, "but I think Jimmy was spiritual. Not that he was a spiritualist, but after his mom died he got pretty blue and dropped by our house from time to time.

"He'd get so blue he couldn't sleep and he'd go past our house on his way out to the old homestead, the old Dean farm, to converse with the ancestors. He'd go out there about midnight and he'd pray. He'd go out and spend some time; it'd give him courage. He got hold of the Almighty God and the Almighty God helped him out.

"After he got his motorcycle he'd drive out at night past my house and he'd yell, 'Hhheeyyy Bing!' Get me awake, see. After a while, maybe fifteen minutes, I'd hear him coming back into town. But as he got to my house, which is the city limit, he'd have to cut the noise to go through the town. So I'd wait for him to cut the noise and then I'd yell, 'Hhheeeyyyy Jimmy!' Boy, he got a bang out of that! And I always waited for him, 'cause I didn't want to disappoint him."

Jimmy got his first bike in 1947–a Czech model with a horse and a half of power–able to hit a top speed of fifty miles per hour. "If he'd fallen only once," Marcus mused, "things might have been different. Trouble is, he never got hurt and he never found anything he couldn't do well almost the first time he tried. Just one fall off the bike and maybe he'd have been afraid of speed. But he was without fear."

Jimmy wasn't the only kid in Fairmount to have a motorcycle; a small group of neophyte bikers would congregate on weekends or odd afternoons at Marvin Carter's Cycle Shop on Fairmount Pike, just two doors away from the Winslow farm. There among the engines and oil the boys would tinker with their motors and race around the back lot.

When he tired of that one day, Jimmy asked if he could use the shop's loudspeaker system and proceeded to introduce a phantom race: the pacing, the flash of the starting flag and *they're off!*

One of the boys remembers that "he'd get us all lined up, tell us what kind of weather it was, who got the jump, who crashed at the first turn, whose motorcycle was bursting into flames. Damned if he didn't make it sound so real, I had to look twice to make sure I wasn't really racing."

Jimmy loved to perform. Make-believe was an easier way to communicate with his friends. He wanted to be like them, but as he began to rely on acting to express himself, it only made him more different.

"Everything is cut and dried from the beginning," was the old Fakir's warning in *The Monkey's Paw*, "and there warn't no getting away from it." In his sophomore year at Fairmount High, Jimmy played Herbert White in this play full of overstuffed terror, acting out the strange presentiment of his own end: a boy killed by a mother's foolish wish. The play's clanking plot revolves around the irony that the wish is fulfilled, but only at the cost of the son's life. For the want

of one hundred quid, poor Herbert falls victim to a fatal accident: he gets caught at the flywheel in a factory and is mangled. The moral of the story, in case you might miss it, is that "there's nothing you can wish for that can't have bad luck about it."

The following year Jimmy had a good part in *An Apple from Coles County*. "He had a grand time," Mrs. Nall recalled. "He painted the flats and set them up. There was supposed to be a bullet hole in the wall and don't you know he put a real hole in my set! Oh! I could have killed him! *I* would have painted it in, but not Jim. He wanted everything to be exactly right. He nearly caused a riot by keeping the kids rehearsing one night until nearly midnight. And the next day . . . my goodness, did those parents call the school and raise heck! Even then Jim's attitude was, 'If you want to act, you have to give up everything for your acting.'"

Senior year, Jimmy impersonated the down-to-earth wisdom of an old-timer in his role as Grandpa Vanderhof in *You Can't Take It with You*. While the play actually takes place in New York, it could have been Fairmount as he says grace to bring the play to a close and sums up the grand ol' Hoosier bluntness and self-sufficiency that put his ancestors on a sort of first-name basis with the Almighty:

Grandpa: Well, sir, we've been getting along pretty good for quite a while now, and we're certainly much obliged. Remember, all we ask is just to go along and be happy in our own sort of way. Of course, we want to keep our health, but as far as anything else is concerned, we'll leave it up to You. Thank you.

Jimmy had his own grandfather, Charlie Dean, in mind when he interpreted the part. His grandmother remembers him as a child mimicking her husband Charlie's every move, crossing and uncrossing his little arms as his Granddad did and marching behind him, every movement in tune. "It was more than a child's playful mocking," she said. "Even then, Jimmy seemed to be able to be another person!

"Jimmy sure took after my husband, Charlie, when it came to cars," said Grandma Dean. "Charlie bought his first car in 1911 and horrified the town by scorching along at thirty-five miles an hour. Jimmy learned to drive a tractor first, and then his bikes. If you start an Indiana boy with a jackknife, you know, he'll end up with a house and lot. Jimmy swapped his whizzer for a little foreign cycle and after that his motorcycles kept getting larger and larger."

Jimmy began his senior year at Fairmount High in September 1948, and the class captured its minor events and major wishes in the still-life prose of its yearbook: "We opened our senior year by selecting class officers September 15, 1948. . . In November we had our pictures taken for the annual. . . in December a Christmas party was held in the Home Ec. room . . ." The time in between the lines was filled with days that began with homeroom and ended with last-period study. Notices of acceptance or rejection from colleges. Basketball practice and homework. The Marathon Farm Show came through town, featuring Uncle Ezra and Elinorie Chief Little Fox, a comic, probably the only Indian west of Mississenewa still laughing.

There was only AM music at that time and the hit parade included "Cow Cow Boogie" (The Ink Spots), "Open the Door, Richard" (Louis Jordan), "Filipino Baby" (Tex Tyler) and the really big hit, "Hillbillies are Sweet Williams Now," by the Hoosier Hotshots.

The Lions Club met and Ralph W. Pack talked about the Boy Scouts. The organization was formed, he said, with the knowledge that boys liked companionship—to be "in a gang" (a pack?) and that this trait was quite desirable as long as their enthusiasm and energy were properly directed. And a committee of six was assigned to study the issue of juvenile delinquency. Their solution was to "find a place suitable to be flooded," a skating rink for the kids.

An old gothic structure built as simply as a declarative sentence, Fairmount High School stands a little ill at ease on the corner of North Walnut and Adams, waiting each September for the herd of students to pour in, while the floor the janitor spent all summer polishing trembles at the thought of well-heeled shoes and boots.

In October, the sign outside the gym that read "Quaker Power" had its big bold letters changed to orange and black for the annual Halloween festival. Inside the gym the audience of students and parents sat in the bleachers while the drama society presented *Goon with the Wind*, a monster parody in which Jimmy had the starring role of Frankenstein, spending hours on his costume and make-up to get the right look. Like the "gory odes" of the WCTU, Jimmy relished the chance to screech and howl, express his "pretended" anger and anguish at being trapped in an alien body in a strange land. As Fairmount's Frankenstein he could well portray the monster's dilemma—the creature that doesn't fit in anywhere. It's no surprise that teenagers thrive on monster stories. No matter how scary they might be, monsters are fearless and can do whatever they want! Smash down the house, grab the girl, squash the mad scientist, swallow a supermarket and disappear without a trace!

The festival was held to raise money for the senior class trip to Washington, D.C. Barbara Garner Leach, Jimmy's classmate, recalled: "The class made enough money to go on the trip to Washington at the end of the year and everyone went except maybe one or two . . . Someone told us the best way to get to see Washington was to take a taxi ride, so when we got there we mostly just rode around. I didn't see Jimmy too much during our free time—he mostly hung around with the boys who were in a music group he belonged to. The first thing we did was to go see a movie—*A Connecticut Yankee in King Arthur's Court*, with Bing Crosby.

"Up until the year we were seniors, the prom had always been held at a more 'sophisticated' place. But in '49 we decided to take this class trip instead of a big, fancy prom, so that's why our senior prom was kind of cut-rate; it was held in the gym. I think a group of boys from

Jimmy as a teenage Frankenstein in Goon with the Wind.

the class played the music—they had a group, and if I'm not mistaken Jimmy was one of them. He played the drum. I don't think he brought a girl. He didn't date a lot during school. Oh, the girls liked him, but I guess he wasn't interested.

"We didn't even have anything to eat at the prom. We just danced. We didn't do much dancing. The prom was the only dance we had; it just wasn't part of the social scene. We mostly just listened to music in the car. I think we went out after the prom to the Hill Top, a drive-in place in Marion, for something to eat."

Jimmy wrote in the old Black and Gold yearbook, "I bequeath my temper to Dave Fox," which was his way of making up for knocking Fox down some stairs. Seems a quiet day in advanced speech class had been loudly punctuated by Fox's criticism of Jim's recitation. Jim responded by punching Fox in the mouth and was temporarily suspended.

The Winslows treated the incident with a Quaker's sense of "leaving well enough alone." Joe Hyams, in *Redbook* magazine, put together a believable interpretation of how they treated Jimmy's suspension:

Jimmy revisited Fairmount High School in 1955 and found things hadn't changed very much.

The boy on the motorcycle sped past the Back Creek Friends Church. Then, hardly slowing down, he skidded the machine into the driveway of his home. As he entered the barn, the sound of the machine and the rumble of its wheels on the boards caused the cows to move restlessly in their stalls. Stomping heavily on the boards, he shuffled into the house. From the kitchen Ortense called, "That you Jimmy?"

"Uh-h-h," he said.

Marcus was in the living room, reading the evening paper. To go to his room, the boy would have to pass him. Rather than do that, he sat at his place at the table and waited for Ortense to announce that dinner was ready.

It was a good meal, eaten for the most part in silence. Knowing nothing would be said at the table, he tried to prolong the minutes before Ortense would begin to clear off.

When Ortense got up, he offered to help with the dishes. She was firm in refusing his offer. Marcus had gone into the living room, and the boy decided to try for the stairs and his room.

"Jimmy!" Marcus had been waiting for him.

He paused at the foot of the stairs and murmured, "Yes."

"Why don't you take your gun tomorrow and spend the day hunting?"

The moment he was dreading had come and gone. That was all Marcus intended to say about it. Jimmy mumbled "Okay" and climbed the stairs to his room. But he left the door ajar slightly so he could hear what was said in the living room below.

"What did you say to him?" Ortense asked her husband.

"I told him to take his gun and go hunting."

"But Marcus, he's been expelled. This is serious."

"What else can I do? I can't hit him—he's too big for that. And besides, it would do no good and you know it. I don't know how to reach him, let alone punish him."

Quietly Jimmy tiptoed to the door and shut it. He took off his boots and lay down on the bed. The unsatisfied feeling was in his chest again. He hadn't wanted to come home and face the hurt he knew would be in Marcus' eyes. But he didn't know whether he had wanted to be scolded and punished, or hugged and kissed, or ignored. He had wanted something—and it hadn't happened.

Jimmy's trouble in high school was the kind of adolescent agitation that parents and teachers thought normal for every kid—low-key trouble like scuffles and cutting class and smoking in the john.

"They were wholesome, you know what I mean? No dope, no liquor. They didn't need it," said Adeline Nall. They weren't reared with that kind of need. Uh-huuuummmmm. Jimmy got on his

Jimmy breaking the pole-vault record for Grant County.

motorcycle; that's true. But we didn't think about his 'tearing around.' I don't know that he was a wild rider. No, it was a means of communication. And it was fun too."

Marcus said about Jimmy's trouble in school, "He smashed fifteen pair of eyeglasses in tryin' to be an athlete. Breakin' em as fast as I could get 'em ... I was called into the principal's so many times I almost moved into her office."

During his last year of school he became hard to handle. "We didn't know what was the matter," Marcus said. "He didn't take stock in us anymore and refused to help out. We were at wits' end. *He was no longer one of us.*"

Jimmy was a precocious and effective alchemist who made the most of his adolescence by retaining the magical principles of childhood and asserting them with his expanding knowledge of the world.

He had been a delicate child when he'd first come to live with the Winslows, but he transformed his frailness to overcome his physical defects. Not only did he want to be the best in everything, he wanted at the same time to hide the struggle, make each championship seem as easy a trick as a rabbit being slipped out of a black silk hat. His ability to succeed, especially on a physical plane, confirmed his belief in the mastery of magical action: he got a letter in baseball during his sophomore year; ran high hurdles on the track team; was champion pole vaulter (despite his size and indifferent strength, he broke the record for Grant County) and became a basketball star though he was only five feet eight inches.

Red-blooded American games have always been considered more "normal" than the arts and, socially, sports compensated for his sensitivity. In a small town even a non-conformist is forgiven if he's a top scorer on the team; so the gap that was developing between Jimmy and Fairmount, between him and the Winslows, suspended during basketball season.

"Jim is our regular basketball guy, and when you're around him time will fly." That's what it said under Jimmy Dean's yearbook picture. On the court, though, Jimmy really had to work extra hard to be a "regular guy." Because of his height, Jimmy *had* to be off the ground and into the air most of the time he played basketball in order to score as well as he did. In the best game of the season he earned a sports writer's label of "firebrand."

It was the sectional tournament against the Marion Giants, and the Fairmount Quakers were feeling pretty much like the forefathers they'd been named after—shakin' and prayin'. In the first half the score was deadlocked seven times. Just before the break Jim scored for the Quakers. He'd leapt up and caught the ball as it bounced off the boards when a Giant missed his shot. The Fairmount fans roared. Jim, confident and unruffled, got into Marion territory and was headed for the basket when a Giant got in his way. But Jimmy was moving like a black and gold streak, and with one quick shot that made the guard swear the pigskin was greased, he slipped the ball to Quaker teammate Rex Bright. Closer to the goal the two teams ran, bouncing and dodging and sweating. As two Giants closed in on Rex, out of the corner of his eye he caught Jimmy across the court, making wild, windmill gestures. He shot the ball back to Jim, whose guard had temporarily lost him, and Jim tipped the ball through the hoop and racked up two points. The Marion Giants called time out.

The cheering squad ran out on the polished floor with a swirl of black and gold skirting, their fists and syncopated saddle shoes punctuating their appeals for screams:

We're yelling for you, Black and Gold,
We're yelling for you, Quakers bold!

Coach Paul Weaver wasn't worried. He knew the Quakers would make a good showing. He tried to give the boys a quick pep talk over the noise of the cheerleaders and the five thousand fans in the stands. "Listen, boys," the hub of the huddle began, "we've only got to sink a few more baskets and we'll kill those Giants and then git us a crack at the championship against the Kokomo Wildcats. . ."

In the third quarter the score was deadlocked again when the Giants began to pull away. Drake Circle hit a pivot shot and then a teammate got two free throws to give the Giants a 30–26 margin at the three-quarter mark. At the start of the fourth quarter the Giants stretched their lead to nine points. Don McCroskey hit a one-hander on a drive-in attempt, Pat Klein tallied after taking a rebound and Bayard King cashed a foul toss to put the Giants in front, 35–26. But the Quakers weren't through.

Jim Grindle, now Fairmount's Chief of Police, connected on a free throw, Jim Dean hit a one-hander and Bud Cox converted a foul attempt. Then when Cox faked around the pivot and drove in to hit again, the Quakers were trailing by only three points, 35–32.

"Jim is our regular basketball guy,
and when you're around him time will fly."

"For a time Saturday night," the *Fairmount News* reported, "it seemed that the Quakers would continue their role of 'Giant-killers' and the spirit was willing, but the flesh and bone of the small squad could not endure." Handicapped by the height of the Giants and the reserve strength of the Marion quintet, Fairmount fought valiantly until the gun signaled the end of the game and the final score of 40–34, Marion's favor.

Despite the loss, it was the best game of the season, with Dean listed as one of the outstanding performers in the tournament. He took scoring honors with fifteen points on five field goals and the same number of free throws. Cox was another heavy scorer for the Quakers, collecting eleven points for the team.

"Unless you've lived in Indiana, you have no idea how big basketball is," Jimmy's friend Barbara Leach pointed out. "When I came to Indiana from Long Island I'd never been to a basketball game, and no one could believe it! Going to the game was the usual Friday-night date. Most of the kids didn't have their own cars, but they'd borrow their dad's for a weekend date." (A '39 Ford at the time cost $584.)

Several years later, a sports writer from Marion who'd watched a

Jimmy was headline news in the spring of 1949.

television airing of *East of Eden* remembered that game and what a great basketball player Jimmy was. He called Paul Weaver for an interview. The former coach recalled the game, right down to the number of baskets and free throws. About Jimmy he said, "He was a heady player and a good competitor. He was what you would call a clean-cut, All-American type boy. In his movies you see quite a bit of what he actually was—quiet, soft-spoken and reserved."

Despite his prowess in athletics, it was his speaking ability which made Jimmy headline news in the spring of 1949. He'd won first place in the state competition of the National Forensic League held in Peru, Indiana, which entitled him to enter the Nationals to be judged in Longmont, Colorado.

Reading in his room at night with a flashlight, he memorized and rehearsed the piece he'd chosen, "The Madman," from Charles Dickens' *Pickwick Papers*. Accompanied by Adeline Nall and sponsored by the people of Fairmount, he left with everyone's wish for "Good Luck at Longmont, Jim" headlining the week's newspaper. The article under it gave a log recorded with loving precision. "Jim and Mrs. Brookshire [Nall] began their journey Wednesday at 11:30 A.M. (CST) and arrived in Chicago at 2:30 P.M. Taking the Burlington Zephyr at 5:30 P.M. from Chicago, Jim and Mrs. Brookshire arrived in Denver, Colorado at 8:30 A.M. Thursday. From Denver, the journey turned north and . . ."

He was out of Fairmount and away from its confines, beyond the reach of Jonesboro Pike, which had been the border of the known world. Nothing is so sure to breed monsters as confinement, and the scream he let out that day was the wild cry of the "thing that grows on the green side of the heart," a shattering of all the layers of varnish that a small town will lay on you:

"*Aaaarrraaaeeeaayyyyhhhaa!*"

The judges flinched. He used the scream to wake them up, then began his recitation.

Yes! A Madman's! . . . the blood hissing and tingling through my veins, till the cold dew of fear stood in large drops upon my skin, and my knees knocked together with fright! Ho! Ho! It's a fine thing to be mad! To be peeped at like a wild lion through the iron bars—and to roll and twine among the straw, transported with such brave music. Hurrah for the madhouse! Oh, it's a rare place.

Jimmy traveled through himself to find that lunatic state—an inner transporter he'd secretly been building while other kids played games or began dating. Now, in his senior year, it was ready to be unleashed on the world! Jim McCarthy, another debater at the meet, remembered how he tried to convince Jimmy to change what he was wearing:

All day I kept trying to talk him into changing clothes. I'd brought my best suit and four white shirts and a couple of ties. So had everyone else, because we'd had it hammered into our heads that appearance counted for a lot and we had to be properly dressed. Jim was wearing an open shirt and jeans when I met him, and that's the way he went into the tryouts every time. At first he told me he just couldn't be bothered changing. But finally he admitted, "Look, Jim, this bit I'm doing is a wild one. It's a Dickens thing called 'The Madman' and I've got to go crazy in it. How the heck can I go crazy in a shirt and tie? It wouldn't work."

"You won't win," I told him. "You've got to go along with what they want you to look like if you want to win."

"Then I won't, that's all," he said. "I don't need to win. Only I can't do the piece if I don't feel it, and I can't feel it all duded up."

"His reading really *was* different," Mrs. Nall said, relishing the opportunity to revisit the past, "and Jimmy was wonderful. He would be very crazy and the next minute perfectly sane just like an adjustable lunatic. But it was the *subtlety* of the change. He really loved it. And like I say, it was a monologue but it had about as many emotions as you could use in a reading. You never get more than five or six characters in a reading, and he had at least that many moods and voice changes."

She sat watching from the back of the room in a school in Longmont as Jimmy took off his thick glasses so that cadaverous face and those malignant-looking eyes would loom out. She'd warned him that the piece, at twelve minutes, was too long.

"Perfect for *Long*-mont," he'd replied sarcastically.

In the preliminaries Jim got a good critique, but in the second round they told him it was too long. So Adeline Nall tried to cut. "But you couldn't have cut it like it should have been," she said, still uncomfortable when she thinks about it, wiggling her glasses up and down on the bridge of her nose in telltale gesture. "I knew it . . . by then. But you know, you can't tell 'em anything. You can never tell these kids; they know so much more than you do. So. I don't know if that's what was against Jim or not, but something was against us."

52

Even so, the day after the competition the *Longmont Times Call* printed a picture of Jim Dean on its front page as the sixth-place winner in the Dramatic Declamation Contest, and quoted Mrs. Nall with dramatic irony as saying, "Certainly great credit is given to Jim for interesting Fairmount students and citizens in speech . . . and I hope this is only the beginning of much more fine work in this field."

Jim hadn't won first place, but something remarkable had happened. He'd bitten of the apple and sat at the table of fame, and its apparitions tantalized him. He had let *it* out. The beast had talent and his eyes were bright. He would humor it and perhaps in gratitude it would lead him out of the labyrinth of smallness, far from all he knew and trusted.

Mrs. Nall said he never forgave her for not having been more adamant in insisting he cut his reading. "The only thing I'm getting today is the glory," she said a little wistfully. "I touched the life of this young genius."

Debating, plays and speech class were particularly active pastimes in Indiana in the forties, a residue from the FERA program instituted during the depression to stimulate homemade entertainment.

"The Voice of Youth" was heard every Sunday on WBAT radio in Marion, and when Fairmount was invited to debate Marion High School, Jim and Barbara Leach were selected to defend the Black and Gold. Barbara, a transplanted New Yorker, had just moved to Fairmount in the beginning of her senior year.

"It was like going to a completely different world," she said. "In New York I had one hundred seventy-five students in my graduating class and in Fairmount there were forty-nine. I wasn't very happy at first, but after a while I liked Fairmount. Everyone was very friendly. The main difference was that in Fairmount everyone participated. Until then, I'd been pretty much of a bookworm.

"Oh, most of the class was in the senior play," she modestly said about her role in *You Can't Take It with You.* "They tried to involve as many seniors as they could; so I was involved as a senior, not a thespian. For Jimmy, of course, it was different. His big thing in school was the Thespian Club. He was a fairly good *artist*, but drama was his big thing."

Barbara and Jimmy worked closely together researching their topic for the WBAT debate: "The United States President should be elected by a direct vote of the people." They made quite an effective team and were told off the air that they'd won; but when the moderator announced the conclusion of the show, he told the audience there would be no winners.

"Jimmy and I felt cheated," said Barbara. "We were convinced that it was just because Marion couldn't stand the thought of being beaten by little ol' Fairmount. But later, at the end of the year at an NFL banquet, we got a plaque that said 'Winner' so we felt a little bit vindicated."

It's ironic that Jimmy's greatest triumphs in high school should've been in speech and debating, since he was often criticized for being inarticulate in his movies.

"None of that mumble bit as far as any of my training was ever concerned," Mrs. Nall said. "I don't know where he got it. Was it his natural way of speaking? Heavens no! Well, just listen to me. *I* articulate like crazy and *he* knew how to articulate."

When graduation day came Jim's grandmother admitted, "It was becoming plain to all of us that acting was the thing Jimmy was best at. He'd won declamatory contests, even a state one; but the thing that convinced us that he was an actor was his appearance in a church play called, *To Them That Sleep in Darkness.* Jimmy played the blind boy. Well, I'll tell you, I wished he wasn't quite so good at it. I cried all the way through."

Consistent with the Quaker way of letting people find themselves, Jimmy's family in Fairmount offered no resistance to his vision of an acting career. If the boy wanted to act, let him learn to do it well.

In June 1949, when he was eighteen, Jimmy left the peaceful nimbus of Fairmount with its quaint old-fashioned ways, not knowing he could return only as an exile.

We are grateful that Fairmount was intimate enough to give us this last glimpse of him in the following piece from the *Fairmount News*:

JAMES DEAN WAS HONORED AT FAREWELL PARTY MONDAY NIGHT
A farewell party was held Monday night in honor of James Dean who left Tuesday for Santa Monica, Calif., where he will enter the University of California at Los Angeles, planning to take a course in dramatics and fine arts.

Joyce Wigner and Barbara Middleton acted as hostesses at the party.

Games were played and Donald Martin played the piano while the guests sang "California Here I Come," and "Back Home Again In Indiana."

Refreshments were served to Mr. and Mrs. Charles Dean, Mr. and Mrs. Marcus Winslow and son, Jerry Brown, Kenneth Bowers, Donald Martin, Virginia Payne, Joan Roth, Wilma Smith, Ethel and Edith Thomas, Norma Banister, James Dean, Joyce Wigner, Barbara Middleton, Phyllis Wigner, Mr. and Mrs. Denzil Thompson and Mrs. Cecil Middleton.

The party was brought to an end with the guests offering their best wishes and singing "Now is the Hour."

The Fairmount Jimmy said farewell to was hardly a training ground for rebels. If anything, it underlined the values of conformity. "One of the many meanings of democracy," read the *Indiana State Manual for Elementary Schools* (1943), "is that it is a form of government in which the right to revolution has been lost."

Geographically remote from the centers of change in America, Fairmount, because of its isolation, preserved a way of life that had disappeared from the cities almost a decade before. While Jimmy's contemporaries at Hollywood High School were forming the sort of subculture that was to be depicted in *Rebel Without a Cause*, Jimmy graduated from a school where hayrides and penny suppers were a thrill.

Jimmy left his protective garden for a country boy's version of Eden, the jewel-encrusted palaces of America's Babylon: Hollywood, California. True to the pattern of the classic American hero, he begins his adventures and enters his destiny from the outskirts. "The American hero as Adam takes his start outside the world, remote or on the verges; its power, its fashions, and its history are precisely the forces he must learn, must master or be mastered by," writes R.W.B. Lewis in *The American Adam*. "Oedipus, approaching the strange city world of Thebes, was in fact coming home; the hero of the new world has no home to begin with, but he seeks one to come."

"Why, gentlemen, didn't you never hear tell
of the Golden Valley that's located somewheres
in these here mountings?"

"What about it?" asked Thurston.

"What about it! Why, nothing at all,
only it's just paved with solid gold,
and there's so much of it that all the miners
in Californy, . . . couldn't pack it away. I tell
you, gentlemen, the prospector that first
tumbles to that ar valley, and sights the
dazzle of its wealth, won't need ask no odds
of the King of all the Injuns, for he'll be
the best fixed galoot in this little old
round world."

–from Kirk Munroe, *The Golden Days of '49*

CHAPTER FOUR

The '49-er
1949–1951

Living with his father in California;
college theater; a Coke commercial and a small part
on television; leaving his father's house;
a fraternity at UCLA; early dates and movie bits;
Jim moves to New York to study acting.

G iven its way, the true American leg will always walk west. It's the native instinct, the legendary continental drift. People and things were pulled west willy-nilly in its magnetic wake–prairie schooners, legs, sunbeams, gold diggers–and by 1949, the year Jimmy set out by Greyhound across America, the periodic table itself was making the move west. (Element 98, californium, was born to its parent, curium, by way of a neutrino at the University of California in 1950.)

As the silver bus pulled out of Fairmount onto Route 37, the panoramic heartland folded itself like a collapsing table, the warm, familiar universe eclipsed; and, after four days in the sweaty metal container, Jimmy arrived at the gates of Los Angeles. It was a ferociously hot day in June: somewhere a brush fire was eating fake mahogony, a tremor ground its granite teeth and sprinklers dribbled in pink sun courts. Beyond these, other images swelled in their tides. The mirage rose and settled; Jimmy entered and inhabited it.

Jimmy waited at the bus station for his father to come and collect him, anticipating this reunion with apprehension for he'd seen his father only briefly during the past ten years. They corresponded rarely and, then, rather formally.

Winton Dean had remarried four years after Mildred's death, and lived with his new wife, Ethel, in a squat little stone house in Santa Monica. Jimmy was polite enough to his stepmother, but she was a woman he never became close to; and, in the new family situation, they occupied mutually distrustful corners. Ethel never became one of Jimmy's "Moms" and is as absent from his story as his own mother is spectrally ever present.

Winton had selected Santa Monica City College as the school in which Jimmy should enroll for the fall. It was nearby and offered a good practical curriculum—business, teaching, physical education—courses you could use to earn a better living. Winton didn't realize that one of the reasons Jimmy had come to Los Angeles was because Indiana's Earlham College did not have a theater arts major. When Jimmy announced his desire to act, Winton didn't want to hear about it. The nine-year separation created a huge communication gap—Jimmy didn't want to fight with his father now that he was finally living with him again, and Winton had no idea how talented Jimmy was on a stage. Jimmy gave in to his father, but hoped to change his mind by the time fall registration came.

Winton Dean and Jimmy . . . a photograph apart.

Jimmy's relationship with his father and stepmother was subtly, but obviously, strained. Within Marcus and Ortense Winslow's sphere of influence Jimmy's chemistry had remained stable, but now, confronted with his father and stepmother, he began to show the signs of stress that were to recur frequently throughout his short life. What charges this unhappy reunion set in him we can only read in the seismic record of his films.

Bill Bast, who roomed with Jimmy a year later at UCLA, said, "Jimmy's father is very mild-mannered. Very quiet. I knew him in California because he was working at Sawtelle Hospital. But if you're looking for the source of Jimmy's dynamism you can forget his father.

"Jimmy related 'nicely' to his family. *Very nicely.* I can't imagine there ever being a family feud unless it was over something he couldn't have. He was always respectful and very kind. Overly kind, overly considerate. And generally gentle with his father. I don't think there was ever an unpleasant scene. Maybe once I think there was a little friction over the car. But not the kind of dynamic friction we would imagine.

"I couldn't see any family problems, though I know they were there. His father was very hard to approach and I know Jimmy wanted to extract more from him. And if you've met Marcus and Ortense, you can't imagine that they were very demonstrative or physically affectionate either. He looked for more, especially as a budding young actor. Jimmy was learning to respect the ability to value and demonstrate love and emotion."

The idea of a father seemed to be something of an abstraction to him, an enigma that he read in cold terms as if he didn't know what the relationship might consist of, what his part was or how to participate in the ritual. His attitude shifted wildly from one extreme to the other, from the freckled innocence of "Gee, Pop!" to the righteousness of "You're tearing me apart!" It was, of course, this very quality that made him such an adolescent idol.

"I don't think there were any specific difficulties between Jimmy and his father," Bill Bast recalled, "but I always wondered why they didn't talk to one another more. We'd go over to the house to get something done and no one would say anything. We'd be there an hour and five words would be exchanged. And later Jimmy would interpret for me. 'Oh, he'll give it to me.' And I'd think, 'Really?' I never heard him say anything about it. They had their own language."

Winton bought Jimmy a '39 Chevy in an attempt to bridge their differences about Jimmy's desire to act. But Jimmy went ahead anyway and joined the local summer stock company, where he acted under the stage name of Byron James in a musical production called *The Romance of Scarlet Gulch*.

Not a month had passed since his farewell party, and Jimmy was still within range of Fairmount's umbilical eye. In the tradition of small country towns where letters home get read aloud in the general store, his gradual achievements were faithfully printed in the *Fairmount News*.

JAMES DEAN JOINS THEATRE GROUP AT SANTA MONICA, CAL.
Mr. and Mrs. Charles Dean received a letter last week from their grandson, Jimmy Dean, who recently went to Santa Monica, Calif., to make his home with his father, Winton Dean. He stated in his letter that he was enjoying his vacation bowling and playing golf with his father, and also wrote, "I have registered for summer and fall sessions at UCLA. I take a subject A English examination Monday. I am now a full-fledged member of the *Miller Playhouse Theatre Guild* troop. I wasn't in time to be cast in any production but my knowledge of the stage and the ability to design and paint sets won me the place of head stage manager for the next production of four one-act plays, starting Thursday."

At the end of that summer Winton won—and Jimmy didn't go to UCLA but reluctantly enrolled at Santa Monica City College as a physical education major. He tried to compensate by signing up for as many theater courses as he could, and in one of his drama classes he found a sympathetic spirit. Drama teacher Jean Owen took Jimmy under her wing and encouraged him. She saw him as the guileless product of a gentle upbringing, as lighthearted and wholesome as a transplanted golden bantam. Mrs. Owen spoke fondly of Jimmy in "An Unforgettable Day with Jimmy Dean," an article that appeared in *Movieland* magazine:

I never knew him to be a complex and difficult personality . . . Jimmy was not moody, temperamental, unpredictable or rude. These terms did not describe the Jimmy Dean I knew. When I read some of the stories about Jimmy, it is almost as though I were reading about another person entirely. I do not understand why so many write about him as though he were a sort of juvenile delinquent. He was never that. I never knew him to be untidy or rebellious. He was always polite and thoughtful; his enthusiasm for everything that pertained to the theatre was boundless.

Jimmy in his Santa Monica City College yearbook.

Jimmy was in my radio class . . . When I first met him, I wasn't particularly impressed by his looks. He just seemed to be another college boy—quiet, shy, not prepossessing in size—and, of course, he always wore glasses. I never realized what arresting eyes he had until I saw him on a TV show in 1951. He was never aware of his good looks. It was one of his more charming qualities.

One day in class, Jimmy read some scenes from Edgar Allen Poe's "Telltale Heart." He was magnificent—but then he always had a spectacular emotion for any scene he played. Later, during that same class, I asked Jimmy to read some scenes from *Hamlet*. That night when I returned home I informed my husband that I finally found the right student to play *Hamlet* as I felt it should be played. That student was, of course, Jimmy Dean.

Jimmy was beginning to experiment with himself, expanding his repertoire of gesture and impersonation. He watched the way the California kids behaved, mimicking a beach boy's bop or a freshman's moon-faced stare. He wanted a reaction, an environment in which he could grow, but Winton and Ethel suffocated him with their lack of response. Bill Bast: "Like anybody when they first learn something, Jimmy went home and tried it out on the folks, and the folks recoiled. They didn't want to deal with anything like that. They didn't *want* to feel. They didn't want to express something they're not used to expressing."

Jimmy's need for feedback and the ensuing ferocities of rejection were never expressed against Winton but waited for release in *East of Eden* and *Rebel Without a Cause*.

In 1950, during his freshman year at Santa Monica City College, Jimmy brought home A's from his gym classes. His coach, Samuel Crumpacker, remembered him as a guy with bad eyesight who didn't like to wear glasses and who had to develop an acute sense of balance to make up for it.

"Jimmy's presence on the basketball court," said Coach Crumpacker, "was concise, authoritative, perceptive and alert to all that was around him. One day he came to practice late, looking confused and withdrawn. I pressed him for an explanation and the boy tearfully explained that he had failed a screen test at a local studio. At that time he wanted more than anything else to get into acting."

During summer vacation, Jimmy worked in one last sweaty burst of physical education as an athletic instructor; but in the fall he left Santa Monica for a theater arts major at UCLA and he left Winton

Dean's home for a room at Sigma Nu fraternity.

A new life began in the fall of 1950: he was a theater arts major; he was living on his own and he landed a part in *Macbeth*, UCLA's first big theatrical production.

"The biggest thrill of my life came three weeks ago," he wrote home to Marcus and "Mom," "after a week of grueling auditions for U.C.L.A.'s four major theatrical productions, the major one being Shakespeare's *Macbeth* which will be presented in Royce Hall (seats 1600). After the auditioning of 367 actors and actresses, I came up with a wonderful lead in *Macbeth* the character being Malcolm (huge part). . . . "

Macbeth's last dress rehearsal was running well past midnight, and as the tired actors went through their paces, student Bill Bast watched Jimmy from the darkened audience of Royce Auditorium. Bill was totally unimpressed with the kid on stage and wondered how he got the role in the first place. "James Dean," Bill remarked to himself, "a name to forget." (Bill's first book was titled *James Dean*, a story about their five years as friends.)

After *Macbeth* opened, the theater arts newsletter, "The Spotlight," was no more charitable to Jimmy than Bill had been and said Jimmy as Malcolm had "failed to show any growth and would have made a hollow king."

"I directed Dean in *Macbeth*," Dr. Walden Boyle, a professor at UCLA, said. "He wasn't at UCLA very long; he just worked on that one show.

"I didn't think he was happy in school. I guess the university life was much too slow for him. I got the feeling he wanted to act and nothing more than that, so he didn't take to the rest of the academic requirements."

Jimmy's college days in California slip out of focus from reel to reel in a hazy flashback where grainy rooms and sandy beaches swallow him up with their tiny grey mouths. Just a colorful trailer of coming attractions made up mainly of news events: the Incredible Sun Demon captured while doing his homework!

A friend at Santa Monica, Richard Shannon, actually spoke of Jimmy using images of light: "He was like a rainbow. You don't ever see one color; you see a maze of them. Nothing stands out in my memory of Jimmy but a bright light."

Later that year, Jimmy got his first professional acting job—a

"The world's worst Malcolm." Jimmy in the UCLA production of Macbeth.

"I'll have a choc malt, heavy on the choc, plenty of milk . . ." Jimmy in Has Anybody Seen My Gal?

commercial for Coca-Cola–through a classmate, James Bellulah. The one minute spot was filmed in Griffith Park, the same place he would film the planetarium sequences in *Rebel Without a Cause* three years later.

Ken Dicen, part of the crew who worked on the commercial with producer Jerry Fairbanks, said, "We had all these kids that we got from schools so we didn't have to worry about SAG (the Screen Actors' Guild). We gave them lunch and ten bucks and had them riding around on the merry-go-round. The gimmick was to grab the ring and then they'd get a bottle of Coke, and we had Jimmy handing out the Cokes."

The reason Jimmy had been chosen for the commercial was because the Coke people were looking for all-American teenagers. Little did they know that Jimmy was *the* teenage boy and that his face would become as classical an American image as the Coke bottle itself.

"The director spotted Jimmy," said Dicen, "and took a lot of close-ups of him. Why? I guess he seemed more animated. They wanted action and reaction and I guess he came through as the best. The next day they filmed an interior spot . . . I think it was a playroom and the kids were laughing and scratching around a jukebox playing rock music–or at least it had a kind of rock feeling. We brought Jimmy back as well as Nick Adams and Beverly Long Dorff [who were both later in *Rebel*] and a few of the other kids from the day before to 'live it up with Coca-Cola.'"

Fairbanks' office soon called on Jimmy again. This time they wanted him for an episode of Father Peyton's TV Theater, a holiday special called "Hill Number One." It was first telecast on Easter Sunday 1951, and although it got good reviews, it seems a little dated today. It had a good cast–Gene Lockhart, Roddy McDowall, Ruth Hussey, Michael Ansara–most of whom seem ill at ease in their djellabahs.

Scene: Easter Sunday, spring rain, mud, World War II.

Plot: A disgruntled platoon trying to capture an anonymous hill takes a break for holiday beans while the army chaplain tries to cheer the boys up. "War is a crucifixion," he says. "It shakes the earth, darkens the sun and makes men look for a meaning in life. Why don't we think a moment about the first hill–hill number one. It was taken by one man alone. (Bells begin to chime here.)

At this point allegorical mists descend and a flashback hurtles us through time to Joseph of Arimathea and Pontius Pilate, who are having a ghoulish discussion about Christ's corpse.

Jimmy played John the Apostle, and we get our first image of him seated at a table with the other disciples, who have gone into hiding. Under the pressure of Pilate's scourges the apostles are thinking of disbanding. Jimmy, with hair tightly curled around his head and a supernaturally deep voice brought on by a cold, angrily rebukes them.

"Was it for this we gave up our nets?! Just to go back to our boats again?"

Later in the teleplay when the apostles discover the stone has been rolled away from the tomb, Jimmy proclaims with eyes rolling heavenward: "He will bring us enlightenment! Come, we must spread these good tidings quickly!"

Jimmy as St. John in his first filmed drama, "Hill Number One."

Jimmy appears in "Hill Number One" only briefly—in the entire teleplay he has perhaps three lines—yet because of his cold and laryngitis, there had to be a nurse on the set with spray. During his scenes, Jimmy anticipates his lines almost audibly and seems extremely nervous. His quality—that vulnerable intensity—is unmistakable.

"You only have to put an actor on camera for a few seconds," director Howard Hawks said, "to know if the camera likes him. If it does, it picks up everything he does. Stars are not necessarily great actors; they are great personalities and you can recognize that instantly."

"Hill Number One" brought Jimmy his first fan club and his first religious following: The Immaculate Heart James Dean Appreciation Society. The girls at the Immaculate Heart High School had been required to watch the television show, and they thought Jimmy's St. John was divine. They contacted him through his agent (though his Malcolm was a critical failure, agent Isabelle Draesmer had taken him on as a client) and requested he attend a party in his honor.

Bill Bast went along with him to the party, which was lucky for Jimmy because they ended up pushing his car the last block and a half. "A lot of giggling went on as far as I recall. They made a cake for him," said Bill. "The girls were between fourteen and eighteen. It was one of those embarrassing affairs where everyone just stands around a lot. Jimmy got to play the star to the hilt and he loved it, and don't think he didn't take full advantage of the situation."

Meanwhile, things had gradually deteriorated at Sigma Nu. While adept at pulling friends into his personal atmosphere, Jimmy was less successful in packs. The very structure resisted his form of magnetism, their diffused mass offering him no focal point and their number giving them bearings with which to get a bead on his oscillating nature. In his secretness and vulnerability they read buried hostilities—a flickering, wakeful eye while Argus sleeps. His association with the fraternity is almost a paradigm for his future relationship with Moose, Goon, Crunch, etc. in *Rebel*: an explosive mixture of the desire to please and be accepted tempered with a characteristic defiance, a pathetic wish to ingratiate himself and be part of something combined with an ingrained distrust of others. Still, like many others his age, he wanted to be part of them at any cost, to be one of the pack—that snorting, ferocious, collective organism of integrated action—the one for all, all for one.

As a pledge, the "brothers" made fun of Jimmy and were fond of calling him the house "plowboy." When he undressed to skinny-dip with the other guys, instead of the neat white strip across his torso, he was comically half brown and half white from his habit of always wearing blue jeans, even at the beach.

Initiations usually consisted of filling rubbers with cigarette ashes, pissing in fishbowls, painting the insignia on pink desert boulders and other slobbering rituals. But the "brothers" decided they'd let Jimmy join if he passed a special test. The idea was to go down to the bottom of the pool and lay spread-eagle across the drainage vent. Then they would turn on the drain and he was supposed to escape its whirlpool. Jimmy went down and didn't come up. It became apparent that he was drowning, and it took longer than it should have for one of the "lifeguards" to jump in and rescue him. He pulled Jimmy out and dragged him into the locker room to administer mouth-to-mouth resuscitation. Alone in the showers, leaning over Jimmy, his rescuer paused for a moment and looked at the limp body, the sleek wet shoulders, the pebbles on the spine. He glanced up at the pale, still face coming to . . . he threw him his clothes from the locker room door and . . . walked out.

These Trojan knights, Jimmy found, lived in a hail of oaths, ate up Woody Herman and relished the blood-on-blonde-cunt-hair art of Mickey Spillane. They seemed to spend most of their time hoarding up juicy jokes for future business lunches. Sigma Nu was better than living at home, but not much. He did not wish to participate in their stiff, mechanical world, vulgar and cruel, yet lacking the grace of violence.

By the end of the semester Jimmy's interests were mainly in the theater. His brothers resented the fact that he spent so little time in their sweaty realm and found his obsession a little suspicious, for they were as gossipy about genders as a Latin grammar. What was he spending all this time in the theater for anyway? Didn't he know those guys were all *fruits*? They didn't want any ballerinas coming around *their* fraternity house. It was a sensitive point and Jim ended their bitchy insinuations by punching a brother in the nose. He was excommunicated and had to move.

Like most drama students at UCLA, Jimmy spent his spare time in Hollywood and Burbank looking for bit parts that would lead to a contract with a major studio. Returning from one of these hunts for a chance as a human prop, he ran into Bill Bast again on a late afternoon bus. They were both vaguely attending UCLA, and both struggling young actors competing for the same kind of parts. "Hey, dontcha think we'd make a great *team*?" said Jimmy breathlessly, sitting down in the seat next to Bill as if, delirious from a day of crowd work, he'd let the idea of humanity become an obsession. "Team?" answered Bill, a little alarmed.

Jimmy had a capacity for binding apparent strangers dramatically into his toils and making them almost his closest friends on the spot —even those who did not care to become involved in his life—as casually as fate. "In the flat glare of the bus lights I could see his intense blue eyes peering out at me from behind his thick lenses, magnifying the sincerity of his expression," Bill recalled. Jimmy outlined his irresistible scheme to Bill and, like D'Artagnan and Porthos, they found themselves in their steel carriage hurtling toward some unknown destiny.

Since he was evicted from Sigma Nu, Jimmy now needed a place to stay. He confided in Bill about the kind of apartment he'd be comfortable in: "a place I know is pretty close to perfect, a place where this whole messy world should be, could be, if it'd just take the time to learn," he said a little piously. "Meet another inmate," said Bill, and soon the two had set out to materialize their dreams. "A place out of which was to grow a whole new life of adventure."

At last, after searching for many days, the two youths came to a white courtyard apartment. A middle-aged woman appeared. All she could offer them, she said, was a dark little room with drab furniture. They were about to go away despondently when, with a special look on her face, she called them back. "I think I might have something you boys would like," she said. Up a flight of stairs they went, across a catwalk, and behind a reedlike curtain of palm fronds . . .

"There before us," Bill remembered, "aloof and apart from the world below, was an almost miniature penthouse apartment which had been constructed atop the main building. Perhaps it was the whole mood that had been created, or the seemingly unsupported stairway and high catwalk, or the singular aloneness of the structure, or just my vivid imagination, but I had the feeling that the entire penthouse was suspended in air. The view to the front was of housetops, treetops and, untouchably beyond, the ocean. What a superior, elevated sense it gave!"

Bill found living with Jimmy a stimulating, but rather unnerving, experience. For one thing, he could turn off his magnetic charm as abruptly as it had appeared. He employed its surging power defensively and aggressively, and often almost ruthlessly, rarely staying long enough in any one place or with any particular friend to form a lasting bond. This way he became a tantalizing blur, irritating those upon whom he intruded and infuriating those who would have liked to know him better.

Far from being the promised "team," Bill found Jimmy secretive about almost everything he did—and the more tense Jimmy became about his role as an actor, the more furtive he would be, reluctant to discuss his sullen art. "I sometimes had the feeling that he thought that by talking about the job, or admitting that it even existed, he would lose it," Bill said. "Once or twice it seemed to me that he was hoarding his pleasure and excitement for fear that I, or someone else, might steal it from him if he left it unguarded."

Bill was working at CBS in the radio workshop (CBS was *only* radio at the time), and Jimmy, in order to stay close to what was going on while he went to UCLA, took a part-time job as an usher. He liked watching the shows, but he didn't like the "monkey suit" he had to wear or being told what to do—and a week later he was fired. He soon found a more congenial job parking cars in the CBS lot.

"I thought," said Bill, "how odd it was that this guy, whom I hadn't intended to cultivate as a friend, had slowly become an integral part of my life in just a few weeks. I reasoned that it was purely a matter of circumstance. We had been thrust together a good deal because of our girls, who were close friends and had taken to the idea of double-dating, one of America's most unfortunate social customs, a procedure I had always considered to be a subtle manifestation of our society's psychological maladjustment."

Eight years later, on the cover of *Modern Screen* for March 1957, a beaming girl arm in arm with a clean-cut Jimmy Dean asks, "I Almost Married Jimmy Dean. Who Am I?" (In the same issue are Sal Mineo's "Dating Do's and Don'ts": "a girl's kiss doesn't mean what it used to . . . but I never think a girl is 'bad' if she kissed on the first date.")

The girl in the picture is Beverly Wills, one of Jimmy's dates, who was articulate and sensitive enough to give us a picture of Jimmy during what must have been one of the most insecure periods of his life. She is the daughter of the late comedienne Joan Davis. Bill had met Beverly at CBS, where she played "Fluffy Adams" on a weekly radio show. She first met Jimmy on a double date—Beverly with Bill, and Jimmy with Jeanetta Lewis, a classmate from the Theater Arts Department at UCLA:

I thought he was pretty much of a creep until we got to the picnic and then all of a sudden he came to life. We began to talk about acting and Jimmy lit up. He told me how interested he was in the Stanislavsky method, where you not only act out people, but things too.

"Look," said Jimmy, "I'm a palm tree in a storm." He held his arms out and waved wildly. To feel more free, he impatiently tossed off his cheap, tight blue jacket. He looked bigger as soon as he did, because you could see his broad shoulders and powerful build. Then he got wilder and pretended he was a monkey. He climbed a big tree and swung from a high branch. Dropping from the branch, he landed on his hands like a little kid who was suddenly turned loose. He even laughed like a little boy, chuckling uproariously at every little thing. Once in the spotlight, he ate it up and had us all in stitches all afternoon. The "creep" turned into the hit of the party.

They double-dated for a while and Jimmy would often drive Beverly to work if Bill had to work. Finally, one hot summer night, Jimmy and Beverly picked Bill up from work:

"Bill, there's something we have to tell you," she said without looking at him. "It's Jimmy and me. I mean, we're in love."

There was a long pause, during which I [Bill] imagined I was supposed to react. I could think of nothing to say. I wasn't shocked by the announcement, since I had not become emotionally involved with Beverly. I seriously doubted 'love' would have been the word Jimmy would have chosen . . . I knew him better than that. But he made no effort to correct her.

"We tried not to let it happen," she explained with all the sincerity at her command. "But there was nothing we could do. These things just happen."

Beverly was only eighteen at the time and she had seen a lot of movies.

It seemed, however, that Jim was still dating Jeanetta, and when she heard the news, she flew into a rage and convinced Bill to move out of the penthouse immediately for such a sneaky double cross.

The incident created quite a scene—Jimmy shaking Bill and slapping Jeanetta—but when Bill and Jeanetta finally stalked out, Jimmy was left with tears running down his face.

Jimmy was forced to move again since he was unable to afford the penthouse on his own. He moved in first with Ted Avery, another usher at CBS, and then stayed for a time with Rogers Brackett, a young CBS director. Brackett was sophisticated and successful and used his influence to get Jimmy a few bit parts on CBS radio shows such as "Alias Jane Doe" and "Stars Over Hollywood." Eventually, Jimmy began getting parts in movies.

His first bit was in a Korean War picture, *Fixed Bayonets*. "There we were, " Jimmy said, "all crouched down behind this hill, covered with dirt and sweat. And it was night, raining, real Hollywood, you know. I had exactly one line. It went: 'It's a rear guard coming back.' What a part!" The line was eventually cut, so all that remained was the dirty face.

In *Sailors Beware*, a Martin and Lewis comedy, he again didn't have any dialogue, but appears suddenly behind Jerry Lewis with a disgusted expression as if to say, "How the hell did he get the lead?"

In Universal's *Has Anybody Seen My Gal?*, however, his little bit was left in. Playing one of the twenties wise guys hanging out at the small town drugstore, he says to Charles Coburn (who is being trained to work behind the fountain by soda jerk Rock Hudson): "Hey, Gramps, I'll have a choc malt, heavy on the choc, plenty of milk, four spoons of malt, two scoops of vanilla ice cream, one mixed with the rest and one floating . . ." To which Coburn replies: "Would you like to come in Wednesday for a fitting? Thank you."

But Jimmy was one of a group of students who weren't satisfied with bit parts or "moss-walled academicians" as Jimmy later referred to the university atmosphere. They wanted the kind of experimental classes that Strasberg and Kazan were conducting at the Actors Studio in New York. Bill, in a rare burst of youthful steamrolling, talked to actor James Whitmore and got him to agree to give classes in the Stanislavsky method. Jimmy, of course, went to these weekly meetings which were held in a rehearsal hall at Twenty-sixth and San Vincente.

Never one to give credit to anyone but himself for his ascendancy ("No one helps you," he said to Hedda Hopper in a reverse switch on long-established Hollywood pieties. "You do it yourself."), he nevertheless considered Whitmore—at that time an up and coming actor from the New York school—a great catalyst in his career.

I owe a lot to Whitmore. I guess you can say he saved me when I got all mixed up. One thing he said helped more than anything. He told me I didn't know the difference between acting as a soft job and acting as a difficult art.

People ask me these ridiculous questions like, "When did you first decide to become an actor?" . . . I don't know that there was ever any such time. I *realized* I *was* an actor because of James Whitmore.

There's always someone in your life who opens up your eyes. For me, that's Whitmore. He made me see myself. He opened me up, gave me the key.

Whitmore advised Jimmy to go to New York and test himself against the uncertainties of an actor's life in the theater, refine himself and if possible become a member of the Actors Studio.

In the early fifties, Hollywood was wading through one of its most gelatinous periods of cotton-candy musicals and Bible epics. The only place where acting was still taken seriously, and deadly seriously, was New York. Jimmy was too ambitious, impatient and aware enough of his own talent to want to wait through another year of the kind of fluff he was being cast in, and had made up his mind to leave for New York in the fall. He seemed more or less optimistic about his forthcoming departure. But as the summer of 1951 approached and the jobs in Hollywood got scarce again, Jimmy's elated mood deflated into gloom. Beverly, then his "steady," recalled:

I soon learned that it was nothing for Jimmy to run through a whole alphabet of emotions in one evening. His moods of happiness were now far outweighed by his moods of deep despair.

He was almost constantly in a blue funk. He still couldn't get an acting job and he was growing increasingly bitter. I hated to see Jimmy become so blue. When he was happy, there was no one more lovable. When he was depressed, he wanted to die.

These low moods became so violent that he began to tell me that he was having strange nightmares in which he dreamed he was dying. The nightmares began to give him a certain phobia about death.

"If only I could accomplish something before I die," Jimmy told Beverly.

Jimmy spent most of his free time with Beverly and in the spring took her to her high school prom:

Jimmy was working as an usher at the time, and although he was in debt, he managed to put aside a few dollars every week so that he could rent a tuxedo. He asked me to go with him to the place where you rent these things, and when he saw all the dinner suits on racks he acted like a little boy in a candy store.

Although we sat out most of the dances, Jimmy was in wonderful spirits the night of the prom. Some of the kids at school joined us and he laughed a lot and told funny stories. My mother stopped by with some friends for a few minutes, and even she was fascinated by Jimmy's personality that night. He jumped out of his chair when she came to our table and even helped her off with her stole. "Good heavens, I've never seen him like this before," said Mother, flabbergasted, but charmed.

Their love affair lasted until the summer of 1951, when Beverly went to Paradise Cove to stay with her father at his beach house. It ended in a sudden outburst of petty jealousy, the result of gradually aggravating pressures.

One night at the cove Beverly said yes to one of the boys who asked her to dance, and it was enough of a trigger for Jimmy to explode. According to Beverly, "Jimmy saw red. He grabbed the fellow by the collar and threatened to blacken both of his eyes . . . I ran out to the beach and Jimmy walked after me, scuffing angrily at the sand, complete misery on his face. We had an argument and I pulled his gold football off the chain."

A few days later he called her to say goodbye, that he was leaving with a friend for New York. "I was glad he called," she said. "I had been thinking of Jimmy ever since we broke off, and I realized more and more that this was a hurt and misunderstood boy. I wanted to remain his friend. I wished him luck."

It wasn't a comfortable place for Jimmy. Intense and moody in contrast to the surfers and beach bunnies, with unruly looks and wearing that same blue jacket and gray pants, he could never hide the fact that he was an outsider among the golden sons and daughters of Southern California. "Somehow in this happy-go-lucky atmosphere, surrounded by boys and girls who didn't seem to have a care in the world, Jimmy stuck out like a sore thumb," said Beverly. "The whole crowd was very cliquey, and when Jimmy came by they looked at him as though he didn't belong."

His two years in California had been a series of steadily deteriorating relationships—first with his father and stepmother, then the grotesque parody of brotherhood at Sigma Nu, then the alienation of his only intimate friend, Bill Bast—and by the end of the summer he had managed to sever himself from Beverly too. He had shrunk to a pulsing nuclear knot, a critical mass waiting to explode.

"Jimmy was very sensitive and it hurt him very much to be looked down on," Beverly said about the way her friends at Paradise Cove treated Jimmy. "He sensed their patronizing attitude and withdrew deeper and deeper into a shell. I think he wanted to hurt them back too. I've often wondered if he recalled this period in his life when he portrayed the sensitive feelings of the rejected youth in *Rebel Without a Cause*."

These tiny slights—the wrong clothes, hair that just won't do, a shyness that keeps poking through—are the huge animals of the teenage nightmare, the agony of exposure, grafts that will not take. It is a misery in which monsters crawl. Jimmy later relished his role as loner, but it was something else to be helplessly impelled toward it. In his films he played this mirror image of his own life against solid backgrounds, but here he was stripped of all Method handles in an unnerving, slippery free fall. He depicted this sensation of a person being absorbed into an element he cannot recognize in a painting described by Bill Bast: "It was an oil and portrayed the skeleton of a man, stretched over with nothing but horrid green skin, who was standing waist deep in the mire which flowed through a long sewer-like tunnel that diminished in perspective. His head and one arm raised upward, as if pleading to be saved, he was slowly melting into and becoming part of the very mire that flowed beneath him. Jimmy titled the picture 'Man in Woman's Womb.'"

This spectral scene is the last souvenir of his college days in California. Hopelessly exposed, Jimmy floats nearly invisible in the flatland dimension of boardwalk postcards. He is a victim of Technicolor poisoning, but the colors cannot hold him.

In the fall of 1951, Jimmy left California for New York City. Beverly's recollection of her goodbye to Jimmy reads like a transparent poem as he ambles forlornly toward an eastern vanishing point:

> I kissed him
> on the cheek, wished
> him well, and watched
> him walk down the street.
> He
> kicked at some stones
> like a little boy scuffling
> down the street, and he
> stopped under a lamppost
> to light a cigarette.
> Then
> he squared his shoulders,
> turned the corner,
> and was gone . . .

The strain of it!
Horse would be dog!
dog would be swallow!
swallow, a wasp
wasp would be horse!
And I, on the eaves,
who strain to be fiery seraph, and am—
while on the ceiling, plaster flowers
so invisible, vast, and so small—
strain not at all!

—from Federico García Lorca,
"Introduction to Death"

CHAPTER FIVE

Persistence of the White Bear
1951

Lean days in Manhattan;
"Beat the Clock"; admission to the Actors Studio;
Jimmy learns The Method.

"**A**stonish me with the size of your vision! Feed me with your gargantuan fantasies!" the city seemed to say to Jimmy with its hooded, hidden voices the day he arrived in New York. "Find my secret equator and I will change you in the shape of your desires."

Jimmy came to New York with a farmboy's daydream of a vast city—a great abstraction overflowing with teeming crowds, salt-shaker skyscrapers, endless tribes of ball players, gangsters, tootsie wootsies, fabulous riches, a colossal Venus with a sugar-cone torch. When Jimmy met a real New Yorker for the first time—on the bus trip to the Colorado speech finals in 1949—he expressed surprise that anyone actually *lived* there.

"'Manhattan?'" Jimmy said [to Jim McCarthy, his busmate]. "All of a sudden he looked like a wistful little boy—I never saw such a change come over a face. '*You live right in Manhattan?*'

"We could have been driving through the prairie for all the notice he took of the scenery after that . . . I told him about the crowds and the school I went to and the theaters and night baseball games.

"'Where'd you see night baseball?' he asked.

"'Oh, at all three ball parks—Ebbets Field . . . Yankee Stadium . . . Polo Grounds.'

"'Three ball parks,' Jimmy said. 'Three ball parks in one town.

77

Geez.' He sat there for a while; then he said, 'I'm coming to Manhattan some time.'

"'Sure,' I said, figuring he was kidding. 'Look me up.'

"'Yeah, I will,' he said. 'I don't know when, but I'm coming.'"

Two years later, in the fall of 1951, Jimmy arrived in New York. He was entering a fallen world and, with it, the domain of time and its consequences. Things began to move forward at an alarming rate. It was as if he had been in a state of suspended animation for the past twenty years. Like the insect who hatches from his larval state after what seems like centuries to squander its energies, it seemed to Jimmy that his whole life had led up to this. New York awakened him to his moment of being.

In California Jimmy seemed unfocused, his particles jiggling helter-skelter, and he came to Electron City seeking form, ready to offer himself up to the spin and charge of its powerful centrifugal forces. Jimmy wanted his lines of force to be polarized and condensed, and from the rubble of former selves he would begin to construct his creature. It is here in New York that Jimmy gathers visibility. He would no longer be anonymous. Within two years he would "press the Broadway theater to its feet," within three years he would "conquer Hollywood" and within four years he would be dead.

At first Jimmy felt only solitary fears, living in a zone where all correspondences were hopelessly lost: "For the first few weeks I was so confused that I strayed only a couple of blocks from my hotel off Times Square. I would see three movies a day in an attempt to escape from my loneliness and depression. I spent most of my limited funds just on seeing movies . . ."

His "funds" had come from Marcus and "Mom" and James DeWeerd, whom he had stopped to see on his way east from California. With this money, Jimmy got a room at a midtown YMCA and waited for the city to begin its irreversible process. Whatever It was out there, Jimmy was eager to merge with it and emerge out of it changed.

The pains of adaptation were eased by Jimmy's discovery that he and the city had something in common. Its delirium and his own turbulence coincided. The city was a giant metaphor for his own inner state. It mirrored his melancholy, and he participated in it with the amused detachment and terror of a ludicrous nightmare. Jimmy later wrote to a lover, Barbara Glenn:

. . . across from Leon and Eddies, and above the so called Brown Derby and the Flamingo, and the Famous Door, and the Harem, and . . . It's so lovely! In the pensiveness of night the cheap, monotonous shrill, symbolic, sensual beat of suggestive drums tatoos orgyistic images on my brain. The smell of gin and 90 cent beer, entwine with the sometimes suspenceful slow, sometimes labored static, sometimes motionless, sometimes painfully rigid, till finally the long awaited for jerks and convulsions that fill the now thick chewing gum haze with a mist of sweat, fling the patrons into a fit of supressed joy. The fated 7 days a week bestial virgin bows with the poise of a drunken pavlova. Rivilets of stale persperation glide from and between her once well formed anatomy to the anxious, welcoming front-row celebrities who lap it up with infamous glee. The Aura of Horror. I live above it and below it. It is now 6:30 monday morning and if I wish; the drawer to my left, 2nd from the bottom is filled with a collection of not so subtle representation of the more imaginative. Photographs and drawings. I did not ask for this; I did not seek it; it is. It is my Divine Comedy. The Dante of 52nd Street. There is no peace in our world. I love you.

I would like to write about nicer things or fiction but we shouldn't avoid reality should we? The things I have just written are the truth. They are very hard to write about. I am lonely. Forgive me. I am lonely.

Although Jimmy had brought with him a letter of introduction from Rogers Brackett to a television director in New York, it wasn't immediately helpful and he began to "make the rounds." Sometime during his first year in the city, Jimmy was hired by "Beat the Clock," a television game show that was as absurd as the climate of the city. His job was to test beforehand the stunts to be used on this weekly show where contestants were rewarded for their bizarre, insane behavior. "Beat the Clock" was one of the most popular shows on the air at that time. Audiences love nothing more than to watch normal people making fools of themselves for money by attempting "impossible" stunts.

But they *were* possible, and week after week for one year, one person single-handedly solved all of them, thereby justifying the impossible logic of nursery rhymes, of dishes and spoons, cows and moons, candles and cats. The conjurer who mastered all of these feats was, of course, Jimmy Dean, that athlete of transcendence.

Working in pre-show "lab" sessions, Jimmy, along with other struggling young actors and actresses (Warren Oates among them), rehearsed the feasibility of these contests of man, matter and moment before they were sprung on guests by cryptic host Bud Collier.

"What I remember most about Jimmy was his dogged determination never to let anything beat him on the show," said Frank Wayne, a writer who created about five thousand of these dramas. "We had an extra hard stunt we used to call the "Bonus Stunt." It would be used at the end of every show until someone finally got it. It was worth $1000 for each try and, just to give you some idea of how hard it was, one stunt was up to $64,000 when someone finally won it!

"Well, if Jimmy couldn't do a stunt in the lab session, he would stay on his own time doing it over and over again until he finally got it, and then he'd come over with this championship grin on his face and say, 'Frank, I've got it!'

"He had that same determination about becoming a star. It wasn't conceit or a bragging, but a matter-of-fact confidence that some day he was going to be a star. It was like it had been ordained somewhere that Jimmy Dean was going to be a star and he'd been tipped off that that was what was going to happen."

Jimmy quickly, but carefully, selected what he wanted from the city's elements, and bit by bit he literally made himself up—Jimmy into James Dean. The man who invented himself!

He was both mechanic and machine, and his creation was to have monstrous proportions, for, as Victor Frankenstein had said, "with the scarcity of parts these days, why make a midget?"

Even before he tried out for the Actors Studio, Jimmy was a student of the Stanislavsky method. Combing the city streets with a derelict's fever, Jimmy would pick up a soft, round moment from a fat lady at a Nedicks lunch counter or steal a wink from an orphaned eye. Stanislavsky, the founder of "Method" acting, recommended collecting these awful treasures to his students—a repertoire of gestures and mannerisms—the material of life from which an actor can build a character:

Both a cat and an elephant can walk, wiggle its ears, wag its tail. But each has its own distinct way of doing it. Master these differences. Ask yourself—is it hard for a fat man to turn his neck? How does he sit down, stand up? Does he eat and drink in a certain way? Do not pretend; do not overact *as if* you were fat. Observe fat men in life and try as correctly as possible to reproduce them.

Apersonalization is the technical word for such aberrant behavior. "One may have as many body images as clothes," says a clinical text.

Jimmy collected and arranged these gaudy bits of body images like costumes he would use for future performances, pinning each one softly in a separate mental case.

All artists obsessed with their craft see the world as a storehouse of objects provided expressly for their use, and Jimmy was no exception.

The transformations he worked on himself during this early period in New York, as treacherous as they were to the fabric of his personality, were also creating a marvelous metamorphosis in him. In a letter he wrote to Reverend DeWeerd, Jimmy compared the pain of his evolving state to a fish scraping its flesh on sand: "We are all impaled on the crook of conditioning. A fish that is in the water has no choice that he is. Genius would have it that we swim in sand. We are fish and we drown. We remain in our world and wonder. The fortunate are taught to ask why. No one can answer."

Few mutants deliberately create conditions for themselves so severe that they must either transform themselves or become extinct; but in his experiments and tests of himself, this is exactly what Jimmy did, and his face and body took on the fluid grace of flesh modeled by his adaptions. Jimmy thought of his body plastically. It was capable of changing shape at will like a soft statue whose limbs would be ground and polished by the city's abrasions.

Jimmy emerged from his three years in New York a different person. Not only was he no longer a country boy, his physical appearance had radically and irreversibly altered. New York was his laboratory, where pieces of himself flew apart and blended together in arbitrary mutations like the horsedogswallowasp of Lorca.

Jimmy was never very good at making casual acquaintances, but when his little room at the YMCA became stuffy and the street full of untouchable city girls seemed forbidding, he would set out on starless nights to cast his spell in one-act plays of his own devising.

"I remember I was sitting in the lounge at the Rehearsal Club," said Dizzy (Elizabeth) Sheridan, recalling how she first met Jimmy. "Boys were allowed to visit the girls until eleven or twelve o'clock. There were two couches in the lobby facing each other, and I was sitting in one and Jimmy was sitting in the other. We were both reading magazines, and for some reason he quoted something out of a magazine. Like 'I admit in retrospect that my methods were unorthodox to say the least.'"

Dizzy answered from something she was reading and a disjointed conversation began:

"Hardly any of my best friends are peasants, except in the popcorn eating, TV-watching sense."

"You seem to know all about the crime. Please tell me about yourself."

"Who invented Truman Capote, that's what I want to know!"

Once cast in this mutual production they became friends.

"He asked me if I wanted to go around the corner and have a Champale with him at this bar. I remember the red and white tablecloth and the way he looked at me across the table. We sat in a booth and talked for a while and then we started drawing pictures on a napkin. I was very impressed with the way he could draw. Jimmy could do almost anything. But I wasn't so good at it and I drew the only thing I knew how—a tree.

"When we met I was very ready to be involved. I guess he was too. He seemed very 'lost,' which is attractive. I was working with two boys at the time—we were trying to get a dance trio together—and he came to see me and that clinched it for *him*, because I was a good dancer. But we reached for each other; we really did.

"Isn't it funny how I can remember what the booth at Jerry's felt like under me, what we drank and sort of falling in love across the table, but I can't remember a damn thing about what we said.

"He had a pair of jeans and a raincoat . . . a brown suit that he never wore. But he had a magnificent face. And I always told him I liked him better without his glasses. They were always slipping down. He was shorter than I was, you know. But he was intense, and that was also attractive. And at the same time very tender. Now that's not the Jimmy Dean you've probably heard about."

Dizzy and Jimmy became inseparable and, if not together, they were on the telephone; so to save on time and telephone bills, they decided to share an apartment together on Seventy-second Street. Dizzy, daughter of pianist Frank Sheridan, was studying dance and lived on the small salary she got working part time at the Paris, a movie theater across the street from the Plaza Hotel. Jimmy would come to visit her at the theater and she would fill him with the coffee and donuts the management gave to guests waiting for the next feature.

Dizzy witnessed Jimmy's features change, his habit of taking whatever he needed to complete the image he kept of himself in his mind's eye. She said of his larcenies: "He would take from people—he took their voices, their expressions, their gestures, and it would become part of him without his having to work on it. I don't think he did it so much as it overtook him because he was so impressionable.

"Sometimes he would come home and be a completely different person. Like later when he was in *See the Jaguar* [his first Broadway role] and was working with Arthur Kennedy, who's kind of big, blustery, drinks and is loud—which Jimmy isn't. Well, that wasn't so good. But fortunately these stages would never last too long."

After a few months, Dizzy and Jimmy left the apartment they'd shared because of the two things that had brought them together—time and money.

"We couldn't afford the rent on the apartment, so Jimmy left to live with Jim Sheldon, a friend of Rogers Brackett, which he didn't want to do—but that's another story. I got a room on Eighth Avenue that was about as big as this coffee table.

"Jimmy came and spent a couple of nights there, and we would have a ball pretending we knew Elsa Maxwell and we planned a big party and made lists of all the people we were going to invite. You couldn't even open the door all the way in this place because the bed got in the way.

"I guess it was time for us to break up, because when we were together we were both hiding out. We stayed in a lot and clung to each other. But you can't live that way for very long. Our lives were full of fantasy and we were so young, with long futures ahead of us, and of course we would be together forever to share it. There's a point in your life when everything seems to be forever. And you should never lose that. But it's good to pull yourself together once in a while and realize that it's not forever."

Jimmy fell in love with New York's fertility, its generous varieties of work, entertainment, decadence, violence and community. While he was scurrying across its parallel latitudes, Nick Adams (who would work with Jimmy in *Rebel Without a Cause*) was still a teenager hanging around on the street corners of Hoboken as Nick Adamshock. Though he didn't know Jimmy in New York, Nick loved to repeat stories about Jimmy living on twenty-five cents a day: "I don't know whether he ever starved—you know Jimmy wouldn't dramatize too much about himself—but I do know he must have gone through some pretty meager times for long periods."

With Quaker stoicism, Jimmy never elaborated on the lean days in New York. Other people would have to tell those stories.

"Once I found out he'd gone for two days without eating," said television writer Frank Wayne. "You know how I found out? Well, we had a sponsor that made tapioca pudding. And we always had gallons of it around because the commercials were live in those days. And after the show we'd throw it away. So one day Jimmy came up to me and said, 'Hey, Frank, if you're gonna throw that pudding away, can I have it?' And I said, 'You sure you want to eat a lot of tapioca?' And he said, 'Man, anything would taste good right now. I haven't had anything to eat in two days.' So I gave him the pudding and took him out to dinner as well."

No distracting calls to adventure came and few alternatives presented themselves to Jimmy as he made the endless rounds of agents. He would take any bit parts that came along, and if he was ever forced to take temporary jobs as dishwasher, busboy, waiter or hustler, he never told anyone. The work was transient and he never stayed long at one job, drifting in the grey azores, little islands of filth and degradation. This kind of sweaty, irritable climate had been enough to make Little Richard (working at about this time in a Greyhound bus-station kitchen in Macon, Georgia) erupt into sheer abstraction with: "whopbobaloopa whopbamboom." But it was even harder on Jimmy since he came from proud stock and up to this time had never experienced want of any kind.

A parody of this life as artist-sent-to-the-kitchen-door was delightfully illustrated in a comic-strip biography entitled *The Tragedy and Triumph of Jimmy Dean*, where, piled high with plates and colliding with coffee cups and chairs, Jimmy is railed at by a porklike proprietor: "Hey you! Snap it up! What the hell you think I'm paying you for—to come here and write poems maybe?"

Jimmy did write poetry. In a spare moment, perhaps between clearing tables, Jimmy scribbled this poem to an unknown lover on the flyleaf of a paperback:

Sight is bent to lick
    your heart;
A liquid mouth dilutes
    my thought.

Souls knit a nebulea mat
We live here in every world
Secret loft in azure habitat.

The average inhabitants of a small town soon learn the harsh limit of what is possible to them, and Jimmy, from the perspective of the city, began to question the collective littleness and carefully maintained equilibrium that made people shrink from any act of imagination that might separate them from the rest. Behind the deliberate action and cautious good sense of most of the people in a town like Fairmount, he recognized the great fear which he had to face, pushing himself every day to face it again. He became outraged at their hypocrisy in the drag of righteousness and their impotence posing as sobriety, and, after living in New York for about a year, wrote a poem called "My Town" on the inside of his copy of *Lorca* by Edwin Honig:

My town likes industrial impotence
My town's small, loves its diffidence
My town thrives on dangerous bigotry
My town's big in the sense of idolotry
My town believes in God and his crew
My town hates the Catholic and Jew
My town's innocent, selfistic caper
My town's diligent, reads the newspaper
My town's sweet, I was born bare
My town is not what I am, I am here

In the summer of 1952, an old friend came from California. Jimmy had written to Bill Bast earlier that year, telling him in the form of a spectacular collection of fantasies what a glittering world awaited him if he would only come to New York. But Jimmy had his own reasons for wanting Bill to come East. It would alleviate some of the loneliness of his life in New York and could extricate Jimmy from a situation that he did not know how to get out of by himself. At the time Jimmy was sharing a loft apartment in the West Twenties with Jim Sheldon, the television director Jimmy met via a letter of introduction from Rogers Brackett.

Bill had wanted to come to New York anyway to try to make it as a television writer, but when he finally got to the city that summer he found things quite different from the way Jimmy had described them in his letters.

10

Serving as a pie-target wasn't getting him anywhere. He made his way t[o]
York, determined to attend an acting school. To keep body and soul to[gether]
he got a job as busboy in a cheap cafeteria. The hours were long, the[work]
dreary. At night he was so tired he could hardly drag one foot after an[other]

"When I came to New York he was living under very unpleasant conditions, and I rescued him from that," Bill said. "Well, I didn't rescue him; he used me as an excuse to leave. And that very same day—my first day in New York—we went out and found a place to live together."

Searching along Forty-fourth Street for an apartment, Jimmy spotted Roddy McDowall, whom he knew from a casting call lineup. As they stopped to talk, Roddy told them he was staying at the Algonquin Hotel. "Why don't we get a room there?" Jimmy suggested to Bill. It was soon apparent that the Algonquin far exceeded their means and they settled for the Iroquois Hotel, a neighboring tribe which is cheek by jowl with the Algonquin on West Forty-fourth Street between Fifth and Sixth Avenue.

"I didn't want to stay at the Algonquin anyway," Jimmy said to Bill as they settled into their green-grey, twin-bedded room. "Only Indians stay there."

"Why, what do you mean?"

"Well, when I walked up to the desk, the man asked me if I had a reservation."

Their room was 802, and it cost them ninety dollars a month. It's probably very much the same today as it was back in 1952. It is still spartan, with no TV and minimal furniture. A chest, a chair, a pitcher and two irrational paintings that hint at a secret life of birds and flowers that could never survive here.

In this pea-green fog, part time and part old paint, the image of Jimmy grows vaporish, condenses itself into the ghost of a boy lying on his back, chain-smoking on a phantom bed. There is something here of the nausea and claustrophobic, suggestive climate of the first black-and-white screen test Jimmy made with Dick Davalos for *East of Eden*. He stares into the blankness of the ceiling and there releases the little creatures of his mind, mentally scribbling an absent-minded Method exercise: Keep your attention riveted on a spotty, uneven place on the wall for about half an hour, trying to constantly feed your attention with new material.

If times were hard, Jimmy thought, it was just the price one had to pay for a new life. Nothing could be sadder, more filled with pretense and despair, than run-down hotels—full of old ladies in their half-mad grooves and solitary lives with disappointed pasts. After a few months at the Iroquois, Jimmy and Bill moved around the corner to West

Forty-fifth Street into an apartment they shared with Dizzy Sheridan.

"The night we moved we were particularly broke because we had to make an advance payment of the rent," Bill Bast recalled. "We had between us less than a dollar on which to eat. So, like scavengers, we took all the leftovers from the refrigerator and made a stew into which Jimmy dumped a half a package of old vermicelli. Our stomachs were singing out in a discordant chorus of hunger cries, and as we sat eating the mess, not one of us would acknowledge the presence of the tiny bugs floating atop the broth. Each of us surreptitiously dipped out the little intruders and continued to eat in silence."

When Jimmy and Bill moved into the new apartment they had no furniture. From friends they assembled a mattress or two, some dishes and pots and a few towels to set up housekeeping. Without a radio or TV or money to go out, they invented ways to entertain themselves —and what better combination could there be than a scriptwriter, a dancer and an actor?

If they weren't rehearsing something or imitating someone, Bill and Dizzy would usually get bullfighting lessons from Jimmy. "But I didn't learn very much about bullfighting from him," said Dizzy, "because Jimmy always made me the bull."

Jimmy had come to New York, encouraged by advice and intuition, to find work and to find himself through acting. "New York's a fertile, generous city if you can accept the violence and decadence," he said, setting out to discover all the opportunity contained in its seething cauldron.

In the jittery market of the entertainment business, it always helps to have an unyielding personality behind you—someone to push, encourage, express faith, make deals, keep you out there. Jimmy found such a person when he met Jane Deacy, the woman who became his agent and a rock-like mother figure in his life.

Television director James Sheldon, whom Jimmy had lived with before Bill arrived, was impressed with Jimmy's looks and acting ability, but couldn't use him. He did, however, refer Jimmy to a talent agent, Louis Schurr, who could turn Jimmy on to endless producers and directors if he liked him and wanted to take him on as a client. But Schurr was not impressed. Jimmy didn't fit into any of his "files": he was too short, wore glasses, didn't talk or act like a "juvenile" and certainly wasn't ready for a "mature" part. Nevertheless, Schurr's assistant, Jane Deacy, recognized the *James Dean* in Jimmy right away, and there and then began a business relationship that would last until the end of Jimmy's career.

Jane Deacy is the not so mysterious element in Jimmy's rise to fame. Because if Jimmy had talent, it was Jane Deacy's persistence that put him in places where he could reveal it. She had the insight to see what he might become, the limitless faith to drive him, and she calculated his value wisely enough to be sure he was never exploited.

One day Jimmy walked into Jane Deacy's office and saw Christine White, an attractive young blonde, typing something at the front desk. He'd never seen her there before and tried to get a look at what she was doing. The following dialogue ensued.

"What is that?"

"It's a scene."

"What's your phone number?"

"I don't know." (still typing)

He doesn't look like an actor, she thought to herself, not with that slouch and those thick glasses. But Jane Deacy (who, it turned out, was her agent as well) told her who Jimmy was.

Jimmy's drawing of a bullfighter.

Later that afternoon, over a cup of coffee at Cromwell's Drugstore, Christine told Jimmy that she was an actress working on a scene to use in her audition for the Actors Studio. Since James Whitmore had told him about the Studio, Jimmy had been trying to figure out a way to approach it. By the end of the afternoon it occurred to Chris that she needed a partner, and, with apparent casualness, Jimmy wrote himself into her little existential drama.

Chris had already written a scene, and when Jimmy created his character they reworked it—adding dialogue, expanding characters—finally naming it "Roots." They rehearsed it for five weeks straight, inflicting it on anyone, anywhere, who would give them a reaction. For little old men and ladies at the automat, to uncomprehending drunks in bars, for Jerry at Jerry's Tavern and among their friends. When it was good enough to be mistaken for a lovers' quarrel they decided they were ready.

Jimmy was so nervous the day of the audition Chris was almost sure he would run out on her. But a few beers (conveniently written in as props) cured pre-audition shakes. Jimmy, with a can of beer in hand, ran on stage. "Without his glasses on he couldn't find center stage," recalled Christine, "and was almost in the opposite wing. He was out of both overhead amber lights, but the scene was supposed to be nighttime anyway. I waited twenty seconds out of the five minutes we were allowed, ran out and plunked down center stage and refused to look at him. I knew he was startled, but he immediately made the adjustment. He rolled over twice on the floor, laughed and said, 'Hi!' which wasn't in the script."

The action takes place on an island just before a hurricane. A young girl trying to get away from her parents runs into a beach bum lying in the sea wheat. Facing the storm together gives them immediate intimacy, and they begin to speak in words that Christine and Jimmy wrote for themselves:

Chris: (*pause*) . . . There are no stars tonight.

Jimmy: They went behind that big black blanket, but they'll peep out again.

Chris: I'm sure I'm nuts! People were evacuatin' the other way and we just roared off into the darkness . . . wind . . . and unknown . . . what're you thinking about? (*silence*) What have you been doin' most of your life?

Jimmy: Ripping off layers to find the roots. How about a beer? Do you mind it out of the bottle?

After some small talk about boyfriends, the hurricane and parents harldy less threatening, she asks him what he's thinking about again:

Jimmy: I'm thinking you are in despair. You've come to me with the emptiness of your world.

Chris: I know, I know. What can I do? I need your freedom. (*She takes his hand.*) You've been runnin' away all your life and knockin' the world down with your fist. Warm and tender hand.

Jimmy: Come inside 'cause you're new at runnin' away.

Chris: (*She starts to cry.*) I hate you. You made me grow up in a twinkling of a second. (*drops his hand*) No, it is not you I hate. It is me. It is me! (*She runs off into the darkness.*)

This story of isolation, which takes place appropriately on an island, ends with the man, alone again after the girl runs off.

Jimmy: (*He chuckles and starts throwing the beer can up in the air several times; then he tosses it away.*) You see, Clayton (*he begins to shout*), you can toss your whole life away and nobody will care! Don't you hear me? (*His robust movements subside to a slump.*) It is *me. We* . . . all of us . . . are alone . . . .

Out of the one-hundred-fifty aspirants for the Actors Studio, Jimmy and Christine White were two of the twelve chosen as finalists, and out of that twelve, they were the only two accepted.

The Actors Studio was the most desirable and prestigious school and showcase of the 1950s. Elia Kazan, Arthur Miller, Marlon Brando and Marilyn Monroe were all associated with it during this time, and it became an intellectual and political barometer of the New York theater, a center for everyone who was looking for new stars, or looking to be a new star.

The Studio had emerged from the Group Theater of the 1930s, which had taken its philosophy toward acting from the great Russian actor and director, Konstantin Stanislavsky. Stanislavsky and his brother had evolved through their work, their school and their theater a new "method" of acting: a trained discipline toward building a character, the aim of which was not to imitate but to become the part, by drawing from the reality of your own life.

The Group Theater had enormous influence in the thirties and forties through playwrights like Clifford Odets and Bertolt Brecht and actors such as John Garfield, Morris Carnovsky and Kazan himself.

The Studio is in a white building on West Forty-fourth Street that looks like a converted church. Students gather in the small room that serves as front desk, lobby and lounge to wait for Strasberg to arrive, before proceeding to class. There is a kitchen for coffee or tea and bathrooms marked "Romeo" and "Juliet." When the magus enters, the students follow silently up the stairs for the two hour drama / discussion / dialogue in which all are supposed to participate.

Perhaps the quiet, matter-of-fact appearance of the Actors Studio is maintained so as not to violate its socialist origins in the Group Theater, which had set out in the thirties, with some political intent, to be "a mirror of contemporary life" and to change it. This influence has spread to some of the Method's most notorious products—Odets, whose plays are exotically drab; Marlon Brando, well known for causes and social involvements; and Kazan, who was once a member of the Communist Party. Jimmy too had his causes, but they were more far-reaching in influence and effect by virtue of not being political.

In the Actors Studio Strasberg later opened in Hollywood, there are huge blow-up posters of Marilyn Monroe and Jimmy Dean, seductive herms at the temple of Method, worshipped by the aspiring actors and actresses who still enroll under the aegis of Strasberg, hoping that a little of the aura of Monroe and Dean will fall on them. But one of the ironies of the Actors Studio is that these stars rarely took part in the sessions. Kazan recalls Jimmy as a student only vaguely: "To begin with, Dean was scarcely at the Studio at all. He came in only a few times. I remember him sitting in the front row, a surly mess. He never participated in anything."

Jimmy stomped out of a session after doing one scene and then having his performance analyzed by students and Strasberg. For an actor whose method was so totally personal, it was a scraping and slicing he couldn't sit still for.

"If I let them dissect me, like a rabbit in a clinical research laboratory or something, I might not be able to produce again," he told Bill Bast. "For chrissake, they might sterilize me!"

Though the reputation of the Actors Studio as an institution rests on its stars, Strasberg readily admits that neither Brando, Clift nor Dean ever trained themselves rigorously there: "Perhaps they didn't need it; perhaps their talent was enough. But Jimmy would sit and watch. He didn't work much; I think he was a little bit afraid of the work. But you'd see him sitting there, watching."

The Method is a system of acting which demands that its disciples use every kind of feeling from their real life in the parts they are to dramatize: every detail of the past, every experience, every sensation, pains and angers and raw wells of feeling are all drawn upon to "build the character."

In the Method, a character is created out of the emotional content of the actor's own body. The actor is warned not to let himself be sucked into what is known as "the existential fallacy" of confusing himself with his creation, but a performer like Jimmy, who has an imbalance in his own chemistry, is susceptible to this form of theatrical cannibalism. He can suddenly find himself consumed by the persona that evolves out of being cast consistently in a certain kind of role.

Europeans have always avoided the existential fallacy, at least in the theater, by allowing the actor to walk away from his mask, to be "merely an entertainer." Stanislavsky insists the actor keep this distance. "An actor does not surrender himself on the stage to some such hallucination. On the contrary, some part of his senses must remain free from the grip of the play to control everything. He does not forget that on the stage are decorations. He says, 'I know that all around me is a rough counterfeit of reality. It is false. But *if* all should be real, see how I might be carried away, then I would act!'"

In America, the Method had a different effect. The American culture, in its relentless consumption and its image of the theater as an entertaining commodity, has made its artists into commercial products, and success for a star means a financial and social class equivalent to the royal heirarchies of Europe.

Many of these stars, created by the movies and by rock, have not been able to resist seeing what it would be like to be carried away on the riptide of illusion. American superstars have fallen victim to the "existential fallacy" because, unlike Europe, where most successful performers are treated as artists, here in America we *want* our heroes to give themselves up to the roles they play.

A film star is always the model of something in extreme—they are victims of implosion who, no longer able to reach the inner limits of their own personalities, dissolve. Marilyn Monroe described this state of mind as something like waiting for an accident: "I think that when you are famous every weakness is exaggerated. This industry should behave to its stars like a mother whose child has just run out in front of a car. But instead of clasping the child to them, they start punishing the child."

It is hardly accidental that three of the four major stars in Hollywood's last era who grew out of the Method fell victims to suicides of one variety or another: by attrition, as in the case of the self-destructive Montgomery Clift; by intention, as in Marilyn Monroe's case; or "suicide by inadvertence," as Jimmy's death has been described.

Jimmy practiced the "Method" on himself almost daily, continually taking himself apart, tearing away the superfluous tissue of his body image and examining that crystal skeleton at the center in its bone-white light: *ripping away layers to find roots*, as he wrote for himself in his audition.

Close friends saw that such hair-raising experiments must lead to a final dissolution. It was just a sum of all the little destructions that he worked so relentlessly on himself.

Barbara Glenn, who was one of the few people in whom he would confide, said, "Jimmy was a terribly destructive person. Our relationship was destructive. I knew he would destroy himself in the end and that's why when it came, it wasn't a surprise; it was as though my reaction to it had happened long before. From the first time I met Jimmy I felt it. Whenever I waited for him I always wondered, 'Is he going to make it?'

"He bought a new bike and said, 'I'm going to go home.' It was winter. 'How?' I said. 'Please, if you're going to die, why don't you do it around here?' 'No, I've got to try it. It's great. Don't worry.'

"So Jimmy went to Indiana and I didn't hear from him for a couple of weeks. He went through the snowstorms and through the ice and practically froze to death, but drove all the way out and back. I was doing rehearsals one day and I looked in the back of the theater and saw him and just said, 'Whew! Okay.'"

Don Quixote said, "Actors live in a magical universe. They mean no harm by their deceptions." But somehow in the magical universe of movies we have used actors like canaries that are watched closely in deep mines, allowing them to be carried out onto the dangerous reefs of fantasy, and in these extremities they sacrifice themselves to show what we are about to become.

The treacherous toying with illusion that Method preparation encourages and the destructive effects it has had on those stars who let their lives spill over into their roles and their roles into their lives, is inherent in Stanislavsky's system. One can play one's part *too* well, and the price one pays can be deadly. It is as if the fictional personality and the real personality are anti-images which cannot co-exist—one of them has to go—and for an actor obsessed with his work it's obvious which one will disappear.

The brothers Stanislavsky were themselves aware of the lurking danger of fusing "real" with "make-believe" and they gave it a recognizable shape by creating the chilling specter of the white bear.

"My favorite story about Stanislavsky and his brother," Dennis Hopper said, "is a game they played at together that they could never succeed in. The game was this: they would go and stand in a corner and for five minutes try and *not* think of a white bear. They tried to do that all of their lives and never once succeeded."

Most actors shrink from the specter of the white bear. Jimmy embraced it as he worked at building the character of *James Dean*, not realizing that in self-creation are the roots of self-destruction.

. . . the *qaumaneq* consists of "a mysterious
light which the shaman suddenly feels in
his body, inside his head, within the brain,
an inexplicable searchlight, a luminous
fire, which enables him to see in the dark,
both literally and metaphorically speaking,
for he can now, even with closed eyes, see
through darkness and perceive things and
coming events which are hidden from others" . . .

—from Mircea Eliade, *The Two and the One*

CHAPTER SIX

An Orthicon Ghost
1952–1954

*Television in the early fifties;
making the rounds; Jim's major roles on television;
friends and lovers.*

I n 1951, television's first year of general programming, most of the shows broadcast over its "airlanes" originated in New York City, and almost any promising young actor could get a part in something. The infant medium quickly became a predatory monster, munching indiscriminately at whatever talent it could find: old character actors, saccharine starlets, scholars, idiots and dogs. What it couldn't find, it invented: game shows, quizzes, basseto-toned newscasters, series for nighttime and soaps for daytime.

The arrival and instantaneous acceptance of television broadcasting caused a panic in Hollywood. Burbank's moguls tried to outdo the cocky cathode by astonishing the public with larger than life spectaculars—3-D movies, Smell-O-Vision, Cinerama and CinemaScope. Tallulah Bankhead tartly suggested they go back to the silents. But this last gasp was to no avail. The Colossus of the Hesperides was mortally wounded and sadly limped off into its final Metro sunset. It was against the glow of this last burst of Hollywood's Red Giant that Jimmy's ascendancy as a star took place.

Though television was spiriting away the movies' audiences, it did provide the industry with a new breed of serious young actors—Rod Steiger, Grace Kelly, Anne Bancroft, Paul Newman, Eva Marie Saint—all had the cool style of New York studios. Television offered more roles to actors and commissioned more scripts to writers—some five hundred live dramas were presented in 1952 alone—than in several years of Broadway theater productions, and it created for the first time in America a kind of national theater in which a repertory of talent could experiment. There was less at stake for television producers: costs were minimal and they had the advantage of being newborn—and the excitement attracted many truly talented people.

"In the days of live TV," said Rod Serling, the television writer best known now for "Night Gallery" and "The Twilight Zone," "you had unexpected things happening all the time, like profanities, missed cues, leftover air time. But nobody at the stations let it bother them too much. Also, we were a close community in New York—the live writers. We compared notes; we socialized together. We used to practically hold hands with a story as it went through final rehearsal and onto the air. Now when a writer does a TV script, he's usually flying to Europe by the time it gets broadcast."

In its random gathering, television also picked up plenty of unknown grubs like Jimmy, who first appeared on camera May 11, 1952 on an NBC show called "Prologue to Glory." In 1953, records show he had at least fourteen major roles, and how many shows he appeared in as one of the "others" is a memory kept by those who worked with him, since few records of television shows were well kept during this time. Jimmy was evidently encouraged to get in as many productions as possible by his agent, Jane Deacy, but only determination could have helped him win so many roles in such a short period of time.

The following list includes all available credits for shows that Jimmy appeared in, including reruns and two posthumous tributes.

Appearances on NBC-TV

May 11, 1952	U.S. Steel Hour—"Prologue to Glory"
Jan 15, 1953	Kate Smith Hour—"Hound of Heaven"
Jan 29, 1953	Treasury Men in Action—"The Case of the Watchful Dog"
April 16, 1953	Treasury Men in Action—"The Case of the Sawed-Off Shotgun"
July 17, 1953	Campbell Sound Stage—"Something for an Empty Briefcase"
Sept 11, 1953	"The Big Story"
Oct 4, 1953	"Omnibus," aired Oct. 4, 1953 (reviewed in *Variety*, Oct.

7, 1953, with Alistair Cooke, Hume Cronyn, Jessica Tandy, Carol Channing, Elliot Reed and others. Ninety-minute emphasis on legit shows with film clips of *Oklahoma* and *Glory in Flower* (a preem of a William Inge play for TV)

Oct 14, 1953	Kraft TV Theater–"Keep Our Honor Bright"
Oct 16, 1953	Campbell Sound Stage–"Life Sentence"
Nov 11, 1953	Kraft TV Theater–"A Long Time Till Dawn" (written by Rod Serling)
Nov 17, 1953	Armstrong Circle Theater–"The Bells of Cockaigne"
Nov 23, 1953	Johnson's Wax Program–"Robert Montgomery Presents Harvest" (a Thanksgiving special, co-stars Dorothy Gish and Vaughn Taylor)
Sept 5, 1954	Philco TV Playhouse–"Run Like a Thief"
March 14, 1955	Lever Brothers' Lux Video Theater–"The Life of Emile Zola" followed by an interview with Jimmy
Nov 27, 1955	Posthumous award presented on Colgate Variety Hour by *Modern Screen* magazine in honor of its twenty-fifth anniversary
Oct 14, 1956	"Steve Allen Show"–Tribute, including film clips of Fairmount, music from *The James Dean Story* and excerpt of television show Jimmy did (Campbell Sound Stage's "Life Sentence")
Jan 4, 1957	Repeat of "The Big Story" aired Sept. 11, 1953

Appearances on ABC-TV

Jan 4, 1955	U.S. Steel Hour–"The Thief" (with Paul Lukas, Diana Lynn, Mary Astor, Patrick Knowles)

Appearances on CBS-TV

April 14, 1953	Danger–"No Room" (with Martin Kingsley and Irene Vernon)
Aug 17, 1953	Studio One Summer Theater–"Sentence of Death" (with Thomas Walsh and Adrienne Spies)
Aug 25, 1953	Danger–"Death is My Neighbor" (with Betsy Palmer)
––, 1953	Danger–"The Little Woman" (with Mildred Duavod)
Nov 9, 1954	Danger–"Padlocks" (with Mildred Dunnock)
Dec __, 1954	General Electric Theater–"The Dark, Dark Hours" (with Ronald Reagan)
___ __, 1954	General Electric Theater–"I Am a Fool" (with Natalie Wood and Eddie Albert)
May 6, 1955	Schlitz Playhouse–"The Unlighted Road" (Pat Hardy, Murvyn Vye, Robert Williams, Charles Wagenheim)

June 1, 1956	Schlitz Playhouse—"The Unlighted Road" (repeat)
Nov 16, 1956	Schlitz Playhouse—"The Unlighted Road" (repeat)
Nov 18, 1956	General Electric Theater—"I Am a Fool" (repeat)
July 4, 1958	Schlitz Playhouse—"The Unlighted Road" (repeat)
Feb 4, 1959	Schlitz Playhouse—"The Unlighted Road" (repeat)
March 21, 1959	Schlitz Playhouse—"The Unlighted Road" (repeat)

From the beginning of his career as a New York television actor, Jimmy received enthusiastic responses, even for his earliest roles. "You should read some of the letters I got," he told Bill Gunn, "from old ladies watching television. They tell me about how they want me to wear tighter pants. They have this television club of ladies from fifty to seventy-five and they sit there checking the cats out, then write these dirty letters. It's really hard to believe."

"That was really blowing his mind. People were *proposing* on the telephone," Bill said. "It was very strange. But you have to discover yourself on that level, especially if you're very young, like he was. Before that you're all wrong—too short or too tall, wear glasses, or don't wear the right, bright clothes. You've already decided to become an actor, so when you get up on stage your head is already there. But then you get to the studios and you're all wrong again. Again you don't fit in, you don't look like they think you should, the image. But then when suddenly everybody starts responding to you on the level they have just rejected you on, now that's a mind blower."

Among actors, television work was hardly considered respectable. There was a definite stigma attached to it, probably for good reason. The talents employed by the stations (Gore Vidal, Paddy Chayefsky, Rod Serling) couldn't write everything. There were more original scripts turned out in a month of television than in the entire golden age of Greek theater, and some of the "mellers" could be pretty corny. If those in the legitimate "theatah" looked down on Hollywood, television was to them quite beyond the pale—a subhuman sink full of slutty, singing cigarette packs, slobbering dogs and perky pills.

Perhaps this was why Jimmy liked his friends to believe he only walked through most of his television dramas the way Marlon Brando is supposed to have strolled through *Desire*. But it is hard to believe that he treated anything he did well as flippantly as he liked to pretend. In fact, Jimmy often seems to have welcomed the chance to lose himself in his parts, and he enjoyed inventing in the theater of preparation as in the following story told by "Poppa" Lucci, the owner of a tavern where Jimmy ate every night.

"One Sunday afternoon I was on my way home—I lived on Fifty-fourth Street and Sixth Avenue—and it was bad weather. Rain. And he's there, in the doorway waitin' for me. I say, 'Whatsa the matter with you? You crazy? It's rain'! Look at you, wrinkled shirt. Whatsa the matter, you drunk?'

"So he came upstairs and I tried to give him some coffee, but he wouldn't take it. He kept lookin' at the time. Finally he said, 'Look Pop, I gotta go now, but I'll be back. You put this station on the TV and watch my show, okay?' So we all sit down and watch the television and about fifteen minutes later we see Jimmy on the screen, look' jest like he did when he was here. He played the part of a drunkard, some drunk man who had an accident or something. But he appeared so natural! He was jest like he was when he was here, sittin' with us. He'd been playin' like he was drunk. I'd never seen him drunk before and I'd been a little worried about him. But he was playin' drunk like he was drunk for TV.

"Then he came back here and walked in laughin' like hell. That's the way he liked to do things."

If Jimmy was just little more than an inkling on television's granulated plane, back in Fairmount he was still big news. His grandparents bought a TV set just because of him, and the local newspaper kept everyone posted on Jimmy's progress, as in this article announcing his appearance with Ronald Reagan:

JAMES DEAN TAKES PART IN TV SHOW

James Dean, . . . gave a convincing performance as a "hep-cat" killer in a supporting role Sunday night during the General Electric hour.

The television play, "The Dark, Dark Hours," starred Ronald Reagan as a physician whose sleep was interrupted by the appearance of the "hep-cat" at his door with a mortally wounded companion. Constance Ford appeared as the physician's wife. The physician was forced, at the point of a gun, to remove the bullet, but in vain. After death of the wounded companion, the "hep-cat" was overpowered by the physician and disarmed.

Impressive as this report seemed back in Indiana, Jimmy's career in television was really pretty uneven. A more personal picture of what he was like at this time can be read in a letter to Barbara Glenn:

In a scene from "Teen-Age Idols" in the TV series Danger . . .

To the sweetest one ever,
Dear Barbara,

Don't be surprised if a lot of people like the Lindburger cheese. Whether the play is good or bad you will have had the chance to play a role quite outside yourself.

I guess I'm alright. Got another cold. Have been staying with a friend in Manhattan will move when new dramatist reading is finished. Scarecrow will resume its run in two weeks. That means Frank will not go upstate N.Y. and will commence rehearsals for Scarecrow. He informed me that I would play the scarecrow in August. I don't have a TV job yet. Still hoping $.

Received your check. Haven't cashed it yet. Will tomorrow. Thank you. Sorry you had to go thru all that trouble.

Still holding MGM off. [He had turned down a part in *The Silver Chalice*, which Paul Newman later played.] See if I can get a play. Got a new pair of shoes honey. Black loafer "Weejuns" Shit! I'm so proud of them. Got a pair of pants too, not too good, but alright. My uncle sent me $30.00 and besides I deserved it. Made me feel good just to go in and get something.

I would like to see you very much. I miss you too. Didn't figure on that too strong. But you just can't tell always I guess. I'm getting sleepy. You write me real soon. You hear? Then I'll write you again.

Love,
Hayseed Jim

P.S. Send it to the old hotel, I go by there every once in a while,
Love,
Jim

(oh, I said that)

. . . Jimmy collapses in the rat-tat-tat of machine guns.

With the letter he enclosed a clipping from *Variety*, September 2, 1953:

CBS-TV exec producer William Dozier brought in two top stars, Sir Cedric Hardwicke and Walter Hampden, for his Tuesday night crime block, "Suspense" and "Danger," last week, but a comparative newcomer, James Dean, stole the spotlight from both of them. Dean, cast with Hampden on "Danger" in the role of a psychotic young janitor, delivered a magnetic performance that brought a routine meller alive.

Play was "Death is My Neighbor," by Frank Gregory, in which Hampden, an aged janitor, was teaching Dean the ropes. When Betsy Palmer moves into one of the apartments and discloses that Hampden is going to be fired after fifteen years, Dean is disturbed. And when Miss Palmer rejects his advances, he attempts to murder her and place the blame on Hampden. The police find out, however, and Hampden's job is saved in a happy wrapup.

Dean's performance was in many ways reminiscent of Marlon Brando's in "Streetcar," but he gave his role the individuality and nuances of its own which it required. He's got quite a future ahead of him.

One of the most painful experiences for a young actor is the constant rejection from agents, casting directors and producers. Jimmy tried to deflect this by pretending it didn't matter. "Across the front page of the portfolio Jimmy carried around," said Dizzy Sheridan, "he printed a headline, 'Matters of Great Consequence,' under which he listed his statistics and credits, you know, a resume. But it was really Jimmy's way of saying it was a matter of no consequence at all; it was all bullshit."

Still, the daily dismissals could be abrasive and Jimmy was often turned away because he was too short, sloppily dressed or wore glasses. Most humiliating of all were the mass auditions.

Martin Landau remembered, "We used to call them cattle calls. You get a number and file past the casting director—if they like you, they would call you back for a reading.

"Jimmy and I saw each other out on the street after an audition and recognized each other from that common humiliating experience. And, believe me, it *was* humiliating. We started to walk around the streets and stopped at a construction site and said, 'Well, if we're gonna be out on the street, let's act like we belong out on the street.' So we started to pretend we were construction foremen and shouted orders to the workmen. That lasted about twenty minutes. Then we went to Rockefeller Plaza skating rink. There was a cute girl skating and doing tricks; so we applauded her and cheered, and she became like a queen and turned to us and bowed and we applauded some more."

Paul Newman, Steve McQueen and Jimmy Dean often bumped into each other at casting calls for television and Broadway. They were all whittling at a similar, but undefined, image. In the meantime they found themselves lumped in the same general file. They were a cluster of types, a slow refining of Brando into a kind of existential cowboy. A new kind of hero was coming into being, and it was inevitable that a lot of people shared the same idea. Jimmy liked to equate the situation to a quote from his favorite philosopher, Elbert Hubbard: "Geniuses always come in groups because groups produce the friction that generates light."

The three young actors turned out to be quite different quantities in the end, but in the beginning of their careers their personas were just drawing boundaries and they were sensitive about being compared to each other.

Steve McQueen especially resented Jimmy, who was always slightly ahead of him. His jealousy took an ironic turn when he later shamelessly adapted Jimmy's mannerisms in movies like *The Blob*. When McQueen was introduced to Landau at a Hollywood party, he said, "Oh, sure, we've met before. I remember the first time I saw you, though you may not remember me. You came into a garage on West Sixty-ninth Street on the back of a motorcycle Jimmy Dean was driving. I was the mechanic."

Jimmy was considered one of the top working "juves" in New

York. He frequently found himself being cast when the writer was looking for a character to replace Hollywood's Andy Hardy (Mickey Rooney) stereotype. In Jimmy's first starring television role, however, a Kraft Theater episode entitled "A Long Time Till Dawn," Rod Serling was looking for an adolescent who could portray one of his characteristically weird creatures.

"The main character," said Serling, "was a terribly upset, psyched-out kid, a precursor to the hooked generation of the sixties, the type that became part of the drug / rock culture—not that I'm making a connection between drugs and rock, although there could conceivably be a connection made.

"We were trying in those days to make a legitimate composite figure of the youth. The movies were still portraying kids as bobby-soxers and cheerleaders, chewing gum and driving jalopies. I was only in my early twenties then and close enough to know that this picture didn't bear any resemblance to reality.

"There was a post-war mystification of the young, a gradual erosion of confidence in their elders, in the so-called truths, in the whole litany of moral codes. They just didn't believe in them anymore. In television we were aware of this and more in touch with what was happening. We could portray it immediately too—write a script one week and have it on the air the next.

"Jimmy Dean played the part in 'A Long Time Till Dawn' brilliantly. I can't imagine anyone playing that particular role better. I think this was his first big role in television and his behavior was very restrained and uncomfortable, but even then there was an excitement and intensity about him that he transmitted viscerally to the television audience."

Jimmy obviously revelled in the conspiracy between himself and the character. Martin Landau recalled how Jimmy prepared for the role Rod Serling had written: "I'll never forget one day I was at the studio watching dress rehearsals for a show Jimmy was going to do for the Kraft Theater. He played a character that had regressed to childhood and had become dangerous. After rehearsal the actors had about an hour break for dinner, and then they went on the air. The shows were broadcast live at the time from the East Coast, and a kinescope was sent to the West Coast. Jimmy was very depressed. He'd done the part okay but he couldn't seem to get a handle on it. So we went to Jerry's Tavern and Jimmy ordered three doubles. It wasn't like him to drink like that.

"I said, 'Hadn't you better take it easy? You know you've gotta go on in an hour.' I got the feeling he wanted to bolt and run away. I said, 'Instead of sitting there feeling sorry for yourself or getting depressed, why don't you try to get a handle on it?' Jimmy had this habit of biting on his collar, like this, just sticking the tip of it in his mouth. And so I said, 'You know, you do that all the time and it's good. I know! It's your mother's tit!' And he looked at me and then said, 'I'll see ya,' and he ran out.

"A little while later, I'm still finishing my dinner in Jerry's when I hear the Kraft theme song come blaring out of the TV and see the Kraft logo flash across the screen. And there's Jimmy. And you know what he did? It was beautiful . . . he would put his collar in his mouth right before he got violent. In each scene he'd just put his collar in his mouth, then there'd be violence. Then he had this love scene with his girl, and he was talking to her and getting closer to kiss her, and while he was talking he slipped the tip of his collar into his mouth. It was a brilliant dramatic move. I saw the people at the bar in the restaurant literally back away from the set. And, sure enough, he did get violent. And the police came or something and he wound up jumping out the window and running away."

Steve Allen, who did a filmed tribute to Jimmy after his death, recognized this distinct and totally different character Jimmy portrayed so well in television.

"I can still recall the first time I saw him," Allen said, "and I don't think that's true of any other actor of our time. Jayne and I were watching some dramatic show, I don't now recall what the series was, but it was one of those thirty-minute adventure/suspense things. The plot of the story was one that quickly became a cliché of the fifties (three books, six movies and seventeen television shows used the same story line), it involved the invasion of a family's home by some sort of criminal.

"In this case, one of the invaders was a tough teenager. His use of the authentic hip language, his naturalness, were so impressive that I said to Jayne, 'I must find out who directed the show because he's done something absolutely brilliant. No *actor* I know could speak that language as authentically as this kid. I think the director must actually have gotten some boy off the streets and somehow made him play himself.' "

That "kid off the street" was, of course, James Dean.

Jimmy was not, however, beyond playing on the delicate balance between absurdity and involvement that Method acting so precariously calls for. "One time he played a prisoner on death row for Studio One," Martin Landau added, "and he wanted to vomit on camera. They thought that would never do since the show went into people's living rooms. Then he asked if dry retching would do. They said, no, that wouldn't do either. I never did figure out if he was putting them on or not."

Jimmy was always solitary, awkward and shy at rehearsals, and, even in his "loosening up" with other actors, his clowning often became a self-parody that he would hide behind. In a series of photographs taken by Roy Schatt on the set of a U.S. Steel Hour production of "The Thief," Jimmy is captured as he acted out his own fragmented state of mind by pushing his glasses to the side of his face so he seemed to have three eyes. He turned to Roy and yelled, "Hey! I'm a Picasso!"

He was perfecting his style, able to learn rapidly in the fast-paced

"Hey, I'm a Picasso!" Jimmy rehearsing "The Thief" with Diana Lynn.

world of television. Whereas a movie might take four months or longer to shoot, Jimmy could be a different character every week in television. When he played in this production of "The Thief," his interpretations were often infuriating to other members of the cast.

"I found out how hard it was to work with a mumbler," Mary Astor, his co-star in "The Thief" wrote in her biography, "when I worked with Jimmy Dean.

"Live television was a very precise business, with word cues for camera cuts. Timing had to be accurate in word and action—or you could find yourself off the air or with time left over to be filled with a short subject on the love life of the wildebeest.

"We were doing a final dress rehearsal," Mary Astor remembered. "Jimmy was six feet away from me in one scene and I could barely hear what he was saying, and what I could hear seemed to have very little to do with the script. I looked over at the booth, my palms up in a 'Help!' gesture.

"'What's the trouble, Mary?' asked the director, his voice booming impatiently over the loudspeaker. Paul Lukas, that excellent actor, came to my rescue.

"He said, 'De trouble iss dat ve don't know vat de hell he's saying, ven he's going to say vat, or vere he's goint to be ven he says anything.' You could understand Paul.

"Our answer came over the speaker. 'I'm sorry, people. That's the way Jimmy has to work. Do the best you can. It's marvelous in here.'

"The cast felt superior to this inconsiderate 'whippersnapper' or 'vippersnopper,' as Lukas called him. But the vippersnopper was the one who got all the notices and we were just lumped together as 'cast.'"

Besides his attempt to recreate the stumblings and pauses of real-life speech, Jimmy had a few other habits that actors and often directors would find irritating. He would quiz the director constantly about the character, wanting to get a handle on him, a way to relate to something in himself that would give the character a special depth. Often the character became such a part of him that his interpretation would vary, depending on his mood and the other people who were in the cast.

Mort Abrahams, who was producer of "I Am a Fool" for the General Electric Theater, said, "This very well-known actor was once acting opposite him, and Jimmy would come up with a different

The mask of tragedy meets Son of Casanova. *On the set of "The Thief."*

character each time they did the scene. Finally this actor grabbed Jimmy by the tie, no, I mean the shirt front because Jimmy never wore a tie, and said, 'Listen, you son of a bitch, if you give me another interpretation next time, I'll wipe the floor with you.'

"But that was just a tough moment. There was no continuing anti-Jimmy feeling in TV or in the theater far as I know. Jimmy was just relating to what was going on in his head, and things were whizzing through his head a hundred miles a minute—they sped through him. And he didn't have the sense at that time to discriminate. That was the director's job—to see the right interpretation and say, 'That's it! Now freeze on it.' Jimmy was always thinking about his character, and every time he did he would discover new things about him that he'd want to say. I think it always stemmed from an honest attempt to perform."

Jimmy also tended to come in late for rehearsals, but "not noticeably," said Abrahams. "Maybe he'd drift in fifteen to twenty minutes late. He was a loner, didn't mix much with the cast. I frequently would go over and chat with him, and he was always amiable enough but not very communicative. He just wanted to be by himself, and if you got that signal, well, you just left him alone.

"But he was never any trouble. I knew him pretty well, and the stories about him being troublesome as an actor are errant nonsense. He was an enormously imaginative and spontaneous actor. And this, of course, causes disruptions, delays, but it comes from an artistic effort. He was just beginning to get discipline of choice and he still had trouble holding a character once it was set. If I had to make a list of my five most temperamental actors, Jimmy would definitely *not* be on it.

"I think you have to remember there was a general jealousy among younger actors too, for the fifties was a period of style—the Method, you know. An introspective kind of acting—which Jimmy came by naturally—was popular, and for a lot of actors it didn't come so naturally and, as actors, they came off very badly. It was an acting style developed from his own personality. A lot of personal stuff got churned up when Jimmy acted, and when that happened he got very emotional and his life became involved in his acting.

"But he would never deliberately foul up a production, never do anything unprofessional. Of course, he was a little crazy. You could never tell if he was going to be manic or depressive; but if you knew this was Jimmy and not an act, then it was okay."

While working in New York, Jimmy could almost always be found sometime during the day slouched in a phone booth in "the actors' drugstore," more exoterically known as Cromwell's, in the NBC building at Rockefeller Plaza. Cromwell's was, *mutatis mutandis*, the Schwab's of Sixth Avenue, a limbo for resting, budding or aspiring actors who hung out there to gossip, check the lists in *Variety* and *Show Business*, call their answering service and only incidentally have a quick cup of coffee.

"Oh, sure, coffee was drunk at Cromwell's, a lot of coffee, with a cinammon stick, of course. But its real function was a sort of actors' living room," said Billy James, who left acting and was later a publicist for the Byrds. "All the really deep discussions about life and art, that kind of stuff, took place there accompanied by an appropriate amount of anguish. It was the anguished era and the beats were out there on the road somewhere. All very intense."

Outside of rehearsals (and even at these he kept pretty much to himself), Cromwell's was the only social life Jimmy had, the only

Jimmy and Martin Landau have breakfast at the Croyden, right next door to the Iroquois Hotel.

place where he ran into others casually and was forced to interact with people. It was here that the jealous, secret self and its obverse side—the clowning, prankish other—presented their binary natures. These were the two most prominent varieties of Jimmy's public behavior. Those who knew him only from a distance, and were less tolerant of such ambivalence, saw in that most painful line of defenses only the exhibitionist.

In Cromwell's steamy atmosphere people and events came and vanished rapidly on the backs of tongues. It was a barn astir with little crises. Stars were born over morning coffee, featured for a moment and were gone in a wink. Once a girl had come gushing into the drugstore saying, "Isn't it great about Biff Elliot? He just got the lead in a Mickey Spillane film!" Within seconds everybody at the counter was agog with repeating it. "Isuntitgraydabowdbiffelliot?"

Something in it appealed to Jimmy's sense of the absurd and he turned it into a private joke with Martin Landau. A few days later, sitting at a staged distance at the counter, Jimmy yelled down to Marty, "Isn't it great about Merv Paine?" For days people would mention the name of the little man Jimmy had let loose in Cromwell's, and whenever he met anyone who was "nowhere" he'd say to Marty, "Y'know, this guy reminds me of Merv Paine."

Billy James says of these days, "Tremendous bravado was displayed by unemployed actors in drugstores. We would take up a cause and often our causes were each other's. With Jimmy, it was his personality that got people off rather than his acting ability. He had that extra momentum—that wild streak that made us believe he was going to make it. He liked to make statements that attracted people's attention. He had a conspiratorial laugh that made the listener feel like an accomplice, and brought him within range of an area he wouldn't normally walk into.

"Or he'd do something completely offbeat, like the ash-tray crucifixion he created, using two matches placed on top of a heap of sugar he'd poured into the ash tray. When he lit this miniature Golgotha, it would carbonize and make the sugar bubble and crackle into a disgusting, black, oozy puddle. Jimmy loved to put on these kinds of childish performances."

For someone as deeply shy as Jimmy was, these games and the laugh that hinted at something beyond itself were devices that helped take the place of more casual behavior. Often enough, though, he

Jimmy's painting of Bill Gunn.

could be simply offensive–aggressively sullen.

"Maybe he used his sometimes perverted humor," said Bill Gunn, "to hide a sense of morality that most people would misunderstand. Jimmy had a high sense of morality–high in the sense that there was no pressure coming from anywhere. It was all inner, but it was very strong."

It was in Cromwell's that Jimmy met most of the people he was closest to during his life as an actor–Barbara Glenn, Bill Gunn, Martin Landau, Leonard Rosenman, Billy James. They shared a silent conspiracy; it was a time when they were all involved and wanted to share their involvement. "That's what Cromwell's was really about," said Billy James. "The show would be over, but the dream lingered. We wanted the feeling to go on."

Along with the prankster, there was the distrustful "other" that Jimmy sometimes wouldn't bother to disguise.

"He was nasty in that he wouldn't communicate," said Barbara Glenn. "Somebody would come up to him in Cromwell's and say, 'Hey, Jimmy, whattaya think about this?' And he'd say, 'Uh.' Or he'd turn away and do something else. It was almost as if suddenly you ceased to exist and he couldn't care less. You were an annoyance. And it was something, when he did it to me, that I just couldn't cope with."

When Jimmy didn't want to be disturbed, he could make his friends suddenly invisible.

"If he didn't like you, Jimmy wouldn't even give you the pleasure of his anger," said Bill Gunn. "You just didn't exist. You could be in a phone booth with him and you wouldn't exist.

"One night we were up at his apartment. He was into something and I was hungry and I kept saying, 'Let's go get something to eat, let's get something to eat, let's eat.' But he wouldn't answer. I was really starved. A couple of times he said, 'Okay, okay.' Then he'd go back into it. Then he took to not answering again. So I said to myself, 'I'm not here, right?' I started out and got halfway down the stairs when he came out and said, 'Where are you going?' It was then I realized I was there. I said, 'I'm going to get something to eat,' and he closed the door and came down the stairs and we went to eat."

Jimmy could turn people off, and those who weren't his friends had little time and effort to spend dealing with it. "Of course Jimmy had his reasons for what he did," said Barbara, "but, really, who needs that shit? Nobody wants to break their back. The worst horror was watching people who *did* break their backs as he started to become *James Dean,* and *then* did the groveling and fawning begin.

"We were products of World War II, and people were not sure what they really wanted, what life was about. People were . . . well, they were lost. They had no goals. It was like holding your breath.

"We were starting to question the moral principles we'd been brought up with. Many of us had immigrant parents who were very strongly opinioned about what people are. Everyone had a category—a nice girl is, a bad girl is . . . I was very much a product of that.

"I think that was one of the major things that Jimmy did; he disregarded all the old assumptions. Most people were frightened by this, and there were people who hated him for it because he got recognition for it. So they hated him and said he was doing a Brando 'bit.' Oh, some of it *was* a bit; but, by God, most of the time he was just very comfortable and that was it! And if you didn't like it, fuck it. It was that simple. But it wasn't really that simple, because I think it really did bother him. He would never let it show that it bothered him though.

"Jimmy wasn't a very social human being, or a nice person to a lot of people, and some people approached him with a chip on their shoulder, trying to prove they would find what they didn't like in Jimmy.

"Jimmy was not good at reaching out, and you just *knew* that anything could be mistaken for a rejection. I felt like I was walking on eggshells at the beginning of our relationship because I so didn't want to disturb him. He was so frightened of anything that was extended, of letting people in. He'd show you some of himself, you'd really share something, and then you'd feel him backing off, and about an hour later coming to grips with himself. Like, 'Why did I do that?' 'Is it alright that I did that?' 'Will she use it against me?'

"He was incredibly vulnerable is what I'm trying to say. Yet people were always giving me advice like, 'What are you doing with *him?* He's the sickest boy I ever met . . .' 'You'd better keep away from him, he's sick . . .' No one ever said, 'Oh, Jimmy, yeah I know Jimmy,' and left it at that. No, sir, people either loved him or got violently angry about him. It was very flipped out and he knew it. He sensed his isolation, though he would often cause it.

"It wasn't what Jimmy wanted, but he just didn't know. He was

Jimmy's ethological paws in "Teen-Age Idols" (left) and Rebel Without a Cause *(right).*

terribly afraid of approaching people. He used to say that he needed no one, that he cared for no one, which of course was not true."

What's left of the beginnings of television and Jimmy's professional acting career are mere fragments, a few scattered artifacts of our electronic history that one might come across only if sifting diligently through the magnetic ruins. The television stations and sponsors have lost or destroyed old kinescopes and films. There are a few photographs taken for formal records or publicity releases. Some clippings from newspapers. A bootleg LP with the complete sound tracks of "The Unlit Road" and "Diary of a Young Fool" (titles thinly disguised for copyright reasons) which was put out by "Movie God Records" strictly for "Dean's Teens and Eternal Lamp Clubs, a Collectors Issue for His Faithful Flock Only."

A brief scene from one of his original television shows is preserved in a 1960s documentary called "Teen-Age Idols," which is part of a David Wolper series, *Hollywood and the Stars.* This tribute begins with a series of stills; then suddenly Jimmy is screaming . . . screaming . . . slamming a door and roaring with laughter as he flops onto a bed while cradling a football and a pistol. More angry screaming as the cops arrive, and Jimmy, at the window, collapses in the deafening rat-tat-tat of their machine guns. Though it is an inaudible and blurry flash, the intensity of Jimmy's performance is startling after the mute pictures that precede it, and his laugh and ethological mannerisms (paws curled in submission to unseen head wolf) are easily recognizable.

In one of Hollywood's rag and bone shops, those halfway homes of sad, old magazines, there languishes a photograph of another scene from one of Jimmy's television shows, an ardent fan's attempt to photograph Jimmy's fleeting image directly from the TV tube. In this snapshot his milk-white face is an almost indistinguishable blob dissolving in the surf of the rolling electron bars. But the identifying fragments of Jimmy can be picked out: a wasted mouth, the tilt of the head and those Mickey Mouse ears of his. If we are in doubt, just the earnestness of this almost invisible photograph should persuade us it is *him*.

It's almost possible to say what the scene is—a room perhaps drifts somewhere in the blind optical space enclosing him. In front of a couch (also suffering from advanced electron decay) he hovers like a magnetic insect about to alight on this pitted surface. A luminous froth bubbles at his mouth.

The almost total absence of detail in this photograph gives it the spectral reality of a psychic event, as if this *thing* of indeterminate mass and frequency had nosed up to the glass to look at its fleeting reflection, an opalescent image wandering through insubstantial space, which then departed back into its murky magnetic world and rubbed a white shadow of James Dean from the screen to leave us a ghostly orthicon image on the pane of time.

In one of my previous cases, the
patient complained that a picture of
his body had been taken, and was kept
in a far-distant town under the
influence of an investigator. Whenever
a perception was offered to this
picture, it went to him. His thought
went into this picture. The
investigator could then read whether the
patient was a pervert or not.
According to Tausk, machines symbolize
the body. The picture of the patient
is just such a machine. It is like a
picture in the mirror, a part of himself
outside. There is a community between
my picture, my image in the mirror,
and myself. But are not my fellow
human beings outside myself also
a picture of myself?

–from Paul Shilder,
The Form and Appearance of the Human Body

CHAPTER SEVEN

Diary of a Face
1952–1954

Jimmy becomes James Dean;
first Broadway part in See the Jaguar;
an award-winning performance in The Immoralist;
Jimmy wins the screen test
for East of Eden.

B y the spring of 1954, Jimmy had nearly completed the evolution of that inner image of himself, James Dean. His body, face and behavior had become a conscious vehicle for the expression of that fabrication of the self–personality. How literally Jimmy modeled himself can be seen in a well-known photograph which, almost twenty years later, was used as a huge blow-up dominating the center stage of *Grease,* a musical about the fifties at the Royale Theater, where Jimmy played his last Broadway role.

In the photograph Jimmy is wearing a black turtleneck sweater, his head twisting to the side in a painful dislocation. His eyes are brooding and ringed with dark circles. It is a self-conscious portrait: sensual, spiritual, heroic and tortured. Though it appears to be an unrehearsed revelation of Jimmy's innermost feelings, he was deliberately arranging himself.

"We were doing this series of portraits," said photographer Roy Schatt, "and Jimmy suddenly said, 'Wait a minute, I want to try something.' He turned his head slightly to the left and looked down. I asked him what the hell he was doing, it was such a strange pose. He said, 'Don't you see it? I'm Michelangelo's David.'"

In this photograph Jimmy crystalized the evolution of his fantasies. In New York he had begun a curious metamorphosis: he had arrived with a face of American bedrock, as pure and strong as a block of Carrara marble, and from this matrix he shaped himself. His features expanded and contracted until they grew into that form of himself which he projected into the magnetic patterns that flow around his face and body. Through them he could express all the complexities of the creature within.

The phases of Jimmy's body landscaping can be seen in the series of portfolio pictures taken by theatrical photographer Joseph Abeles during the three years Jimmy lived in New York. In the first sitting, in 1951, Jimmy still looks like a farmboy. When Abeles asked him to smile, Jimmy bared a slightly self-conscious row of teeth. By the second sitting, in 1952, the granite had begun to soften. His hair is no longer the smoldering, unruly bush, but is beginning to take the shape of that jagged wave which later burst into the pentecostal flame that became his symbol. Not only has he commanded his hair, but his features no longer are contained in a vicelike grip. They have relaxed sufficiently to be malleable. By late 1953 the transformation is clearly visible. His eyes have deepened, and their expressions varied; his mouth is more fluid. He has learned to animate this liquid mask into patterns of his own devising.

"Jimmy never liked the way he looked in photographs," said Abeles. "But when he saw this picture (the profile) he looked at it and asked softly, 'Is that really *me?*' and he grabbed it and kind of hugged it to his chest."

Though always aware of how he looked through the lens of a camera, Jimmy had difficulty when he had to pose for pictures. "You never see a good *portrait* of Jimmy," said Dennis Stock, a photographer friend. "He didn't respond well to studio-type situations. He couldn't relate to that; it was too clinical. He had to have a handle, something to react against. He couldn't stand the blankness of a studio, the no-scene backgrounds. He performed best when he could react to what was around him—a three-hundred-pound hog, a book, a fence post, a taxi, *anything*. His best photographs are really little pieces of theater."

A classic piece of Jimmy's staging is the photograph Dennis Stock took in Times Square. He slouches along the iron railing that divides Broadway and Seventh Avenue, hunched like a fugitive and dressed

120

Joseph Abeles' portfolio pictures: top, 1951; middle, 1952; bottom, 1953.

with a deliberately sloppy air, like a Chaplinesque dandy. Without Jimmy, this picture would be pointless, the sightless crowds and grey buildings hurrying into undeveloped spaces. But Jimmy exploits these elements as his vast stage and they lean on him as if he had put them there as props. He is always the verb in these photographic sentences, a role only a master director of his own image can play.

The Times Square photograph is a perfectly realized image of what Jimmy tried to do all his life: set up a situation in which he would play the starring role. He enters the selected scene—a rainy, cold city street—wearing an oversized coat with collar turned up, frail body slightly bent, preceded by a wet seallike shadow. It tells his story: the loner in the city, exuding nausea, sensitivity and inner pain. Yet Jimmy does not despair; he walks *into* the picture, inviting us to follow with a rakish tilt of his cigarette. That trademark cigarette, dangling from his mouth, was adopted from the cover photo of an Albert Camus paperback Jimmy owned. With its oblique angle, this image represents everything Existentialism stood for to American youth—a fantasized hero out of *The Myth of Sisyphus* and *Being and Nothingness*!

"If Jimmy had ever mentioned Existentialism to me, I would have laughed in his face," said Roy Schatt. But even if Jimmy could not quote the tenets of Kierkegaard's gloomy *Either/Or* nor *Fear and Trembling*, he could embody his own idea of them. Existentialism meant something quite different to American youth in the fifties than it did to French intellectuals. It was adopted by "beats" as the first philosophy of the young. Like the audience of *The Sorrows of Young Werther*, only the very young, vigorous and hopeful could afford to wallow in the "gloomy depths," and American youth had converted the stoic philosophy of Sartre into a hip form of morbid self-pity.

Schatt didn't think much of Jimmy, either as an actor or a human being ("He was no more than a plain show off!"). Jimmy was not a star at the time he was taking these photographs, but Schatt must have guessed that Jimmy was on his way or he wouldn't have so diligently recorded his life in New York. "I took hundreds of pictures of him. He was fun to hang around with," said Schatt. "But he was always making romance with his own activities. He made romance with the fact he didn't eat or dress like other people ... Sometimes I feel that he was writing a biography at that time about himself, you know, and that moment was entitled 'This is the Way

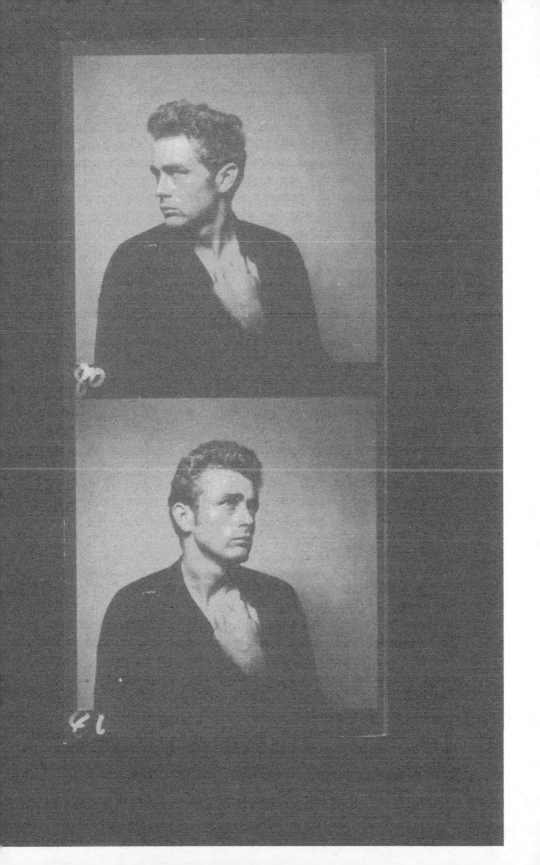

Jimmy Dean Prepared for His Role in . . .' That's the feeling I got! Like I was his Boswell.

"Y'know Jimmy was like one of the characters in *The Man Who Came to Dinner*. This guy walks into the room, a slightly fey character, blows in like a breeze and says to Sheridan North before he can say anything, 'Stop, Sherry. I've got only a few moments, so let's just talk about me.' It's a helluva theatrical line. And unless Jimmy were talking about himself or things were happening for him, it wasn't happening."

One of Schatt's photographs shows Jimmy nibbling anxiously at his fingers. His hair is short, the curtains cast disturbing shadows and the atmosphere is dense and eerie.

"I began to take pictures of him at TV rehearsals. In one picture, I said, 'Hey, Jimmy, I want to shoot some pictures of you against this curtain.' He said, 'Hey, you know, man (he used 'man' all the time the way people do now who think they've discovered it), I'm doing this cowboy for TV and this guy's got to pull his gun. Got to pull his gun fast, you know. So I gotta have quick fingers.' So he bit the tips of his fingers to get them sensitive."

Schatt was one in a long line of temporary tutors. From him Jimmy tried to learn the secrets of photography.

"Did he study photography with me?" Schatt asked almost incredulously. "I'd say study was a bad word. He always was studying photography with me—if every now and again when the moment would hit him he'd ask a question meant studying. But then it would be too much for him and he'd let it go, and we'd be talking about something else—bullfighting, motor racing or some other damned thing which I wasn't interested in. Oh, he took pictures all right, but if it came to developing or printing, he'd just throw his hands up in his Jimmy Dean way and say, 'What the hell!'"

A few photographs taken by Jimmy still exist. The more contrived of these are quite bizarre in composition. Usually shot from extremely low or odd angles and involving knives and mirrors, they look as if some undisclosed crime is being committed. "They were very overly poetic," says Schatt, "as if he tried to shoot a scene from a Jean Cocteau movie; pure fifties melodrama, very intense, symbolic stuff, generally meaning about nothing at all.

"Jimmy loved shock and surprise. I remember Martin Landau, Bobby Heller, Bill Gunn and Jimmy and I were sitting at the kitchen table drinking coffee and talking, and we didn't notice Jimmy leave the room. A couple of minutes later there was a helluva lot of noise outside the window. Horns were blowing and people were yelling. Someone got up to see what was going on, and there was James Dean in one of my living room chairs sitting right in the middle of the street. Nobody took a photograph of this, although I imagine that was Jimmy's general idea."

How seriously Jimmy considered the way he was photographed and later filmed and how carefully he organized the elements of his poses and costume can also be seen in the way he composed and photographed other people. One snowy morning around 5:30 A.M., he decided he *must* shoot a picture of his friend Bill Gunn with his newly acquired Leica.

"We walked all the way down to Thirty-third Street and knocked on Roy's door," Bill said. "While Roy was walking around rubbing his eyeballs wondering what the hell was going on, Jimmy put me in front of the white background screen. My pants were frozen with snow, so he pushed them around till they looked the way he wanted them to, and then he pulled my jacket down. He shaped my clothes, like a sculpture. Then he brought the fire iron over . . . I didn't know what that was for."

The idea of directing movies appealed to Jimmy, and once he even began shooting one with a Bolex 16-mm. camera in Roy Schatt's back yard. When asked what became of it, Schatt said, "Nothing, absolutely nothing, like everything else he started. He didn't have the patience to finish."

Every day Jimmy would set out for midtown from his nile-green chamber to begin his "rounds": casting calls, a stop at his agent's office, a coffee at Cromwell's and perhaps the afternoon at the Museum of Modern Art. Then he would scurry back to his room to examine the awful treasures his day had yielded.

After dark, Jimmy often headed for the Algonquin Hotel on West Forty-fourth Street. "New Yorkers know that if you could make it past 6:30," Dorothy Parker of the Algonquin's literary "Round Table" used to say, "you could make it through the night."

In the twenties the Algonquin became famous for the "Round Table" in its elegant lounge, a hive of literary, social and theatrical figures. By the fifties its aura had tarnished, but the Algonquin was still a fashionable watering hole and Jimmy used it as a baroque inkwell in which he would dip himself to refine his public image. Among this polished horde of bores, Jimmy shone like a refreshing imp, and with a mixture of disdain and desire, they embraced him.

"You have to remember that Jimmy was still something of a hayseed," said Frank Casaro, an actor friend of Jimmy's at the time. "Wide-eyed at the whole scene. He was fascinated by *me* because I was not American and he was totally American apple pie.

"He was this hayseed guy, and I was this big, wild, wordy wop running around. He was a pain in the neck in the beginning ... He would always be hovering around me. But he *was* talented, that I could see."

Bill Bast said, "This was his 'Getting to Know You' period. He was playing 'Bye Baby Bunting' or 'I Was a Clever Darling' all over New York! Oh, there were some very effete games going on at the Algonquin! And everyone 'schpoke quite liiiike that,' stiff upper lip and all that. When he'd come home, I would ask him, 'What is *that*? What have you got, marbles in your mouth?'"

It didn't take long for Jimmy to develop a hard and gorgeously colored shell to wear among these vitreous creatures. It was an armor that protected his own jealous inner self and zealously guarded his deeper vein of shyness. Without it, he might have slipped into inarticulateness.

Bill described this as Jimmy's high-wire act, "very daring, suspended in midair. He walked around as if someone might spill him. It was sort of, 'Do you like my red cloak? Well then, how about my blue one?' Jimmy desperately had to make it in this scene, as if it were back to the farm if he didn't."

There's something incongruous about this combination solitary dreamer and pandering trickster, but these people *were* useful to Jimmy. His motives were apparently quite calculated, and if he had to play an unlikely role at times to appease their vampirish appetites, it would become not just a flighty game, but an actor's exercise.

Whether enjoyable or painful, it was through this connection that Jimmy got his first Broadway role. One Sunday afternoon in 1952, Rogers Brackett took Jimmy on a social call to Broadway producer Lem Ayers and his wife, Shirley. The young man they met that day was witty, charming and entertaining—a side of Jimmy that would arise when conditions were favorable.

While Jimmy "put on the Ayers," he also set his own course, letting their mutual paths cross with apparent casualness of fate. It was through Lem Ayers that he eventually landed his first Broadway role, but in order to manipulate the preliminary stages, he employed two impersonations—the mild-mannered country boy who turns out to be an "experienced" deck hand and the deck hand who later turns into a budding actor—and set the scene by utilizing some heavy props: a yacht, one balmy summer, a Massachusetts peninsula and a group of theatrical producers hungry for young talent.

After the Ayers invited Rogers and his friend back to their house a few times, they asked Jimmy if he'd like to crew as a cabin boy on their yacht. This invitation was a credit to his acting ability, since he'd never been sailing before. He wrote to Barbara Glenn, who was traveling with a summer stock company: "Got my annual thrill. Yacht racing for the New York Yacht Club. We had a storm. Had to lock ourselves to the helm. I'm a great sailor you know. I got seasick, wasn't worth a god damn."

But he was to be rewarded. At the end of the season Jimmy accompanied the Ayers on another week-long cruise to Cape Cod, and it was during this trip that Jimmy let slip the fact that he was an actor, a "surprise" for Mr. Ayers, who happened to be producing *See the Jaguar* that fall.

When Jimmy returned to New York, he talked to his friends about boats and navigation, but carefully avoided any personal discussions. The Ayers cruise was to remain a mysterious voyage. Jimmy was a great believer in the retention of ideas, secrets and dreams, and his attempts to avoid dispersing his energies were usually mistaken for psychic hoarding.

"I had learned," Bill Bast said, "that it was natural to avoid direct discussions of his private life. Jimmy was guarded, protective and always testing you to see if he could really trust you."

But his unfolding plot worked much the way he'd written it, and when Lem Ayers told him to come for a reading, Jimmy wasn't surprised. After a series of impersonations and transformations, when the night of the audition came, the materialization of his schemes seemed almost too real; its suddenness caught him off guard.

Bill Bast wrote:

His nerves were showing the night of the reading. He rushed around the apartment in a state of panic, trying to get dressed in a totally disorganized manner.

"Oh, no!" he bellowed. "Oh, my God!" he roared, and threw himself on the floor.

"Now what?" prodded Dizzy, losing her patience.

"I haven't even got a clean shirt to wear! I haven't got a goddam *shirt*!" he wailed.

"Go nude," Dizzy suggested. "At least you'll have their attention."

" . . . Dizzzzzy!" he screamed like a tortured man.

Dizzy rushed into the bathroom and helped him untangle his hands from the massive knot in which he had caught them trying to tie his tie. Then, while he bounced and bobbed like a nervous little boy, she tied the tie for him, combed his unruly hair, tucked in his shirt, gave him a pat on the behind, and sent him on his way.

"We'll wait for you at the Paris," she shouted after him, as he dashed down the street toward the wrong subway entrance.

The initial reading at some midtown hotel went very well and he was asked by the play's author, N. Richard Nash, to come back again to read at the theater.

He came to the reading at the theater wearing glasses," said Nash, "and one of the lenses was cracked. He read very haltingly and very badly. He'd just read for me the day before and had done very well. I couldn't understand it. So after his reading I asked him to come to see me. Then I asked him what had happened. He told me he'd broken his glasses and couldn't see. I promised him another reading and told him to go fix his glasses. 'I can't. I haven't any money,' he said. So I gave him ten dollars and set up the reading.

"Two or three days later he came in and his glasses were still broken. But he'd memorized the entire thing so he didn't have to read. He got the part. Afterwards I said to him, 'You son of a bitch, why didn't you get your glasses fixed?' And he pulled out this vicious-looking knife and said, 'I saw this knife and I've been wanting one . . . I just had to have it. But I figured I couldn't betray you entirely so I memorized the script for the reading.'"

Jimmy's behavior during the early readings had just the combination of naive trust and hint of violence that director Michael Gordon was looking for.

"When Jimmy read, I was immediately taken with his qualities. He had the naiveté of a newly hatched chick . . . I interviewed over a hundred young actors for that part and I was at my wits' end. I knew what I was looking for and it was a very difficult part to cast. When Dean came in, I knew he could handle the strangeness of the part."

See the Jaguar is the story of Wally Wilkins, a boy who is locked in an ice house by his mother and released just before she dies. Like a child born a teenager, Wally Wilkins wanders from his shack and collides with all the elements of a small southern town.

The story is loaded with charged elements from Jimmy's own childhood, the emotional details jumping out with relentless coincidence: the hovering, protective mother; the release from a charmed circle into corrupt city living; an innocent of the world at the threshold of adulthood. These similarities are not purely coincidental, however. Writers were becoming concerned with the theme of innocence and, specifically, original American innocence. Jim Stark in *Rebel* or Holden Caulfield in *Catcher in the Rye* are more refined examples of this archetype.

"Wally Wilkins was one of the world's innocents," said playwright N. Richard Nash. "He'd never done any harm; he'd never seen any. His mother was half-demented, half-sage, and was trying to keep him from the bestiality of the world. But in the end she fails.

"Dean read the part of Wally beautifully. In fact, he was the only person in the play who caught the spirit of it, I'd say He had it from the beginning. There's a great difference, you know, between a simple-minded person playing a simple-minded role and a complex person playing a simple-minded role. And if the complex man has it, like Dean did, then you have a great richness in the part. There were scenes of deep puzzlement, and you have never seen such puzzlement as portrayed by Dean. He had it. It was deep down and quite beautiful."

The idea behind Wally Wilkins is a sort of rural Sleeping Beauty waking up to that strange dislocation of time and place. It's the kind of feeling common to most teenagers in the early fifties.

As Bill Gunn remembered: "In those days you had nowhere to go. You had no drugs. You could drink, but sometimes it didn't work. Sometimes you went nuts, because you didn't want to go to sleep. Who wanted to go to sleep? You'd been sleeping for eighteen years while you waited to get out of the house. So you wanted to wake up, talk things out, stay up all night, fuck a lot.

"Jimmy and I were reading Kerouac; we were relating to that kind of breaking out. It was the only thing to read unless you went back to Fitzgerald or Hemingway. And we were busy getting rid of that Hemingway big-game hunting thing. Jimmy read Kerouac, but he was too ambitious for an *On the Road* trip. He wasn't about to wander around the country for a moment."

While Jimmy waited to hear if he got the part, a hazy, goose summer ambled into New York City late in 1952. Invisible apples and a phalanx of phantom corn stalked through Jimmy's head as Fairmount slowly materialized itself. He had to see autumn and knew just the place to go, so he asked Dizzy and Bill to come with him to the Winslows' farm.

With only ten dollars among them, hitchhiking was the only way to get to Indiana. They got a ride almost all the way with baseball star Clyde McCullough of the Pittsburgh Pirates, who was on his way to Des Moines.

"A not insignificant motive in this expedition," said Dizzy, "was that it was around Thanksgiving as I remember, and people like Jimmy's aunt and uncle, of course, really knew how to celebrate it. It was a country feast. There were no leaves on the trees by then and Indiana can look pretty desolate, but Jimmy was completely happy back there.

"You could see how simple he was. He really loved the animals, the way of life, even the dirt on the farm. Jimmy's dad, I remember, came all the way from California to see him and to fix the two front teeth that he had knocked out when he was a kid. I never saw any animosity between Jimmy and his father. They seemed to get along fine. After all, he had come *3000* miles just to see him.

"People say that Jimmy was always car crazy . . . they think he got into it because of the Indy 500 or something, but I never saw that side of him. Jimmy couldn't have cared less about cars when I knew him. In fact, whenever we went anywhere in a car, he always made me drive."

At the end of a week in Fairmount, Jane Deacy called from New York to tell Jimmy he'd been chosen for a part in *See the Jaguar* and had to get back right away. Jimmy, Dizzy and Bill left the next morning.

See the Jaguar opened at the Cort Theater on December 3, 1952.

THE CAST

Hilltop	Philip Pine
Yetter	David Clarke
Janna	Constance Ford
Grampa Ricks	Roy Fant
Mrs. Wilkins	Margaret Barker
Dave Ricks	Arthur Kennedy
Brad	Cameron Prud'Homme
Harvey	George Tyne
Frank	Arthur Batanides
Meeker	Ted Jacques
Mrs. Meeker	Florence Sundstrom
Wally Wilkins	James Dean
JeeJee	Dane Knell
Sam	Harrison Dowd
Andy	Harry Bergman
Carson	Tony Kraber

The action of the play takes place at Brad's gas station and in the nearby mountains of a western state.

The time covers about twelve hours, from morning to night, of a day in early spring in the present time.

See the Jaguar begins as a young boy about sixteen, who has been kept locked in an ice house all his life by his mother, wanders out for the first time and stumbles into town. His only connection with the outside world is a note his mother gave him before she died, addressed to the town's good-hearted teacher: "Dear Davie Ricks. This is my son Walter that I hid from all the meanness of the world . . . Maybe I was wrong to hidden him this way—maybe I was right. But I loved him dear and didn't want for hurt to come his way."

Dave takes a look at this boy and says, "I've always wondered, if I could see it new what would it look like?" And Wally says, stretching out one hand to the bigness, 'You can't *touch* nothin.'"

Director Michael Gordon said, "He can't understand why everything is not within his grasp. To be someone who's discovering that for the first time was what Jimmy could do. He was able to use that magical quality, that *as if I were*, and make it happen to himself."

Jimmy had no trouble learning the part of Wally Wilkins. But since he was tone deaf, he found it practically impossible to sing the little

131

song which Alec Wilder had composed for the show. "Rehearsals helped him with the acting, but nothing could help him with the singing," Bill Bast said. Bill and Dizzy spent long torturous hours going over it with Jimmy and would often hear him in the middle of the night moaning it over and over again, trying to get it right:

> I won't cry in the daytime.
> I won't think of Ma.
> I'll think of her at night time
> And cry then.

Other than this, Jimmy seemed delighted with his role. He fit the part perfectly, and the producer and director were behind him. But during out-of-town tryouts a story circulated that Jimmy pulled a knife on someone during a rehearsal.

"In Hartford, the ruckus began during the rehearsal of the third act," said Michael Gordon. "The tension during that scene was pretty high and Jimmy took out after a prop man. I was sitting down in the audience. I jumped up on stage because there was a commotion, but by the time I got there it was all over. I think Jimmy actually pulled a

Jimmy as Wally Wilkins in See the Jaguar *with Arthur Kennedy.*

switchblade on the guy, but I never did find out."

Arthur Kennedy, who played the benevolent Dave Ricks, later told writer Ed Corley that Jimmy had pulled a knife, the same switchblade Jimmy had bought with the money Nash had given him for glasses. "Kennedy supposedly took the knife out of Jimmy's hand," said Corley, "and broke the blade, with stern instructions 'not to pull any of that crap in *my* show!' Jimmy, who was impulsive rather than violent, may have been relieved the matter was taken out of his hands and his 'number' had a quick resolution."

When *See the Jaguar* opened in New York, Jimmy felt as if it were the first Broadway opening night in history.

"His feet never touched the floor," said Dizzy Sheridan, who went with Jimmy to Sardi's for the opening-night party. "He just flew from table to table, talking, laughing. I watched people's eyes pouring adulation all over him; they loved him.

"But it was a very crushing night for me. We left together, we wanted to be together, but he was staying at the Royalton that night and after we got upstairs they called and told him he couldn't have a woman in his room. So we ordered something to drink and then he walked me downstairs and put me in a cab. I had the feeling that things were starting to move for Jimmy and I would never be able to catch up. I saw him two or three times after that and then I left for Trinidad."

Reviewers found the play obscure and silly, "a contrivance of jejune symbolism." The critic for the *Daily Mirror* said, "The advance notices spoke of this play as an allegorical western without a horse. Come to think of it, maybe that's what was missing." The reviewers pretty much agreed that the plot was so torn between forthright story and lofty parable that it was completely unsuccessful in both.

But James Dean was recognized for his wraithlike portrayal of Wally Wilkins: "overwhelming as the boy from the ice house" ... "played the part with sweetness and naiveté that made his tortures singularly poignant" ... "makes childish young fugitive believable" ... "adds an extraordinary performance in an almost impossible role ... "

It's revealing to look at the photographs of him as Wally Wilkins. Although the character so closely matched the conditions of his own life, he has created an inner character who has his own face. It's not just the way his hair is combed down, but his expression, the aperture of his eyes, his loose jaw and open mouth. Jimmy has regressed here some five years, just as he later aged himself over twenty years for the part of Jett Rink in *Giant*.

Jimmy's growing restlessness, his taking things to the edge and his inherent sense of fatalism are expressed in an interview he did with Jack Shafer for a New York radio station the Sunday night before *See the Jaguar* opened.

Jimmy showed up at the interview with his glossy Golden Mentor paperback on the Aztecs and startled Shafer by talking about Aztec sacrificial dramas, a people who sang under torture, a culture where suicides were sacred beings and had their own heaven and patroness, Ixtab, goddess of the rope:

"Well," he [Jimmy] somewhat reluctantly explained, "I've always been fascinated by the Aztec Indians. They were a very fatalistic people, and I sometimes share that feeling. They had such a weird sense of doom that when the warlike Spaniards arrived in Mexico, a lot of the Aztecs just gave up, fatalistically, to an event they believed couldn't be avoided."

"Like the Arab philosophy of Kismet?" I [Shafer] asked, *"what is written, is written?"*

"And for them, the arrival of the Spaniards was written!" Dean went on, his enthusiasm bubbling to the surface. "They had a legend that their god Quetzalcoatl had predicted they would be conquered by strange visitors from another land!"

"Well, no wonder they were fatalistic about it then," I [Shafer] said. "But what's this about *your* being fatalistic, too?"

"In a certain sense I am," Dean admitted. "I don't exactly know how to explain it, but I have a hunch there are some things in life we just can't avoid. They'll happen to us, probably because we're built that way—we simply attract our own fate . . . make our own destiny."

"I think I'm like the Aztecs in that respect, too. With their sense of doom, they tried to get the most out of life while life was good; and I go along with them on that philosophy. I don't mean the 'eat, drink, and be merry for tomorrow we die' idea, but something a lot deeper and more valuable. I want to live as intensely as I can. Be as useful and helpful to others as possible, for one thing. But live for myself as well. I want to feel things and experiences right down to their roots . . . enjoy the good in life while it is good."

In the *Journal American*, the reviewer ended his story with the advice that "if you want to 'See the Jaguar'—you had better hurry." The play closed after five performances.

Out of work again, Jimmy answered as many casting calls as he could. Not every casting director he read for, though, recognized *James Dean* when he walked through the door. But these rejections had some positive aspects. Imagine if Jimmy had been cast as Clarence in *Life with Father* or a singing and dancing Curly in *Oklahoma*. What would living out *those* roles have done to Cal Trask/Jim Stark/Jett Rink? Still, it can't be said that he didn't try.

The first time actor Bill Hickey met Jimmy was at an audition Jimmy didn't pass: "I was working for the director who was casting for the show and Jimmy came in for an audition. As the actors were waiting to get called to read, he flopped down on the floor and rested his chin on his hands and started reading the script. Most of the actors and actresses just sat around chewing the fat with each other. One of them said to me, 'Get him out of here.' I asked why. Maybe it was unseemly conduct to them or something? I guess it could be a bore having to step over him. But he wasn't in anyone's way, so I didn't say anything.

"Jimmy just lay there and laughed. When it came time to read for the part, he did that—he sprawled out on the floor for the scene. So, you see, he wasn't just lying around waiting for an audition, he was making a *physical adjustment*.

"But he didn't get the part anyway because they wanted a *juvenile* juvenile. Who was ready for James Dean?"

Jimmy spent most of his time doing television and trying out for Broadway roles. Movie parts were a little harder to come by, and when a chance came up for a role in *Battle Cry*, Jimmy spent days getting ready.

"I did the screen test for Jimmy for a movie called *Battle Cry*," said Bill Orr, then an executive in charge of talent for Warner Brothers. "He came in wearing these . . . 'battle fatigues' . . . a dirty cap, days' worth of beard, dungarees. He was goddamned *dressed* for the part! And he gave the most fantastic reading I'd heard. It wasn't a reading, it was a performance! He *became* that character.

"I gave him the script and he looked at me and said, 'Don't just hand me this, tell me who I am.'

"So I told him, 'You're a young Polish boy being shipped off to war. You're leaving the next morning and have to say goodbye to your girlfriend, and her father hates you. What do you do?'

"And he was electric! Fantastic! He would walk away with an

agonized look, turn his back, then wheel quickly around and grab her. He portrayed such torment—the kind of emotion it might have taken another actor a week to do. But he didn't get the part unfortunately. Tab Hunter finally got it. He was well known and he had a contract with Warner Brothers, etc. The studio finally decided it wanted a name for the picture, so Hunter was used.

"At that time there were 100,000 people who all thought they were Marlon Brando, but Jimmy Dean wasn't one of them. If Jimmy Dean had never become what he did, I would still remember him. He was really different and left a powerful image with me."

Though *See the Jaguar* had closed after a week's worth of performances, it had given Jimmy enough confidence and promise of work to move into a small place of his own. The excitement of communal living had begun to wear into a cramped arrangement that demanded constant consideration of the other fellow—a trait neither Bill nor Dizzy nor Jimmy possessed in unlimited supply.

"If we weren't battling over the maze of bras, panties and stockings that were making access to the bathroom impossible," said Bill, "we were haggling over the unwashed dishes, the open windows, the closed windows, the selection of food, topics of conversation, etc."

In Jimmy's first apartment on the top floor of 19 West Sixty-eighth Street, the first thing one sees upon entering is a porthole window, the room's one eye which fixes you with a camera's inflexible gaze. A wall of books and record albums faces forward in geometric squares and on the floor there's a regimental cot for a bed. On the wall is a mounted pair of bull horns and a matador's cape.

What strikes one are its absences. Aside from the bed and built-in desk with its practical piano stool, there is no furniture in the room. It is cluttered, but lacks the murky oppressiveness of most living rooms with their heavy curtains and carpeting. There is no domesticity here—no armchair or couch, and no TV, although this was not so unusual in the early fifties. Yet this den speaks eloquently about the creature who inhabits its spartan Quaker atmosphere. The functional bed folds into a simple bench. Everything in the room Jimmy *used*, including the cape and the bull's horns, the castanets and the recorder above his desk, which he later used in a screen test for *East of Eden*.

It is a student's room, dominated by heavy tomes, collections of recorded classics and dense paperbacks on Western civilization, the kind of books Rimbaud described as "Miss Europe with her ancient parapets." It is a sheltered fastness against the insecurity of life in New York. The room breathes intimacy, peacefulness, work, silence and security, and yet it is modeled on an absurd idea: a boat adrift in a city!

In this fantastically blank space, Jimmy would spin his dreams—conducting a recording of Berlioz's *Harold in Italy*, intoxicating himself with Rimbaud, leafing through a dozen books at a time: *Some Faces in the Crowd* / *The Seven Storey Mountain* / *Heavenly Discourse* / *Learn Chess Fast* / *Dance to the Piper* / *A Saki Sampler* / *García Lorca* / *A Goddess to a God* / *Flowering Judas* / *How to Sail* / *Franz Kafka* / *I Go Pogo* / *The Burns Mantle Best Plays* / *The Creation of the Universe* / *Moulin Rouge* / *Baudelaire, Rimbaud, Verlaine* / *Los Torros*.

In reaching out for things he could not grasp, he loved all books, but mostly those that were profound, obscure and intense. Although he had little patience and rarely read them, he looked on books as talismans, elusive substances, a sort of plasma connecting him to his past and his mother.

"Jimmy had a chapter heading of knowledge," said Leonard Rosenman, who wrote the music for *East of Eden* and *Rebel* and most recently has composed scores for two *Planet of the Apes* films. "One night Jimmy was at my house reading Kierkegaard's gloomy *Fear and Trembling*. I noticed that after about five minutes he was still on the first page, painfully following every word with his finger and forming the words unconsciously with his lips. When I suggested that he might try a little lighter introduction to the subject, he slammed the book shut and stormed out in a rage."

He was accumulating things and he was in a hurry: he studied Bach with Frank Casaro, dance with Katherine Dunham and played bongos with Cyril Jackson. Despite the way Roy Schatt felt about Jimmy's attention span, Bill Gunn would watch him focus on the drums: "He would sit in the corner with a set of bongos and stay there for hours. He had the most incredible sense of concentration. Changing beats, figuring a rhythm. He'd get into a piece of music and nothing could distract him."

In black turtleneck and blue jeans, Jimmy was intense one moment, impatient the next. His interests drove him one way, then another; so unconnected that in the day-to-day world the resources of their experiences would be reserved for dreams, exercises and building characters.

"An actor," Jimmy said, "must interpret life, and in order to do so must be willing to accept all experiences that life has to offer. In fact, he must seek out more of life than life puts at his feet. In the short span of his lifetime an actor must learn all there is to know, experience all there is to experience—or approach that state as closely as possible. He must be superhuman in his endless struggle to inform himself."

Bill Bast was becoming discouraged in New York. He had wanted to write scripts, but they kept him in the public relations department at CBS. By Christmas he decided to return to California. Jimmy and Bill had a last cup of coffee together and said goodbye:

"Just forget about end results," he [Jimmy] advised. "Remember, the gratification comes in the work, not in the end result. Just remember who you are and what you are, and don't take any of their crap out there."
Then, suddenly, he announced, "I've got to go," and left the drugstore.

As Bill walked back to the Iroquois Hotel, he heard someone call out. It was Jimmy. He had three books in his hand.

"Here," he said to me, "read the one called 'Harpies on the Seashore' in the *Maurois Reader*."
I looked down at the books I held. The two pocket books were *Orlando* by Virginia Woolf and *The Heart is a Lonely Hunter* by Carson McCullers. The other, a hardbound edition, was *The André Maurois Reader*. On the inside cover was written: "To Bill—While in the aura of metaphysical whoo-haas, ebb away your displeasures on this. May flights of harpies escort your winged trip of vengeance."

The pattern of Jimmy's sex life at this point was definitely not taken from Sal Mineo's "Dating Do's and Don'ts." Though he was still fundamentally naive and retained remnants of his puritan upbringing, he managed to treat sex in his usual ironic manner.
"One night we were at some girl's house," Bill Gunn recalled. "Music was playing and the wine was being poured in paper cups. Jimmy called and said, 'What are you doing?'
"'We're having an orgy.'
"'Ha ha.'
"'No, really, we're having an orgy.'
"'I'm coming right over.'

"So he hung up and we all decided to pretend we were having an orgy. The guys rolled up their pants legs and took off their shirts. The girls dropped their blouses, and we put a blanket over us. But nobody was naked. All our clothes were disguised. You know, that's where *we* were at.

"So the doorbell rings and a girl says, 'Come in!'

"And Jimmy comes in, the lights are down and we're all lying around trying to look like we're doing something we'd never been involved in before. And he looks around, I don't know if he believed it or not, but he looked at us, closed the door, opened his pants and took out his thing, shook it and said, 'Okay, let's go!'

"All our faces were like we'd just been fucked with. Put us right in our places. But then we just went back to what we'd been doing—listening to music and pretending we weren't teenagers."

In music, Jimmy and his friends discovered the beat. "We were still swinging each other out and pulling each other back," said Bill. "I'll never forget the first time I heard Big Maybelle singing 'Tweedlee Tweedlee Tweedlee Dee.' That blew my mind. I thought that was terrific. Jimmy and me were in a taxi. We were always in a taxi—when

New Year's Eve party 1953–54 at Roy Schatt's studio. From left: Barbara Glenn, Bill Gunn and Jimmy.

we had a dollar we jumped in a taxi—and on the cab radio came 'Tweedlee Tweedlee Tweedlee Dee' and I said shut up, shut up and listen to this, it's incredible. And it was really something new. Big Maybelle was really knocking it out. Jimmy said, 'That *is* really incredible!' and the next three months he was walking around singing 'Tweedlee Tweedlee Tweedlee Dee.' He couldn't get that out of his head. That was the big song. The thing was, when a black entertainer did something and it started on up, then a white entertainer would record it and that would become a hit, and the black artist would disappear. So Doris Day finally did 'Tweedlee Tweedlee Tweedlee Dee' and Big Maybelle disappeared back into the jungle."

Jimmy came closest to finding a match for his own unstable nature when he met actress Barbara Glenn.

"I was in Cromwell's at the counter, and over in a booth there was this little, pathetic figure huddled in a corner," she said. "I asked a friend, 'Who's that over in the corner?' and he told me it was Jimmy Dean, an actor in *See the Jaguar* (which was opening that night). I looked over at Jimmy and he seemed so alone I just couldn't stand it. I asked my friend to go over and ask him to eat with us, and he came over and we all got a table together.

"There's something so different about Jimmy. It's so hard to describe when you first meet him . . . the little boy quality. Insecure, uptight, but *very* involved. Trying very desperately to make conversation, badly. I found him utterly fascinating."

Barbara and Jimmy dated steadily—traveling, living together and frequently fighting—until Jimmy left for Hollywood in 1954. Jimmy's earlier relationship with Dizzy Sheridan, a tall, sensuous girl, had been relatively calm because of her basic good nature, humor and sensible attitudes. That had been a time when there were few pressures on Jimmy. As Dizzy herself said, "We were hiding from the world when we were together."

With Barbara, though, things became more chaotic. Tall, thin, hyperactive Barbara was as volatile as Jimmy, who once affectionately referred to her in a letter as "my neurotic little shit." Their mutual combustibility incited constant fights and created a pattern of break-up and make-up that was ideally suited to Jimmy's temperament.

"We had a lot of fights," Barbara Glenn said. "I was very emotional; I cried and screamed a lot back then. But Jimmy never screamed back. The hardest thing for Jimmy to do was to be angry. He could never show anger. I remember he told me how afraid he was before he shot *Eden*, afraid of the anger he'd have to go through and worried that he wouldn't be able to do it.

"We would fight every time we were going to be separated. Once I was going away to do stock and everyone decided to have a party for me, and it was going to be at Jimmy's apartment. And he said, 'What the hell is all this party crap? She's only going away for two weeks.' The night of the party he just got nastier and nastier and surlier and surlier. Jimmy just sat in the corner and sulked until eventually everyone went home. I was left there with a friend and Jimmy wouldn't talk to me, wouldn't relate to me. So I said, 'Okay, Jimmy, if you're around when I'm back, I'll see you.' He just grunted, so I walked out.

"I walked down the street to Jerry's Tavern and we were sitting in the booth having a drink, tears streaming down my face, and, of course, in a few minutes Jimmy walked in. He didn't have much to say, but he held my hand and we sat there—and then we spent the night together and that was it. There was never very much said at our partings, but they were intense because there was a cutting off."

When Barbara went away for summer stock, Jimmy stayed in the city, determined to find work. Despite looking for work, learning to sail, his friends and endless interests, Jimmy missed Barbara and in August wrote to her:

Dearest Barbara,

I never suspected one could know as few nice people as I know. My own damn fault. Lamas and scientists may fume and quander. Everything is not just illusion. You are my proof. You have gone to Israel but you have not. I am very lonely for you. I am alone. Thoughts are sweet, then wicked, then perverse, then penitent, then sweet. The moon is not blue. It hangs there in the sky no more.

Please forgive me for such a sloppy letter, I'm a little drunk, drink quite a bit lately. You see, I don't know what's going on any more than you do. Remarkable lot, human beings. I care too.

In antiphonal azure swing, souls drone their unfinished melody... When did we live and when did we not? In my drunken stupor I said a gem. I must repeat it to you loved one. Let's see "great actors are often time pretentious livers. The pretentious actor, a great liver." (Don't get a headache over it.) God Damnit!! I miss you... You're terribly missing. Come back. Maybe I can come up and see you. You think you need understanding? Who do you think you are. I could use a little myself.

You're probably running around up there with all those handsome guys. When I get my boat, you'll be sorry.

Hope you're ok up there. Working pretty hard I guess. More than you can say for us poor thespians back here in the city.

Got to move out of this crappy old apartment. Can't get along with nobody I guess. Makes you feel good when you're not wanted.

Love, Jim

The steamy grey of a New York summer turned into the grey New York autumn, with sharp currents of alternating hot and cold. Barbara came back and Jimmy landed a few television parts; then at the end of the year another Broadway show with a part for him came along.

It was right after Jimmy heard he'd won an audition for the role of Bachir in *The Immoralist* that he met Bill Gunn at Cromwell's Drugstore.

"After I landed the part in *The Immoralist*, I went to Cromwell's and was busy telling my friends I'd been hired for something and how terrific it was—Louis Jourdan was going to be in it and Geraldine Page, and I was sure I was going to be a big success," said Bill. "A friend of mine came in and Jimmy was with him, so he introduced me, and I started telling them about the play and that I had to understudy this guy who was going away, and they were very nervous because he was riding a motorcycle and I didn't know who they were talking about. So my friend said, 'Jimmy's doing a play too.' And I asked him what it was."

"'I'm in *The Immoralist*,' Jimmy said.

"'So am I! What part are you playing?'

"'Bachir.'

"'Hey! *I'm* your understudy. I'm playing this guy named somebody else and I'm also your understudy.'

"'Oh, that's terrific! Do you know anything about Arabs?'

"'No.'

"'Let's get into the Arabs,' Jimmy said. 'Let's find out what that's about.'

"All they'd told us was that if you were an Arab and you got caught stealing, they chopped off your hand," Bill said. "So we went off and started talking about the Arabs. We hit it off because he was blonde and I was black, and we were both playing someone we'd never heard of.

"We saw each other a couple of times before the first rehearsal. The first rehearsal is like the coronation and everyone behaves very badly. The cast sits around a table and there's always this older man eating Life Savers. And Louis Jourdan comes in and everyone holds their breath, and then Geraldine Page walks in. It was incredible . . . I was sitting there, my heart was pounding—I was the only black person in the cast. Billy Rose had informed the director that there were to be no black people in the cast and he didn't know how *I* got in there. All the Arabs were played by whites with their hair and their skin dyed. Except for me. There I was. Finally I got fired, after we opened, thank God, so I *did* get into the program.

"So when Jimmy came in the door, I said, 'Oh boy, somebody I know.' So I said hello to him, and then he looked at me and turned away . . . He didn't speak to me! I almost died, I almost really died, especially since I was alone. Later I realized he knew what he was doing. He was doing a number. He was always doing a number. I didn't realize it then, of course. I know what it is to do it now, but he knew what it was *then*. Of course in those days you had to do it in bigger terms or nobody would notice it."

The part of Bachir, "a colorful, thieving, blackmailing, homosexual Arab houseboy," was Jimmy's last live performance on Broadway. The script of *The Immoralist* was adapted by Ruth and Augustus Goetz from the autobiographical novel by André Gide. The main characters are Michel, a French archeologist (played by Louis Jourdan), and his wife, Marcelline (played by Geraldine Page). The story revolves around the problem of homosexuality. As a boy of eleven, Michel had been expelled from school for "misconduct" with a fellow student. "At that moment," he recalls bitterly more than a dozen years later, "they cut me away from other human beings and I have never been able to find my way back."

On his honeymoon in Africa, the "problem" comes to the surface. At first Marcelline attributes their barren relationship to her husband's cough and fever, but the real "illness" becomes apparent with the intervention of the corrupt Arab houseboy (James Dean), who introduces Michel to an avowed native homosexual, Moktir (David Stewart). The play concludes with Marcelline, an alcoholic as a result of the conflict, returning pregnant and alone to France determined to find a "middle way."

In adapting Gide's covert novel, the Goetzes make the theme of homosexuality more explicit by emphasizing the roles played by James Dean and David Stewart in the seduction of Louis Jourdan. Typical of the fifties, the writers deal with a bold subject, but treat it with lyrical restraint:

Bachir: Soon the warm season will come and I can spend the nights in the orchards.
  Michel: The orchards?
  Bachir: Yes, sir—the trees are filled with fruit; dates, figs, oranges, everything grows in the orchards. Many boys tend the crops, the earth, the goats. They are very beautiful, those places.
  Michel: Where are they?
  Bachir: They are out there beyond the walls. It is always green and cool and they live like a thousand years ago.
  Michel: (*interested*) And do the whole families live there?
  Bachir: There are no families. Only men and boys. Beautiful men . . . They live without women.
  Michel: (*shocked*) Oh—(*coldly*) That is not very interesting.
  Bachir: You asked me, sir.
  Michel: You misunderstood me! (*Turns away*) And you eat disgustingly, Bachir!
  Bachir: (*smiles*) Yes, sir. I think so. I am very healthy and disgusting.

Jimmy was dressed in a long, loose burnoose and heavily made up to look very brown and to accentuate his lips and eyes.

Bill Hickey, who was in Philadelphia with a show while *The Immoralist* was having tryouts, said, "The way he did the role of Bachir was that he created a mystery about the character so the audience's reaction was, 'What is it about this kid?' He wasn't a bit effeminate, so that when he said to Jourdan, 'Do you want me to dance for you?' it was like being in a restaurant and a waiter comes up to your table and stands there for a minute, then says, 'Do you want anything else?' 'Do you want your check?' 'Do you want me to dance for you?'"

In this scene, which is the only physically suggestive scene in the play, Jimmy plots to steal a pair of scissors from the house while the mistress of the house is out. Playing on the weakness of Michel and the sexual desires he is trying weakly to suppress, Bachir tempts him with a tour of all the night places. "I know them all. With money you can buy anything that pleases you . . ." Bachir says.

Michel refuses and Bachir says, "Then maybe I amuse you sir. I dance for you." Then he takes scissors from the taboret where he had put them down and snips them in a rhythm, then slips the scissors in his burnoose and continues the rhythm by snapping his fingers and dancing sensuously, his arms extended into the air.

"When he did the dance with the scissors," said Hickey, "it was very slow and very deliberate, and very *man to man*. When it was over, he just stood there and waited for Jordan to react. Being an Arab and all, you might think he'd be tempted to overact and be very vampy, but Yvonne de Carlo he was not."

Whenever anything was bugging Jimmy, Barbara said she could count on a letter or a phone call at four in the morning, and Jimmy's first letter from out-of-town tryouts for *The Immoralist* in Philadelphia was a cry for help. On St. James Hotel stationery, he starts his letter with "Don't worry about me. I'm O.K.?" Next to the first line is a little drawing of a man with mechanical brains coiling out of his head. The rest of the message read:

Reason you didn't get a call Sat. morning was because (as usual) I just made the train.

Rehearsals are quite confusing at this point. Lighting etc. Can't tell much about the show yet. Looks like a piece of shit to me. Stereophonic staging and 3-D actors. Probably be a monster success. Please write to me about next week-end. Please come and see me. Have to get back to rehearsal now.

Love, Jim

How do you feel honey?
Hate this fucking brown make up.

Jimmy still pulled ironic and testy little "numbers" as he developed his creature during final rehearsals. For a traditionalist like Daniel Mann, who was brought in to replace the original director of *The Immoralist* during out-of-town tryouts, it was an annoying repetition of destructive games that infuriated him to such a point that once during a rehearsal in Philadelphia he jumped on the stage and chased Jimmy out of the theater down the street!

"I had this strange young man who was defying the whole company. Well, there's only so much you can take. I would ask him to do what he had to do, try to communicate with him, but it was extremely difficult. But I wouldn't sugar-tit Jimmy because I had a play to do in a certain amount of time. He was a rebel, and that has a negative connotation if rebelling is against progress, and *the play meant progress*. You have to play the play, not your own whims. If you're playing music . . . if someone stands up and plays the wrong notes or holds his note too long, he's gonna stick out, right? That's what Jimmy did to get attention. Jimmy would decide to play a scene differently—but it wasn't interpretation, it was defiance! Jimmy played what came to his mind and nothing was ever the same twice. He had an attitude toward me that I was a policeman, worse than a policeman, a pig. But it was a big loss for him because I would have helped him the way I helped Louis Jourdan if only he would let me. But I couldn't make him understand that my approach was a positive one, that the director's job is to help an actor help himself.

"He had all these adolescent notions about being a man—he carried a knife, he rode a motorcycle around—but it couldn't have nourished him very much or else he would have been much calmer and enjoyed it. I thought he was a very, very disturbed, very compulsive young man."

Martin Landau gave Jimmy a call to see how he was making out in Philadelphia.

"How's rehearsals?" Marty asked him. "What's it like to work with Louis Jourdan?"

Jimmy's letter to Barbara Glenn while rehearsing for The Immoralist.

"Oh, Louis is great," Jimmy told him. "He really loosened up. He raised both hands at the same time!"

In Philadelphia, the play did get good reactions, and Jimmy wrote home to Barbara:

I am now a colorful, thieving, blackmailing Arab boy played by James Dean. Don't know who the hell *I* am. They are rewriting alot. In rehearsals I was working for the elements of tragedy. A real tragedians role, pathos etc. I turn out to be the comedy relief. The Leon Erroll of the show. "balls".

Some of the drama in *The Immoralist* went on offstage, clearly the most important part as far as Jimmy Dean was concerned. After Daniel Mann had replaced Herman Schulman as director, the play underwent extensive rewriting, and after the first performances Jimmy's part was cut considerably. He had a showdown with producer Billy Rose but got no support from Mann in his argument. After a backstage argument, Jimmy walked out just before curtain time. Bill Gunn was called to stand by and thought for a moment he'd really blow Rose's mind by going on as Bachir. But Jimmy knew he'd be expelled from Actors Equity if he had quit then, so he returned to the theater.

A dance with scissors in The Immoralist.

Just before the play opened in New York, Jimmy went to visit Jim McCarthy, the "native" boy who'd tried to convince him to wear a suit and tie for the Longmont judges five years earlier.

"We kidded him a lot about being an Arab from Indiana," said Jim McCarthy, who was then a law student, "and Jim imitated every star in his show. There was never anything mean about Jimmy's imitations and they were really great.

"He dug into his pocket and came up with a pair of tickets to *The Immoralist* and handed them to me. They were for opening night, the next evening. When he left, I walked him to the door. 'Try to be a good actor tomorrow,' I kidded.

"He turned around and put his hand on my shoulder. 'Mac,' he said slowly, 'I don't want to be a good actor. I want to be the best actor there is.' Then that quick change again. He punched me lightly. 'Told you I'd get to the big town some day,' he said, and ran down the stairs."

The Immoralist opened in New York to a preview audience on February 1, 1954 at the Royale Theater:

THE CAST

Marcelline	Geraldine Page
Dr. Robert	John Heldabrand
Bocage	Charles Dingle
Michel	Louis Jourdan
Bachir	James Dean
Dr. Garrin	Paul Huber
Sidma	Adelaide Klein
Moktir	David J. Stewart
Dolit	Bill Gunn

The action takes place during a period of approximately one year beginning in November, 1900, and alternates between a village in Normandy, France, and Biskra, North Africa.

Minutes before curtain time, Jimmy parked his motorcycle at the backstage door of the Royale and ran up the iron-railed stairs to put on his Arab make-up. That night he gave a performance which won two Broadway awards—the Antoinette Perry, better known as the "Tony," and the Daniel Blum Award—both for most promising young actor of the year.

"I remember the opening night of *The Immoralist*," said Barbara Glenn. "I was all dressed up for opening night—and I met his aunt and uncle there from Indiana. After the show I went backstage and asked Jimmy what he wanted to do. He said, 'They're all going to Sardi's, do you want to go?' as he was putting on his torn dungarees and his tee shirt. I said, 'Jimmy, you can't go to Sardi's that way; they won't let you in.' 'C'mon, they'll let *me* in,' he said. And of course they didn't.

"So he said, 'What do you want to do?' I wanted to go in, so he told me to wait there for him, that he'd go home and change. So he got on his bike and went home, and came back in a suit—one of the rare occasions—and he even had on a tie! And it was funny because I couldn't relate to him that way—it was *weird*. In the meantime I'd been sitting at this table—and it was like a bad Hollywood novel, everybody gossiping and bitching—and I'd gotten so uptight that when he walked in the door in his little choir boy's suit I just stood up and said, 'I'm leaving.'

"We had a violent, violent fight. I can't tell you what a sacrifice this was, for Jimmy to go home and put on a suit. We didn't talk to each other for two days after that. The reason I bring it up is that Jimmy never dressed up for any occasion or for anybody. I think that was the only time I ever saw him in a suit. But I had no choice. I didn't know it would be the nightmare it was. It sounded like so much fun—a party full of stars. Ugh."

Unlike *Jaguar*, *The Immoralist* opened to excellent reviews. Its social theme was considered especially relevant. Homosexuality, along with racial prejudice, juvenile problems and other social "diseases," were just surfacing in the theater of the fifties. *Tea and Sympathy*, also with a homosexual theme, was playing on Broadway at the time.

Critics recognized the boy who had been "so exceptional last year in *See the Jaguar*," though this time, instead of a shy, naive mountain boy, he was playing the witch boy, "a corrupt he-slut with a hundred itchibay tricks." His portrayal of "an unpleasant irregular" was so effective that some of the more bitchy members of Cromwell's community insinuated it was only another instance of typecasting.

Jimmy was touchy about the sexual undertones of his part as the effeminate Bachir, and it has been suggested that he was uneasy about the sexual ambivalence of the role. A great deal of speculation has focused on Jimmy's sexuality, but the form it has taken has usually been self-conscious, using Jimmy as a libidinous mirror—from Kenneth Anger's apocryphal "Human Ashtray" to the alleged porno photographs which have circulated for years and were once published in *Screw*. These fuzzy snapshots of "Jimmy" sitting nude in a tree with socks and a hard on, have more to do with the anonymous poser's idea of Jimmy, on whom he has modeled himself, than with Jimmy's real sexual habits.

The "Human Ashtray" is an image Kenneth Anger created in his book *Hollywood Babylon,* based on a rumor that Jimmy liked to have people put out cigarettes on his body. As Bill Bast points out, Jimmy would never have punished himself so literally.

"Kenneth Anger wishes that Jimmy Dean would have put out cigarettes on *his* body," Bill said. "It's not that Jimmy was above, shall we say, game-playing, but I can't see Jimmy sitting still for something like that. It's a little out of character. If Jimmy had idiosyncracies, and he did, I'm afraid they were much more conventional.

"Jimmy made a drawing once of a human ashtray; I suppose that's where the story got started. He was always making nasty drawings . . . He smoked too much and so did I, and in the morning our apartment was always like the black hole of Calcutta. We woke up to the stench of cigarettes and ashtrays. So Jimmy drew a picture of an ashtray and up out of the center is the head, arms and torso of a man. Jimmy called it the 'Human Ashtray.' Through the head there was a hole and the cigarette would rest in his mouth."

Both fictionalized accounts of Jimmy's life (*The Immortal* by Walter Ross and *Farewell My Slightly Tarnished Hero* by Ed Corley) contain obligatory homosexual incidents, meant to satisfy the voyeuristic readers of pulp biodramas. In Ross' book, one of "Johnny's" girlfriends tells "in her own words" how she barged in on him one morning and was horrified to find him in bed with a man. Corley's book "recreates" a New Year's Eve party in Hollywood where lead character "John Lewis" picks up a transvestite named Dick Devine and retires to the upstairs bedroom.

Fantasies such as these feed on innuendo. Jimmy's real sexual life had more to do with his relations with himself and the androgynous image he projected, wandering in and out of different personalities, than it did with his gender. What these fantasies distort is Jimmy's sexual ambivalence. Jimmy's own answer to someone who asked him if he were gay was, "Well, I'm certainly not going through life with one hand tied behind my back." Jimmy was collecting experience and wouldn't be prevented from trying anything.

Whatever sexual aspects Jimmy contained within himself, they were unfissionable parts of his personality, an innate ambiguity which shaded everything he did, revealing and reveiling his intense inner self. The conflicts arising from his refusal to be only one part of himself caused him a great deal of personal anxiety. He felt that he was both prey to his latent homosexuality and attracted to it, and wrote with his usual ironic tone to Barbara Glenn:

I'm staying in a guy's apartment while he flies to London. No dear . . . by airplane! He's a TWA purser not a vampire. At least not a full-fledged one. That's why I have to leave tomorrow. He's coming back. I'm sure he considers me a victim. I do not wish to move to _____'s apartment now. He has been staying here with me. He also considers me a victim. I refuse to be sucked in to things of that nature. (pun, ha ha) Street urchin again.

Jimmy had a number of homosexual roommates, and it has been insinuated that he even got some of his early parts through these connections. Though he did move around a lot during the later part of his life in New York, Bill Bast said about the "Jimmy Dean slept here" stories: "I once made a list of all the people who claimed to have lived with James Dean and added up the time they lived with him, and if they were telling the truth, Jimmy would have been one hundred and forty-seven years old when he died.

"Jimmy *was* a dabbler, he *was* learning through experiment, and if he wanted to play the role in *The Immoralist* as best he could, well, maybe he did some experimenting. But to say he was gay? That's ridiculous.

"Another thing you should remember about people who say they knew Jimmy is that unless they knew him on a one-to-one basis, *they did not know James Dean*. Because in a group or in a social situation it was impossible for Jimmy to relate. More than one person and you would see a personality instead of a person. You got a show."

Androgyny is the traditional sexuality of the classic performer. Jimmy's interest in his own body has the autoerotic quality of all great actors. The relationship of an actor with his audience takes place in a zone of sexually-charged reciprocal currents, and the androgynous character of Jimmy's roles in his movies is a fusion of both male and female elements. It was the material out of which he created, composed, his polymorphous body. All vices have claws and can be traced through the unerasable hieroglyphics of the features and gestures, but Jimmy's shape-changing was a projection, an idealized union. His body is a performance, not a record.

Jimmy's performance in *The Immoralist* was clearly one of the best in the show, but he still managed to infuriate director Daniel Mann.

"On opening night he came forward at curtain call, and when he stepped up to take his bow, he lifted the robe he was wearing up to his knees and did a little courtsey to the audience. They laughed, but I could have killed him," said Daniel Mann, annoyed to the end. "Jimmy was not without a gift. Not without talent. He may have been a genius for all I know. But I'd rather have someone with a thirty-percent capacity who uses twenty-eight percent of himself than someone with a seventy-five-percent capacity who only uses twenty percent of himself."

Daniel Mann had said Jimmy was disturbed, but what he meant was that Jimmy had been a *disturbance*. At that time nobody talked back to a director. They talked behind the director's back maybe, but Jimmy would say what he thought right to his face. And opening night was no exception: Jimmy gave his two weeks notice.

Geraldine Page, who had become great friends with Jimmy during the show, was very upset when he left and screamed at the producer, "How could you let pure gold walk out on you like that?"

Jimmy tracked down Bill Hickey: "I just wanted to tell you I quit the show. Go and get the part."

When Bill Hickey had asked Jimmy why he gave his notice on the opening night of a successful play, Jimmy had answered cryptically: "I'm taken care of."

"He was very excited about something," Bill Gunn said, "but couldn't tell us what it was. He said, 'No, I can't tell, I can't tell.' I thought he was replacing someone in *Tea and Sympathy* on Broadway, so we all decided that's what it was."

But it wasn't Elia Kazan's Broadway production of *Tea and Sympathy*. It was Kazan's next big film, *East of Eden*.

— "Nobody'd heard of *East of Eden*, except for Steinbeck, and who knew they were going to make a movie out of it?" said Bill. "Originally as a film they were trying to pair Marlon Brando with Montgomery Clift as the twin brothers, which would have made it an older picture . . . and a very strange one! I mean, they couldn't decide who was going to play the *good* one. So they threw that out. That was stupid."

Kazan was secretive about casting *East of Eden*. He had already assembled a group of established actors for the older parts. But the central characters would all be juveniles, and it was important that he find three young people whose chemistry was just right.

Kazan said later, "We'd decided to take just the last ninety pages of the book's about 560 pages. That made the story just about the sons. I started looking around and it was just impossible. I got nowhere. Then a friend of mine told me about a kid that was playing a bit in a play on Forty-fifth Street. I went down and saw him, so then I got him around and got talking with him and I realized it wasn't a matter of could he or couldn't he: he was it.

"I got to talking with him and he had the same problems with his old man, and I rode around on his motorbike, I hung around with him. I just got to know the guy. He was ready to do anything."

Kazan's previous blockbuster movie had been *On the Waterfront*, and Marlon Brando, its star, had gotten his start in Kazan's production of *Streetcar Named Desire*. "I get a kick out of working with unknowns, people who are hungry," Kazan said. "They're like fighters on their way up. It's a life or death struggle for them and they give their utmost to the role. This quality disappears later. They become civilized and normal."

Kazan had seen Jimmy during his brief appearance at the Actors Studio and had recognized his talent. It was the very qualities that Kazan had disliked about Jimmy as a student—his sulkiness, rebellion and pride—that made him want to test Jimmy for the part of Caleb in *East of Eden*.

The "friend" who first suggested Jimmy to Kazan was Jane Deacy, and it was possibly through her efforts that Kazan was convinced Jimmy should initially audition for the part. Because she made a vow never to talk about Jimmy after his death, it is difficult to confirm just how instrumental she was. After just one good part in a poor play and a poor part in a good play, it would seem that Jimmy stormed Hollywood miraculously with superhuman, superstar strengths. But this analysis strains his real nature, contaminates his *truly* remarkable adventures and slights those who helped prepare him.

"I couldn't imagine Kazan being initially attracted to Jimmy," said

Bill Gunn. "I know Jimmy would have been attracted to Kazan, from the fact that Kazan had directed Brando. Kazan was gold. Every New York actor dreamed of being found *anywhere* doing *anything* by Kazan. Kazan was the ultimate. If Brando was the God, then Kazan was the Godfather."

The preliminary readings for *East of Eden* were held in New York and narrowed the possibilities for the three leading roles down to about a dozen actors and actresses, among them James Dean, Paul Newman, Dick Davalos, Joanne Woodward and Julie Harris.

In one important test, Jimmy and Newman are filmed side by side. Newman is dressed in a white shirt with a spotted bow tie, cigarette behind his left ear, and Jimmy is in a casual sports shirt, with his glasses tucked in his top pocket. The following is the actual sound track:

Off-camera director: Hey, you two queens, look this way.
(They profile for the camera.)
Paul: I don't want to look at him, he's a sourpuss.
(Muffled giggles from the crew.)
Director: Oh, he's only doing his job. Turn the other way then.
Jimmy: I don't like *him* either.
Director: Okay, how about looking right into the camera?
(Jimmy and Paul peer into the lens.)
Director: Look at each other.
(Paul and Jimmy crack up as they turn face to face. Jimmy is nervously flipping something in the air, catching it as it tumbles back into his hand, then tossing it up again.)
Director: Paul, do you think Jimmy will appeal to the bobbysoxers?
Paul: I don't know. Is he going to be a sex symbol? (Paul gives Jimmy a quick once-over.) I don't usually go out with boys. But with his looks, sure . . . sure, I think they'll flip over him.
Director: What about you, Jimmy, do you think the girls will like you?
(He doesn't answer right away. There's a trickle of a giggle. The strange object he slips into the air comes into focus as a switchblade knife.)
Jimmy: Sure. All depends on whether I like them . . .

Dean and Newman engage here in a skirmish of images loaded with tension. All seemed playful because, unlike the other tests, there was no script. But both actors knew that this filmed encounter was a battle for currency in a magnetic field, a serious match in which their phantom antlers locked in a deadly combat—the territory they fight for is the imaginary, future kingdom of Eden.

Screen test for East of Eden *with Paul Newman.*

What determined the winner was his face: both Jimmy and Paul Newman were nascent icons with features that were to become as easily recognizable as Christ, Mao or Mickey Mouse. But in this test, Jimmy's entire countenance rippled with expression while the signals of Newman's eyes and mouth were almost vaudevillian numbers restricted to isolated parts of his face. Newman's expressions were typecast into smile, frown and cool stare, but Jimmy's face resisted and relaxed in alternating currents.

Though approximately the same age, Newman looked like a young adult while Jimmy's face expressed the vulnerability of adolescence. Newman's focus was cool: "The thing I carry is Ivy League," he said later. Newman didn't look like he would do anything unpredictable or uncontrollable, but Jimmy looked like he was about to erupt.

Jimmy got the part of Caleb Trask in *East of Eden* and left immediately for Hollywood. His creature had been completed and had passed its first test. The chrysalis was opened and the sidereal body ready for flight. Jimmy had created a powerful telegraphic system for transmitting his most important message–his face.

∞∝

AND Adam knew Eve his wife; and she conceived, and bare Cain, and said, I have gotten a man from the LORD.

2 And she again bare his brother Abel. And Abel was a keeper of sheep, but Cain was a tiller of the ground.

3 And in process of time it came to pass, that Cain brought of the fruit of the ground an offering unto the LORD.

4 And Abel, he also brought of the firstlings of his flock and of the fat thereof. And the LORD had respect unto Abel and to his offering:

5 But unto Cain and to his offering he had not respect. And Cain was very wroth, and his countenance fell.

6 And the LORD said unto Cain, Why art thou wroth? and why is thy countenance fallen?

7 If thou doest well, shalt thou not be accepted? and if thou doest not well, sin lieth at the door: and unto thee *shall be* his desire, and thou shalt rule over him.

8 And Cain talked with Abel his brother: and it came to pass, when they were in the field, that Cain rose up against Abel his brother, and slew him.

9 ¶ And the LORD said unto Cain, Where *is* Abel thy brother? And he said, I know not: *Am* I my brother's keeper?

10 And he said, What hast thou done? the voice of thy brother's blood crieth unto me from the ground.

11 And now *art* thou cursed from the earth, which hath opened her mouth to receive thy brother's blood from thy hand.

12 When thou tillest the ground, it shall not henceforth yield unto thee her strength; a fugitive and a vagabond shalt thou be in the earth.

13 And Cain said unto the LORD, My punishment *is* greater than I can bear.

14 Behold, thou hast driven me out this day from the face of the earth; and from thy face shall I be hid; and I shall be a fugitive and a vagabond in the earth; and it shall come to pass, *that* every one that findeth me shall slay me.

15 And the LORD said unto him, Therefore whosoever slayeth Cain, vengeance shall be taken on him sevenfold. And the LORD set a mark upon Cain, lest any finding him should kill him.

16 ¶ And Cain went out from the presence of the LORD, and dwelt in the land of Nod, on the east of Eden.

CHAPTER EIGHT

I'm Just a Human Bean
May–August 1954

Alone in Hollywood;
Jimmy's role as Cal Trask in East of Eden;
working under director Elia Kazan; comparisons to Brando;
Jimmy becomes a star.

E den.

In the Bible, Adam was guilty of the first breach of man from God by biting into the fruit of knowledge. By slaying his brother, Cain committed the first violence of man against man. Cain thereby destroyed humanity's first nuclear family and set out to begin a new society.

"What a strange story it is, and it haunts one," John Steinbeck wrote in his *Journal of a Novel* the day he came up with the title *East of Eden*. "This one story is the basis for all human neurosis—and if you take the fall along with it, you have the total psychic troubles that can happen to a human."

In Steinbeck's novel, Eden is a romantic evocation of a paradise lost in a mechanical world, and finding this kind of Peaceable Kingdom has been a persistent American delusion. But the idea of Eden as a simple country garden is a city-dweller's hallucination. Those who live in the country are more likely to envision Eden as a jeweled paradise filled with gold—encrusted palaces. Steinbeck magnified the contradictions of our vision by making his Eden correspond to the Biblical version, a garden bristling with anxieties.

In the movie based upon Steinbeck's allegory, Jimmy Dean, as the Cain son, portrayed the role of Caleb Trask. Director Elia Kazan used

Jimmy as an erotic, demonic force to dominate the anxiety of Stein-beck's schizophrenic Eden. And in the best Method tradition, he utilized the urban versus rural consciousness which was so obviously a source of tension in Jimmy's personal nature. Warner Brothers, the studio that produced *East of Eden,* took this schizoid coupling a step further and played up its contradictions. They promoted their new product—James Dean—in two directions: he was both a simple country boy and a neurotic movie star.

"Only a few years ago James Dean was a farm boy in Fairmount, Indiana," his first studio biography began. "Today he is farming again, but this time in his starring role of Cal in *East of Eden,* Warner Brothers' CinemaScope filming of the John Steinbeck novel. In this, his picture debut, Dean is being acclaimed as one of the brightest acting finds in many years."

The rural connection was justified, but his life with the Winslows soon became oddly stressed, stamped out like a toy farm for a greedy press. Jimmy's own statement was sweet and simple, a typical piece of Indiana humor:

Cows, pigs, chickens and horses may not appear to be first rate dramatic coaches, but believe it or not I learned a lot about acting from them. Working on a farm gave me an insight on life, which has been of tremendous help to me in my character portrayals.

But in the same press release, Jimmy made a startling statement rarely found in Hollywood bios:

A neurotic person has the necessity to express himself and my neuroticism manifests itself in the dramatic. Why do most actors act? To express the fantasies in which they have involved themselves.

The dualism of these statements is strange and unexpected. Many stars came out of the Midwest, but most of them wanted to forget about it. And few stars ever reveal their highly guarded feelings of inner turmoil. This kind of promotion was a signal of Hollywood's desire to create a new image: offbeat, disturbed, even aberrant behavior at least made interesting copy. And though Warner Brothers was packaging the image, Jimmy supplied the quotes.

Elia Kazan accompanied Jimmy on the trip west to begin the shooting of *East of Eden.*

"I took Jimmy out to California," said Kazan. "He hadn't been there since he was a kid. I picked him up in a car and he had his clothes in a paper bag. He'd never been in an airplane before. He kept looking down over the side of the fucking plane, just watching the ground. He was totally innocent. It was all new to him."

Kazan and Dean arrived together in Hollywood in March of 1954, and both lived on the Warner Brothers lot. "After we were in Hollywood for a while, he got upset and it was affecting his work," said Kazan. "I was alone, my wife wasn't there, and I told him I didn't want to live in the hotel anymore and got into the dressing room next to him—so we lived in adjoining dressing rooms on the lot. The star dressing rooms were rather luxurious. We both had these two-room apartments with a toilet and a place to cook. I kept my eye on him night and day."

Before long, the publicity mill was grinding out stories about Kazan's "new genius," the temperamental star who would be coached by Kazan, live in isolation at the studio and be protected by a closed set. It was true that Kazan and Jimmy didn't want anyone hanging around while *Eden* was shot, but the reaction was to make sensational comparisons to Greta Garbo:

Hollywood is just getting to know James Dean, who was surrounded with the mysterious air of a Greta Garbo during the making of *East of Eden* at Warner Brothers. The "I want to be alone" girl had nothing on Dean, who remained very much to himself.

The early bios also included a hint of what Jimmy looked like before official studio photographs had been taken:

VITAL STATISTICS

Born: February 8, 1931   *Where:* Fairmount, Indiana
Height: 5' 10"   *Weight:* 155 lbs.
Eyes: Blue   *Hair:* Blond

Inflated by publicity, locked in a room on the Warner Brothers lot, Jimmy's connections to a familiar world were severed. He waited there for the fulfillment of his dreams, his apotheosis, and like the wolf man Lawrence Talbot, longed for death:

4/26/54
Dearest Barbara
    I don't like it here. I don't like people here. I like it home (N.Y.) and I like you and I want to see you. Must I always be miserable? I try so hard to make

people reject me. Why? I don't want to write this letter. It would be better to remain silent. Wow! Am I fucked up.

Got here on a Thursday went to the desert on Sat, week later to San Francisco. I DON'T KNOW WHERE I AM. Rented a car for two weeks it cost me $138.00 I WANT TO DIE. I have told the girls here to kiss my ass and what sterile, spineless, stupid prostitutes they were. I HAVEN'T BEEN TO BED WITH NO BODY. And won't untill after the picture and I am home safe in N.Y.C. (snuggly litttle town that it is) sounds unbelievable but it's the truth I swear. So hold everything stop breathing, stop the town all of N.Y.C. untill (should have trumpets here) James Dean returns.

Wow! Am I fucked up. I got no motorcycle I got no girl. HONEY, shit writing in capitals doesn't seem to help either. Haven't found a place to live yet. HONEY. Kazan sent me out here to get a tan. Haven't seen the sun yet. (fog and smog) Wanted me healthy looking. I look like a prune. Don't run away from home at too early an age or you'll have to take vitamens the rest of your life. write me please. I'm sad most of the time. Awful lonely too. (I hope you're dying) BECAUSE I AM.

Love

Jim (Brando Clift) Dean

Steinbeck's *East of Eden* is a contemporary story of Adam—Adam Trask. Though it is the most popular retelling of the Biblical story, it remains one of Steinbeck's lesser achievements, essentially a potboiler with one of its leading characters, Kathy Trask, Adam's wife, an unmotivated monster of willful destruction, based it is said, on Steinbeck's suppressed hatred of his own mother.

In the original novel, Kathy marries the pious Adam but is more attracted to his "evil" brother, Charles, and on her wedding night she slips something into Adam's wedding drink and sneaks off to enjoy the first night with Charles. Steinbeck implies that her twin boys are fathered separately—Aron by Adam and Caleb by Charles.

Kazan's production of *East of Eden* only hints at Adam Trask's complex background—the fact that his wife wounded him with a gun, left him and the newborn babies and fled the farm they began together in the Salinas Valley. Adam falls into such despair that he doesn't even name his boys until after they're a year old. By the last quarter of the book he is just coming out of his self-isolation, and it is at this point, with Adam moving into town and his sons ready for college, that the movie begins.

East of Eden was Kazan's most controversial film since *On the Waterfront*. The film concentrates on the story of father versus son and the theme of rebellion. Although the allegory doesn't confront any real social problems of the fifties, the film struck a nerve in many sons who were beginning to question the values of their fathers' generation.

Kazan always wanted to film stories about America. He has made a movie on just about every period in twentieth-century America, from the poetic story of his grandfather's passage to this country (*America, America*) to the personally exploitative sinerama of his own sex life (*The Arrangement*). He's also attracted to Christ figures and thought of both Stanley Kowalski in *Streetcar Named Desire* and Terry Malloy in *Waterfront* as versions of Christ. Caleb as Cain is another Christ-like anti-hero, a scapegoat who sacrifices himself to benefit others.

Kazan has been a prime creator of the anti-hero in American movies. He democratized and linked this rebellious figure to root American values by using such fundamentally recognizable types as Brando and Dean–*i.e.*, Brando as a dock worker, Dean as a farmboy. For Kazan, *East of Eden* was not only a symbolic vision, it was also a vehicle for change. He has always believed that movies "change human life," and through movies like *On the Waterfront* and *East of Eden*, he tried to show how the discordant, disruptive elements of American society could effect wide-ranging changes in attitude, behavior and awareness. By making Jimmy the pivotal character in the central American story of *Eden*, he identified him with the original spirit of revolution of America.

Cal–defiant, disobedient and uncompromising–provokes the conflict around which the movie revolves. He is the one who must be punished, who seeks the truth about his supposedly dead mother and finds it, who is sensuous in his every approach to life and who is secretly envied by his brother.

Kazan used Dean to embody the theme of rebellion and exploited Jimmy's nervous system to make his most radical point: Cal as Cain as juvenile delinquent. Kazan thereby made Jimmy a social weapon to play out the director's own visions.

Steinbeck himself had never intended any portrayals of a youthful hero. He vehemently condemned juvenile rebellion in *America and Americans*: "Actually, the whole American approach to the young has extended adolescence far into the future, so that very many Americans have never and can never become adults."

But Kazan and Jimmy had a common cause: confrontation with the father, the father as repressive society and society as an oppressive patriarchy. Cal distilled and embodied the feelings toward parents they both felt.

"*East of Eden* is more personal to me," said Kazan, when comparing it to his previous films. "It is more my own story. One hates one's father, one rebels against him; finally one cares for him, one recovers oneself, one understands him, one forgives him and one says to oneself, 'Yes, he is like that' . . . one is no longer afraid of him, one has accepted him."

The difference between Jimmy and Kazan, however, is that Jimmy never forgave and never accepted. By using Jimmy as the protagonist in this movie, Kazan had unwittingly selected a lethal weapon that would eventually be used to cut away the debilitating compromises of the family. "I chose Jimmy because he *was* Cal Trask," said Kazan. "There was no point in attempting to cast it better or nicer. Jimmy was it. He had a grudge against all fathers. He was vengeful; he had a sense of aloneness and of being persecuted. And he was suspicious."

"I want to make folk movies," Kazan told a reporter from the *New York Times,* "not folksy movies. Odets described the Bronx, but no one has described America."

From his experience in documentary films such as *People of the Cumberlands,* Kazan had acquired a taste for neo-realism—"photographing non-enacted drama"—and a knack for using the raw material of his actors' psyches as the principal drama of his films and plays. But in spite of a self-proclaimed interest in "naturalism" and his Method training, *East of Eden* looks staged. Not surprisingly, it is a favorite movie of both art directors and set designers. There are no "process" shots in *East of Eden*—that is, no simulation of reality—which is very unusual in a movie with so many outdoor sequences. But Kazan could never get the furniture out of the garden. The real landscape is used like layers of scrim, giving the effect of a tableau. It is an illusory *trompe l'oeil* painting, a lyrical stage set which seems to be framed by a proscenium arch, curtains and stage. Nature is organized into planes, as if beyond the range of the camera's f-stops reality dissolves into unfocused space. The finished product is an urban artist's reverie of Americana. Kazan even used color romantically, as if he were tinting a huge black and white photograph.

The quality of this cinematic Arcadia worked *for* Jimmy rather than against him, its wide-screen artificiality making the inner drama of Cal Trask seem larger than life. In his starkness, Jimmy stands out, a silhouette in this lush technicolor garden.

When Kazan brought Jimmy onto the Warner lot in March, no one was quite sure what kind of impact the boy would have, though Kazan instinctively calculated Jimmy's latent powers. "I was going to take some photographic tests," Kazan said about the preliminary work, "and see how he behaved in front of a camera. Well, the crew came out and they thought he was the stand-in. Standing in for whoever was going to play the lead. Then I told them this was the boy who was going to be the star of the movie."

Kazan's desire to have a "realistic" movie did not prevent him from improving upon nature in order to obtain his cosmetic effect. To achieve a "natural" look, he ordered Jimmy to go to Palm Springs before the actual shooting started so he would look like a "real" farmboy.

"Kazan sent Jimmy to the desert to get a suntan and made him drink a pint of cream a day," said Bill Gunn. "It was kind of ironic to fatten him up to make him look like a farmboy, because he was a farmboy. He had that lean look from doing it. And suddenly he had this rubber tire. And this suntan. I'd never seen him suntanned! But this was Kazan's conception of the farmboy. Healthy. Fat. Cornfed. I think he got the pigs mixed up with the farmers.

"Jimmy hated it. They cut his hair, fattened him up, put make-up on him, all this stuff. Maybe to make up for the fact that he wasn't six foot."

But Jimmy got his revenge.

"Every morning we would run into the john and rub our make-up off," said Dick Davalos. "Jimmy taught me how to rub our faces here and there so they wouldn't notice. I don't think we had any make-up on at the end of the day."

There were many efforts to capture "reality," but Kazan was most successful in building the psychological tension between the leading characters which would drive the film on to bursts of anger, confusion and desire. In selecting the people who would trigger these buried reactions in both themselves and in the audience, he was a subtle, deliberate chemist mixing the electric fluids of personality.

· Dick Davalos, who played Abel to Jimmy's Cain, had come to Hollywood straight from a job as an usher at a movie theater in New York. Kazan sensed that Dick would be Jimmy's ideal foil.

"Gadge's [Kazan's] genius is that even before the actors knew each other, he knew how they would react to each other," Dick said. "It was like chemistry. As a unit, this was the singularly most important event in my life. It was a mind blower, truly.

"We were so into those roles, me and Jimmy . . . it took me two years to get over that part."

To produce the necessary relationship between the brothers, Kazan had thrown Jimmy and Dick together long before the film went into production. The tension Kazan had to build couldn't derive only from sibling rivalry, but from the sexual ambivalence between the brothers, so he paired Jimmy and Dick to see what would happen. The earlier black and white test had bristled with latent sexuality.

"Jimmy and I got very close during the testing," Dick continued, "and did the black and white bedroom test to see how it would work. I stayed at Jimmy's house the night before that test so we could work most of the night.

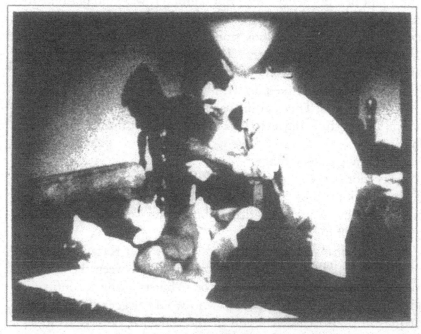

Screen test with Dick Davalos, who plays Aron, Cal's twin brother.

"Sure the test we did had homosexual undertones, but no one has ever said it before, though some people reacted wildly to it when they saw the rushes. That's why it was never put into the film.

"During *East of Eden* Jimmy and I shared a one-room apartment over the drugstore across the street from Warner Brothers. And we were Aron and Cal *to the teeth*. It crept into our social life. He would do something and I would reject him, and he would follow me down the street about twenty paces behind. I went through many numbers, baby, but it was worth it."

Jimmy's first appearance in *East of Eden* is silent. Slouching, prowling, lurking on the street corners of Monterey, he follows a woman he suspects is his "dead" mother. Without saying a word, he fills the screen with a sense of precocious and troubling sensuality. His anxiety seeks us out, and when the camera brings us close to his face, his presence is riveting.

Raymond Massey, who played Jimmy's father, Adam, was dignified, poised and temperate enough in real life to embody all the rigidity Jimmy railed against. Massey had not been cast by Kazan, but had made it a condition for accepting a role in *Battle Cry*, agreeing to play in the war movie only if he could also appear in the more prestigious Kazan film. Massey is not a Method actor and found Jimmy's long preparations for the scenes—exercising, shaking his wrists, bouncing up and down, long meditations in the dressing room—both excessive and unprofessional. He found Jimmy, who would sometimes not talk nor acknowledge someone's presence if he were "in character," rude and offensive.

Kazan played on this mutual opposition in one of the early key scenes when Adam asks Cal to read some verses on repentance from the Bible as a punishment for impulsively and senselessly pushing blocks of ice down the chute of his father's newly purchased ice house.

Cal, Aron and Adam are sitting at the table and Cal begins to read the text, first rushing through the verse, then emphatically punctuating the numbers at the beginning of each passage. Adam tells him to read more slowly and to forget the text numbers, visibly controlling his temper.

Cameraman Ted McCord framed the discord between father and son by shooting the scene at an angle so that the asymmetry of the actors is itself a source of tension. Kazan wanted the saintly Adam to finally explode as Cal continues to defy him, but Massey remained impassive; so Kazan employed one of his classic techniques to provoke the reaction he wanted.

"I was on the set when they shot that scene," said Leonard Rosenman, who wrote the score for the movie. "They must have done six takes and Gadge still wasn't satisfied, so he took Jimmy to the side and whispered something to him. Jimmy came back and they started rolling the cameras, and Jimmy looks down at the Bible and starts to say, 'The Lord is my shepherd, I shall not suck cock, up your ass, fuck you, shit, piss...' And Massey! Well, the old man from the old school started to turn purple! He jumped up from the table and started to yell, 'Gadge, I will *not* play with such a person. You'd better call my lawyers and...'

"And Kazan said, 'Cut! Cut! Calm down, *I* told Jimmy to say that.'

"But he'd gotten Massey fighting mad, and that's what he wanted. He got the reaction he'd wanted on camera and later they dubbed in the dialogue."

Family quarrels are temporarily set aside when the father and his two sons work together on Adam's idea to pack lettuce—the most abundant product of the Salinas Valley—and send it back East, where they can only grow it in season. Adam puts everything he's got behind the project, filling boxcars with ice and lettuce to be shipped across the country. The whole town turns out for the send-off. Leonard Rosenman, infected with the director's desire for realism, reflected the local life in his music: "We got a local Salvation Army band to play at the station when the train takes off. Usually in scenes like that a couple of guys are playing a simple tune and later it's dubbed in by a symphonic orchestra. But I was interested in realism and so we left it in, sour notes and all."

Adam fails in his lettuce venture, but Cal recoups the money by secretly investing in war-time beans so he can surprise his father and hopefully win back his love and respect. Cal visits his crop regularly, and as Jimmy dances Pan-like in a field of new sprouts, his body speaks with its own sensuous language, bringing its redeeming message of pent-up energy.

A good deal of vegetable manipulation went into this sequence. Kazan had to synchronize the shooting with a local farmer so that the bean crop would be precisely three inches high when filming began. Then the sprouts (actually mustard plants), had to be replanted every five minutes since during the shooting they would wilt and discolor.

This stage-set farm where Jimmy lay down in the dirt and played with his bean crop is the Winslows' favorite scene in their favorite of Jimmy's movies. "It's most like the way he was," said Marcus.

Kazan was sensitive to the strenuous effort Jimmy was making in his first starring role. "Jimmy wasn't easy to work with because it was all new to him. He was like an animal might be. Fretful, uncertain. But Julie Harris was very helpful because she was terribly patient and understanding. When Jimmy sensed affection and understanding and patience, he got awfully good."

Julie Harris played the coquettish Abra, engaged to the worthy Aron yet attracted to the animalism and mystery of Cal. She understood Jimmy's anxieties better than most people, having made her own reputation as an adult–child in Carson McCullers' *Member of the Wedding*.

Abra finally admits her attraction for Cal when they are stopped atop a ferris wheel at a carnival where, waiting to meet Aron, she impulsively goes for a ride with his brother. This scene in which they sit and talk and finally kiss would traditionally have been done in a studio with a film projected behind them showing the twinkling

Jimmy in the beanfield.

lights of the fairground below. Instead, Kazan rented a real ferris wheel from a carnival, set it up on Warner's back lot, then borrowed a giant crane camera Walt Disney had used in filming *20,000 Leagues Under the Sea* and hoisted lights, sound equipment and precariously balanced sound engineers into the air to capture the unfolding romance.

Jimmy prepared in his own way. "He really wanted to look up-tight," said Dennis Hopper, who worked with Jimmy in his second movie, *Rebel Without a Cause*. "So to get himself really uncomfortable, he told me he didn't pee all day until they did the shot." Ironically, one reviewer later compared Jimmy's performance to "Baby Snooks reciting while waiting to go to the bathroom."

Kazan's final cut of the film omitted some of the very real undertones of sexuality: he didn't use any intimate scenes between the brothers and he didn't include the most sexual scene Jimmy Dean ever put on film.

In a black and white test for a scene following a fight with Aron, Cal gets drunk and, infatuated with Abra, climbs up on the roof outside her bedroom window. She is asleep, but he climbs inside.

In a screen test, Jimmy fondles Abra's slipper.

There he violates the privacy of her bedroom and crouches beside her, fondling one of her slippers, which seems to become sexually alive in his hands. The fetishistic quality of this act, so explicit and suggestive of Cal's character, are lost in the final, color version where the scene is reduced to coy banter on the traditional balcony.

After their scene on the ferris wheel, Cal and Abra plan a surprise birthday party for Adam at which Cal will give his father the $5000 he's secretly earned. As Cal hands his father the small, ill-wrapped package, Aron, as if sensing a propitious moment, interrupts him by making a surprise announcement of his engagement to Abra. Adam goes over to kiss them both, forgetting the gift he holds in his hand, and Cal, standing alone on the other side of the room, is once again outside the family circle. But Abra gently pulls away from Adam to remind him of Cal's package.

Cal brightens again as his father fumbles at the ribbon, and what follows is the most touching and explosive dialogue in the movie:

CAL: (*grinning*)
Open it.

ADAM:
Yes, yes . . . (*As he fumbles with ribbons, Cal watches him like a cat.*) . . . I don't want the money, Cal. I can't take it. I thank you for it though.

CAL: (*wildly*)
I'll put it away. I'll keep it for you . . .

ADAM:
No, I won't ever want it. (*He looks up at the nearly crazed Cal.*) I would have been so happy if you could have given me, well, something like your brother has—something honest and human and good. Money, even clean money, doesn't stack up with that . . . (*Cal stares at Adam, unbelieving and torn.*) Don't be angry, son. If you want to give me a present, give me a good life. That would be something I could value.

Cal then breaks down on his father's shoulder, crying and trying to hug him as he lets the money cascade down Adam's chest. The puritanical father is horrified and pushes him away, and Cal, like a monster who has caught a glimpse of himself in a mirror fragment, runs sobbing out of the house and into the dark.

The original script called for Cal to "stare at Adam slowly, as though in a trance . . . walk over and pick up the money, then give a loud, choking, agonizing scream and run out of the room." But in this climactic moment Jimmy went far beyond the script and allowed his

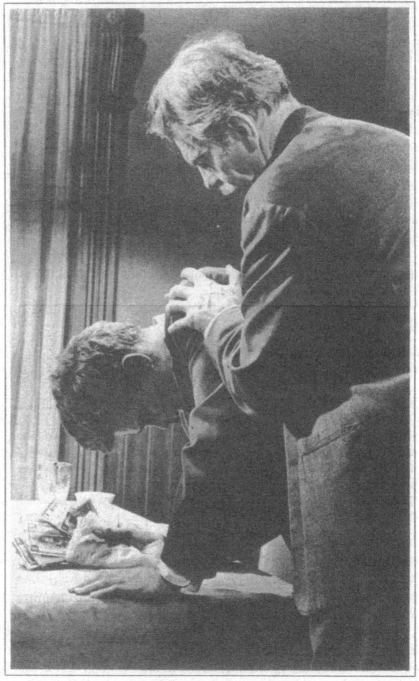

Adam (Raymond Massey) rejects his son's offering.

deepest longings to surface. All the years of his life that he missed a father, the love he longed to give, the anger he couldn't scream, welled up and overflowed onto Massey. Jimmy's clinging, his look of pain, the weak fluttering of the money as it clung to his suit—all unrehearsed and unexpected—horrified Massey, and the camera captures his spontaneous reaction of shock and withdrawal from such an intense expression of emotion.

"Jimmy was always improvising and he cried a lot during the movie," said Dick Davalos. "He loved to do that and he could do it very well. Most of the time Kazan would just let him go through with it and then carry on with the scene. But in the birthday scene Kazan left it in, and it really worked there."

Rejection was something Jimmy had experienced in the unfathomable loss of his mother, compounded by having been sent away at an early age by a father who never called him back. Jimmy tried to bury those fears so no one could see the pain. He could let it all out through Cal, but in his own life his typical, earthly reaction was to reject and yet long for the thing he rejected. In a letter sent to Barbara Glenn during rehearsals, Jimmy wrote:

Have been very dejected and extremely moody last two weeks. Have been telling everybody to fuck off and that's no good. I could never make them believe I was working on my part. Poor Julie Harris doesn't know what to do with me. Well, to hell with her, she doesn't have to do anything with me. Everyone turns into an idiot out here. I have only one friend, one guy that I can talk to and be understood. I hope Lennie comes out here. I need someone from New York. Cause I'm mean and I'm really kind and gentle. Things get mixed up all the time. I see a person I would like to be very close to (everybody) then I think it would just be the same as before and they don't give a shit for me. Then I say something nasty or nothing at all and walk away. The poor person doesn't know what happened. He doesn't realize that I have decided I don't like him. What's wrong with people. Idiots. (I won't fail please.)

While Jimmy's emotional valves fluctuated crazily, causing moodiness and irritability, his screen brother, Dick Davalos, was also suffering from the psychological reality they had created.

"The worst scene for me to do in the entire movie," Dick said, "was when we have an argument and Cal hits me. Jimmy didn't really hit me, but it was so real . . . and I *believed* he hated me, I *believed* he hit me, because it was real for him too.

"I went off the set after the take and cried and cried for about four hours, I was so upset. Julie Harris had to come over and try to calm me down.

"We all play that fucking game where we can be our own worst enemies. We can destroy ourselves, and Jimmy had that in him too. And he got caught at it."

Even Kazan, though he knew he'd tapped a rich, natural resource right from the beginning, was amazed at Jimmy's intensity. "God, he gave everything he had in that film. He didn't hold anything back. At the very end of the shooting, the last few days, you felt that a star was going to be born. Everybody smelled it; all the publicity people began to hang around him. Then he began to spoil, I thought, a little bit. By the next film I thought something in his character was spoiling."

Kazan is notorious for drawing out emotional tensions and resources for dramatic use. If Jimmy began to spoil after *Eden*, Kazan, who drew on the lush bottom land of Jimmy's childhood for four intense months of shooting, had something to do with it. He took from this ripe moment of Jimmy's life the plasma for his film. Kazan himself recognized the loss of vitality suffered by his victim.

"The more success an actor has," said Kazan, "the more he acquires the look of wax fruit; he is no longer devoured by life . . . I try to catch my actors at the moment when they are still, or again, human. And if you have a human actor, at that moment, you can slip your hand inside, touch him and wake him . . . Jimmy Dean . . . was just a young fellow who prowled about the front offices. But he had violence in him, he had a hunger within him, and he was himself the boy that he played in the film."

Long before *East of Eden* was released, it was well known in the movie world. "I was only a young clerk at the time," said reviewer Howard Thompson of the *New York Times*, "and the way to get ahead was to go after something on your own, something that would be a knock-out. I was always reading the trades (*Variety, Show Business, Backstage*) and heard that Warner Brothers had high hopes for the newcomer James Dean. I'd seen Dean on Broadway in *The Immoralist*, and I remembered him from that. It wasn't so much his performance, because he had very few lines in it, but it was his *presence*. So I arranged to go to a screening of *East of Eden* and expected the usual reviewers and trade people would be there. But it turned out to be a private

screening requested by Steinbeck and his wife! Just before the movie went on, I had a chat with them; they were perfectly lovely and I asked if they'd seen it before. She said yes, and I asked how they'd liked it and Steinbeck said, 'I think it'll be a classic.'

"The picture went on and it just left me cold, all the way through to that awful scene at the end where the father and son are united. I looked over at Mrs. Steinbeck and she was just bawling . . . I got out of there before the lights came up.

"At that time I'd only done two interviews before—one with Marlon Brando and. one with Montgomery Clift. And I thought Dean was of that line, that texture. I found out who his agent was. Turned out Jimmy had never been interviewed by a newspaper before. The picture hadn't opened and Warner Brothers hadn't put any pressure on him to be interviewed yet—he wasn't to be bugged, I gathered. I was new at interviewing too."

The story ran:

ANOTHER DEAN HITS THE BIG LEAGUE

James Dean is the young man who snags the acting limelight in "East of Eden," which arrived at the Astor last week. Its opening has started a lively controversy over his histrionic kinship with Marlon Brando—and his professional competence. At any rate, 25-year-old Dean, a product of an Indiana farm, Hollywood, television and Broadway, has made an impression and now owns a Warner Brothers contract.

Count his supporting chore in last season's play "The Immoralist" as having threefold significance insofar as the rapid rise is concerned. It netted him the Donaldson and Perry awards, and, indirectly, the attention of director Elia Kazan, then scouting leads for "Eden," and finally, his flourishing reputation for unvarnished individuality. In a recent chat at his agent's apartment, west of the Yorkville area, Dean gave ample evidence that he was prepared to maintain that individuality.

He sat quietly, awaiting the first query. The slender frame and boyish features suggested a Booth Tarkington hero. The black corduroy shirt and trousers and a penetrating neutrality of expression, magnified by large, steel spectacles, did not. Had he caught "Eden" yet?

"Sure, I saw it," came the soft, abstract reply. His verdict? "Not bad."

"No, I didn't read the novel. The way I work, I'd much rather justify myself with the adaptation rather than the source. I felt I wouldn't have any trouble—too much, anyway—with this characterization once we started because I think I understood the part. I knew, too, that if I had any problems over the boy's background, I could straighten it out with Kazan."

Asked how he happened to turn to acting, Dean hoisted a jodhpur over one knee and lit a cigarette. "It was an accident, although I've been involved in some kind of theatrical function or other since I was a child—in school, music, athletics." He rose and began pacing the room. The words came slowly and carefully.

"To me, acting is the most logical way for people's neuroses to manifest themselves, in the great need we all have to express ourselves. To my way of thinking, an actor's course is set even before he's out of the cradle."

An only child of non-professionals, Dean was raised by an aunt and uncle in Fairmount, Ind. "My father was a farmer, but he did have this remarkable adeptness with his hands," he said, flexing his own. "Whatever abilities I may have, crystallized there in high school, when I was trying to prove something to myself—that I could do it, I suppose. One of my teachers was a frustrated actress. Through her I entered and won a state oratorical dramatic contest, reciting a Dickens piece called 'The Madman.' What's it about? About this real gone cat," he chanted, "who knocks off several people. It also begins with a scream," he remembered casually. "I really woke up those judges.

"All these things," he went on, "were good discipline and experience for me. After graduation, I went to live with my father in Los Angeles—Mother had died when I was a kid—and just for the hell of it, signed up for a pre-law [*sic*] course at UCLA. That did call for a certain knowledge of histrionics. I even joined a fraternity on the campus, but I busted a couple of guys in the nose and got myself kicked out. I wasn't happy in law either.

"Then I tried my luck in pictures, contacted an agent, got some small parts in things like 'Has Anybody Seen My Gal?', a Korean War film, 'Fixed Bayonets,' and one TV play.

"I came here at the suggestion of Jimmy Whitmore, a fine actor and a good boy, a real New York boy, who wasn't too happy out at Metro." For what he learned at the Actors Studio, while edging into prominence on television and his Broadway bow, "See the Jaguar," Dean pointedly credits director Lee Strasberg, "an incredible man, a walking encyclopedia, with fantastic insight."

Would he compare the stage and screen media? "As of now, I don't consider myself as specifically belonging to either. The cinema is a very truthful medium because the camera doesn't let you get away with anything. On stage, you can even loaf a little, if you're so inclined. Technique, on the other hand, is more important. My real aim, my real goal, is to achieve what I call camera-functioning on the stage.

"Not that I'm down on Hollywood. Take pictures like 'The Ox-Bow Incident,' most of the Lubitsch ones. Gadge (Kazan), of course, is one of the best. Then there's George Stevens, the greatest of them all. I'm supposed to

175

do 'Giant' for him. This guy was born with the movies. So real, unassuming. You'll be talking to him, thinking he missed your point, and then—bang! —he has it."

How did his Warner contract read? "Nine films over a six-year period." Story approval? "Contractually, no—emotionally, yes. They can always suspend me. Money isn't one of my worries, not that I have any.

"Don't get me wrong. I'm not one of the wise ones who try to put Hollywood down. It just happens that I fit to cadence and pace better here as far as living goes. New York is vital, above all, fertile. They're a little harder to find, maybe, but out there in Hollywood, behind all that brick and mortar, there are human beings, just as sensitive to fertility. The problem for this cat—myself—is not to get lost." Dean's smile spread as far as his lenses.

East of Eden officially premiered in New York as a gala benefit for the Actors Studio. Ticket-holders paid $150 apiece to see Kazan's latest monster and were escorted to their seat by celebrity usherettes: Marlene Deitrich, Eva Marie Saint, Anita Loos, Terry Moore. The only sensation missing from "this biggest turnout ever" was James Dean, who, much to the consternation of everyone, had disappeared.

Jimmy had seen the movie earlier with Bill Gunn and Marty

Jimmy with Howard Thompson of the New York Times. *His first interview.*

Landau, the three of them walking past the Astor Theater in Times Square a couple of times to check out Jimmy's name in lights. He sat in the dark theater tugging on Bill's sleeve. "Whattaya think? Do ya like it? Huh? Am I okay?" Before the actual premiere he became nervous, however, and escaped, stopping in Fairmount to see Marcus and "Mom" before returning to Hollywood.

The movie hadn't opened in Fairmount yet. But when *Eden* did open in Marion on Easter Sunday 1955, it received a fanfare as indigenous to the region as the one in New York had been.

"Even if Jimmy Dean weren't a hometown boy," the *Fairmount News* began, "*East of Eden* still would be one of the most powerful productions ever released by Warner Brothers . . . Packed houses have seen *East of Eden* every place it has played and in our opinion this will be true from Fairmount to Timbuktu."

The extremes and intensity of reaction among movie critics was evidence that the picture either strongly attracted or repelled. There was little middle of the road reaction:

Library Journal: One of the best films of this or any year, a film which gives deeply disturbing insight into what psychologists call the feeling of rejection.

Time magazine: They've taken the novel and stuffed it into a tight little psychoanalytical pigeonhole—a father problem.

William Zinsser, *New York Herald Tribune*: Kazan lets his characters unfold slowly, and when they finally erupt into anger or violence, you know exactly why. This is the secret of *East of Eden*."

Bosley Crowther, *New York Times*: Why there should be a lack of harmony between Adam and Cal is not clear. Neither is it apparent why they are reconciled at the end. The solution is arbitrary, as is most of the plotting of this film.

James Dean as Cal Trask was the pivotal subject of all reviews. The rest of the cast is lumped together and identified only with their role: Julie Harris as "the country coquette," Raymond Massey "still playing the Lincoln we all know and love" and Jo Van Fleet as the "cold and vengeful" mother. Dick Davalos suffers most; although he played opposite Jimmy, he is rarely mentioned and in some cases is completely ignored. Dick becomes invisible when the story ends because he, like Aron, is the forgotten brother. Though we blame Cain, we follow him out of the garden and into the cities and, as his descendants, keep him alive in our legends.

Jimmy was identified with legend even by the reviewers who most objected to his performance as Cain. Bosley Crowther said in the *New York Times*:

The people in *East of Eden* are not sufficiently well established to give point to the anguish through which they go. Especially is this true of James Dean in the role of the confused and cranky Cal. This young actor, who is here doing his first big screen stint, is a mass of histrionic gingerbread.

He scuffs his feet, he whirls, he pouts, he sputters, he leans against walls, he rolls his eyes, he swallows his words, he ambles slack-kneed—all like Marlon Brando used to do. Never have we seen a performer so clearly follow another's style. Mr. Kazan should be spanked for permitting him to do such a sophomoric thing. Whatever there might be of reasonable torment in this youngster is buried beneath the clumsy display.

Comparisons to Marlon Brando followed Jimmy relentlessly, and there seemed to be no way to counter them at the time. "If you waited between two lines you were Marlon Brando," said Bill Gunn, "but the *funk* of Jimmy Dean was important. He bridged the jump we made clear from the fifties to the seventies. Sure, he probably watched Brando and took things from him, but imitating someone is also a way to become yourself through an endorsement of yourself."

One reporter asked Jimmy what he thought of being compared to Marlon Brando, and Jimmy countered with, "How do *you* like being compared to Walter Winchell?"

Paul Newman, who was just a step behind Jimmy and inherited the Brando tag when Jimmy died, confronted these absurd comparisons: "I was pigeonholed as a Brando, which really bugs me, not because of the comparison, which I rather enjoy, but because it's what I refer to as lazy journalism—'He's a Brando type.' So when they would say that to me, I would say, 'Well, what do you think is Marlon's basic quality? What do you think he carries around with him as an actor? If there's a comparison, then how can we be compared, on what level?' And I would see a lot of blank faces, a lot of blinking eyes. Unless you know what Marlon's basic quality is, then it's ridiculous to make comparisons with him."

Given the expediencies of time and skill, it's easy for writers to ignore detail or serious observation. Critics were used to two-dimensional characters on the screen. "People had a tendency to watch

Jimmy," said Bill Hickey, "watch his mannerisms and say, 'Oh, another Brando.' But what they really meant was, 'Oh, another virtuoso.'"

Jimmy tried to simplify the issue for a hometown reporter: "People were telling me I behaved like Brando before I knew who Brando was. I am not disturbed by the comparison, nor am I flattered. I have my own personal rebellions and I don't have to rely on Brando's. However, it's true I am constantly reminding people of him. People discover resemblances: we are both from farms, dress as we please, ride motorcycles and work for Elia Kazan. As an actor I have no desire to behave like Brando—and I don't attempt to. Nevertheless, it is very difficult not to be impressed, not to carry the image of a highly successful actor. But that's as far as it goes. I feel within myself there are expressions just as valid and I'll have a few years to develop my own style."

Jimmy did develop a distinct "style," but it didn't take years—it took only eighteen months. Kazan's own overpowering ideas and reputation dominated *East of Eden*, and though Jimmy managed to affect some scenes, he went through his first movie like a stowaway in the Hollywood Vehicle, an infiltrator who would risk everything to learn.

Strasberg said about the comparisons of Jimmy to Brando: "Never! They're two totally different kinds of personalities. What was common at that time was the *characters* they played. I don't care what the authors may have intended, they brought onto the stage what we call today the anti-hero, the person who cannot express himself, the person who is not a hero in the ordinary sense of the word."

Jimmy's new type of hero had an immediate appeal that was so strong it even surprised Kazan: "The balcony was full of kids at a Hollywood preview who had never seen Jimmy before, and the moment he came on the screen they began to screech, they began to holler and yell and the balcony was coming down like a waterfall. Every time he made a move it was like ... like Janis Joplin might have affected an audience, or Frank Sinatra when I was a young guy. Every move he made ... it was a landslide.

"I've never seen anything like it in the movies in my whole life, including Marlon Brando."

Jimmy's message was transmitted before he said a word on screen.

Throughout *East of Eden* Cal Trask is an unpredictable and wayward son dedicated to finding truth in his life. As he tells his father, "I've got to find out who I'm like." When Adam brutally rejects him, it seems to be a confirmation of his most dreaded fear that his father will never understand nor accept him. This realization triggers his ultimate blow against his father's hypocrisy. Cal takes his brother to the whorehouse in Salinas, where Aron finally meets his mother.

Aron's state of mind is shattered by this sudden confrontation. As he leaves town on a troop train, he smashes his head into a window in a drunken fit of monstrous laughter, showering his father with fragments of glass. Adam, who'd come to the station to try to prevent Aron's decision to join the war, collapses in Cal's arms, and as the movie concludes, he lies in bed, paralyzed and mute from a stroke.

This is a climax true to character: Cal has destroyed his brother, who has accepted all the compromises of his father, as well as his father, whose legacy was a life conditioned by lies. But Kazan tacks on a last-minute reconciliation between Adam and Cal, and as the movie concludes, Cal is sitting at Adam's bedside, happy to stay home and take care of his father.

One suspects that Kazan, by concluding with this complacent piece of fakery, either gave in to his own sentimentality or backed away from the consequences of the forces he had unleashed. *East of Eden* should have been a radical film for adolescents because it exposed the real issue of Cain's plight: no sacrifice to the past will alter the future, and nothing good can ever come of appeasement toward something in which you cannot believe. Kazan revealed in an interview what he concealed in the movie's conclusion: "If your parents raised you wrong, you should realize this as soon as possible and go your own way."

Critic Pauline Kael objected to this climax, but failed to acknowledge how out of context it really is:

This is a complete negation of previous conceptions of heroism: the hero is not responsible for his actions—the crazy, mixed-up kid becomes a romantic hero by being treated on an infantile level. And the climax of the film is not the boy's growing beyond this need or transferring it to more suitable objects, but simply the satisfaction of an infantile fantasy: he displaces his brother and is at last accepted by his father.

Always attuned to the social extensions of a scene, Pauline Kael's

A new type of hero . . . Jimmy prowls the streets of Monterey.

response to Jimmy was one of moral outrage, as if she had been conned into a cracker-barrel version of Freudian theory: "Lack of love did this." She recognized a new dimension of heroism in Jimmy's Cal, but objected to the film's pseudo-analytical intimacy:

This is a new image in American films: the young boy as beautiful, disturbed animal, so full of love he's defenseless. Maybe his father doesn't love him, but the camera does, and we're supposed to; we're thrust into upsetting angles, caught in infatuated close-ups, and prodded, "Look at all that beautiful desperation."

Kael's reaction was similiar to Massey's. She was repulsed by the success of Jimmy's telegraphic system. "A boy's agonies should not be dwelt on so lovingly," she said indignantly, but Jimmy's neurosis cannot be so easily debaptized. Her objection was actually the highest compliment she could have paid his ability; his performance *disturbed* her.

Some critics are offended when ideas don't precede behavior and evolution continues intuitively without a plan. But intuitive behavior is often political, and it was, in fact, a social evolution that Jimmy forecast in his performance as Caleb. He created a new model, an adolescent who seemed destined to fail, yet in the end became the hero—what the mass media later termed an anti-hero.

Jimmy symbolized the scapegoat who draws the lightning upon himself. His "bad" behavior was really a rebellion against an old definition of good and evil. Kael objects to a movie star leading a nihilistic movement that lacked a premeditated program. But Jimmy had taken the first step. He had the courage to just say, "No, I don't believe it. I have to find out for myself."

East of Eden is a moral allegory and Jimmy is its symbolic agent of disturbance and change: Cain, the mythical destroyer of illusion. Cain has traditionally been thought of as a killer, but the Kabbalist commentary upon Genesis suggests that Cain does not actually slay his brother. In this interpretation, Cain is called *Yaqam,* meaning he is elevated, raised and exalted above Abel. This makes clear why God accepts Abel's offering and rejects Cain's. Abel is a conditioned man content to be a herder of sheep, but Cain, as first tiller of the soil, imitates God by creating new life in the garden. By then offering to the Lord the fruit of his labor, Cain recognizes his own Godliness but commits an act of self-worship—and so his efforts are rejected.

"Qaheen [Cain] establishes a relationship between YHWH [God] and himself," says the *Cipher of Genesis*. "Hevel [Abel] then imitates him and produces offerings to YHWH. There is nothing wrong with Hevel; since he cannot help being a specimen of ordinary, petty, humanity, YHWH accepts his offerings. But Qaheen, being YHWH itself, incarnate but in a state of amnesia, worships an image of himself, which he projects, thereby creating a distance between himself and himself. Since this form of worship reflects a lack of self-knowledge, it is rejected."

Cain is condemned to wander over the face of the earth, and live, as Lord Byron wrote in his play, *The Tragedy of Cain*, "in the shadow of an eternally postponed fruition."

A restless wanderer himself, Jimmy was the vital germ planted in a Technicolor garden, and through him we receive the true message of Cain. The Eden which Steinbeck and Kazan created was a stagnant idyll from which Jimmy recoiled instinctively. The word "instinct" comes from the past participle of the Latin verb meaning "to incite," and in a religious paradise insurrection can only be demonic.

"Cal is a hero who is humanly demonic," Jimmy told the *Marion Chronicle*. "The picture is a study of dualities—that it is necessary to arrive at goodness through a sense of the satanic rather than the puritan." Finally, emphasizing his awareness that a destructive force in nature can often be a dynamic one, Jimmy said, "I hate anything that limits progress or growth."

East of Eden marked the beginning of Jimmy's movie career, an intense period in which he made a total of three films. His portrayal of the errant son was important to Jimmy, not only because it was his first starring role, but also because he identified so strongly with its heroic theme. In this role, Jimmy relied on his ability as a chameleon to slip from mask to mask, occasionally giving us an intimate glimpse of the vulnerable spirit who would flash a look as if to say, "Well, I'm really human too, or had you forgotten?" as one reviewer noted.

Drawing from his own experience and skills as an actor, Jimmy used this hero to communicate what he couldn't say in his own life, "since human speech is like a cracked kettle on which we beat out tunes to make bears dance, when our desire is to touch with passion the stars."

He soars . . . sways back and forth
some more . . . he's giving it hell
up there . . . he sails . . . backs . . .
throwing off glimmers from his limbs. From
his sockets green, blue, yellow . . .
he's enveloped in flashes . . . a fleshless
arpeggio . . .
     The trick is to amuse the demons, to
dazzle them, stun them, possess them,
possess them through joking, and
when they're having a good time, all
shaking with laughter, to
slip behind them, knock them out with
whacks of bamboo! BAM! On the head!

–from Louis-Ferdinand Céline, *Guignol's Band*

CHAPTER NINE

Hollywood Babbles On
1954–1955

*Big Bang theory of publicity;
Dating Do's and Don'ts; the romance
with Pier Angeli.*

J ames Dean was Hollywood's Terminal God. He arrived at a time when the movie industry desperately needed a new star. The old giant of the Hesperides was tired; rivaled by television and plagued by aging idols, it drowsed in its penultimate Metro sunset. The old glamour had long since been rinsed away, and even the city, with its dirty, ice-cream houses and dusty, coffee-can parade of palms, looked tacky and tawdry in the corrosive light, like the crumbling Shangrilas on studio lots. Tinsel Glocca Morra was slowly melting, and in this Pompeian atmosphere Jimmy's ascendancy stood out in sharp relief. James Dean was the last mega-star of the movies before the old solar system was finally eclipsed.

Hollywood believed in the Big Bang theory in the order of its universe, and the publicity build-up Warner's thrust upon Jimmy immediately triggered the conditioned metaphors of celestial dimension. "James Dean, hailed as a second Brando, who we predict is going to be more than a meteor in the Hollywood sky..." said Louella Parsons.

James Dean was the last star Hollywood used to excess, along with technical devices like 3-D, Cinerama and Smell-O-Vision, in an attempt to cure the self-delusions of its old order.

The state of the business was diagnosed in the *New York Times:*

Hollywood has a new kind of crisis on its hands—a shortage of stars. At present, big studios have at least twenty-five major stories ready to face the cameras. But the studios can't cast them properly. The reality is that time has caught up with most of the front-line stars. Middle-age paunch, disappearing or graying hair, sagging facial tissue have blunted the romantic appeal of too many top-rated stars. They are trying harder than ever, but the rapport between stars in their forties and fifties and the broad mass base of the film audience, which ranges in age from fifteen to twenty-five, just isn't as close as it should be.

Hollywood's publicity machine was working hard. It even managed to exploit those who resisted it. Greta Garbo had been the classic example of a star whose attempt to escape notoriety only encouraged it. In the fifties, Brando was the model for actors who, by resisting publicity, generated it. In Jimmy's case, his resistance became far more insidious because of his collusion. "I didn't come here to charm society," Jimmy was fond of saying. "I came here to work." While it was true that he genuinely despised the infernal gossip combines, he was aware that by creating his own personality, he was making good copy.

Hedda Hopper was one of the first to fall under his spell. When the studio publicist first told her, "We think he's a genius, more or less," she reluctantly went to meet the latest on the long list of would-be's. At the Warner cafeteria, where they met for lunch, Jimmy *dared* her to write what she saw—and she did, but not until after he had worked his magic on her in *East of Eden*.

The latest genius sauntered in, dressed like a bum, and slouched down in silence at a table away from mine. He hooked another chair with his toe, dragged it close enough to put his feet up, while he watched me from the corner of his eye. Then he stood up to inspect the framed photographs of Warner stars that covered the wall by his head. He chose one of them, spat in its eye, wiped off his spittle with a handkerchief, then like a ravenous hyena, started to gulp the food that had been served him.

"Would you like to meet him?" said the studio press agent who was my escort.

"No thank you, I've seen enough. If that's your prize package, you can take him. I don't want him."

An invitation came to see the preview of "East of Eden."

In the projection room I sat spellbound. I couldn't remember ever having seen a young man with such power, so many facets of expression, so much sheer invention as this actor.

In his own way, Jimmy courted those powerful ladies by alternately titillating them with outrageous activities, then charming them with his unexpected good manners. Jimmy admitted to Joe Hyams, another Hollywood writer, that he really didn't like Hedda, but that she was his "voice in court."

"You're right," he explained to Hyams, who knew Jimmy had many unkind things to say about ass-kissing actors, "but look at it as protective coloration. If I conform to myself, the only one I'm hurting with the press is myself. So, instead, I'm a nice, polite, well-raised young boy full of respect—which is what Hedda likes. Instead of being on my back, she'll be on my side and she'll defend me against the other press, the people who say I'm just an irresponsible, no-good rebel."

His perceptions were correct, and Hedda, a tough old turkey so ruthless to many, became his ally, his "confidant," an advocate for the troubled boy she felt she "understood." He had done a consummate job of acting and achieved the impossible. He had turned the wicked witch into his "mother"!

In the end, however, Jimmy's own ambivalences were turned against him. The game he had allowed himself to play had hidden traps. He found himself "on" all the time. He had made his personal life into a performance, extending his roles into his everyday life in Hollywood, where he had few real friends to ground him. The anxious character he had played so effectively in *East of Eden* was very much a part of himself, and when it became good copy, he found himself underlining it: "I'm a serious minded and intense little devil—terribly gauche . . . and so tense I don't see how people stay in the same room with me. I know I wouldn't tolerate myself!"

Jimmy was intellectually attuned to this collaboration without realizing how emotionally involved he was becoming. It was almost an excuse to avenge some of the indignities he had suffered as an unknown, particularly from casting directors and agents. "Dick Clayton, Jimmy's Hollywood agent, had obviously been primed for Jimmy's arrival," said Bill Bast, "because he didn't show the usual signs of shock when Jimmy was brought into his office. But Jimmy still blew his mind. He walked in, and without even introducing himself, sat down on the desk with his back to Clayton and made a personal phone call. After we'd left I said, 'What are you doing? Are you crazy?' Then Jimmy surprised *me* by saying, 'Aw, they love it, they eat it up.'"

Jimmy was lovingly creating his monster, but Kazan realized it would ultimately lead to his own undoing. "It's almost impossible for anybody to take that kind of attention and adulation and crowding," Kazan said. "But Jimmy was more vulnerable than anybody I've ever seen. He was terrifically narcissistic. After the palomino and the motor-bike, he bought himself a lot of camera equipment, and I remember him standing in front of a mirror taking pictures of himself. He'd hold the camera under his chin and take picture after picture of himself in the mirror with a long lens. That sort of self-consciousness fitted that part. He became very aware of what sort of image he created."

Hollywood's publicity machine had its own Homeric catalogue of press agents, public relations officers, paparazzi, movie magazine writers and gossip columnists, and they all synchronized smoothly in the creation of outrageous, trumped-up stories, folksy anecdotes and intimate details of the stars to satisfy the voracious appetites of millions of fan magazine readers, playing upon the yearnings of teenage girls and sentimental middle-aged women. Jimmy was nauseated by the blatant exploitation of these contrived situations, but for a very short time he played his obligatory part in the tawdry subculture, going on prearranged dates with starlets and attending premieres dressed in a tuxedo.

Jimmy appeared at one prefabricated event with Terry Moore, a darling of the movie magazines, whose utterly malleable personality threw him into a state of panic on their first "date." The mutant meets the humanoid!

"They arranged a date between Jimmy and Terry Moore," said Bill Gunn. "Terry Moore was a young sex ship, bombshell type, and Jimmy later told me that a limousine picked him up and then they went by to pick up Terry Moore. And she came out all propped up in this huge dress and she sat down and he smiled and said, 'Oh hello,' and she looked at him, turned away and sat straight up. The limousine went all the way there and he's sitting in the back seat, terrified, thinking what the hell is going on? She's not saying a word, but about two minutes before they pull up in front of the place, a big smile flashes across her face, she turns her head and takes his arm and begins to talk into his ear, just bllalalaaahalalla. And he's going through this and he doesn't know what's happening. They got out and they go through the whole evening like this—she watches the

The mutant meets the humanoid—a date with Terry Moore.

movie, they come out, then they get back in the car, she sits straight up, doesn't say a word to him, he takes her home and she gets out—and she'd never spoken to him the whole night."

One of the first women to be romantically linked with Jimmy in Hollywood was Vampira, a female version of Zacherly. She had a television show in which she introduced horror movies and cultivated a bizarre, trendy image. "It was like a Halloween thing that stayed around for a while," said writer Logan Smiley. "Everybody didn't take down their decorations right away if you know what I mean. It was kooky and it was fun. Everyone was getting into pills too. She was from Europe and she was pushy. It was a very sure way for her to break into the business, but I don't think she and Jimmy were as close as her 'planters' made it out."

Jimmy was not sucked in. He did not even date her. "I don't go out with witches," he said to Hedda Hopper, "and I dig dating cartoons even less," alluding to the Charles Addams character on which she had modeled herself.

"I have never taken Vampira *out*, and I should like to clear this up. I have a fairly adequate knowledge of satanic forces, and I was interested to find out if this girl was obsessed by such a force. She was a subject about which I wanted to learn. I met her and engaged her in conversation. She knew absolutely nothing! She uses her inane characterization as an excuse for the most infantile expression you can imagine."

Vampira was furious. This was like putting a stake in her heart. Had she not tried to help this mortal, built an altar to summon the dark powers to his aid? Vampira believed that Jimmy was killing himself and that his friends might help prevent it.

"Vampira wanted me to make this altar for Jimmy because she said he really needed help and that we had to help him find out who he was and stop him from killing himself," Smiley said. "This was about seven months before his death. I said okay. She didn't tell me what to do, I just found this poster that said, 'Blessed are they that go around in circles, for they will be called big wheels,' and I used that as the centerpiece and then put up lots of pictures of him and some candles. I made this in the bathroom. Not that it was a put-down, but just that the bathroom was pretty big, and what I wanted to do was bring him into perspective. Everybody around him was telling him he was a god. He was spinning around, they were building his ego up, but nobody was *relating* to him as a human being. So, what I did was a clarification thing, not a worship thing."

Vampira cut off all her hair in a last attempt to get his attention, but Jimmy would not respond to her trick-or-treat threats. Finally she actually cast a spell on him! O, Ye Powers of Mwuetsi Moon Men, come to my aid! She drew magic Oola-Oola signs with thrice-charmed ashes. Snakes and lizards! She was using black magic against James Dean! She administered the dreaded rites of the eight-by-ten glossy, cutting out his eyes and ears from photographs with a little gold dagger, incanted fiendish curses (by the Fates of Ghastly Guchkakunda!), made a black and white voodoo doll to represent his body and performed other macabre ceremonies in her room, which was said to resemble "some witch doctor's shack in Haiti."

Finally she sent him a picture of herself seated in front of an open grave. "Darling," the inscription read, "come and join me!" He would see, even a comic-strip strega has her powers!

For a time Jimmy enjoyed the frivolous nonsense. It was a novelty, and as Bill Gunn said, "You have to have a good time out there. If you start to take it seriously, you are going to get into trouble—I mean

Vampira digs Jimmy.

those plastic flowers on the highway can run you right off the road."

Practically anything Jimmy did became reading material. "Kandid Kendris" wrote in her column: "Plenty of the younger glamour dolls are dying for dates with Dean, who's been playing it like he couldn't care less. No doubt it's this disinterest plus the fact that he's so different from the average charm boy, that intrigues the gals.

"One cutie pie told me, after a brief introduction in which Dean did little more than nod to her, 'He sure appeals to me. I guess because I'm the type that likes to take in stray cats and dogs.'"

But despite the "glamour dolls," Jimmy was still writing homesick letters to Barbara Glenn in New York:

5-8-54

Was very pleased to hear from you. That's putting it mildly. Gadge Kazan and Williams *are* nice but I wouldn't trust the sons-a-bitches far's I could throw em. They can take advantage of you like anybody else.

Honey!!! I'm still a Calif. virgin, remarkable no. I'm saving it—H-bomb Dean. A new addition has been added to the Dean family. I got a red 53 MG (milled head etc. hot engine). My sex pours itself into fast curves, broadslides and broodings, drags, etc. You have plenty of competition now. My motorcycle, my MG and my girl. I have been sleeping with my MG. We make it together. HONEY.

Jimmy was an enigmatic figure at Hollywood's, Googie's and Schwab's Drugstore, meeting places, like Cromwell's in New York, for aspiring young actors. Jimmy would show up there after work and became one of the "night watch."

"Jimmy was always a night person, and Googie's and Barney's Beanery were the only places in town that were open after twelve o'clock," said Bill Bast. "You start out by talking to someone because they're kooky or interesting and you wind up getting to know them. I think he was interested in these people because they were not bourgeois, mundane, ordinary people. He was like a writer sitting and interviewing people. Jimmy was *always* doing his research, getting involved with his research."

Jimmy was elusive about what he was doing. His friends knew he had a part in *East of Eden*, but when the film came out, even the night watch was shocked.

"I had offered Jimmy a chance to get in the background of a layout

I was doing of Debbie Reynolds for a movie magazine," said photographer Frank Worth. "It was pretty common for out-of-work actors to get in the background, hoping to be spotted. I thought I was doing my friend a favor because we'd never talked much about what he was doing. He turned me down. 'No thanks, Frank,' he said with a mysterious smile on his face." Slightly pissed, Frank said, "Well, it's your loss." Then he added sarcastically, "Maybe someday I'll take a layout with you in the foreground!

"Well, a week later I saw *East of Eden* at a screening. I don't think I've ever felt like such a complete jerk before or since."

Secret star became instant celebrity, and Sidney Skolsky, the Hollywood gossip-monger who had his office above Schwab's Drugstore, reported the scene:

Jimmy found that, if he went to Googie's or Schwab's, his favorite hangouts, he was no longer "just there." Everyone came to his table, and more often than not he was left to pick up the check. Fan magazine writers and photographers were after him continually. The girls he dated were pestered by writers wanting to know what he was really like.

Suddenly everything he said was considered important, and he was misquoted or quoted out of context so often that he became afraid of interviews. The things he said at parties or on dates began appearing the next day in gossip columns.

The vulnerability Jimmy so effectively conveyed in his movies was jealously hidden from the press. Frank Worth, who took a lot of pictures of Jimmy after *Eden*, caught him once in an unguarded moment. Jimmy looked at the photograph Worth had taken and suddenly made a big X over the picture. "I don't want that printed," Jimmy told him.

"I couldn't figure out what was wrong because it wasn't a bad photo except that a bit of his underwear was slipping out of his pants," said Worth. "But Dean has been photographed with *nothing* but underwear on, so that wasn't it. The photo showed Jimmy bent over his car. There'd been some trouble with the engine and he disappointedly was working on it. The picture showed him with his head turned away for a moment. 'It makes me look like a kid,' Jimmy stammered, 'a helpless kid who just got his finger banged or his best toy busted and he wants his mother. It makes me look like I'm hurt and I'm crying out—not out loud—but just crying for someone to come and help me. I don't want people to see me that way.' I was aware of a quiet, imperative tone in his voice. 'Maybe later, much later, you can print the picture, but not for a long, long time,' Jimmy said."

Jimmy was wary of being typecast, but found it was almost impossible to avoid. Because of the pressure of deadlines, the nature of gossip, the catalogue of types and laziness of most columnists, Jimmy found that even if he consented to an interview, the myth would arrive before he even talked to the writer.

When Jimmy met with a reporter for *Seventeen* magazine, the writer reacted as if he were seeing double. "When you meet him for the first time, your eyes take a second to fuse your already photographic image with flesh and blood reality." Hinting that the writer would get an accurate story if he just cleared his eyes and listened, Jimmy said, "People sit and listen to me until I say something that fits in with what they figure I'd be like. That's the part they write down. Then they say, 'Dean, ughh! That character!'"

Like the press, the Hollywood community only saw fragments of Jimmy Dean and isolated the pieces they wanted according to their own discontent. Whatever his peers thought of Jimmy personally, though, acting was always something else, and they respected that ability separately. "Jimmy had the patience of a farmer when he was working," said Logan Smiley. "It was serious business for him. It was like getting in the crops."

Jimmy told Dennis Hopper as they were filming *Giant* together, "Y'know, I think I've got a chance to really make it because in this hand I'm holding Marlon Brando saying, 'Fuck you!' and in the other hand saying, 'Please forgive me,' is Montgomery Clift. 'Please forgive me.' 'Fuck you!' 'Please forgive me.' 'Fuck you!' And somewhere in between is James Dean."

Jimmy met both Clift and Brando after he had become a star in filmdom's synthetic galaxy. Brando visited the *East of Eden* set, and in Jimmy's first and only photographs with him, everyone is smiling except Jimmy, who seems numbed by the idea. When Jimmy and Brando met again at a Beverly Hills party, Brando, at the insistence of their hostess, took Jimmy aside for a "fatherly" chat.

"Dean was never a friend of mine. But he had an *idée fixe* about me," Brando told Truman Capote in an interview. "Whatever I did, he did. He was always trying to get close to me. He used to call up.

(Brando lifted an imaginary telephone, put it to his ear with a cunning, eavesdropper's smile.) I'd listen to him talking to the answering service, asking for me, leaving messages. But I never spoke up. I never called him back.

"When I finally met Dean, it was at a party where he was throwing himself around, acting the madman. So I spoke to him. I took him aside and asked him didn't he know he was sick? That he needed help?"

Leonard Rosenman described Jimmy's playful retaliation: "There was one record Jimmy loved—Elvis Presley singing 'You Ain't Nothin' but a Hound Dog.' In the middle of the night he'd call up somebody and put the phone to the speaker, and then when they answered and said, 'Hello?' he'd put the record on. 'You ain't nothin' but a hound dog . . .' He did it to Brando once."

Jimmy's elusiveness also led to the quasi-cosmic question that all fan magazines purport to answer—"Who is the *Real* James Dean?"

"While the petty quarrels rage as to what is the real James Dean, the big judgment that has shaped up with a dissenting voice is that a young lad is marked for greatness," an anonymous fan magazine writer predicted. "Whether he also is marked for happiness is another question. Unlike the proverbial cleavage between East and West, there are times when the twains do meet. After all, Hollywood is the land of the happy ending."

Jimmy's one real romance in Hollywood was with Pier Angeli, an Italian actress who was appearing in *The Silver Chalice* with Paul Newman. Jimmy and Pier met on the set of *East of Eden* and were soon observed holding hands in the Warner Brothers lunchroom. Some columnists thought this was too good to be true. Was the demon of the East really "going steady" with the shy young starlet? Cal York remarked in *Photoplay*:

Woo-some Twosome: Some still say it's a publicity romance, but Cal knows a secret! Pier quietly bought Jimmy a gold wrist watch, a gold identification bracelet and a miniature gold frame with her picture in it. No, they don't exactly go with his levis and sweat shirt (the new school uniform!) but he was very pleased just the same. So help us, pretty Pier now wears a pearl ring on the second toe of her left foot! Cal tried to ask her if she was engaged—but the words just *wouldn't* come out!

Jimmy was living on the lot, and he entertained Pier with passes at imaginary bulls, while dressed in a matador costume and cape that had been used in *The Sun Also Rises*. They carried on their secret love affair in hideaways along the Pacific Ocean.

Pier confessed to the *National Enquirer* fourteen years later:

We used to go together to the California coast and stay there secretly in a cottage on a beach far away from all prying eyes.

We'd spend much of our time on the beach, sitting there or fooling around, just like college kids. We would talk about ourselves and our problems, about the movies and acting, about life and life after death.

Sometimes we would just go for a walk along the beach, not actually speaking, but communicating our love silently to each other.

We had complete understanding of each other.

[She put a handkerchief to her eyes to wipe away the tears as she told the story of her young love.]

We were like Romeo and Juliet, together and inseparable. Sometimes on the beach we loved each other so much we just wanted to walk together into the sea holding hands because we knew then that we would always be together.

It wasn't that we wanted to commit suicide.

We loved our life, and it was just that we wanted to be that close to each other always.

We didn't have to be seen together at film premieres or nightclubs.

We didn't need to be in the gossip columns or be seen at the big Hollywood parties.

We were like kids together and that's the way we both liked it.

We saw a great deal of each other when we weren't making films. We were young and wanted to enjoy life together and we did.

Sometimes we would just drive along and stop at a hamburger stand for a meal or go to a drive-in movie. It was all so innocent and so emphatic.

Their love, alas, was destined to be star-crossed. Huge forces moved against them. Pier's mother disapproved of Jimmy's tee-shirted appearance, the late dates, the fast car and, *worst* of all, he was not a Catholic. His manners left even more to be desired. On a particularly late outing, Mrs. Pierangeli remarked that such behavior was not permitted in Rome. Jimmy mumbled sarcastically, "When in Rome do as the Romans do; when in Hollywood . . ." But it wasn't only Pier's mother who disapproved. MGM, where Pier was working, felt the relationship was not a good idea, and Jimmy's business "mom," Jane Deacy, advised him against marriage. "If you marry her, you'll be

Mr. Pier Angeli," she warned him. Shades of the Montagues and Capulets!

Jimmy had told Pier that he didn't want to get married. "We'll work something out," he said naively. Pier, the columnists said, was beginning to "civilize" Jimmy. He became neater, started wearing suits, grew concerned about what the press was saying and even planned to join the Catholic Church. But it was not to be.

After completing *East of Eden* Jimmy took a quick trip to New York, and while he was away Pier announced her engagement to singer Vic Damone. The wedding, which would be in two weeks, came as a shock to both Jimmy and the press.

The day of the wedding, Jimmy sat on his motorcycle across the street from St. Timothy's Catholic Church and gunned his motor as the bride and groom emerged.

THE SAD AND THE GLAD

James Dean, the boy who was cooing it up with Pier Angeli just before she switched to Vic Damone, has been seeing Pat Hardy, the girl who was mighty cozy with Vic until Pier came along. Sort of a change-partners deal.

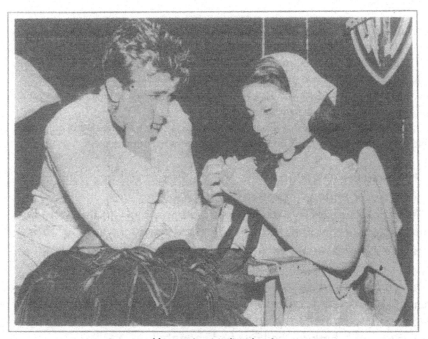

Star-crossed lovers. Pier Angeli with a dreamy Jimmy.

But Jimmy makes no secret of the fact that he still hankers after Miss Pizza, as he used to call Pier. "You might say I'm not exactly delighted and happy over her marriage to Vic," says the young actor. "I've seen Pat Hardy a few times and I'd say she was a little hurt, too. I guess she and Vic were practically engaged. He'd called her parents and everything. She was surprised when Vic and Pier announced their engagement.

"But something happened," explained Jimmy. "I figure that when I went back to New York after finishing *East of Eden* her family and friends got her ear and changed her mind about me.

"I won't try to pretend I'm not sorry—Pier's still okay with me. She broke the news to me the night before she announced her engagement but she wouldn't tell me who the guy was. I was floored when I learned it was Vic Damone. Oh, well, maybe she likes his singing. I hope they'll be happy."

What mothers can do in the name of what's "right"! Though Pier's mother disliked Jimmy, her daughter's marriage to Vic Damone turned out to be one fist fight or child custody scandal after another, and in 1959, five years after her "storybook wedding," Pier divorced Vic Damone. She was married again in 1962 to musician Armando Trotajoli, and when their marriage ended after four years, Pier openly blamed Jimmy Dean:

He is the only man I ever loved deeply as a woman should love a man. I never loved either of my husbands the way I loved Jimmy.

I tried to love my husbands but it never lasted. I would wake up in the night and find I had been dreaming of Jimmy. I would lie awake in the same bed with my husband, think of my love for Jimmy and wish it was Jimmy and not my husband who was next to me.

I had to separate from my husbands because I don't think one can be in love with one man—even if he is dead—and live with another.

In September 1971, thirty-nine-year-old Pier Angeli was found dead of an overdose of drugs, reported "accidental."

Why *did* Pier hastily marry someone else if she and Jimmy were so much in love? Leonard Rosenman suggested a sinister reason for their break-up: "Jimmy would get drunk on a couple of glasses of wine, and when he got drunk he could become very nasty. His personality completely changed; he was completely uncontrollable and could get vicious. It was very Jekyll and Hyde. He also became violent, and he had a reputation for beating up his girlfriends. He did this to Pier once too often and I think she had just had enough."

Another possible answer was revealed in 1973 by Joe Hyams in his book *Mislaid in Hollywood*:

I drove by Jimmy's house the Wednesday before the races to wish him well. As I pulled into the driveway, none other than Pier Angeli passed me, coming out of Jimmy's driveway in her car.

I waved and honked but she only nodded to me and her face looked tear-stained. Jimmy, too, looked distraught when I went in. I felt it was best to leave him alone.

Before going out, I asked if there was anything I could do.

He clenched his fists tightly, over and over again.

"It's already done," he said in a choked voice. "Pier's going to have a baby," he blurted out.

I was stunned by the news. I knew he had seen her from time to time since her wedding. I thought I knew what was on Jimmy's mind, that perhaps it was his baby—and there she was, married to another man. I stood there feeling at a loss, not knowing what to say.

Then Jimmy started to cry, and for the first and only time in my life I took a man in my arms and I held him to my chest and rocked him.

Jimmy lived alone in Hollywood after *East of Eden*. He'd found a place as close to a hunting lodge as you can get in Sherman Oaks, a suburb of Los Angeles. Again it was just one room, a huge A-framed house with a balcony and a sleeping alcove. Jimmy, accustomed to small living spaces, had moved from the Warner Brothers lot only after being forcibly ejected by Jack Warner himself.

"After *East of Eden*, J. L. [Jack Warner] said that he'd heard Jimmy was still living on the lot," said Bill Orr. "He was always against people staying on the lot because we had no insurance to cover that, and there'd been a fire not long ago after some party that caused a lot of damage. He'd made an exception in Jimmy's case because Gadge had asked him, but after *Eden* he wanted Jimmy off the lot.

"I was talking to Jimmy every day because he'd asked me how he could get a weekly salary and I told him by signing a long-term contract—which meant we could use him for more pictures, but then the salary would be the same through the year instead of per picture. J. L. called and told me to have Jimmy off the lot by the end of the week. On Friday I asked the guard at the gate to let Jimmy in until Monday, that he still didn't have a place to live and was working at finding one, and he'd definitely have a place by the weekend.

"When Jimmy came back to the lot on Monday, all his luggage and clothes were waiting at the gate for him. He asked permission to go into the dressing room, and he reached into a vase and pulled out a couple of thousand dollars he'd been hiding—I think it was about $3500.

"From that day on Jimmy never spoke to me voluntarily. He never came into my office again."

After Pier, Jimmy sought male companionship for a while, giving his old friend Bill Bast a call. "He called and said, 'Let's go to dinner,' and we went to the Villa Capri. I didn't realize he'd been frequenting the place until he went in—through the kitchen! He knew the chefs, the maitre d'; it turned out he had a real family relationship there. Later, when we were eating, I asked him why this place, and it turned out that Pier had first brought him to the restaurant.

"Jimmy could be very sneaky. I'd be at his house and the phone would ring, and he was very careful not to let you know who it was. They might be long, intimate conversations, but you would never know if they were male or female, or what they were talking about, or if it was the same person who called or twelve different people. Maybe

Jimmy dines with "the female Marlon Brando," Ursula Andress.

it was his mechanic for all I knew.

"But I didn't pay much attention, because if you knew Jimmy well enough, you knew enough not to. Because it was being done for that, and I didn't want to give him the satisfaction of knowing he had me hooked."

Joe Hyams had become Jimmy's close friend and one night he introduced Jimmy to Humphrey Bogart, thinking "they would hit it off because they were both masters of the 'I don't give a damn' attitude." But Hyams later admitted he was wrong: "Bogie was a master at hiding whatever insecurities he suffered from, while Jimmy's uncertainties were expressed in almost every word and gesture he made. Bogie did most of the talking while Jimmy sat, literally, at his feet, mumbling pleasantries and agreeing with everything that Bogie said. It was a surprise to me to realize that my young friend was as star-struck as any tourist, and I liked him all the more for it."

Jimmy took out a lot of different women—Lilli Kardell, Katy Jurado, Leslie Caron, Pat Hardy, Ella Logan, Marilyn Morrison—and got the stereotyped reputation: "Jimmy's got a new line for his dates—he doesn't say come up and see my etchings, his line is, 'I'll help you with your part,' or 'Come on over and I'll show you my bullfight poster.'"

But there was only one other actress Jimmy saw frequently and that was Ursula Andress. She was fresh from Europe at the time, still shaped like an ideal Brunhild, and in her first Hollywood interview she claimed to be "the female Marlon Brando"!

In the midst of all this Jimmy wrote to Barbara Glenn: "I haven't written because I have fallen in love. It had to happen sooner or later. It's not a very good picture of him but that's "Cisco the Kid" [a thoroughbred palomino horse that Jimmy bought], the new member of the family. He gives me confidence. He makes my hands strong. May use him in the movie. I'm very lonely. Your card smelled so good. Please don't do that (dirty trick, I'm still a Calif. virgin.) I *hate* this place."

Oh! the old swimmin'-hole! where the crick so still and deep
Looked like a baby-river that was laying half asleep,
And the gurgle of the worter round the drift jest below
Sounded like the laugh of something we onc't ust to know
Before we could remember anything but the eyes
Of angels lookin' out as we left Paradise . . .

Oh! it showed me a face in its warm sunny tide
That gazed back at me so gay and glorified,
It made me love myself, as I leaped to caress
My shadder smilin' up at me with sich tenderness . . .

                              When I last saw the place,
The scenes was all changed, like the change in my face;

The bridge of the railroad now crosses the spot
Whare the old divin'-log lies sunk and fergot.
And I stray down the banks whare the trees ust to be—
But never again will theyr shade shelter me!
And I wish in my sorrow I could strip to the soul,
And dive off in my grave like the old swimmin'-hole.

—from James Whitcomb Riley,
"The Old Swimmin'-Hole"

CHAPTER TEN

No Different Flesh
Fall 1954–Spring 1955

Two last television shows;
New York revisited; Jimmy's final trip back
to Fairmount and the Winslow farm.

A fter finishing *East of Eden*, Jimmy wanted to go home: first to New York, where he had consciously begun molding himself, and then to Fairmount, the hometown where his quest had begun. But in his careful way, he arranged this occasion to be more than just a visit with friends and family. It became a photo essay for *Life* magazine—an opportunity to present his image to the world and redefine it for himself.

Jimmy made the trip with Dennis Stock, a young Hollywood photographer he'd met at the Chateau Marmont, a Hollywood hotel on Sunset Boulevard. Although they became friends, as in his relationship with all photographers, Jimmy determined what was to be recorded on film.

"Jimmy invited me to a preview of *East of Eden*," said Dennis. "I'd met him at a Sunday soiree at Nick Ray's bungalow at the Chateau Marmont, and I really didn't know who he was. But once I saw that beanfield scene, I knew he was going to be a really big star, and I wanted to do something with him.

"I saw an awkwardness of purity there that I wanted to capture. I wanted to get to the roots of that earthy quality he had. You know, I photograph what most people usually step on—things like weeds. And that's what Jimmy was—a weed. He grew like crazy and should have kept on growing. When I went to New York and Indiana with him, I didn't think he'd ever stop growing."

While he was in California, between the shooting of *East of Eden*, which ended in August 1954, and the beginning of *Rebel Without a Cause* in spring 1955, Jimmy made his last two television shows: *I Am a Fool* and *The Unlighted Road*. Both are corny and contrived melodramas, but in both Jimmy played characters with personalities much like his own. In *I Am a Fool*, he loses the love of his life by creating a fictitious personality which is his own undoing, and in *The Unlighted Road*, he escapes a life of crime by honestly confessing to a murder of which he is innocent.

At the time, *I Am a Fool* was considered a very progressive production. The teleplay was adapted from a short story by Sherwood Anderson and reconstructed as a sort of two-toned soliloquy. Seated in the foreground of a stylized, Hollywood Shenandoah set, an old man (played by Eddie Albert) reminisces about a love lost years before, while a plaintive harmonica accompaniment whines in the background. Jimmy acts out the story, playing Albert as a young man.

"There I was, nineteen years old," Albert begins, "too big to hang around the house, and there was no job in town I could get. So I decided to move to another town. I knew if I wanted to amount to anything, I had to get outta there. That's all there was to it."

At this point the spotlight switches to Jimmy, who is sitting on an old-fashioned porch in the background. Amidst a mother's tears and kisses, he gets ready to leave home. Then he hops on a train to a neighboring city, where he finds a job as a stable boy. Grandiose and sinful ideas begin to fill his head, however, and he takes the money he's saved, buys a suit and goes to town. With a big cigar in his mouth and after a whiskey or two, he meets a group of society toffs and invents a fictitious identity—"Walter Mathers, from Mariettah, O-hi-ah." This ruse eventually backfires, since among his new-found friends is Lucy, the girl he's destined to fall for.

Lucy was played by Natalie Wood in her first "grown-up" role, and as a result of this teleplay, she was later considered for the part of Judy in *Rebel Without a Cause*.

Natalie nervously awaited the arrival of *James Dean* the first day of rehearsal for the show.

"Everyone arrived on time except Jimmy," Natalie said in a *Photoplay* story called "You Heaven't Heard the Half about Jimmy

Dean." "Like everybody else in Hollywood, I'd heard the stories and was frankly afraid of him. The longer we waited the more frightened I became, and as I went through the script I found that he was going to make love to me.

"After a half hour with everyone watching the door for Dean's arrival, he came in—through a large window of the building. All I could think of was, 'He sure knows how to make an entrance!' He was dressed in a dirty sport shirt and had a large safety pin across the front of his pants—jeans, of course. He jumped down on the floor, looked around, picked up a script from the table and sat in a corner. The director said, 'C'mon Jimmy, sit next to Natalie. You're going to have to make love to this girl.' Jimmy didn't even look up. He just grunted."

Their love scene, which takes place at a train station, is the exasperating climax of the drama. Walter realizes that Lucy is about to go home without even knowing his real name. If he ever wants to see her again, he has to tell her the truth right there on the platform. Birds twitter anxiously like a gossipy chorus while Walter whines and stutters every word of his gnawing confession, as the distant train, that gloomy pack of cars about to deal its fateful hand, whistles and shuffles closer and closer.

Walter: Lucy! (*He grabs her and kisses her.*) Oh . . . Lucy, Lucy . . .
Lucy: I know what you want to tell me.
Walter: (*very surprised*) You do?
Lucy: You want to tell me you love me. Don't you? Isn't that it?
Walter: (*growing more desperate*) Well, yes, yes, I do, but . . .
Lucy: (*aggressively dreamy*) And I love you, Walter. (*Breathlessly*) I'll . . . I'll always love you.
Walter: (*starting to grow weak as the train arrives*) Oh Lucy . . . but . . . Lucy, I don't know where to write.
Lucy: I know where. *I'll* write. Walter Mathers, Marietta, Ohio!
Walter: But Lucy, (*the train starts to pull out of the station*) I'm not . . . Wal . . . Walla . . . (*she's waving goodbye*) . . . Ma . . ." (*He's left alone in the train's wet, smokey wake.*)

In this agonizing scene, Jimmy's lines drag along slowly, spaced by painful pauses that stretch out like an empty track, as Jimmy's voice jerks out—half word, half noise—in a glotteral grinding of gears.

"Natalie was pretty young at this time," said the show's producer Mort Abrahams, "and she didn't quite know how to deal with this man who roared up on his motorbike every day. He could be alternately jolly, charming and funny, then twenty minutes later off by himself 'sulking.' But he only *appeared* to be sulking – he was actually inside of himself.

"I thought it might throw Natalie, who was such a neophyte at that point. But Jimmy was very good with her. He was always kind to Nat, never rough with her at all."

After the first rehearsal, Jimmy came over to Natalie and they shared their lunch break.

"We found a café," Natalie said, "and, like most actors, gabbed about the script we were working on and the show.

"Then in the middle of his sandwich he said, 'I know you. You're a child actor.' I said that was true, but it's a lot better than acting like a child. He didn't get it for a moment. Then he started to laugh. Then I started to laugh, and that's how our wonderful friendship began."

Though Jimmy was considered a "hot property" in Hollywood, television producer William Self didn't even know who James Dean was when his secretary suggested him for the part he eventually played in *The Unlighted Road*.

"I called Dean's agent, and she asked me what the top money was for the show," said Self. "We were making fifty-two shows a year, so the most I could offer was $2500, but I told her I had no intention of paying that much for someone I'd never heard of. So she said fine, then he wouldn't do it.

"Then I called up Steve Trilling at Jack Warner's studio and Steve said, 'Man, he's *terrific*! We've got him under contract, and if you want to buy him out for $100,000 per picture, we wouldn't sell.'

"So I called back the agent and said, 'Okay, you've got a deal.'

"I think our schedule was one day rehearsal and three days shooting. Dean showed up on his motorcycle dressed very . . . uh, casually. He *was* professional, though a bit indifferent, I felt. He shrugged his shoulders when given direction, then went ahead and did his own thing. He did a good job for us and that was it."

The Unlighted Road was Jimmy's last role on television. Again, he is the young innocent thrust into a corrupt, adult world. Jimmy plays Jeff Latham, a hitchhiker who strays into a sleazy roadside diner for a cup of coffee and a sandwich. The jukebox is cha-cha-ing a Latin number, and two sinister men "with bright, animal-like eyes" are sitting in a corner booth. The owner, impressed by Jeff's ability to fix his stubborn coffee urn, offers the boy a job plus free meals and a place to sleep. Jeff says, "That sounds okay to me." But he soon becomes unwittingly involved in a hijack scheme when one of the bright-eyed pair in the corner offers him a part-time job making "collections" of supposed car payments.

One night, while Jeff is making his usual collections, a "police car" starts to chase him. Jeff is puzzled when the shooting starts, but decides he'd better not stick around to ask questions. He speeds through the dark country roads until the car behind him misses a sharp curve and smashes into a tree. Jeff then goes back to the diner, where he breathlessly recounts the story to Egan (the diner owner) and Schreiber (the hijacker). The two older men go to check on the accident and find Schreiber's ex-partner trapped with a broken leg in the phony police car. He had tried to double-cross them, so they heartlessly finish him off with a bullet in the brain and push his car into a lake. This gruesome pair returns to the diner and tells Jeff *he's* killed the policeman by causing the "accident."

Unable to live with this crime on his conscience, Jeff tells his girlfriend, Ann (played by Pat Hardy), he's going to turn himself in.

Ann: Will they believe it was just an accident?

Jeff: I don't know. I gotta take my chances. I just had to tell you before you found out . . . I know I shouldn't have come up here, but I wanted to see you and say good-bye.

Ann: Oh, Jeff . . .

He confesses to the police chief, then learns the true story of the complicated crime.

Cop: Latham, you don't know how lucky you are. If you didn't have the courage to come in here and confess, you might have spent the rest of your life working for Schreiber, sweating out a murder you never committed. As it is now, you'll probably get off with probation.

Jeff: Can I see Egan's confession?

Cop: Sorry, that's against regulations. But there is one thing I can do for you. There's a young lady who's been out here for hours, just waiting to see you. *(He opens the door to reveal Jeff's girlfriend.)*

The Unlighted Road was eventually shown in 1956 and rerun at least six times until CBS lost the original print.

In late January 1955, Jimmy and Dennis Stock left for New York.

Jimmy thought of Manhattan as his second home, but after nearly a year in Hollywood, he had changed so much that he felt out of place.

The scenario began with Jimmy visiting his old haunts—coffee houses, Cromwell's Drugstore and Jerry's Tavern. Then Dennis photographed Jimmy playing bongos with Cyril Jackson, taking dance lessons with Eartha Kitt and drifting alone down the mean city streets. He appears against billboards, below Forty-second Street movie marquees, in front of a paddy wagon and reading in his room. Jimmy's room on Sixty-eighth Street had been cleaned up for the formal photograph by Dennis Stock, but Christine White recalled how the room looked in its usual state: "Across the room on the shoulder-high shelf that ran the width and length of the entire side of the room were empty beer cans, an open peanut butter jar, an album cover of *Romeo and Juliet*, a baseball bat, a hot plate, a bunch of dried leaves stuck in a Maxwell House can, several sheets of music and a bust of Jimmy gazing down upon a new chrome music stand."

Jimmy loved to improvise, often using a random crowd as his audience. "We were walking down Broadway one afternoon," Stock recalled, "and Jimmy stopped outside this furniture-store display window. He said, 'Wait right here, I'm going inside,' and then went in, walked into the display window and sat down in a chair. Pretty soon a crowd collected, peering, pointing, wanting to know what was going on, while Jimmy just sat there completely motionless for about ten minutes while I shot pictures of him. When he had created the desired effect, he just got up and walked out.

"He was a bastard sometimes," Dennis said, "but I liked him well enough so that when he got into one of those moods, I would just pull away and not get near him for a while. Don't forget, I was very young then [eighteen] and I had a lot to learn, so I didn't mind doing what he told me to do sometimes."

Jimmy had looked forward to seeing his old girlfriends, but Dizzy Sheridan recalled some uneasiness.

"Jimmy heard I was in town—I was staying at a friend's apartment. We were having a party and he called and said he was with Rosenman and Jane Deacy, and I said, 'Sure, c'mon over.' So he arrived, and I opened the door and he was standing there in a yellow turtleneck and I said to him, 'My God, you've gone Hollywood.' And I was only teasing him. It had just leapt out of my mouth, but I don't think he liked it at all. As the party went on and got kind of cocktail partyish and silly, he started getting nasty. Not that he said 'fuck you' to anyone or anything, but he just didn't want to play games. I don't think he was in a party mood. Mostly he just hung onto this long braid I had hanging down my back and wanted to get in a corner and talk.

"After a while, everybody left. He managed to clear the room. I don't know how he did it, but shortly we were the only ones left."

Jimmy still wanted to get into the city's monster hum. One night while on a date with Eartha Kitt, he reached its crystal core. A friend had given him an "upper."

"Jimmy called me from the theater where he was watching Eartha Kitt," recalled Martin Landau. "He hadn't slept in a couple of days, so he took a bennie. It was the first time he ever had one, and he called me at intermission. I heard this voice yell, 'HELLO!' I said, 'Who the hell is this?' He said, 'It's Jimmy! I feel just like you.' I never heard him talk so fast and so loud in my life. He said, 'I FEEL TERRIFIC! Jesus, is this the way you feel all the time?' I said, 'Holy Christ, you're not going to miss the last half of this show, are you?' He said, 'I'LL SEE YA,' and I said, 'Okay, man,' and he hung up and I heard him laughing like hell."

Jimmy's most painful encounter came when he said goodbye to Barbara Glenn. Although he had tried to accept the fact that he "was not the person you need to lead a happy life," he was startled to discover upon his arrival in New York that Barbara was marrying someone else.

"The last time I saw Jimmy was when I told him I was going to get married. And he said, 'All right, I want to meet him.' And I thought that would be very awkward, but Jimmy insisted—so the three of us had dinner together. They got along *famously*. The next day Jimmy called me and said, 'You know, I wanted to hate him, but I don't. He's good for you. You're right. But I can't leave without saying goodbye. Why don't you meet me today and we'll just talk.' Well, I didn't want to, because I was afraid. And I said no, but then he begged me, which was not like him. So I went. And when I got there, he had this suitcase full of money opened up, and he said, 'Take it. Go ahead, take it.' And I didn't understand what was happening. During the two years we'd gone together, I'd loaned Jimmy a lot of money, so I said, 'What are you trying to do, pay me back?' And he said, 'You can't leave me, Barbara. You can't go. We can't end like this.' I told him it could end, and it was ending, and that I was going to get married and that was that. It was over. I said, 'Goodbye, Jimmy. I hope we can be friends sometime in the future,' and I closed the door and started walking down the stairs. And then he opened the door and started screaming—the only time he had ever screamed at me—and started flinging the money—fistfuls of money—down the stairs at me. And the last thing he said to me was, 'And when I die, it'll be your fault.'"

After two weeks in New York, Jimmy and Dennis left for Fairmount.

Jimmy grew up in an Indiana Eden, and its scents and sounds passed through him like a colony of wild things. After *East of Eden*, he came back to look for one last time at the farm, creek, trees and meadowlands. Dean is almost an anagram for Eden, and an old meaning of the word dean is "a deep, narrow and wooded vale of a rivulet" as used in "the wild beauties of the dean" or the Castle Eden Dean in England.

As soon as he got back, Jimmy changed into his old work

Jimmy reading James Whitcomb Riley, that "sly old bramble of a man."

211

clothes—overalls, chino jacket, boots and camel-hair cap. This was his costume for the mini-documentary he and Dennis would direct and shoot during their week in Jimmy's hometown. Most of the film was shot within a mile radius of the farm—listening to Jim's grandfather's tales, sitting in the grain troughs, feeding the pigs, walking in stark, winter weather, visiting the town and the cemetery, and attending a local Valentine's Day dance.

In contrast to the usual Hollywood background of pools and nightclubs, these rural pictures look heroic, earthy and elemental. As Jimmy told Hedda Hopper, he had always thought of the farm as "a giant stage," and he posed for Stock like some solitary Hamlet practicing his soliloquies on the Herefords and Poland China hogs. Anyone who has spent time on a farm knows that cattle, and to a lesser degree hogs, make an especially appreciative audience. Will Rogers used to say he'd try out his routines on animals first, and if they laughed, *anybody* would.

The photographs that appeared in *Life* were wholesome enough, almost *deliberately* wholesome. There's no quality more difficult to maintain than innocence, and though Jimmy had it, he also knew

Jimmy tries out primitive rhythms on the stock.

how to put it on—like his classic "Well, now, then, there" in *Rebel*, as deliberate and slow as four adverbs leaning over the rail at the state fair.

The only exception to this group of photo homilies was a series taken at Hunt's General Store on Main Street. In addition to home furnishings, Mr. Hunt kept a few caskets in stock, and when Jimmy saw them, he jumped into one and insisted Dennis shoot some pictures. At first, Dennis refused, but Jimmy prevailed and posed a number of ways in the narrow mahogany box. First he lay down with his eyes closed and hands over his chest . . . then sat up . . . then smiled . . . then flashed a "V" for victory and laughed.

When Dennis was asked if this were another example of Jimmy's prankishness, he replied angrily, "He wasn't being delightful about death. C'mon! *You* lay down in a coffin sometime and tell me what it's about. It's one thing not to be afraid of death and to be realistic about it, but he was afraid, *afraid*. And this way of dealing with it was to laugh in the demon's face, to make fun of it, tempt it, taunt it. He wasn't being cool about death at all. When Jimmy acted like this, I just wanted to take him by the shoulders and shake him, and say, 'How dare you!'"

But Jimmy understood what he was doing in these photographs and talked about it with chilling mockery. "The creepiest thing about it," he told Dennis, "was that with the lid shut, it squashes your nose."

Back at the farm, the family celebrated its reunion. "None of us will ever forget that last family reunion we had with Jimmy in the spring of 1955," Emma Woolen Dean said. "While we're not ones to do much lollygagging around, kissing and hugging each other, it does seem that whenever we're going to be separated . . . we all have tears running down our faces.

"Thanks to television, we felt we had shared those New York days with Jimmy. We had to buy television sets as soon as he began getting parts in programs. Marcus and Ortense had one of the first sets around here, and then Charlie and I got one. The old grapevine got going every time Jimmy was on Lux or Studio One . . . They'd announce it in school and the neighbors would come streaming in to watch."

Jimmy and his family gathered in the Winslows' dining room. Their "conversations buzzed and hummed like bumble bees tangled in air." Jimmy, his grandmother and grandfather, Marcus and Ortense and little Markie were all captured by Dennis on film, and Jimmy also recorded them on tape with a microphone hidden in his sleeve. His grandparents retraced his ancestry, and Jimmy found out his great-great-grandfather made him distantly related to the country singer Jimmy Dean.

Then Jimmy asked about his great-grandfather, Cal, who died in 1918.

"You know, Grandpa, in the movie *East of Eden* it was so funny, 'cause I played a character named Cal . . . and Cal Dean, he was your father, right? Markie and I went to the cemetery today and saw where great-granddaddy Cal Dean is buried. What was he like? Did he have any interest in art or anything? Was he an arty kind of kid? Or what kind of kid was he?"

"He was one of the best auctioneers I reckon I ever did hear."

"Well, what does it take to be a good auctioneer?"

"You got to be a good judge of stock, you got to be a good judge of human nature and you've got to have a talent at it."

"How do you do it?"

To show Jimmy how it was done, Charlie Dean obliged with the

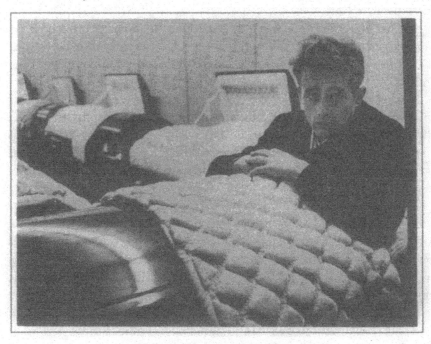

"When they shut the lid it squashes your nose."

non-verbal cadences of the block, a singsong rush of sounds—"Hey, I have three dollars, will you go, will you make it four, will you buy four, I got a three, now four, wuddya go a five, whomake it five, I gotta five howany nowsow leds gititup there do I hearasix now igotta six . . .

"I'll tell you what kills auctioneers . . ." Grandpa Dean told Jimmy. "You take a man who talks to the public every day, he'll eventually get too much confidence in himself. He fools himself by thinkin' he's gettin' by with it, and as soon as the people finds out, they quit him. And that's what kills 'em off."

Jimmy was also delighted to hear there'd been a poet in the family. Cal's brother had written a poem so people could remember all the names of the six Dean boys: Joe Bennel, "Kil" (Achilles), Cal, Harry, Pat and John. It went:

Joe Bennel, Kil Cal, while Harry, Pat and John
Stood off and looked on.

On previous visits, Jimmy had always stopped to talk with Adeline Nall and sometimes even visited her class at the high school. This last time he was too busy taking Dennis around, but she finally bumped into Jimmy at his grandparents' house in town.

"The last time I saw Jimmy was at his Grandpa Dean's house," Mrs. Nall recalled. "Jimmy came over to my car window. What I was trying to tell him was—don't forget to be kind. He was objecting to all the Hollywood commotion. He had no one to go to. No one to encourage him. Or *dis*courage him. Someone should have said to him, 'This is what *you* chose. *You* wanted to be an actor.' But he wanted that and he wanted his own private life too.

"We talked for a while, till I kinda reached the end of trying to explain what I meant, and in the background Dennis Stock was shaking his head, agreeing that Jimmy couldn't fathom it all. We backed out of the drive and I proceeded down Washington Street toward the stop sign, and Jimmy was sailing along behind me. We got to the stop sign and I had to go straight on and then Jimmy made the turn to go out to the Winslows'. He honked and we both laid on the horns, and that was our last communication. We were communicating again."

The photo story was published in *Life* on March 7, 1955. Dennis said the editors did not appreciate his down-home approach. "How can we tell this is a star? How do we know who the hell this is?" they asked. But one editor rescued the story. "Look, this kid Dean is going to be really hot. And Stock's the only one who's got it, so we've got to go with it." They revealed the farmboy's true identity by also including stills from *East of Eden* and an explanatory note on the first page of the story, which they titled "Moody New Star."

"Jimmy knew he'd never be coming back to the farm," Dennis said. "That's why he had me set up the last shot of him in front of the farmhouse, with him looking one way and his dog, Tuck, turning away from him. It was his interpretation of that line, 'You can never go home again.' I don't mean that he thought he was going to die, but that he just felt it was gone. There was no way he could ever return to what he'd been, and that's what the farm represented to him."

Within a year, Jimmy returned to Fairmount and was buried along with generations of Deans, Winslows, Woolens and Wilsons in the meadowland outside of town.

His grandmother said, "When I stand on the hill by Jimmy's grave, I sometimes feel I can look one way and see work done by all the

Jimmy, Charlie Dean, Ortense, Marcus, Emma Dean and Markie.

216

Deans who have been here. Then I can look ahead and see the promise of those still to come. Sometimes it is comforting just to have lived so long in Indiana."

The town of Fairmount was first settled around Back Creek, which runs through the Winslow farm. This stream curls in eddies and pools and widens into a swimming hole where Jimmy and his friends would fish for shiners, red horses and bream.

Like Narcissus at the spring from which all forms flow, Jimmy looked into its mirrored surface and touched his source in a poem he wrote entitled "Old Creek."

I took a little drink from an ample stream
I fear thereby result in fertile jest to her source
Her current swift direct and crystal
There is a want to be there and drink long
Nature's plea, ovum, stem and pistil
But there is more to streams
Than the water to gorge on
Plunge your face in a brook
To wash the desire away
A fool to drink
To drink and not to taste.

Feed, oh feed confidently on the tears and
blood of the adolescent. Blindfold him while
you tear at his quivering body; then after having
listened for hours to his bloodcurdling
cries . . . you will rush into the next room,
pretending you have come to help him . . .
Adolescent, pardon me. Once we have left
this changing life, I want us to
be wrapped in each other's arms for eternity;
to form one being, our mouths glued
together forever.

–from Le Comte de Lautréamont, *Chants de Maldoror*

CHAPTER ELEVEN

Rebel Without a Cause
March–May 1955

The background of Rebel;
Nick Ray and the Cathedral of Adolescence;
Jimmy as Jim Stark: Rebel *as Jimmy's film.*

Rebel *Without a Cause* tells a story as old as *Tom Brown's School Days*: a boy's adventures, travails and triumph on his first day at a new school. James Dean plays the part of the fledgling Jim Stark, a new boy at Dawson High. On the first day of classes, he tries to make friends by offering a ride to the girl next door (Natalie Wood). She snubs him. And when he arrives at school, he finds it is dominated by a group of bullies (the gang) who persecute the weaker boys. The hero then befriends the weakling (Sal Mineo), defends him from the others and emerges vindicated and triumphant in the best tradition of boys' weeklies.

Jim Stark appears initially in the guise of a modest, amenable fellow. Awkward and shy, dressed in a drab brown jacket, he's pegged straight away as a square by the "wheels," though we sense a smoldering resentment which will later burst into flame. Finally, the new boy is forced to reveal his secret powers in a contest of strength—a fight in which the villain is forced to give way.

What makes *Rebel* different from traditional schoolboy adventures is that school is no longer the only relevant field of play. Most of *Rebel* takes place away from Dawson High, late at night, in a teenage underworld of violence, romance and death. There are also new, more powerful authority figures—parents and police—to make the hero's trials more complex and difficult.

By involving police and parents, *Rebel* moves the old story into modern society and portrays Jim Stark's tests and triumphs as a positive social force. Finally, through the hero's bravery and compassion, he convinces his parents to face their self-deceptions, wins the girl's love and takes on "adult" status.

Rebel Without a Cause is clearly James Dean's film. He dominates, absorbs and incorporates its drama as its dynamic, instrumental force. In *Rebel*, Jimmy plays himself. He is both victim and hero, and he injects the film with all the diffuse fragments of his own personality. In his role, he reveals all that we know about Jimmy as James Dean, and in his innocence exposes the corruption and compromise that surround Jim Stark.

At a time when the American character seemed cemented in hypocrisy and violence, Jimmy displayed, in *Rebel*, the reality of our alternatives. Like Hamlet in a hall of mirrors, Jimmy created a hero who is both tender and ferocious, child and man, male and female.

Rebel's director, Nicholas Ray, allowed Jimmy to play these different roles and carry the dramatic and spiritual momentum of the film. By giving Jimmy his head, Ray also gave validity to his own conscious themes.

Jimmy contained a very special tension which Nick Ray had been searching for in an actor throughout his career. "The conflict between giving himself and fear of giving in to his own feelings," was a quality Ray saw in Jimmy and wanted him to reflect in the film, "... a vulnerability so deeply embedded that one is instantly moved, almost disturbed by it. Since infancy he had engaged in this struggle between impulsive violence and a grand defiance.

"I didn't *pick* Jimmy for *Rebel*," Ray said. "We sniffed each other out, like a couple of Siamese cats. We went to New York together so I could see where he lived. You should have seen his room—a tiny place, cluttered with books and boxes. We hung out together for about a week—played basketball, went to the movies, got drunk with his friends. We were really close by the time we came back to start the picture."

Though Ray recognized Jimmy as ideal for the part, he didn't yet realize all that Jimmy would bring to it. Ray had wanted to make a film that would take the problem of juvenile delinquency from the other side of the tracks and move it into middle-class homes. He understood the paradox of rich kids who steal a car while there are two others sitting in the family garage. Ray's film *Knock on Any Door* had envisioned a micro-society in which kids would splinter off from the established pool of moral values and form their own society. But such a doomed outlaw union could only survive in romantic fantasy. He wanted *Rebel* to be a romantic story too, but it would also be a conscious synthesis of what was already happening throughout America, a realistic conflict that could not be simplistically resolved. *Rebel* would suggest alternatives to existing conditions rather than merely oppose them.

"*Romeo and Juliet* has always struck me as the best play ever written about 'juvenile delinquency,'" said Ray. "I wanted a *Romeo and Juliet* feeling about Jim and Judy—and their families. Out of this came a conviction about the shape of the story: 'Try to follow the classic form of tragedy.' The main action would be compressed into one day—beginning in trouble and confusion for Jim and ending in something different. One of my notes was: 'A boy wants to be a man, quick.' The problem was to show, during this day, how he started to become one."

It became Jimmy's monumental task to collect in himself all these conflicts, confront them and resolve the dangerous situation which they so obviously suggest. He would portray a hero who was a constantly moving target, and the center of that target was close to the center of Jimmy's own being.

Rebel Without a Cause was originally a book about a teenage psychopath written by Dr. Robert M. Lindner and purchased by Warner Brothers in 1946. While the first script was being written, William Orr, executive in charge of talent for the studio, went to New York City to cast the lead—a boy in a deluded mental state who is driven to senseless murder by his violent memories of childhood.

"When I did the original screen test for *Rebel Without a Cause* in 1947," Orr said, "I finally gave the leading role to Marlon Brando. The script wasn't even finished, but I knew I was looking for a sensitive, unusual young man and everybody kept telling me, 'You must see Marlo Brinden, or Maylin Brandin ...' No one was really quite sure *what* his name was.

"Someone said he was running an elevator in Macy's, and another person told us that the night before he'd swum across the reservoir in Central Park. We kept hearing these great stories about him and finally found out who his agent was and she came in and said, 'Oh,

Marlon isn't interested in getting into pictures at all.'

"So I looked at her and said, 'Wait a minute, you're in my office aren't you?' After we established the fact that she was there and I was there and Marlon wasn't interested in pictures she set up an interview for us.

"When he came for his screen test, he didn't say a word. He just sat there tearing up an envelope into little pieces. So I figured he must be a genius and signed him. I got back to California, read the script and it schtunk; so we never made the picture, nor did we ever exercise Brando's contract."

The property languished in the script morgue at Warner Brothers until 1954, when a number of things occurred. Juvenile delinquency had become a social issue, and the movie business, always the first to exploit cultural trends, began to produce low-budget, high-gross films like *Blackboard Jungle* and *The Wild One*. When director Nick Ray appeared at Warners with an outline for a juvenile story he said had never been done, Jack and Harry Warner couldn't have been happier. The story was commercial and Ray had just made a box-office hit, *Johnny Guitar,* possibly the weirdest western of all time, with an

offbeat plot that François Truffaut described as "a fairy tale, a *Beauty and the Beast* of westerns." Ray's idea also provided a vehicle for Warner's valuable new property, James Dean.

Nicholas Ray's sensitivity to youth had grown from an innate distrust of his own generation. "We should get rid of the school system for kids over six," he said, "before they lose their 'ESP,' their instincts for learning. Let them live a little in society before we fill 'em with bullshit." Ray reflected this attitude in movies he directed: the first adolescent gunslinger, "Turkey," in *Johnny Guitar* and the first teenage Christ in *King of Kings*.

In *Rebel*, Ray depicted a different sort of adolescent—a kid in trouble who comes from a middle-class background. He collected material from what was happening around him, searching the local juvenile homes, police stations and courts.

"The Culver City Police liked our approach and offered us everything we needed," Ray said. "Talks with social workers and psychiatrists, admission to interviews and courtrooms, going out on riot calls in a police car.

"Out of all this had come confirmation of my original point of departure. In listening to these adolescents talk about their lives and their acts, two impressions always recurred. What they did had a terrifying, morose aimlessness—like the sixteen-year-old boy who ran his car into a group of young children 'just for fun'—and a feeling of bitter isolation and resentment about their families."

Ray had originally approached his friend Clifford Odets to write a treatment for the film, but Warner's latest "wonder boy," Leon Uris, who'd just completed *Battle Cry*, got the job as scriptwriter and worked with Ray on the research for *Rebel*. Despite their investigations together, Uris and Ray had extreme personality differences: Uris wanted to go off by himself and bring back a detailed story whereas Ray conceived of the movie as a pool of information gathered from police, parents and kids. The conflict was irreconcilable and Uris left.

The next writer to work on the script was Irving Shulman—novelist, filmwriter and ex-school teacher. Shulman was also a sports car enthusiast, and Ray hoped this interest would help him get close to Jimmy.

"When we met Shulman at my home one afternoon, though," Ray said, "the result was disappointing. After a brief spurt, the talk of cars dwindled. Suspiciously, rather menacingly, as happened when rapport was not forthcoming at a first encounter, Jimmy withdrew."

Shulman is credited for the story adapted from *Rebel Without a Cause*. He created the middle-class characters, outlined the plot and indicated the major scenes—the planetarium, the chickie run, the confrontation between Jim Stark and his father—and his efforts moved the script from idea to screenplay.

Shulman said, "The basic idea was that juveniles are imprisoned in an adult society which is delinquent, and youth finds itself an unwilling conspirator. Until he is an adult, he is nothing: he can't vote, he can't effect the laws, the mores, the myths and legends. And this makes him anxious to lose his allegiance to youth.

"But when he does, if he's lived an 'Eagle Scout' existence during his childhood and wants to behave that way in adult society, he's immediately told he'll be eaten alive if he behaves that way. He's told to take his uniform and put it in the attic, to forget it.

"I worked for about ten to fifteen weeks on the script and was almost finished by that time, so you can see how quickly I wrote. But I didn't like working with Ray, and the whole project took on a nightmarish quality. So I went to Finley McDermit, the story editor, and I said I wanted to get out. My screenplay was the property of Warner Brothers, but they gave me permission to use the basic story for a novel, which I published as *Children of the Dark*."

"Nick had practically thrown out Shulman's script and was really desperate," said Leonard Rosenman, whom Ray had hired to compose the score. "One day I ran into Stewart Stern, a writer I'd known in New York, and asked him to come with me to the studio to see what we were doing and if he could make some suggestions. And Stewart got the job."

Stewart Stern, in his early twenties and with only one minor film to his credit, turned out to be the missing link. Stern (who later wrote the screenplays for *The Ugly American*, *Rachel, Rachel* and *Summer Wishes, Winter Dreams*) brought together all the diffuse elements and wrote a script which was lean, provocative, psychologically charged and appropriately cosmic. The story was ready for the cameras.

With a writer to give his vision form and with Jimmy to embody it, Nick Ray was not about to sacrifice his film by filling it with stereotypes from central casting. Believable juveniles were rare in Hollywood, and the way Ray assembled his authentic teenage types was a departure from traditional moviemaking. Hundreds of kids turned out to answer the initial casting call and wandered around a stage set that had been used in *A Streetcar Named Desire*, waiting for their individual auditions. Ray and his producer, David Wisebart, personally screened them all, asking unprecedented questions such as, "How did you get along with your mother?" Out of these interviews, nine non-professionals were chosen to play "the gang."

For the part of Judy—the girl opposite Jimmy—Warners sent Ray an unlikely collection of familiar ingenues. Ray passed on Margaret O'Brien because she answered all the questions by professing love for parents and teachers. Jayne Mansfield showed up, but Ray said, "I didn't even put any film in the camera for her screen test. That was just an hallucination of the casting department." Then he tested Natalie Wood.

"I wasn't going to cast Natalie Wood in the picture because she's a child actress, and the only child actress who ever made it as far as I'm concerned was Helen Hayes," said Ray. "But after Nat's interview, she left, and outside waiting for her was this kid with a fresh scar across his face, so I said, 'Let's talk again.' She seemed to be on that kind of trip.

"One night a little while later, Dennis Hopper called me. I hadn't finished casting yet, but Dennis had a part in the gang. He said, 'Now, don't get excited, Nick, but I was out driving with Faye and Natalie and we've had an accident.' I said, 'Dennis, have you been drinking?' and he said, 'Yes.'

"I asked him where he was and he told me the police station, so I said, 'For Christ sake, get the hell out of there! Chew some gum and run around the block a few times before you get yourself arrested.' He said, 'I can't leave. There's been some trouble. Natalie's hurt. I think she has a concussion.'

"'Well, call her doctor right away,' I said, but Dennis told me she didn't want to call her family and she didn't know if they had a doctor. So I said, 'Okay, I'll call my doctor. He'll come down immediately.'

"So I called my doctor, then Natalie's parents, and went down to the police station. When I got there I saw Dennis, my doctor, stretchers being wheeled around in the background, and Natalie's parents came running in. Her mother says, 'Oh, Nick, what's happened? You know this is no good for her father. He's just gotten over a heart attack.' No questions about how's Natalie or anything . . . Then the doctor came out and said she was all right, but she didn't want to see her parents first, she wanted to see me.

"I went in and Natalie was lying down, and she grabbed me and pulled me close to her and whispered in my ear, 'You see that son of a bitch?' and she pointed to the precinct doctor. 'Well, he called me a juvenile delinquent. Now do I get the part?' "

While casting members of the gang, Nick spotted Sal Mineo, an unlikely candidate, lost in the lineup of tough guys. "I saw this kid in the back who looked like my son except he was prettier. I called him over and asked him what he'd done. He said he'd just played Tony Curtis as a young boy in *Six Bridges to Cross*. I asked Sal to take off his jacket and start sizing up those big guys. I called Corey Allen over [who played Buzz, the gang leader], and because of the improvisation they did decided Sal would be great for the part of Plato."

The next step was to see how Jimmy and Sal would relate, since they were to share a key relationship in the movie. "I was almost sick, I wanted the part so badly," said Mineo, who was just sixteen at the time. "I thought I was dressed pretty sharp for those days—pegged pants, skinny tie, jacket—until Jimmy walked in with his tee shirt and blue jeans.

"We went through a scene and nothing happened between us. Nick finally walked over and suggested we sit and talk for a while. When Jimmy found out I was from the Bronx, we started gabbing about New York and then progressed to cars, and before we knew it we were buddies. Then we went back to the script, and this time it went off like clockwork. When we reached a part where we were supposed to laugh hysterically, Jimmy gave out with that special giggle of his, and I couldn't help but follow along. Pretty soon we just couldn't stop laughing."

After three weeks, Nick Ray had assembled the central "teenage" characters detailed by Stewart Stern:

Jim: (James Dean) The angry victim and the result. At seventeen, he is filled with confusion about his role in life. Because of his "nowhere" father, he does not know how to be a man. Because of his wounding mother, he anticipates destruction in all women. And yet he wants to find a girl who will be willing to receive his tenderness.

Judy: (Natalie Wood) The victim and the result. At sixteen, she is in a panic of frustration regarding her father—needing his love and suffering when it is denied. This forces her to invite the attention of other men in order to punish him.

Plato: (Sal Mineo) Son of a divided family . . . he feels himself the target of desertion. At fifteen, he wants to find a substitute family for himself so that he need no longer feel cold, and especially a friend who will supply the fatherly protection and warmth he needs.

Buzz: (Corey Allen) A sadomasochistic boy of seventeen who acts out aggressively his idea of what a man should be in order to hide his real sensitivities and needs. He was probably rejected by both parents and must constantly court danger in order to achieve any sense of prestige or personal worth.

The Kids: All searching for recognition in the only way available to them; all suffering from unfulfilled hungers at home; all creating an outside world of chaos in order to bear the chaos they feel inside. They are soldiers in search of an enemy:

Helen: Beverly Long	*Cookie*: Nick Adams
Crunch: Frank Mazzola	*Mil*: Steffi Skolsky
Moose: Jack Simmons	*Chick*: Jack Grinnage
Goon: Dennis Hopper	*Harry*: Tom Bernard

Rehearsals. Counter-clockwise: Jimmy (in front of TV), Jack Simmons, Jim Backus, Natalie Wood, Nick Adams, Frank Mazzola, Dennis Stock (in front of tape recorder), Nick Ray and Stewart Stern.

One of the more bizarre pieces of casting was Jim Backus as Jimmy's father. Jim Backus is best known as a comedian ("I Married Joan," "Gilligan's Island") and as the familiar voice of Mr. Magoo. In *Rebel*, Backus would play a human cartoon, a caricature of the middle-class father.

"It took a great deal of courage on Ray's part to cast me as the father," said Backus. "When we made *Rebel* we were near the end of the era of the major studio, but the studio still had the power of life and death. If they needed a henpecked husband, they went into their henpecked husband file—and came up with a little man, probably wearing glasses, somebody like Hume Cronyn, no reflection on his talent. When they went into the mother file, they of course came up with Ann Durand. To them, she played *all* mothers. It didn't matter that at the time she was only thirty-five years old, because, you see, to the studio executives time stood still. If they went out on Culver Boulevard, they would disintegrate. But Nick resisted studio pressure and I got the part."

Ray encouraged the kids to hang out together. "Nick's whole thing was to make us a family," said Steffi (Skolsky) Sidney, "to make the movie come from *us*, rather than from his direction. We were not really together as a gang when we started rehearsing. Nick told us we were playing individually instead of together. So we all went out together, except for Jimmy. We went to the beach, climbed around a deserted warehouse one night, to get the feeling of being a group. By the time we were ready to start shooting, we were really thinking as one."

Nicholas Ray's ability to absorb himself in the world of adolescence rather than just make a movie *about* adolescents, marks a turning point in the creation of a fantasy world shared by adults and children alike. The Cathedral of Adolescence!

Like the building of medieval cathedrals, *Rebel* was a community project, lovingly attended and dedicated to a high ideal. Ray encouraged the teenage cast to improvise, change dialogue and suggest scenes, sacrificing some of his original ideas. Stewart Stern admits he'd like to leap at the screen with a dagger in response to some of the lines worked into the movie without his approval. There's no denying there is plenty of corn and cliché in *Rebel*, but its young cast really believed in it, and for that reason it's believable to us.

In one of the early "rumble" scenes, for example, Nick's treatment

230

had originally indicated a near-riot. "Nick had all these kids running down the alley, shouting and carrying on," said Beverly Long, who played the tough, pony-tailed blonde in the gang. "We told him it just wasn't done like that. When gangs rumbled, they didn't invite twelve hundred people. They did it kind of surreptitiously and quietly, otherwise the authorities would come.

"Nick was great because we'd all get excited and he'd make us calm down and say, 'Okay, now what do you want to do with this scene?' Nick was way before his time. Wearing Levi's and walking around in bare feet. I mean, they just didn't *do* that in 1955. Everybody at the studio was in a suit and tie."

Leonard Rosenman participated in the early script sessions: "We'd meet at Nick's bungalow at the Chateau Marmont. Nick and Stewart Stern would tell us what they had planned for a scene and then we'd react. Natalie might say, 'Well, I don't think I should say that.' Or someone would say, 'Why can't Jimmy just go into the precinct . . .' It was a pretty free-flowing discussion. We wrote and rejected and retained. But what really happened was, we got to know each other as people and recognized ourselves as a pretty good team."

Nicholas Ray had grown up in a Midwestern community – La Crosse, Wisconsin – and at one time wanted to be an architect, winning a scholarship to study with Frank Lloyd Wright. He later decided to get into the theater, studied acting and went on to directing – *Lute Song* and *Beggar's Song* on Broadway, assisting Elia Kazan in *A Tree Grows in Brooklyn*, and, in 1947, directing his first feature film, *They Live By Night*, with Humphrey Bogart and James Cagney.

Ray had an artistic vision he pursued relentlessly. He'd always been interested in nuclear break-offs from society, from his first film to the late sixties when he considered directing *Only Lovers Left Alive*, the Rolling Stones' first movie venture, which never went into production. He had begun his career with Orson Welles and John Houseman in the Mercury Theater, a company of artists who generated their creations out of group interaction. Actors, directors, writers—all contributed to the final product. *Citizen Kane* is the masterpiece of this school, and its success indicated how well such a collaboration can work.

In *Rebel*, Ray carried this principle to a new generation. "No director can play all the roles. He's an asshole if he thinks he can," said

Ray. "I always work communally, whether it's with adolescents or adults. While I was working on *Rebel*, I came across a note of Kazan's from when we'd worked on *A Tree Grows in Brooklyn*, and the note said: 'Have to be careful. Fuck acting. Don't direct a natural.' I've always believed that. A director shows the way. He does not manipulate his actors."

The theme of *Rebel Without a Cause* is metamorphosis: the evolution of a new generation. The young cast depicted the biological, sexual and moral shifts of adolescence, the changes from child into adult which are more rapid than any changes since the first year of life. *Rebel* resonates with the energy of firstness and had a transforming effect on many of those involved in the production. It was Jimmy's most significant role; Stewart Stern's first major production; the first time many of "the gang" had ever been in a movie; Jim Backus' first dramatic part and Natalie Wood's first grown-up movie role.

Ray submerged himself in this virginal climate and encouraged a state of mind to assert itself. As the benevolent parent, he allowed this experimental situation to evolve at its own rate. The end result might have been chaos, had it not been for Ray's intuition to let Jimmy take the lead.

"James Dean worked very closely with Nick," Jim Backus later said in *Variety*. "May I say that this is the first time in the history of motion pictures that a twenty-four-year-old boy, with only one movie to his credit, was practically the co-director. Jimmy insisted on utter realism, and, looking back, I sometimes wonder how we finished so violent a picture without someone getting seriously injured."

When Jimmy was in the process of forming his own production company after *Rebel*, he claimed he was the one who actually directed the film. "No, Jimmy was just one character in the story," said Rosenman. "Nick had a much broader concept. He had the sets, the photography, all working at the same time. But Jimmy had to create the most important character, Jim Stark, and Nick Ray didn't know anything about Jim Stark. It was up to Jimmy Dean to find out." This challenge provoked Jimmy to his greatest achievement as an actor, but it also terrified him.

A few days before the shooting began, Jimmy disappeared. "No one knew where he was and Warners was frantic," said Stewart Stern, "threatening to suspend him. Then one morning at about four o'clock my phone rings and I hear this 'Mmmmooooo.' I knew it was Jimmy and I mooed back. Then I said, 'How are you?' And Jimmy said he wasn't going to come back. He asked me if I thought he should do the movie, and I told him, 'If you did it and were miserable in it or if the picture turned out badly, then it would be on my head, and I couldn't take that responsibility.' I told him they were thinking of suspending him.

"Jimmy just said, 'Well, I'm not coming back. Talk to ya.'

"He was gone about ten days, and then one day he just showed up at my office and looked at this perfectly blank wall, stood back pretending to admire an imaginary painting. I think he was looking at Picasso's *Guernica*. He asked me if it was real or a reproduction, and I said, 'Oh, God, it's real of course!' And he said, 'Well, you writers . . . and just because you're a nephew of Arthur Lowe . . .' But he never talked about where he'd been or why he'd come back.

"I don't know what scared him, but I know he was scared."

Rebel finally began filming in March 1955, with cinematographer Ted McCord shooting in black and white CinemaScope. It was a low-budget movie expected to turn a big profit. The final cost was one million dollars, including a forty-percent charge for studio overhead, which meant Ray spent only six hundred thousand dollars.

"Our schedule wasn't very structured," Jim Backus said, "because Warners knew they had a tremendous moneymaker. And it was not an expensive picture to make—no big sets, no battle scenes, no one getting a half a million plus percentages, à la Liz Taylor. In fact, I think I might have been the highest paid actor on the picture. And any time I'm the highest paid actor, you *know* it's a cheap picture."

After almost a week into production, Nick Ray was called into the front office and told to stop shooting. "They didn't know what I was doing and didn't want me to finish the picture," said Ray. "I said, fine, take me off salary and sell me all the rights to the film. The executives hesitated and said, 'We'll call you back.' Then Steve Trilling went to the projectionist and asked him what he thought of the rushes. 'Mr. Trilling,' he said, 'frankly, I think it's the only picture worth something on the lot.'

"So they called me back and said, 'Okay, Nick, finish it.'"

Two days later, Nick was called in again, this time to hear the film had to be made in color, not black and white. It turned out the inventor of CinemaScope had in his contract that CinemaScope could only be filmed in color. The change meant a lot of reshooting. The kids might have been upset by the fact that they'd worked so hard and would have to do it over again, but Nick used the switch to turn them on.

Corey Allen, who'd worked on a knife-fight scene with Jimmy for days before it had been shot in black and white, said, "I was sitting in Hamburger Hamlet and Ray came in and said, 'I saw the rushes of the knife fight and they're really *fantastic!*' So I said that was great and then he said, 'Yeah, they're *so* fantastic that we're going to have to shoot it again, because now Warners wants to do the movie in color!'"

Ray was genuinely delighted to be working in color: "The first thing I did was pull a red jacket off the Red Cross man, dip it in black paint to take off the sheen and give it to Jimmy. Then I sent Natalie to buy a green skirt off the rack, not some $450 designer special."

Bev Dorff remembered that "after the switch to color film, all the guys' blue jeans had to be redyed because in WarnerColor that blue just bled, and it didn't look right at all."

Color plays an important thematic role in *Rebel*, as it does in all of Ray's films: the purple and gold in *Party Girl*, the red and green in *Johnny Guitar* and the red and blue in *Rebel*—the blazing red of rage, passion and fire, and the cool blue of space and isolation. The tones are raw and the combination as abrasive as adolescence itself.

Ray's use of color has been described as apocalyptic, "une palette en feu" as a French critic called it. The colors in *Rebel* change like banners, symbolizing the evolution of the characters.

"I started Jimmy in this neutral brown and he graduated to the blue jeans and red jacket," said Ray. "And Natalie graduated from the gauche red in the beginning to a soft, pink sweater. When you first see Jimmy in his red jacket against his black Merc, it's not just a pose. It's a warning. It's a sign."

Jimmy is the first person we see in *Rebel Without a Cause*, lying dead drunk on the sidewalk, curled up next to a toy monkey he is whimsically trying to cover with a piece of paper, while credits and title flash by in flaming letters.

Without being introduced or identified, Jimmy acts out his own prologue to the movie. He plays an isolated, defenseless child, deliriously enclosed in his own protective fantasy, stranded like some

"Jimmy in his red jacket . . . it's not just a pose. It's a warning, a sign."

235

inhabitant of another world on a grimy concrete ledge. Jimmy modeled his pose on one of his favorite paintings, Manet's *Dead Bullfighter*, and in his slow, deliberate actions, the hero is introduced to us almost in embryo, a child with his mechanical toy who wishes nothing more than to be left alone with his dreams.

To appreciate this endearing improvisation, it isn't necessary to know how the monkey got there or why the police pick Jimmy up, but in the black and white version there had been an explanatory scene. The time was Christmas Eve, and a middle-aged man on his way home is rumbled by a group of tough kids who set fire to his packages. As he drops them, a toy monkey falls out. The gang disperses when they hear approaching police sirens, and it is at this moment that Jimmy rounds the corner and finds the monkey lying in the street. When the film was reshot in color this introduction was cut, and Stewart Stern changed the time to Easter simply because Christmas in Southern California was hard to deal with visually and wouldn't have fit in with the "Anytown, U.S.A." feeling he wanted.

Bev Long watched Jimmy improvise his opening scene: "We didn't have anything worked out for the scene, so Jimmy said, 'Please let me do something here; let me play with it. Just roll it.' And so he came around the corner and the whole thing was an improvisation because nothing had been planned.

"I remember that we'd been working for twenty-three hours straight that day so we could get the dawn light, and we were really exhausted. But we all stayed, as tired as we were, and sat on the curb and watched Jimmy do that scene. And it was so beautiful that we just *wept*."

Dennis Hopper, who played a gang member named Goon, couldn't get over Jimmy's interpretation of the part: "I have a script in my hand that says this guy's in the gutter, drunk, and he gets taken to the police station and is angry about it.

"Well, first of all, the guy is in the street playing with a toy monkey? And doing baby things—trying to curl up, to keep warm . . . Then he's searched, and this angry, drunk guy is suddenly ticklish? Where did that come from? It came from genius, that's where it came from. And that was all him. Nobody directed him to do that. James Dean directed James Dean."

In the course of this night journey, Jim is hauled into Juvenile Hall—a cold, sterile maze with glass partitions and jangling phones, gloomy and bizarre, with endless forms and mechanical procedures. The wards of "juvenile delinquents," we soon learn, are the result of parental indifference and inability to understand their children. Despondently, these young victims wait for the real culprits to collect them. Ray had observed this nightmarish situation firsthand at the Culver City juvenile precinct and tried to reproduce the atmosphere as faithfully as possible. Unlike the producers of *Blackboard Jungle*, Ray had the cooperation of the police department, and the juvenile officer who questions Jim and Judy is depicted as the only responsible adult in the movie. (Not coincidentally, he is also given the director's name.) This neo-Freudian, revisionist cop is sympathetically treated as the long-suffering do-gooder.

Society sends all its youngest casualties to Juvenile Hall. The three principal characters in *Rebel*—Jim, Plato and Judy—find themselves in this decompression chamber, each with very different problems: Jim is drunk, Plato has shot a puppy and Judy, in searing red coat and lipstick, has been picked up for wandering around late at night.

RAY (*the Juvenile Detective*):
Why were you out walking the streets at one o'clock in the morning, Judy? You weren't looking for company, were you? (*She starts to cry.*)
JUDY:
He hates me.
RAY:
What?
JUDY:
He doesn't like anything about me. He calls me . . . He calls me . . .
RAY:
He makes you feel pretty unhappy?
JUDY:
He calls me a dirty tramp—my own father!

When Ray (played by Ed Platt, who became the chief in "Get Smart") dismisses Judy and calls Jim in, the detective immediately recognizes Jim's act: "You don't kid me, pal. How come you're not wearing your boots?" Like a cop in a Sam Fuller movie, he is tough, but benign, assuming the role of father figure and psychologist with all the right answers. When Jim tries to take a swing at Ray, he invites Jim to "blow his wheels . . . take it out on the desk."

Jimmy played this scene with such intensity that when he slammed his fists into the desk with such a violent, sudden and adenoidal fury the first preview audience burst out laughing.

"It wasn't, of course, what we intended," said composer Leonard Rosenman, "and we couldn't cut the scene because it was crucial. So I added about five seconds of music, and when the scene came on the audience started to laugh, but as soon as they heard the music they shut up. It was as if the music was a second voice saying, 'Wait a minute, take another look at this scene. It isn't funny . . .' And that's the only function of music in that scene—to keep the audience from laughing."

This was one of the first scenes shot, and also the first time that Jimmy kept the cast and crew waiting. They sat around for hours while he stayed in his dressing room. "He was preparing," said Jim Backus. "He was drinking wine, hitting a drum and they were trying to get

The hero of the story, a child who wishes to be left alone with his dreams.

him on the set, but he wouldn't come out until he was ready. He kept them waiting several hours. Now, if you keep a set waiting, the executives up in the big building hear about it and descend in a covey of limousines.

"Anyhow, Jimmy walked out finally and said, 'I'm ready,' and he did that whole scene in one take. Beat the desk, broke two bones in his hand and as he walked off the set, the camera crew cheered. And you know what a hard-nosed bunch they are."

After he calms down at Juvenile Hall, Jim blurts out, "If I could have just one day when I wasn't all confused . . . I wasn't ashamed of everything. If I felt I belonged some place." Nick Ray calls this statement the "spine" of Jimmy's dilemma—he is nowhere and yet he is never left alone. Out of place everywhere, and yet trapped.

"An actor should always be on the verge of an explosion," Ray said. "Every line he says should be the first and last time he says it. He's got to be sitting on a keg of dynamite. And Jimmy was."

Stewart Stern had written an earlier version of this scene, never put on film, which stemmed from an original concept of Nick Ray's. The idea was to use a split screen, so that reality would be depicted simultaneously with a fantasy scene to show what was going on in Jim's head. Stewart objected to the idea because he felt it robbed the audience of their own ideas about what Jimmy was thinking. He finally won, but not before writing a scene which bombastically reveals the film's thematic intentions.

"I wrote a scene where Jim was talking to his parents," said Stern, "and suddenly you see a shooting gallery in an amusement park and Jim came up to the shooting gallery, put down a quarter, picked up a gun, took aim and there on the moving belt instead of ducks were his mother, father and grandmother, in 3-D. They were balloons, but very recognizable. He took aim and missed Mom and Grandma, but he got Dad right through the head and all the air went out of him, out of the balloon. Suddenly, Jim was in a panic about what he had done, and he leapt over the rail and grabbed the balloon, threw it in his car, raced it to a service station and said, 'You've got to fix this, you've got to fix it!' And they got the tire inflator out and they start patching this thing and pumping it up, and they get it half-pumped, but the air just keeps going out of it. The station attendant finally says, 'The material's no good. It just won't hold.' And that was the end of the fantasy."

Rebel had intentionally cosmic overtones. Its key sequences revolve around the D. W. Griffith Planetarium, near the Hollywood Bowl in Los Angeles. The tension begins during a lecture on the universe, escalates into a knife fight behind the planetarium and reaches its climax hours later with a floodlit shoot-out on the front steps. The movie is so loaded with psycho-stellar allusions that it's like a CinemaScope Kosmikomic.

"The infinite doom, the divine hand of God, is announced right from the beginning," said Ray. "What's wrong with that?"

This preoccupation with the cosmos was noticed by some reviewers. The *Illustrated London News* commented: "Dawson High is a very odd school whose chief study seems to be astronomy." The only class shown in this "average" high school day is an outing to see a spectacular show about the stars. A planetarium's function is to demonstrate the order of the universe, but the kids pick up on its disorder, its form without comprehensible meaning, its particles verging on self-immolation.

The students sit in the darkened auditorium, confronted with a giant replica of the heavens, listening to the dry, droning voice of a lecturer as insectlike as his projector, and they watch this artificial show, a Hollywood projection of the universe! Then they hear the lecturer unconsciously announce the approach of the film's star, Jim Stark.

LECTURER'S VOICE:
For many days before the end of our earth, people will look into the night sky and notice a star, increasingly bright and increasingly near.

On this cue, Jim enters and says in a stage whisper to the teacher checking names at the door, "*Stark*, Jim *Stark*." The class turns; the lecturer hesitates; Jim slithers to a seat.

LECTURER'S VOICE: (*continuing*)
As this star approaches us, the weather will change. The great polar fields of the north and south will rot and divide, and the seas will turn warmer.

As if descending into his mortal form, Jim lets out a soft, "Whew!" and leans back with, "Once you've been up there, you really know you've been some place." As the lecture progresses, symbols bombard us. Buzz relates to the stars in his own hard-shelled way when Cancer is pointed out. "Hey! I'm a crab!" he says, walks his fingers across Judy's chest and pinches Goon's nose, a gesture which induces Jim to try again at making himself part of the gang:

LECTURER'S VOICE:
. . . and Taurus, the bull . . .
    JIM: (*in good imitation*)
Moo!
    (*He waits for approval.*)

But his daring attempt to horn in on the gang has the opposite of the desired effect: it provokes them and they taunt Jim with the idea that he may be a coward.

Scene: Angle shot of Judy, Buzz and group (seen from Jim's angle). He is in the foreground. They are staring at him. Nobody laughs.

CRUNCH: (*flat*)

Yeah, moo.

BUZZ:

Moo. That's real cute. Moo.

GOON:

Hey, he's real rough—

CRUNCH:

I bet he fights with cows.

BUZZ:

Moo.

With all the symbols that hurtle past our eyes, we are alert that Jim's outburst might allude to Jimmy's farmboy background. Or maybe his love of bullfighting. But it turns out that it was put in as a personal joke between Jimmy and Stewart Stern.

"I was in Los Angeles on vacation in 1954 and went to my uncle's house—Arthur Lowe—and Jimmy was there. I had never met him and didn't know who he was. So I walked over to him and said hi. Jimmy was sitting in one of two revolving chairs my uncle had, and he spun around, said hi and gave me this big smile. He didn't have any front teeth and looked like a really strange character. He told me later his bridge was out getting fixed. I didn't know who he was and I didn't like him. And there was this *terrible* silence. Then one of us mooed and the other mooed back.

"Then we had a mooing contest that went on for a long time. He'd say, 'Can you do a bull?' And I'd say, 'Can you do a calf?' And he could, so I said, 'Can you do a *roped* calf?' He couldn't do that, but I could. Then we turned around and faced each other."

After the boys at the planetarium boo his moo, Jimmy slumps back into his seat. Behind him, Plato, who's trying to make friends, whispers some advice:

PLATO:

You shouldn't *monkey* with him.

JIM:

What?

PLATO:

He's a wheel. So's she. It's hard to make friends with them.

JIM:

I don't want to make friends.

(*He turns back, unhappy at having revealed himself.*)

241

The lecture ends with an exploding star zooming on the screen with 3-D ferocity. It's as if the scene itself, so overloaded with symbolism —impersonal technology, existential smallness, academic apathy, desire for approval—finally explodes with the violence of an atomic holocaust:

(*Music of the spheres is heard—a high, threatening tremolo . . .*)
LECTURER'S VOICE:
Destroyed as we began, in a burst of gas and fire.
(*The sky is blasted by a wild flash of light. Music reaches explosion.*)

The students of Dawson High School watch this demonstration without apparent alarm. But they are neither cold nor indifferent; it is just too much to absorb and react to immediately. They introject their own fantasies of destruction, internalize them and become restless to act them out. The universe in its flagrant self-destruction seems to them like a "JD" on a cosmic chickie run. Worlds collide! Buzz, Goon, Crunch and the other members of the gang aren't satisfied with a flat projection of "the war of the worlds"—they want to enact it, take part in it, collide with its energy.

Stewart Stern, who inherited the planetarium idea from Shulman, sensed the apprehension of fatality this scene can generate: "It's another level of reality . . . the threat of extinction coming from out there, the threat of extinction coming from inside, the threat of extinction coming from everybody around us. It had to do with survival, with immediacy of life, the necessity to make choices. It had to do with humanity versus the machine."

The lifeless professor who manipulates the cosmos with his dumb-bell projector doesn't skip a beat as he ends the world:

LECTURER:
The heavens are still and cold once more. In all the complexity of our universe and the galaxies beyond, the earth will not be missed . . .

Through the infinite reaches of space, the problems of man seem trivial and naive indeed. And man, existing alone, seems to be an episode of little consequence . . . That's all. Thank you very much.

Plato, as his intellectual name implies, responds with existential angst, "What does *he* know about man alone?"

Stewart Stern conceived of Plato as the enigmatic, sexually ambivalent, psychotic crypto-hero of the film and sees in him a star-child who was not able to control his instability: "It's that sense of dimunition, of tininess, that we feel when we are confronted with a universe that is really indifferent to us . . . There's a wonder in that, as well as a horror. It's what Kubrick did, showing what you have to crash through to become the cosmic child. And as frightened as Plato was by the planetarium, that's where he nestled in the end."

Planetarium music weaves throughout *Rebel*, reminding us at odd moments of its doomy portent. "Sure I wrote the planetarium music to be 'cosmic,'" said Leonard Rosenman, "but even if I didn't, it still would be fucking cosmic because that's such a great scene." The score is melodramatic in its suggestion of swelling teenage lust and rage, but the kind of lyrical score Rosenman had done for *East of Eden* was really closer to his own musical temperament. He had trouble with Ray, who wanted a bop number he couldn't compose.

"Before they rumble Jim, the kids are standing around wondering, 'What should we do about Moo?'" said Ray. "And somebody says, 'Moo!' and they start to go around this pendulum saying, 'Moo,' and this big circular thing was swinging around like the rhythm of the earth, and Corey Allen takes out his comb and starts beating a rhythm on the ledge, and then someone takes out a set of keys, then a steel comb, a tube of lipstick and so on until they're going around and around beating this rhythm . . . boom . . . baboom . . . boom . . . baboom . . . And this begins a beat that was to begin a suite that would continue through the fight scene. But Leonard Rosenman couldn't write the suite that I wanted, so without music the scene was cut. It was one of my favorites."

The tribal be-bop which was cut from the final version set the tone for the scene which immediately followed—the switchblade showdown between Jim and Buzz.

Neither Jimmy nor Corey Allen had ever been in a knife fight before. Nick Ray had seen juvenile delinquency where it ends—in the courts—but didn't understand the gang mentality. Frank Mazzola introduced them to the formal world of teen-gang warfare. Cast as Crunch, the gang's second lieutenant, Frank was actually leader of *the* gang at Hollywood High, the Athenians.

"Frank was weeded out of the original lineup by casting directors who thought he was too disruptive. But he insisted on seeing me, and his perseverance paid off," said Ray. "He was head of a gang, but he lived in a better house than either my producer or myself. I was introduced to the inner sanctum as his 'uncle.' We planned a 'war' and Frank made the rules—no knives, no dope, just tire chains. On the night of the 'war,' about seventy or eighty guys showed up at the pizza joint to wait for the yellow Ford—the signal from the other gang. It was the most bizarre thing I'd ever seen. Two girls outside the pizza joint were having a knife fight.

"I'd invented a way of concealing a mini-phone tape recorder in a shoulder holster, with a wristwatch as a microphone so we could get dialogue. I came away from the scene with a very primitive feeling about the whole confrontation. It was a conflict of sex and power."

The knife fight outside the planetarium was a combination of improvisation and choreography. Since Jimmy and Corey were using real switchblades, they wore chest protectors under their shirts. But there was still a possibility of serious accident, and three CinemaScope cameras covering the fight only added to the tension.

"I was so fucking nervous," said Corey Allen. We did take after take and it was just *awful*. Finally Nick told us to take a break. Everybody went for a soda, but I just stayed on the set. I knew what I wanted to say, but I just couldn't do it right.

"Jimmy and I weren't good friends. We weren't enemies, but we just never spent any time together, which was probably good for our roles. But I was always aware of him on the set, where he was, what he was doing, and during this break he walked across the lawn in front of the planetarium to where the crew and sound men were and I watched him. I always knew where Jimmy was every minute. I was hypersensitive to his presence. I knew every move he made.

"Then he started to walk back, and as I watched him come back, I said to myself, 'He's coming over here. That man's coming over to *me*. So Jimmy walked over, walked up to me without saying a word and handed me a drink of water. I took it, drank it and said, 'How did you know I wanted a drink of water?' He said, 'I'm a lot older than you.'"

The tension of sex and power Ray saw in the gang wars is briefly focused as Buzz jabs his knife into Jim's whitewall while Judy's nylon-stockinged leg dangles suggestively in front of the tire. Jimmy, sitting on the parapet with his back to the gang, lets out a slow, painful breath of air. There's no way he can avoid the trouble behind him. He climbs down and moves toward the group:

JIM: (*wearily*)
You know something?

BUZZ:

What?

JIM:

You read too many comic books.

BUZZ:

Hey, he's real abstract.

JIM:

I'm cute too.

(Suddenly Goon starts clucking softly like a chicken. One by one the others pick it up. Buzz, the last, crows.)

JIM:

Does that mean me?

BUZZ:

What?

JIM:

Chicken!

(The group gives a quick, short laugh.)

"Chicken" is another of *Rebel*'s code words, a detonator that sets Jim off. He'd had to leave another school for "messin' up a guy" who called him chicken. He tries to back away, refusing the knife Buzz forces on

The chicken and the coupe. (From left: Sal, Corey, Jimmy, Frank, Natalie and Bev)

245

him, but the gang knows he really has no choice and eggs him on.

BUZZ:
Remember, no cutting, just sticking. Jab real cool.
JIM:
I thought only punks fought with knives.
BUZZ:
Who's fighting? This is the test, man. It's a crazy game.

The two boys circle each other, like wolves vying for territory. Buzz seems to snarl, thoroughly enjoying the encounter, while Jim hesitates, then lunges and gets jabbed in the stomach. Buzz grins. Jim makes another quick leap and is cut again.

During one take Ray suddenly shouted, "Cut! Cut!" and called over a first-aid man to take care of a thin trickle of blood running down Jimmy's neck from behind his ear.

"Jimmy got furious when Nick stopped that scene," said Dennis Hopper. "He started yelling at Nick, 'What the hell are you doing? Can't you see I'm having a *real* moment? Don't you *ever* cut a scene while I'm having a real moment. What the fuck do you think I'm here for?'"

A reporter from the *Los Angeles Examiner* was on the set. The next day (May 22, 1955), in a story entitled "The Fight Was for Blood—and They Got It," Neil Rau recorded the scene and the one brief question he managed to ask Jimmy.

. . . I went over to the chair which the first aid man ordered for Dean. The actor is visibly nervous and is mopping perspiration from his forehead.
"Isn't this pushing realism a bit?" I asked him.
For a moment the intense young man doesn't speak. He closes his eyes and droops his head as though meditating. Then he juts out his chin.
"In motion pictures," he answers, "you can't fool the camera. If we were doing this on stage we'd probably be able to gimmick it up—but not in a picture. Film fans are too critical these days."

Frank Mazzola helped stage the fight, and Mushy Callahan, an ex-boxer who was Jimmy's stand-in, also gave advice. But Ray directed the scene within a traditional context so that the steps, leaps, twists and lunges would preserve the choreographic rhythms of a familiar ritual. The movement in the scene is created by two traditional forms of motion: the dance and the bullfight.

"Jimmy knew how to move," said Ray. "He was really in tune with his body and understood how to use it as a carefully tuned instrument. He learned more studying dance with Katherine Dunham than he ever did from the Actors Studio. He knew what I wanted—the precision of the dance—and I choreographed him and Corey in that scene. I'd done two musicals on Broadway and wouldn't be worth a damn as a director if I hadn't learned how to use dance dramatically."

The planetarium and its quiet grounds in Griffith Park were witness to the different ways *Rebel*'s cast let off steam while they were waiting to perform. While they were taking a break during the strenuous fight scene, Jimmy found a chance to embarrass Bev.

"Jimmy could be vulgar in a little boy kind of way," she said. "He had this tire iron in his hand and came over to where I was sitting on the car and said to me, 'Here, hold this,' and handed me the iron. So I said, 'Okay,' and took it. Then he looked at me and said, *'Have you ever felt anything so hard?'* And everybody just cracked up. I wanted to die! I don't remember what I said—'Wouldn't you like to know' or something like that and threw it back to him.

"Jimmy could be *so rotten,* but then so cute, that I just couldn't stay mad at him though."

Bev had no speaking lines in the movie since, when she was cast, Stewart had her speaking only French—based on a girl he knew who got so hung up on her French course that she would use it all the time. For example, Bev was supposed to say, "Les jeux de combat!" (The games of combat!) when the gang decided what to do about Jim. "Well, you don't say that kind of thing at a rumble, no matter *how* much into first year French you are," said Bev. "So we cut my dialogue completely because it sounded even cornier when it was translated into English!

"None of us were jealous of each other's parts. We all worked together beautifully, with one exception—Nick Adams. Nick was one of the most ambitious actors I've ever seen in my life and was very given to lines that would seem to come out of nowhere, but which often he took out of the mouths of other actors.

According to the cast, Nick Adams was always sure to get in front whenever he could. Though he wasn't close to Jimmy, Nick evidently did encourage Jimmy's impromptu performances for the cast. A movie magazine reported that one day during the shooting:

Jimmy jumped up and said, "Let's plug Bud's (Brando's) picture." Then

Jimmy hollered in a loud voice, "There goes one of the Wild Ones, folks!"

Nick Adams jumped up and started to imitate Brando. Jimmy imitated Elia "Gadge" Kazan.

"Down on your knees, Bud," Jimmy said to Nick. Nick fell down and looked with wide, scared eyes at Dean.

"Y-y-y-es, Gadge," whimpered Nick.

"Now Bud," says Jimmy, "I wantcha tear that grass—tear it out—out by the roots! You hate that grass, Bud! Tear it up! Tear it up!"

Like a madman Nick tears up the grass.

When he made *Rebel Without a Cause*, Dennis Hopper looked like he hadn't even started shaving yet, but there was that hint of madness in his eyes. "Once on the set, I told Jimmy I *had* to know what he was doing because acting was my whole life," he said. "I asked him why he became an actor and he said, 'Because I hate my mother and father. I wanted to get up on stage . . . and I wanted to *show* them. I'll tell you what made me want to become an actor, what gave me that drive to want to be the best. My mother died when I was almost nine. I used to sneak out of my uncle's house at night and go to her grave, and I used to cry and cry on her grave—Mother, why did you leave me? Why did you leave me? I need you . . . I want you.' Okay, well that eventually turned into Jimmy pounding on the grave saying, 'I'll show you for leaving me . . . fuck you, I'm gonna be so fuckin' *great* without you!'"

Rebel is constructed as a series of concentric rings, with Jim Stark trapped in the center. He can release himself only by breaking through these barriers one at a time. By winning the knife fight, he only involves himself in more difficult tests: Buzz challenges Jim's manhood by daring him to a chickie run. This leads to another confrontation when Jim takes his dilemma home.

Unlike Buzz, Crunch, Goon and the other members of the gang, who have apparently abandoned their parents, Jim Stark's relationship to his family is more insidious. He is torn between sympathy for his father's condition and anger at him for not dealing with it directly. By avoiding his responsibilities as a man, Jim's father makes himself more vulnerable to his predatory wife and mother-in-law. Both oblige by "eating him alive." The only solution Jim can see to this incestuous cannibal rite is a drastic one. "I mean if he had the guts to knock Mom cold once, I bet she'd be happy, stop picking . . ." he tells Officer Ray.

Jim's family is caught in a self-perpetuating, vicious circus of lies, hypocrisy and self-serving morality, turning even the most innocuous situation—such as a bowl of spilled soup—into confusions of role, sex and identity.

Scene: Upper hall, Jim's house, as Jim rises into view at the top of stairs. He sees a figure on hands and knees mopping something off the rug. Leak-light from the staircase dims details. An apron is tied around the figure's waist, and its bow sticks bravely up in the air.

JIM:

Mom?

(*The figure straightens and turns around, smiling. It is the father. He is neatly dressed in his business suit but wears a Mary Petty apron.*)

FATHER:

Hiya, Jimbo.

(*Jim leans against the wall, shaking his head and trying not to laugh. The father laughs unhappily, trying to make it all seem a joke.*)

FATHER: (*continuing*)

You thought I was Mom?

JIM:

Yeah!

FATHER:

It's just this get-up. The girl's out and I was bringing Mom's supper.

JIM: (*giggling*)

And you dropped it?

FATHER:

You ever see such a mess in your life? (*Jim shakes his head.*) Boy, will I catch it! "You ruined my very best rug!"

The scenes between Jim and his family required delicate handling because the dialogue played so heavily on psychological clichés. Jimmy was the only real character among a collection of stereotypes, and after preparing for the fine balance of the emotional relationships, he was not about to let a booming cameraman disturb its fragile texture.

"Jimmy wouldn't allow the cameramen to say, 'Speed! Roll 'em,' etc. He hated that loud shouting," said Jim Backus. "And it *could* scare the hell out of you.

"Of course I was still too afraid of Jack Warner to say anything, but Jimmy got them to start the camera with a silent cue, the way they do it with animals. 'Shhhh . . . get the turtle . . .'

"Also Jimmy insisted on a closed set. There were a lot of intimate, very personal scenes being filmed. Imagine you're doing a scene you've rehearsed for a week, giving everything you've got, and there's some shoe manufacturer from Des Moines standing with his wife and four kids watching the whole thing."

These scenes between Jim and his parents required care for another reason. As typical representatives of "momism" in 1950 suburbia, the family portrait was so broadly drawn that such scenes might easily have fallen over the edge of melodrama into sheer farce.

"One of the most crucial scenes we did together was when I was on the staircase picking up the food," Backus recalled. "If that scene—a big man dressed up in an apron—got a laugh, well the whole goddamn picture would go right out the window. When I first put the apron on, the crew laughed—so we did it over and over to make sure it was right. We knew we were walking a very thin line, so we'd do it, watch it, do it over, watch it again. We did it so many times that the lines were no longer cued. It became a real moment between Jim Stark and his father."

The spilled-soup incident borders on the comic, but the next scene approaches pathos as Backus pops his head around the door of Jimmy's room, catches sight of the blood on his shirt and then dithers about helplessly when confronted with his son's crisis:

JIM:
Can you answer me *now*?
FATHER:
Listen, nobody should make a snap decision—this isn't something you just—we ought to consider the pros and cons—
JIM:
We don't have *time*.
FATHER:
We'll make time. Where's some paper? We'll make a list . . .
JIM: (*shouting*)
What can you do when you have to be a man?
FATHER:
What?
JIM:
You going to stop me, Dad?
FATHER:
You know I never stop you from anything.
(*Jim suddenly makes his decision and sheds his jacket for the red one.*)
Believe me—you're at a wonderful age. In ten years you'll look back on this

250

and wish you were a kid again. When you're older, you'll laugh at yourself for thinking this is so important.

But Jim can't believe his state of mind is transitory, and when he grabs his red jacket, it's a turning point in the movie. He runs out of the house to meet his next battle, incredulously repeating, "*Ten years . . . ten years . . .*" Jimmy improvised this repetition as a war cry for Jim Stark.

As Jim leaves the house, he shifts once again from one level of conflict to the next—from the shadowy zone of his parents' ambivalence to the direct plane of a violent test, the chickie-run.

The script sets the tone for the showdown Jim is headed for by evoking the charged atmosphere of a dawn patrol waiting for the signal to attack:

Wind shrieks over the exposed plateau, which is several hundred yards long. It cuts into the darkness like the prow of a ship and ends in empty air. Several cars are scattered about, defining a sort of runway in the center. There are several kids present but very little talk . . . They stand in small clots, murmuring and smoking.

Blind Run was the title Ray had suggested for the film when he originally conceived of this key scene as a mindless race through a dark tunnel. It was also suggestive of his attitude toward shaping the movie—a sort of lunge at the subject. "Irving Shulman made a more dramatic suggestion for this key scene after reading a newspaper item about a chickie run at night on Pacific Palisades," said Ray. "A group of adolescents assembled in stolen cars on the clifftop plateau. Drivers were to race each other toward the edge. The first to jump clear before the rim of the cliff was a 'chickie.' On this night, one of the boys failed to jump in time."

Jimmy drove a raked '46 Ford for *Rebel*'s chickie run. "They weren't supposed to be great cars," said Frank Mazzola. "They were supposed to be cars the gang stole for the run. I'd never had a chickie run like that. When we played 'chickie,' we just drove our own cars down the street at each other and whoever swerved lost. The guy who beat you won your car."

At the designated meeting place, Jim and Buzz break away from the group and share a momentary comaraderie at the edge of the cliff:

Scene: Two shot. Jim and Buzz. Jim is staring below. He is beginning to perspire. He lights a cigarette. Without taking his hand from Jim's shoulder, Buzz borrows the cigarette from his lips, takes a drag and hands it back. Jim takes another puff then tosses it into the abyss.

BUZZ: (*quietly*)
This is the edge, boy. This is the end.
JIM:
Yeah.
BUZZ:
I like you, you know?
JIM:
Buzz? What are we doing this for?
BUZZ: (*still quiet*)
We got to do *something*. Don't we?

(*Long shot of Jim and Buzz with Plato in foreground. Jim and Buzz appear to Plato as two close friends. Suddenly they break and go, without speaking further, to their cars.*)

It's the last time they speak, for during the run Buzz catches his sleeve on the door handle and can't get out. Trapped in his car, he careens over the side, and his life ends in a "burst of gas and flames." Jim, looking over the cliff, realizes he's lost his first friend.

This scene, shot at the Warner Brothers ranch, had a military atmosphere with its detailed manuevers, troops of young faces, meticulous plans for the sequence of events, a full medical unit and even a fresh supply of "corpses."

"It was really cold out there the night we were shooting," said Corey, "and none of us had dressed warmly enough. I went over to the prop truck to get a blanket to wrap around myself and got up onto the back of the truck—and did I get the shock of my life. There in the pile of props were six dead bodies. And they were all me!

"Nobody had told me about them. They had my *likeness* on them, and shit, they were in my wardrobe, which by this time I was very used to.

"Wwwwoooah! I fell backwards. Calm down, I told myself, they're only dummies. But they had *my* likeness and their eyes were all open. Shit."

The Warner plateau actually ends at a ravine, so the edge of an artificial cliff was constructed on a sound stage at the studio. The kids are shot from behind looking down into the "ocean," which was really a black velvet drape.

"When Jimmy was at the studio, he was supposed to look over the cliff and see Buzz down there," said Corey. "But he couldn't relate to the blank cloth, so he took an apple core, covered it with ketchup, threw it down on the floor and pretended it was me."

After Buzz is killed, his girlfriend Judy makes a quick shift of loyalty and accepts a ride home with Jim. In explaining this unbelievable development, Stewart said, "We tried to find a kind of poetic reality. We compressed the whole thing between dawn and dawn because of the energy of events. There was a point where we realized we had one powerful thing after another, and to assemble all that into a linear film which progressed through a school year would be unbelievable. So I talked to Nick and we decided to turn that unreality into an asset. The

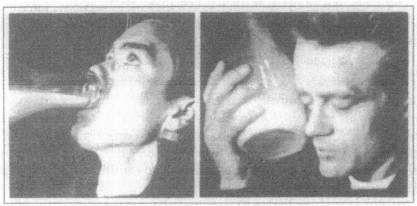

Jimmy cools off an overheated brain.

story became very operatic and it worked the way *opera* would."

Exhausted, but wired by the chickie run, Jim returns home. His own family "zoo" is an ominous cage into which he is lured with bait of food and shelter. Reluctantly, he slips through the kitchen door and approaches the crucial emotional scene of the movie. As if to cool his overheated brain and heal his frayed nerve ends, he rolls the cool glass of a milk bottle across his forehead. "He was always drinking milk because he needed nourishment. He needed a mother," Stewart said. "But the original idea to use the milk bottle was Jimmy's own."

Nick Ray confirms this: "The milk bottle scene was entirely improvised and entirely Jimmy's idea. We did it in my home. I said c'mon over, we're gonna go over this scene. Shulman had written a totally unbelievable scene that was supposed to take place in the mother's bedroom. So I got Jimmy to my house and gave him a contradictory situation: he had to sneak upstairs without getting caught or spill his guts. So he got the milk bottle . . . put it down on the table and began the struggle . . . It was red against red."

The script then recreated the scene worked out between Jimmy and Nick:

Scene: Inside Jim's living room.

The television is on, but only a hum comes from it, and the screen is a flickering gray. The father sits lumpily in a chair by the fireplace, still dressed . . . the sound of Jim's step makes him open his eyes. Fear of facing his son makes him shut them again. The boy comes in, the milk still in his hand. Seeing his father there, he stops short—his impulse is to flee. Instead, he comes in and looks down at the sleeping man whose eyelids, fluttering in the father's masquerade of sleep, make him seem to be having a dream . . . Jim is torn between his desire to leave and his need to speak, then lies down on the couch.

This silent sequence is suggestive and hypnotic in its sexuality and pain. Jimmy caresses himself in an autoerotic embrace, regressing to the infancy which began the movie. But there is a latent aggression here, and in his fetal pain, Jimmy expresses one of his most penetrating private moments—a somnambulist disturbed by dreams which are at once infantile and bristling with hostility. Too many poisons have been taken into his body, and even as he tries to throw them off, they seem to turn him inside out.

In a scene shot from Jim's point of view, his mother enters the room upside down. His parents seem to be in another dimension in this scene and appear almost as figments of his imagination. When Jim tells them he was in trouble out at the bluff, his father removes the immediacy of the situation by acknowledging that a "bad accident" out there had been reported on the television news. The TV set flickering in the background of this scene is the first cinematic treatment of a controversial theory of the fifties: that television is a prime cause of violence and domestic apathy. Jim's parents sit glued to their set, passively absorbing the day's news. But when their son confronts them with the *reality* of what they've been watching, they can't cope with it.

The word "involved" is what detonates this scene:

MOTHER:
I don't want him to go to the police! There were other people involved and

why should he be the only one involved!

JIM:
But I *am* involved! I was in a *crime*, Mom! A boy was *killed*! You don't get out of that by pretending it didn't happen.

FATHER:
You know you did wrong. That's the main thing, isn't it?

JIM:
No! It's nothing! Just nothing! . . .

FATHER:
Son, this is all happening so fast—

JIM:
You better give me something, Dad. You better *give* me something fast . . . Dad? Aren't you going to stand up for me?
(*The father is mute, helpless . . . Suddenly Jim screams.*)
Dad?

Jim puts his hands around his father's throat, drags him down the stairs, pushes him over his easy chair and onto the floor—quite a feat considering the size of Jim Backus. His mother runs after them shrieking, *"Stop it! You'll kill him. Jim! Do you want to kill your father?"*

Jimmy so personally identified with this patricidal rage that he transforms what might have been an Oedipal travesty into a moment of real tragedy. He runs out in search of the only other adult he believes can help him—Ray, the juvenile officer. Ray isn't at the precinct, but the gang is. When they see Jim, they assume he's going to tell all; so Crunch decides they'd better take care of him. Jim doesn't want to go home, but heads back anyway and finds Judy waiting in his driveway. She's run away too.

As he gets out of the car, the disc jockey on the radio announces a request . . . "This time from the boys down at Anna's Pizza Paradise—a new arrangement of a great oldie in rhythm and blues—Jim, this is dedicated to you, from Buzz." "Milkman's Serenade" comes on—a musical jab from the gang for their favorite cow-boy.

Jim turns off the radio, faces Judy, and they recognize a mutual "rage to live."

JIM:
I swear sometimes, you just want to hold onto somebody! Judy, what am I going to do? I can't go home again.

JUDY:
Neither can I.

JIM:

No? Why not? (*no answer*) You know something? I never figured I'd live to see eighteen. Isn't that dumb.

JUDY:

No.

JIM:

Each day I'd look in the mirror and I'd say, "What? You still here?" Man! (*They laugh a little.*)

Like even today. I woke up this morning, you know? And the sun was shining and everything was nice. Then the first thing that happens is I see you, and I thought this is going to be one terrific day so you better live it up, boy, 'cause tomorrow maybe you'll be nothing.

As Jimmy got ready to kiss Natalie—her first screen kiss—he nuzzled his body next to hers as if to keep them both warm and whispered off camera, "You look green, and you know how green photographs in color."

In a line that became the theme song for *West Side Story*, Jim tells Judy that "there's a place" where they can hide, an old mansion Plato had pointed out from the observatory steps. The abandoned villa, with

An imaginary family grows up in the romantic ruins of the mansion.

its sunken gardens, waterless fountains, stone balustrades and rococo candelabra, is a romantic and eerie setting (actually the old Getty mansion used for the movie *Sunset Boulevard*).

The sequence begins with games and charades, a prankishness which lends the light, airy quality of *A Midsummer Night's Dream*, and gives relief from the doomy momentum of the story.

"There's nobody here but us chickens," Jim giggles to a wide-eyed Plato, who arrives to warn them of the approaching gang. Plato picks up on the fun and gives the new couple a mock tour of the property:

PLATO: (*He holds up the candelabra.*)
What do you think?
JIM:
Wow! Well, now, then, there . . . Let's take it for the summer.
JUDY: (*laughing*)
Oh, Jim.
JIM:
Should we rent or are we in a buying mood, dear?
PLATO:
. . . Only three million dollars a month!
JIM:
Why don't we just rent it for the season?
JUDY:
You see, we've just . . . oh, you tell him, darling. I'm so embarrassed I could die!
JIM:
Well, we're newlyweds.

When they joke about the possibility of children, Jim does his classic imitation of Mr. Magoo–"Ark! Drown 'em, like puppies." Warner Brothers, however, didn't find it very funny, and dispatched an executive with the earnestness of a collective Elmer Fudd to the scene, who suggested a somewhat bizarre change.

"One of the boys from the front office came over and went up to Jimmy and said, 'I understand that you're doing Mr. Magoo in this scene?'" Jim Backus recalled. "And Jimmy looked at him like, 'What business is it of yours what I'm doing?' So the executive asks him, 'You know this is Warner Brothers?' And Jimmy said, 'Yeah, I've got the general idea.' And the executive replies, 'Well, as long as this is Warner Brothers, why don't you make it Bugs Bunny?'

"Jimmy's reaction was–get your ass out of here!"

257

Most of the action in *Rebel* takes place at night, "when man and the universe are most resonant," said Nick Ray. It is also a time when the air is full of dreaming. "Not to dream is simply irresponsible," says an ancient proverb. For Jim and Judy, who've finally disengaged from their families, these fantasies are a necessity. Here in the romantic ruins of a past world, they dream of a new society reconstructed from their own intense imaginings, and a generation comes of age.

"The purpose of the film," said Stewart Stern, "was to tell the story of a generation growing up—in one night. That's why I consider it mythic, because it was a night journey.

"It was also a magic world, but it was a magic world built on the armature of Jim's unfulfilled wishes about his parents. He created an idealized family in which he was the father, Judy the mother and Plato the child. He could act out all those things he wished his father could have been able to do—defend him against his own rage, disarm his anger with understanding, risk his life for him. After Jim did this for himself, he was able to look at his parents as troubled people who could never change, but loved him in their own way.

"So it was a mythic experience Jim Stark was creating and living all at the same time. He was creating a legend as he went along. He was author of his own story."

Judy hums a little lullaby to Plato and he falls off to sleep, but his dreams of the future are merely a cruel repetition of his recurring nightmares of loss and rejection. Plato acts as Jim's alter ego in *Rebel*, and embodies the Freudian residue of Lindner's book—the violent, latently homosexual neurotic. That Plato is Jim's mirror image is emphasized when Plato sees Jim in the mirror of his locker next to a photo of Alan Ladd. He adopts Jim as a friend, and by this final scene he has intensified his "platonic love" for Jim by identifying him as a father.

With the emergence of the anti-hero—usually an androgynous adolescent—the fifties explored the topic of bisexuality. By allowing Plato to play a homosexual counterpoint in *Rebel*, the basic question of the movie—How can you become a man?—became more complex. Plato was too unstable to survive, and his violent end becomes apparent as the gang members arrive. He shoots one, screams, "You're *not* my father!" at Jim and rushes off into the bush as the police arrive. Judy and Jim run down the hill after Plato, who has broken into the planetarium and hidden himself inside its dark, empty space. Simultaneously, the cops arrive at the door and there are lights, bullhorns, Officer Ray, Jim's parents, Plato's maid and assorted police to witness this last drama.

Ray decides to talk to the "cookaboo inside with a gun."

RAY: (*into mike*)
I am addressing the boy in the planetarium. I am speaking to the boy inside. This is Ray Framek from the Juvenile Division . . . You are now surrounded. You are surrounded by many armed police. Whoever you are, drop your weapon and come outside.

Jim dashes for the door—Jim's father is able to shout down a trigger-happy cop—and, inside the planetarium, coaxes Plato out from under the same seat he'd crouched behind that very afternoon.

Jimmy is fitted with a chest protector.

"I've got the bullets!"

"Do you think the end of the world will come at night, Jim?" Plato asks, shivering like a puppy. Jim offers his jacket, asking for the gun as a trade. He promises to give it back, keeping it only long enough to remove the bullets. "Here," he says as he hands back the empty revolver, "friends keep promises, don't they?"

Jim takes Plato as far as the planetarium door, but Plato hesitates when he sees the menacing searchlights and faceless crowd outside. "They're not my friends!" Plato sobs as he bolts away from Jim and Judy. The police open fire and the child falls dead. "But I've got the bullets!" Jim shouts with outstretched hands. He goes over to Plato, the second friend he's lost in one day, and zips up the jacket—"He was always cold."

After winding its serpentine way through mythological,

psychological, social, sexual and moral themes, *Rebel* comes to a formal conclusion on the steps of the planetarium, where all these diverse elements were first set in motion: destruction and creation, hot and cold, isolation against union, red versus blue, the micro and the macro.

With classic simplicity, *Rebel* resolves the question with which it began. "You did everything a man could," Jim's father says as he comes over to comfort Jim and Judy. Jim has become a man and found a friend.

All of the wayward threads of the movie are exhausted by the end of this first day at school, and as a rosy-fingered dawn breaks, the scene resembles the last act of a Greek tragedy: a chorus made up of members of the community who comment on the sacrifice which reunites them standing against the pseudo-classical architecture of the planetarium.

The sky lightens, the ambulance and patrol cars pull away and who should approach the "temple" but its high priest—the professor who had projected the end-of-the-universe show. He looks around at the departing cars, parents and newly hatched mutants. He senses that something has happened here, but doesn't quite understand what it is. But this man in a trench coat carrying a satchel is none other than Nick Ray—personally signing his moving "picture."

Nicholas Ray has said that "if *Rebel* has been playing for the last twenty years (and it has), then it can stand as my epitaph." But *Rebel Without a Cause* is really James Dean's epitaph; in it he successfully depicted the most elusive of all human stages—transition.

As the adolescent Jim Stark, Jimmy enacted that "awkward stage" with the intensity of one who has never left it. Adolescence is a biological and social transformation expected to end when we reach our twenties and are released from confusion, awkwardness and pain.

In *Rebel*, however, Jimmy revealed what we would all eventually find out: that this self-conscious transition is a normal state of mind, a continually evolving process not limited to one age group. "Nobody despises adolescence more than adolescents," Ray said, because, as defined by adults, this stage of development denies reality to those who are going through it. It is an alien condition youth is simply expected to wait out. When Jim Stark screams, "I want an *answer now!*" all his helpless father can do is offer time—"In ten years you'll look back on this and ... you'll laugh at yourself for thinking this is so important,"—as if time were a solution in which the poisons could dissolve.

In the fifties, juvenile delinquency was considered a temporary American social disease. It panicked adults who felt they were losing control and authority over their children, and their fears were justified. The adult empire was beginning to topple. By living in a self-sealing sphere, parents of Jimmy's generation were already dead. "You can stop changing now and settle down" was their "adult lesson," but not all of their children would accept it. It was James Dean who acted out our cherished fantasies by rejecting the old models and offering, in *Rebel*, a real alternative.

Rebel Without a Cause is Jimmy's movie. All its forces flow through him and he is the source of its current. Its flagrant symbolism, violence and cosmic metaphors become plausible because we see *Rebel* through his vision. What is going on in his turbulent, enchanted head is projected on the screen, just as the heavens are projected on the planetarium dome. *Rebel* takes place in a teenage cranium, where a boy's wishes, dreams and furies become our own. Jim Stark's fantasies are the *content* of the movie, and *Rebel* infects us with their power.

The spellbinding effect of *Rebel* depends on Jimmy's ability to turn himself into a magnetic field on which all the lines of force are directed. Jimmy's riveting personality was the sum of all the experiments he had practiced on himself as an actor. But in *Rebel* he was no longer mimicking; he had completed the body vehicle and was connecting the invisible threads between himself and the other actors. Personality is not constituted of mannerisms, but wave lengths, and Jimmy realized that by tuning into someone else's wave length, he could become that person. As he shifted from frequency to frequency, he expressed an increasingly multiphrenic and collective personality.

Every scene in *Rebel* is played to Jimmy, not simply because he is the star, but because Jimmy was a mass of energy seeking form, and his need to be at the center was an attraction impossible to resist. Whoever came into contact with him *had* to react, either positively or negatively polarized by the reciprocal forces he put to work. The entire production of *Rebel* was pulled into his magnetic orbit. As a result, Jimmy's iridescent personality is reflected on all the members of the cast. The more frequent the exchanges between Jimmy and the others, the more intense his presence became. He had thrown his nimbus around the entire movie.

Jimmy's personality was ideal for a character in transition, moving from stage to stage and evolving through the course of the movie. *Rebel Without a Cause* reveals the transitions of Jim Stark as he progresses frame to frame from babbling infant to confused adolescent to the father of himself. He is a new creature coming into being, and in his mutation, he rehearses us for all the changes that we must go through. Like the schizont form of a cell which keeps reproducing in its own image, James Dean evolved a new community, and those who saw him became like him and took his message into themselves.

Rebel not only depicts a new society, but the effectiveness of a new community at work is demonstrated in the making of the film itself: it was a collective undertaking in which youthful talents created a film from the reality of their own desires. *Rebel* is also a revolutionary movie because it precipitates violence through a breakdown in communications: between Jim and the gang, Jim and Judy, Plato and himself, Jim and his parents. But these are the crises that mold a new society into a cohesive form. Something new and different can only occur just at that moment when communications break down for good, when the splinter group finds itself so alienated that it turns away and develops from its own resources a new and specific character.

This film was not a comedy, a case history nor a moral allegory, like *The Wild One* or *Blackboard Jungle*. *Rebel Without a Cause* was a realistic war movie—full of all the violence and death which society can inflict upon a family paralyzed by hypocrisy and the denial of feeling. Unlike the conventional war movie, in which the motivation is abstract and the confrontation depersonalized, the hostilities on the home front in *Rebel* are immediate and instinctive, taking the battles to a personal level where they strike a universal nerve.

In *Rebel Without a Cause*, James Dean rehearses his audience for greater battles to come, but is careful to warn us not to confuse street violence with the "true war of the hidden heart." Doing his own research for the part, Jimmy mixed with the teen underworld and found that most of the gangs modeled themselves after movies. He felt a moral obligation to present an alternative to the kids who didn't have a positive image on which to model themselves.

"The thing that interested me in *Rebel*," Jimmy said, "was doing something that would counteract *The Wild One*. I went out and hung around with kids in Los Angeles before making the movie. Some of them even call themselves 'wild ones.' They wear leather jackets, go out looking for somebody to rough up a little. These aren't poor kids, you know. Lots of them have money, grow up and become pillars of the community! Boy," he nodded his head slightly, "they scared me! But it's a constructive movie, it gives some of these kids, the ones who aren't out to be tough guys, something to identify with."

The conclusion of *Rebel* is only an apparent happy ending, one of those cinematic sleights of hand that Ray practiced throughout his career. It begs us to question it. We cannot really believe that Jim and Judy's problems are finally over. What we see is only a lull in the battle, setting the stage for a new war. It is a battle vital to the origin of a new species.

The pain Jimmy so intensely expressed in *Rebel* is the pain of mutation, of the new being who is neither one thing nor the other, yet stretches itself recklessly over the space in between. Unlike his parents, who anesthetize their discomfort with sleeping pills and evasions in an attempt to avoid pain, Jim Stark experiences the pain that comes from the uncertainties of transition and the hazards of evolution. This pain is actually one of the vital signs of life: As Gerald Heard said in Jimmy's favorite book, *Pain, Sex and Time*: "Men alone can still evolve. Therefore, if the creature in pain happens to be a man, because of the high degree of vital energy still remaining in his species to be provided for, it's still unfinished evolution, he must suffer intensely when injured, unless he has found appropriate channels through which to let that pent-up energy express itself."

He has banged into your wall
of air, your hubris, racing
towards your heights and you
have cut him from your table
which is built, how unfairly
for us! not on trees, but on clouds.

—from Frank O'Hara,
"Five Poems for James Dean"

CHAPTER TWELVE

Wall of Air
May–September 30, 1955

Jimmy begins Giant; *he*
wins first sports car race; a new Porsche Spyder;
Jimmy dies in a car crash in Cholame;
Fairmount mourns; Rebel *is released.*

J immy took no time to rest after finishing *Rebel Without a Cause.* Almost a year earlier he had agreed to star in *Giant*, a sprawling saga of Texas based on Edna Ferber's best-selling novel.

George Stevens was to be both producer and director of *Giant*, and this was one of the primary reasons Jimmy wanted to be in the film. Unlike Elia Kazan or Nicholas Ray, George Stevens was an authentic legend of the old Hollywood, a director who'd worked with all the greats: Fred Astaire and Ginger Rogers, James Stewart, Betty Grable, Cary Grant, Douglas Fairbanks, Jr., Alan Ladd, Montgomery Clift, Katherine Hepburn and Spencer Tracy. In this production, Jimmy would have equal billing with two of Hollywood's biggest stars —Elizabeth Taylor and Rock Hudson.

Jimmy had first met George Stevens on the Warner Brothers lot while he was filming *East of Eden.* He knew Stevens was preparing *Giant* and that it was destined to be a "monster" industry production. Although he didn't openly lobby for the part, he did become friendly with Fred Guoil, Stevens' assistant.

Stevens remembered that "when Jimmy was working with Gadge, he would walk back and forth past our office every day, and soon he started to drop in to talk to Freddy Guoil. When he first came into the office, my secretary was a little concerned about him being there; she didn't know him from Adam. Jimmy and Fred talked about cars and fishing and stuff—not a very fast moving conversation, mind you —every five minutes or so somebody said a word.

"When *East of Eden* was finished we went to see it, and the boy was just incredible. I'm not just talking about him as an actor, but it was his acting that made his personality so sensitive.

"So when we cast the role of Jett Rink—which really called for a tough, kind of beefy guy—I said to Fred, 'Hold onto your belt, Fred. What do you think of Jimmy Dean for the part?'

"So the next day I said, 'Here Jim, I want you to take a look at this script and see how you feel about it. See if it's too far out for you.' He said, 'Okay.' There was about a half hour of conversation between us. After no haste at all, he read it, came back to my office, put the book on the table and stood there and shook his head. Now Jimmy Dean had a way of shaking his head so that it could be both positive and negative. He'd shake it up and down, but you'd catch an angle of the negative in it. I could never imitate it.

"Anyway, Jimmy stood there, shook his head and said, 'That'd be a good thing.' We talked some more and he decided to do it."

At a press party to announce the start of production, Jimmy was already getting into his role as Jett Rink, the surly ranch hand who worked for the Benedicts (Liz and Rock). Jimmy sauntered in wearing blue jeans and an old red flannel shirt, cowboy hat, boots and silver-buckled belt. He sat in a corner, his hat pulled down and a cigarette hanging from his mouth, and when Stevens introduced him, he didn't smile or stand up—just sat there.

"He just stared at his boots," said a reporter who was at the party. "When a photographer came close to photograph him, he quickly put on his dark sunglasses."

"Would you be kind enough to remove your glasses, Mr. Dean?" the photographer asked.

Jimmy made out as if he didn't hear.

"Why don't you give the guy a break?" a reporter asked. "After all, he's got a job to do."

Dean shook his head. "I didn't mean to be rude. It's just that I've got bags under my eyes, and I need a shave."

In another corner of the room, a studio representative muttered under his breath, "That's typical of the guy. I hope the Army drafts him and teaches him a little cooperation."

Jimmy continued, "Maybe publicity is important, but I just can't get with it... The newspapers give you a big build-up. Something happens, they tear you down. Who needs it? What counts to the artist is performance, not publicity. Guys who don't know me, they've already typed me as an oddball."

Jimmy was already a star in the Hollywood community before his movies were released to the general public. By the time *Eden* came out, Jimmy had become a genuine celebrity—sought out by writers and fans. This attention distracted him for a while, and when it began making him late for work, Stevens had a talk with him.

"He wasn't really late, but still, other people would have to sit around and wait," said Stevens. "I told Jim I knew what he was going through, but he had a job to do and he'd better figure out a way to do it, and if he couldn't handle it, he'd better go to the front office and see about taking some time off to relax. The lateness stopped and we never talked about it again."

As *Giant* began filming, Jimmy noticed immediately the enormous differences between Stevens and the other two directors with whom he had worked. Stevens is not "an actor's director" and does not construct his films around performers. For Stevens, actors are simply threads in a complex interweaving of elements. Though Jimmy was exhausted by *Rebel*, *Giant* would tire and frustrate him in a different way because he couldn't grow emotionally or participate in the creation of the film. Stevens was in total control of *Giant*. No longer the *enfant terrible*, Jimmy was just another cog in the wheel.

Though Jimmy respected Stevens and his work, he objected to being treated like a prop. Sometimes he would arrive on the set promptly at eight o'clock in the morning, only to wait around all day until Stevens might decide to shoot one of his scenes. Once he waited all day without being used at all. The next day he didn't show up.

Dennis Hopper, who appeared in the movie as Rock Hudson's son, recalled the blow-up that followed:

"Stevens was furious with Jimmy, took him up to Jack Warner's office and threatened to kick him out of Hollywood (after the picture, of course). After they chewed his ass off for about an hour, Jimmy said, 'Are you finished? Well, let me tell *you* something. I am not a machine. I may be working in a factory, but I'm not a machine. I stayed up all night Friday to do that scene. I prepared *all night* for that scene. I came in ready to work and you kept me sitting around all day. Do you realize I'm doing emotional memories? That I'm working with my senses—my sight, hearing, smell, touch? Can I tell you that for every day you make me sit, there'll be two days next time? Then three, then four? You'll pay for it. And you're *not* going to stop me from working. Now let's get back to the set.'

"And you know something? From then on, when they called Jimmy in to work, he worked. He never sat around after that."

Stevens did not understand Method preparation, but Jimmy didn't understand Stevens' problems either. Jimmy was still being uncooperative on the set when Hedda Hopper called him over and tried to explain the situation from the producer's point of view.

Hedda wrote about his visit in her book, *The Whole Truth and Nothing But*:

"I've been reading some bad things about you," I said. "I understand you haven't been showing up for work."

"Right, I haven't. Stevens has been horrible. I sat there for three days, made up and ready to work at nine o'clock every morning. By six o'clock I hadn't had a scene or rehearsal. I sat there like a bump on a log watching that big, lumpy Rock Hudson making love to Liz Taylor. I knew what Stevens was trying to do to me. I'm not going to take it any more."

"I hold no brief for Stevens," I said, "but what you don't know is that there's a man on that set who put the whole deal together. Henry Ginsberg, Stevens, and Edna Ferber are partners. It took Henry two years to do it. This is the first time in Ferber's life she took no money, only an equal share of the profits as they come in. If this picture goes wrong, Stevens can walk out, and those two years of Ginsberg's life go down the drain."

"I didn't know," Jimmy said.

Jimmy tried to repress whatever negative feelings he had, but Nick Ray watched the tension building. "It was really depressing," Ray said, "to see the suffering that boy was going through. *Giant* was really draining him, and I hated watching it happen."

Stevens constructs his movies by shooting each scene from every conceivable angle, then masterfully editing the best shots out of miles of film. Jimmy described this technique as Stevens' "around the clock system." The financial pressures of his huge undertaking only magnified Stevens' autocratic manner of working. The "professional" members of the cast could adapt to his methodical, painstaking procedures which might entail several hours of shooting for a scene lasting only seconds. But it made Jimmy stir-crazy.

"I hate pictures," Jimmy told Bill, "and Stevens is no better than the others. Only he can't go wrong. Do you know he gets more footage, more film, than anybody else at Warner Brothers?. . ."

Not only did Stevens dominate the film, eliminating any contributions Jimmy might make, but his iron will found its way into Jimmy's personal life.

"Three days before we were to go on location for *Giant*," Stevens recalled, "Jimmy was entered in a race at Palm Springs. Fred and I had a talk about it and were frankly worried that he might get hurt. So I had a talk with Jimmy and said to him, 'I hear you're entered in a race. But what happens if you break your arm or something, you can't do the movie with your arm in a cast.' And Jimmy said, 'You mean what if I break my neck, don't you?' I told him I didn't think he'd break his neck, but I didn't want him to break *anything*, because there was too much at stake. So he started the picture without going into the race."

Jimmy Dean had always loved to go fast. After the little Czech

Jimmy withdraws into himself at the Warner Brothers canteen.

269

motorcycle he'd owned in high school, Jimmy went through seven other bikes. In Hollywood, he owned an MG, two Porsches, a Ford station wagon, a Triumph motorcycle and a Lancia motor scooter.

In May 1954, Jimmy bought his first sports car, a used MG roadster, but sold it after six months. During *Rebel* he bought a Porsche, a white Speedster, which was the first car he ever raced.

"The first meeting I had with Jimmy Dean was at a California Sports Car Club race at the Palm Springs Airport in May 1955," said former sports columnist Wilson Springer. "He was entered in the Production "D" Class, which means he had a sports car with normal highway trim (headlights, windshield, normal engine, etc.) instead of being in the faster category of "Modified" Class. At the race, I got to know Dean pretty good because I treated him like any other sports car driver. I didn't know who he was.

"I always took a motorcycle to the races instead of walking my legs off, and Dean was impressed with the British AJS I had, and that's how we started talking. I noticed he was working on his own car and had nobody in his pit area to help him. I asked him about his 'pit crew' and he said he had none, and that the two or three guys hanging around were from Warner Brothers' publicity department, but they didn't know anything about racing. Because it's necessary for a driver in a race to have someone in the pits to give him signals and information about where he is and what's going on in the race, I volunteered to 'pit' for him.

"When the race started, I saw Dean go into the first turn at the airport circuit and said to myself, 'Gad, this guy knows how to handle his car.' By the end of the first lap, after the dust settled, I saw Dean five car lengths ahead of the second-place car. For the next three or four laps, Dean gradually stretched out his lead by a hundred yards and I gave him the 'slow down' sign, because there's no use in overtaxing an engine if you have a comfortable lead.

"Dean won the Saturday prelim race with ease and was very happy. When he came in, he pulled off his helmet, lit a cigarette and just grinned."

The next morning at the track, a winding, three-mile course laid out on the runway of the airport, Jimmy showed up dressed in "whites," which is the traditional outfit worn by professional sports car racers.

Springer pointed out Ed Kretz, Sr., one of the most famous

professional motorcycle racers: "Dean said, 'Jeez, you mean "Iron Man" Ed Kretz?' And then he almost came apart asking if I'd introduce him to Kretz. I led Dean over and made the introduction, and Dean grabs ahold of Kretz like he's meeting the President. 'It is certainly a thrill to meet you, Ed,' Jimmy said. 'I saw you at Hammond, Indiana in 1946 when you were on that Indian, and only got fifth in your heat race, and then in the main you really blew those guys off the track. . .' We took some pictures of them talking, and when they parted Dean acted like he was leaving God.

"In the Sunday finals for the Production "D" Class, Jimmy led the field and it was "NC" (no contest) all the way. Dean was so much better than anyone in the race that he 'ran away and hid,' as the old saying goes," said Springer. "He finished so far ahead in that race, that I'm sure that's why the Cal Club put him in the big car production race later in the day. He finished up third in that race, driving a 96-cubic-inch Porsche against 180-cubic-inch Jags, Corvettes and bigger, faster cars."

Ken Miles, an auto mechanic who competed in these races, felt that Jimmy was a good racer, but that he would never be a great one. "Most people have the idea that sports car racing is principally a matter of speed," Miles said. "It isn't. Speed is a factor, certainly, but this kind of racing is primarily a test of the driver's skill. How cleverly he can maneuver his car at high speed in and out of a pack of other cars, all against drivers attempting to maneuver *their* cars at high speed.

"Dean was always too careful with other drivers. He didn't care about his own neck, but he would not take any risk involving another driver. You can't win races that way.

"Jimmy wanted speed. He wanted his body to hurtle across over the ground, the faster the better. Jimmy was a straightaway driver. His track was the shortest distance between here and there."

As much as he loved the competition, Jimmy loved speed for its own sake. For him, the acceleration hastened and blurred his transition from one moment to the next, creating a sense of weightless flight through space. He wanted to go faster, as fast as light itself, an image flashing toward the silver screen. And in this exhilarating dizziness, Jimmy could paradoxically find himself. "It's the only time I feel whole," he said of his love of racing.

In late May 1955, Jimmy entered the Santa Barbara races. He drew

a bad starting position, but pushed hard until another Porsche cut directly in front of him. To avoid a collision, he swerved and side-swiped two bales of hay which lined the course, shuddered for several feet and then straightened out. He had resumed his pace and was back into fourth place when his engine dropped a valve and was forced to coast off the track. It was his last race.

There's been speculation that Jimmy's speeding was a manifestation of his death wish, a suicidal tendency. But his recklessness, his love of bullfighting (the Dance of Death), the Colt .45 he kept in his room at the Warner Brothers lot, his Aztec fantasies and his poses in a coffin cannot be taken to mean he intended to kill himself. It was simply a matter of going as far as he could as fast as he could.

Jimmy's preoccupation with his own mortality didn't begin when he took up racing in Hollywood. "Jimmy was *always* interested in death as a subject," said Billy James, who knew him in New York. "When Jimmy was living at the Iroquois Hotel, he had a little gallows model with a light behind it. It was specially lit from behind so that it projected this huge shadow on the wall. When you walked into the room, this huge shadow of a noose was the first thing you saw."

Photographer Roy Schatt also said that Jimmy told him he would die young. "Now the astrologists and numerologists, those nuts, would say he could see ahead of his time and all that. *C'mon!* Jimmy was the kind of guy who wouldn't bet you on the next moment. Maybe he had a death wish, but that's a guess. He never told me that. But he did say, in fact, '*I will not live over thirty*,' and you can play around with that any way you like."

Irving Shulman watched Jimmy race at Palm Springs and said that he won, not with skill, but with sheer nerve and a reckless disregard for himself.

"Jimmy was a dreadful driver. He would hit a hay bale every time he went around a corner. That's no way to drive, slamming your car around like a billiard ball. The pit crew who worked in the gas station across from Warners thought he was a bad driver too.

"One day I was in the gas station, and Jimmy came up off the freeway on his motorcycle and down this steep grade that goes onto Barham Boulevard. His brakes failed, and his way of stopping was to cut across the street, run through the gas station and drive into a wall.

That he didn't kill himself or crush a leg was a miracle."

Jimmy was also fond of quoting a line from Nick Ray's *Knock on Any Door*: "Live fast, die young, and have a good-looking corpse." While making *Giant*, he heard about the death of two young stars—Bob Travis in a private plane crash and Susan Ball succumbing to cancer—and predicted to a friend, "Well, three is the number of completion, and I'll be number three, don't worry."

During *Giant*, Jimmy filmed a spot for the National Highway Committee. It was a thirty-second commercial for safe driving made during a short break in the shooting. Gig Young talked to Jimmy, dressed for his role as a cowboy, about his racing:

Gig Young: How fast does your car go?
Jimmy: OOhhh, about a hundred miles per hour, clocked.
Gig Young: You've used it to race, haven't you?
Jimmy: Oh, one or two times.
Gig Young: Where?
Jimmy: Oh, I showed pretty good at Palm Springs. I ran in a basic heat. People say racing is dangerous, but I'd rather take my chances on the track any day than on the highway . . . Well, Gig, I think I'd better take off.

As Jimmy stood at the door twirling his lariat, getting ready to leave, Gig asked him if he had any special advice for the young people who drive, to which Jimmy was supposed to supply the committee's slogan: "Drive safely, because the life you save may be your own."

Instead, Jimmy turned toward the camera and said, "And remember—drive safely . . . because the life you save may be . . . *mine*."

Jane Deacy came to Los Angeles in September to negotiate a role for Jimmy in a television special entitled "The Corn is Green." She completed a substantial new deal with Warners—nearly a million dollars for nine pictures over the next six years.

"That night Jimmy celebrated," said his friend Joe Hyams. "He went with Lew Bracker to buy a new Porsche Spyder he had seen—a two-seater costing more than $6000 with an eggshell-thin, aluminum body, no windshield and no top. It could go more than 150 miles per hour. Jimmy bought it solely for racing. He drove it around Hollywood only to show it off to friends and to put on mileage."

Lew Bracker was one of Jimmy's few friends in Hollywood. He was Leonard Rosenman's cousin and had met Jimmy right after his break-up with Pier. Since Lew had also been jilted, the two hit it off immediately in their romantic self-despair. Coincidentally, Lew was an insurance agent who shared Jimmy's avid interest in sports cars. He encouraged Jimmy to buy the silver Porsche, but also encouraged him to settle his estate now that he was making big money. Bracker drew up a life insurance policy for $100,000.

"Leave $5000 for Grandma and Grandpa Dean, $10,000 for Markie's education and the rest to Ortense and Marcus," Jimmy told him.

"The way it's distributed is for your will, Jimmy," Lew explained. "Did you make that out yet?" Since there wasn't a will, Lew decided the estate would be beneficiary until a formal will was drawn up, and Jimmy agreed to get around to it as soon as he could.

Stevens had prevented Jimmy from racing during *Giant*, but as soon as his part was finished—in mid-September—he entered the races that would take place at the end of the month in Salinas. This news made the columns almost immediately:

JAMES DEAN PLANNING TO GO ON RACING KICK WHEN "GIANT" ENDS
September 16, 1955—In case Warners doesn't know it, James Dean has big racing plans after he finishes "Giant" this week.

"I want to enter at Salinas, Willow Springs, Palm Springs, all the other places," Dean tells me. "Of course, I'll miss some of them because I have to do a TV spectacular in New York on October 18. But maybe I can catch a race back there."

"Will Warners like this?" I asked.

"When a man goes home at night," he replied, "the studio can't tell him not to do what he wants to do."

For the present, Dean will drive his German sports car but he gets delivery from England next month on a Lotus Mark 8.

"This is strictly a racing car," he enthused, "it goes like a bomb. I'll be very hard to catch."

Under his Warner contract, Dean can follow his whims in 1956. He has the whole year off.

Although Jimmy had the Lotus on order, he couldn't resist buying the Porsche Spyder. He had first heard about the Porsche from mechanic Rolf Wutherich, who worked at Competition Motors. In *Modern Screen* (October 1957), Wutherich recalled in detail their first conversation about the car:

He was walking with that slow gait of his, a toy monkey on a rubber band hanging from his wrist, hopping up and down with each movement of Jimmy's arm. Jimmy was in a completely carefree, happy mood. We shook hands, and we talked about sports cars, what else? Jimmy wanted to enter the big-car class in his next race—the class for cars with the large, powerful engines. That was Jimmy's big dream. And he told me about the big Bristol car he had ordered.

That was when I remembered about the Porsche Spyder we had on sale. I told Jimmy about this car—told him how powerful it was and that it might be just what he wanted to make his dream come true. It was September 19, 1955. He drove it once around the block. And really liked it. He made one condition before buying the car—he made me promise that I would personally check it before each and every race he took part in, and that I was to ride with him to all the races. Naturally I said *yes* because I couldn't think of anything I'd like better.

Jimmy loved nothing better than to show off his new car, and one day he drove it over to the Warner Brothers lot. Though Jimmy had finished *Giant*, there was still a lot of work to be done on the film, and Stevens was in the middle of a conference on the sound stage when he felt someone tap him on the shoulder. "I turned around and it's James

Jimmy looks into an ancient mirror. Sanford Roth's house.

Dean," Stevens said, "and he motioned for me to step aside. So I excused myself from the group and he said, 'C'mere, I want to show you something.'

"He took me outside the sound stage, and there was this big Porsche sitting there. He told me he'd seen the Porsche and fallen in love with it and bought it. It was low as a bathtub, and I got in and he took me for a ride around the lot on two wheels. By the time we got back, the sound-stage door opened and everyone else was out there and got all around the Porsche to see Jimmy Dean's new car. It was at this point that I became aware of his psychology. You want everyone to admire your new car, so what do you do? You don't ask your buddy to come out and see it, you shanghai the *director*—so that there's nothing going on inside and everyone comes outside to see what's happening. Sure enough, he had everyone on the set around him.

"By the time we got back, the studio guards had also come over and said, 'You can never drive this car on the lot again; you're gonna kill a carpenter or an actor or somebody.' And that was the last time I saw Jimmy."

During the filming of *Giant*, Jimmy had met photographer Sanford Roth. Roth was in Europe when *East of Eden* was released and didn't even know what Jimmy looked like when he arrived on the *Giant* set.

"I noticed a young man playing with a lariat," said Roth. "He looked as if he had spent his young life close to horses and cattle. This was Jimmy Dean. He watched me as I approached."

When Roth introduced himself, Jimmy looked up over his thick-rimmed glasses and replied, "Are you *Sanford H. Roth*? Did you do the book on Paris with Aldous Huxley?"

That night Jimmy went to dinner with Sandy and his wife, Beulah, and a close friendship began. In their forties, with no children of their own, the Roths welcomed Jimmy as friend and son. They told him of their travels and the European writers and artists they knew, and all three talked of a trip together after *Giant* was completed. Sandy also became involved in Jimmy's racing interests and made plans to accompany Jimmy to the races in Salinas.

Marcus and Ortense Winslow came to Los Angeles in September to visit Jimmy. "He seemed very happy," said Ortense. "He showed us the house he had in Sherman Oaks, the big hunting lodge kind of place with just one room. We had dinner with him, and he visited with us out at Winton's house, where we were staying. But we didn't stay too long, because it's a long drive back to Fairmount. He took Marcus for a ride in his Porsche. I didn't want to try it . . . it's so low."

On Thursday, September 29, two days before the Salinas races, Jimmy started preparations for the drive north. His racing number, "130," was painted in black on the side of the car, and Jimmy impulsively added a nickname which might have been his own —"Little Bastard." He had planned to tow the car to Salinas, but since the car needed 1500 miles to be in perfect racing condition and he had put on only 150, he decided to drive there.

At six o'clock Thursday night, he set out from Los Angeles accompanied by Bill Hickman, who'd been his dialogue coach during *Giant*. By the time they reached Santa Barbara, the fog rolling in from the ocean was so thick they had to turn back. Jimmy stopped to call his father's house. He knew his father wouldn't go to Salinas, but his uncle, Charles Nolan Dean, was visiting. Since his uncle had taught Jimmy to ride his first motorcycle, Jimmy asked if he'd like to watch him race. Charles was planning to leave for Mexico on Friday, so he couldn't go. But he told Jimmy he'd like to meet him for lunch Friday before he left.

Jimmy and Bill Hickman drove back to Los Angeles, stopped at the Villa Capri and finally got home to bed about three in the morning.

The following account of Jimmy's last day, Friday, September 30, 1955, is taken from eyewitness reports, newspaper stories and recollections of people who were with him. We examine the minute particulars of his last day as if by retracing each detail we could find a way to avoid the inevitable.

8 A.M.: Jimmy arrived at Competition Motors with Rolf Wutherich, who gave the Porsche one last check on spark plugs and oil pressure. By ten, the car had had a thorough going-over and Rolf attached the safety belt to the driver's seat. Since there would be no passenger in the race, he didn't put a safety belt on the right-hand side. Then, still undecided about whether or not to drive the car to Salinas, they hooked the Porsche up to Jimmy's station wagon before picking up Sandy Roth and Bill Hickman.

12 NOON: Winton Dean and Charlie Dean showed up to say

goodbye, and the four had lunch at the Farmer's Market on Fairfax Avenue in downtown Los Angeles.

1:30 P.M.: Rolf and Jimmy went to pick up Sandy Roth and Bill Hickman. "He came to my house with his racing Porsche atop a trailer attached to his Ford station wagon," Roth said. "We were happy and enthusiastic at the prospect of the seven-hour drive up the beautiful coast, the races and the weekend to follow in San Francisco. The day was magnificent, and Jimmy thought it a pity to sit cooped up in the station wagon for the long ride. They took the Porsche off the trailer, and Jimmy and his mechanic set out in the car. I followed behind in the station wagon, hauling the empty trailer." They went down Cahuenga to the freeway, then up Sepulveda to the Ridge Route.

They drove along the Ridge Route (then Route 99, now Route 5), stopping at Tip's Diner for something to eat. Jimmy had a glass of milk. Rolf said, "I'd never seen Jimmy so happy. He talked and laughed and seemed very at ease."

3 P.M.: Back on the Grapevine (a grade of the Ridge Route), Wutherich gave Jimmy some advice about driving.

"Don't go too fast!" I said, my face dead serious. "Don't try to win! The Spyder is something quite different from the Speedster. Don't drive to win; drive to get experience!" "Okay, Rolf," he said with a smile, a sort of smile that laughed at me and my fears for him.

Then he hesitated for a moment. He pulled a ring from his finger. It wasn't an expensive ring—just some little souvenir he had picked up, but I knew he had a sentimental attachment to the ring. He handed it to me.

"Why?" I asked.

"I want to give you something," he said. "To show we're friends, Rolf." I was touched. The ring just fitted on my small finger. My hand was much bigger than Jimmy's.

Jimmy's driving was like the best in Europe. When he drove, he drove with his whole being. He had good steel in his hands.

Jimmy pulled over for a few minutes to let Wutherich look under the hood and make sure the highway was not taking any edge off the engine. Sanford Roth and Bill Hickman caught up with the Porsche and warned Jimmy he was going too fast on the winding road. They were barely able to keep him in sight at sixty miles per hour.

Jimmy came off the Ridge Road and went through Bakersfield.

3:30 P.M.: Highway patrolman Oscar Hunter pulled Jimmy over

and gave him a ticket for doing sixty-five in a forty-five-mile-per-hour speed zone. Sandy Roth, in the station wagon behind him, also got a ticket. As they drove off, Jimmy told Sandy and Bill they'd meet in Paso Robles, about 150 miles away, for dinner. Jimmy continued north on 99, went through Formosa and Lost Hills and onto Route 466 (now Route 46).

5 P.M.: They made a fifteen-minute stop at Blackwell's Corner at the junction of Routes 466 and 33. It was a monotonous drive, and both were grateful for a break. Wutherich said:

When we reached Blackwell's Corners, a sleek, grey Mercedes was parked in front of the store, another of the racing cars on the road to Salinas. Jimmy stepped on the brake and we got out. He took a close look at the Mercedes and chatted with the owner, Lance Revson, the twenty-one-year-old son of Barbara Hutton.

Jimmy bought a bag full of apples, and hopped back into the car. He was raring to go. "Non-stop to Paso Robles!" he shouted and jammed down the accelerator without fastening his safety belt. Blackwell's Corners was our last stop.

We had been on Highway 466 ever since we went through Bakersfield and now it was deserted. No car except our Spyder and the station wagon as far as we could see. Jimmy went faster now—a very natural thing to do when you are all alone on a good road in a racing car. It was just past five in the afternoon. The sun, a ball of fire, shone directly in our eyes. It was still very hot and the heat flickered and danced on the sandy brown road. To the right and left of us was desert; in front of us, an endless ribbon of road.

5:30 P.M.: Twilight. Jimmy had averaged seventy-five miles per hour from the time he'd been ticketed, which meant he must have been doing over one hundred miles per hour in some stretches. The road, growing grey in the dimming light, was empty and flat. Wutherich started to get sleepy:

"Everything okay?" Jimmy asked.

"Everything okay," I answered, half dozing. The monotonous hum of the engine was like a soft cradle song.

We were not talking now—not of Pier Angeli or of Dean's mother or of anything. The only thought on Jimmy's mind was winning that race. There was no doubt of that; that's all he talked about.

A few minutes later, they approached the intersection of Routes 466 and 41 in Cholame (pronounced *shall aim*). A Ford sedan going in the opposite direction on Route 466 began to turn left. The driver looked down the road, didn't see anything coming and turned.

Jimmy said to Wutherich, "That guy up there's gotta stop; he'll see us."

5:45 P.M.: Jimmy Dean was dead.

Hickman and Roth arrived at the crash a few moments after Jimmy had slammed into the side of the Ford. Roth described the scene:

I noticed what seemed like some kind of a roadblock far off in the distance. As I came closer, the obstruction took form. It was a sedan, not badly damaged, in the middle of the highway. I strained to look around the immediate area—I was looking for the other car.

Off in a ditch to the right, I suddenly saw what had been the sleek, silver Porsche—now it was like a crumpled pack of cigarettes. But where was Jimmy? My heart screamed. I leaped from the car, only to be confronted by a highway policeman asking questions.

Then I saw it all. Rolf had been thrown clear of the car: Jimmy was dead in his seat. The impact had thrown his head back too far.

The ambulance came and I instinctively began taking pictures. I begged the attendant to keep Jimmy under oxygen on the way to the hospital, but it was no use. Neither was the fifteen-mile race against time to the hospital. Jimmy was dead.

On the side of the road, Donald Turnupseed, a twenty-three-year-old college student from Tulare, California, was white-faced and crying. "I didn't see him ... I swear I didn't see him ..." His car was barely scratched, and United Press News Service said he "escaped the accident with only a 'bruised nose.'"

There were no skid marks at the site of the crash. There hadn't even been enough time for Jimmy to swerve at the last moment. "It was impossible for Dean to avoid the crash," a highway patrolman said later to a reporter from the *New York Post*. "Speed was not involved ..."

Jimmy, trapped in the seat behind the wheel, his head practically severed from his body, died instantly. He was taken to Paso Robles War Memorial Hospital, and a doctor later issued a report that he had suffered "a broken neck, multiple broken bones and lacerations over his entire body."

Saturday morning, the world heard the news—from the bold

headlines of the *Los Angeles Times*—"Film Star James Dean Killed in Auto Crash"—to the small obituary buried in the *New York Times*. In the *San Francisco Chronicle*'s final edition, it was a subheadline—"Crash Kills Film Star James Dean"—under a larger story—"Theories on Mystery Blast Told." The wire services ran "James Dean, Film Meteor, Dies in Crash" and "Dean Feared the Crash that Killed Him."

At this point, the public knew Jimmy Dean only from one film—*East of Eden*—yet all stories agreed that he was a "brilliant young actor" whose loss would "cast a pall" over Hollywood. Even his obituary in the *London Times* began, "Mr. James Dean, who had already been hailed as a great film actor after appearing in only one film..."

Back in Indiana the reaction was, as usual, matter-of-fact: "Fairmount Man Dies in Traffic Accident in West." Marcus and Ortense didn't hear the news until they arrived home from their drive to California.

In the fall, Indiana distills its juices; "the frost is on the pumpkin and the fodder's in the shock." Usually the farming community of Fairmount begins to slow its pace and prepare for the long winter nights ahead. But the crisp atmosphere of feasts and fires was absent from Fairmount in October 1955, as the town prepared to bury James Dean.

Four days after Jimmy's death, Winton Dean accompanied his son's body back to Fairmount. Three thousand people, one thousand more than the entire population of Fairmount, attended his funeral on Saturday, October 8, 1955. The funeral, and the memorial services held a year later, were the largest functions ever held in Fairmount, Indiana. Special details of state police and civil defense police were dispatched to the area just to handle the traffic.

Jimmy's body lay in state at Hunt's Funeral Parlor from Wednesday to Friday, and on Saturday an orderly crowd of some twenty-four hundred people stood outside Back Creek Friends Church (which could only seat six hundred) as burial services were held. Jimmy's coffin was then carried by six former classmates—Paul Smith, Bob Pulley, Bob Middletown, James Fulkerson, Rex Bright and Whitey Rust—four of whom had been on his old basketball team. The procession went only a short way to Park Cemetery, located on the meadowland that lay between the town and the Winslow Farm, fertile ground where James Dean was buried.

Though the people of Indiana rarely ponder out loud on the nature of fame and death, their poet laureate, James Whitcomb Riley, wrote this verse on the subject:

Once in a dream, I saw a man
With haggard face and tangled hair
and eyes that nursed as wild a care
As gaunt Starvation ever can;
and in his hand he held a wand
whose magic touch gave life and thought
unto a form his fancy wrought
and robed with coloring so grand
it seemed the reflex of some child
of heaven, fair and undefiled—
a face of purity and love—
to woo him into worlds above:
and as I gazed with dazzled eyes,
a gleaming smile lit up his lips
as his bright soul from its eclipse
went flashing into Paradise.
Then tardy Fame came through the door
And found a *picture*—nothing more.

Just four days after Jimmy's death, on October 3, 1955, *Rebel Without a Cause* opened. The reviews began to appear shortly after the news of his funeral, and critics unanimously recognized the brilliance of *Rebel*'s star—James Dean.

"Dean projects the wildness, the torment, the crude tenderness of a rootless generation," said Arthur Knight in *Saturday Review.* "Gone are the Brando mannerisms, gone the too-obvious Kazan touch. He stands out as a remarkable talent; and he was cut down by the same passions he exposes so tellingly in this strange and forceful picture."

Jimmy escaped even the acid critique of those who hated the movie: "[It's] written and directed so sluggishly that all names but one will be omitted here," said William Zinsser in the *New York Herald Tribune.* "The exception is Dean ... his rare talent and appealing personality even shine through this turgid melodrama."

The rest of the cast received neither sympathy nor praise. As in the afterglow of *Eden*, Jimmy is so overwhelming that all others seem to take on the role of satellites. Even the bristly Bosley Crowther of the *New York Times* had so succumbed to Jimmy's spell that, although there's another Brando barb in his review of *Rebel*, he so totally accepts James Dean that he never mentions a character named Jim Stark nor makes any distinction between the two: "Mr. Dean . . . is a mixed up rebel . . . Mr. Dean mumbles longingly . . . There is a horrifying duel with switchblade cutlery between the reluctant Mr. Dean and another lad (Corey Allen) . . ."

The reviews could hardly fail to mention the dramatic irony of Jimmy's tragic accident. "In this movie," said *Newsweek* magazine, "he wins an auto race with death. Only four weeks ago, at the age of twenty-four, he lost one." *America* magazine said, "One of the film's chief exhibits of teen-age irresponsibility is a full dress demonstration of a game called 'chicken'. . . . The tragic coincidence that Dean lost his life in an automobile accident a few weeks ago, gives this sequence an almost unbearable morbid ring."

The violence of Jimmy's death and the temper of the times initially perverted the profound image Jimmy projected in *Rebel*. His crash made it seem as if *this* were Jimmy's personal message, and the immediate reactions among teenagers included violent reenactments of the chickie run and the switchblade sequences. Although the real seed Jimmy planted in *Rebel* took years to reveal itself, the initial impact of the film got the juices going inside the greasers, the townies and the "teddy boys," much the same way the end-of-the-universe movie in *Rebel* got the old secretions of adrenalin dripping in Buzz, Goon, Crunch, Moose and the rest of the gang.

Rebel succeeded in creating a new mythology of violence with its own totems—the car and the switchblade—and laid down codes for a new form of ritual combat among adolescents. The knife fight and chickie run are as formal in their ceremonies as any *rites de passage*. In America, there were sharp increases in neighborhood knife fights; Japanese youth obsessed with shuaisei (selfhood) reenacted the cults of *Rebel* so ferociously in the streets of Tokyo that further showings of the film were banned; in London, despite the English censors who cut "inflammatory sequences" like the conversation between Jim and Buzz on the cliff, hospitals were deluged with victims of the English version of chickie runs—head-on challenges.

As a result of disturbances at the early showings of *Rebel*, the film was banned altogether in some countries in the fifties. When it was finally shown in Mexico in 1960, it had to be withdrawn, as *Variety* reported, because "of disturbances in nabe theaters." *Rebel* was banned in Spain, but smuggled prints were screened at secret showings and an underground cult developed. The Spanish censors finally gave the film a permit in 1964, when *Rebel Without a Cause* was voted Spain's film of the year, winning against *La Notte, The Umbrellas of Cherbourg* and *The Cardinal.*

Stewart Stern got a first-hand look at the international reactions to *Rebel* when he traveled around the world to research *The Ugly American*: "Wherever we went, people would come up and start talking about *Rebel.* There was one boy in the Philippines who could speak no English at all, but he had memorized the entire screenplay. I met his parents, and they said he was *crazed* with this movie, 'He made us see it. And we want to thank you for it.' And apparently that was the general experience, that the kids found that movie wherever it was allowed. *Parents would be taken to that film by their children.* It was as if the children were saying, 'I can't say this to you, but this is really what I mean.'"

While youth was reacting to "Rebel," some critics objected to the "Without a Cause."

". . . It would seem that the juvenile gangs of the West Coast have been organized by Cocteau," said *The Nation.* "Rich kids playing dreamy games of suicide, floating hand in hand through ruined mansions, doomed children reading one another through mists of alcohol, comic books and police car sirens." This seems consistent with the standard intellectual *hauteur* toward the "JD" movies of the fifties—*The Wild One, Blackboard Jungle, Crime in the Streets, Green-Eyed Blonde, Running Wild* and hundreds of others trying to cash in on the "lost generation."

"Juvenile delinquents" and intellectuals seemed paradoxically to agree, however, that Jimmy's death underlined the pointlessness of life. Depending on your viewpoint, it either reinforced the prevailing strain of European *Weltschmerz* or suggested that a bit of the old ultraviolence was just the medicine to cure the teenage blues.

As *The New Republic* commented:

It is significant that there is little interest in what Dean might have gone on to do if he had not died. His death was a fitting culmination to his life, senseless, but justified by the story. There was no future for Dean, just as there was no future for Bellow's, Gold's or Baldwin's characters. These contemporary heros are not the intellectual nihilists of Turgenev or Dostoevsky; they are rather the results of the naturalistic-existential schools of writing. In all instances, they are without direction and aims, dominated by the utter helplessness of their positions and unwilling, or unable, to win even one victory.

It's a credit to Jimmy that critics did begin to suggest that because of this "boy who wants to do good but who is confused by a world that doesn't make sense," the term "juvenile delinquent" had become inadequate. Many did sympathize with that feeling of helplessness Jimmy represented, and in search of a term to describe the huge unnamed forces he was fighting, *The New Republic* turned—perhaps influenced by the "sky high poetry" of the planetarium—to the cosmos:

In *Rebel Without a Cause*, rebellion is made not against parents or law but against the universal conditions of life. The children do not rebel against the bad or the good, but against ALL. In search of love, they are acquitted of any breach of the law or morality.

In James Dean, his movie roles, his life and death, there is a general lack of identity. He is supposedly like all the rest of us and to criticize him would be self-criticism.

Perhaps only one critic understood the complexity and significance of Jimmy and his film. And that was François Truffaut:

In James Dean, today's youth discovers itself. Less for the reasons usually advanced: violence, sadism, hysteria, pessimism, cruelty and filth, than for others infinitely more simple and commonplace: modesty of feeling, continual fantasy life, moral purity without relation to everyday morality but all the more rigorous, eternal adolescent love of tests and trials, intoxication, pride, and regret at feeling oneself "outside" society, refusal and desire to become integrated and, finally, acceptance—or refusal—of the world as it is.

Jimmy's death became inseparable from *Rebel Without a Cause*; this movie literally became his epitaph. When *Rebel* was released, only the mythic James Dean remained. His personality now not only dominated the movie, it possessed it with incorruptible grace and extended its meaning, not as a metaphor for violence, but for Jimmy himself.

Jimmy had said that death came in threes, and in the reality of *Rebel*, his death completed the film's own trinity: Buzz, Plato and Jim Stark. Stewart Stern had originally ended the film with the death of Jim Stark, but the final script was changed. "I wanted Jim to be killed at the end when he ran out with the bullets. He was supposed to be gunned down too," said Stewart. "It just exploded into gunfire; nothing was making sense anymore. And his father ran over to him to see if he was alright and started talking to him and said, 'Listen . . . you know . . . it was just, God, I didn't know what was happening. There was no hint. I didn't know how you really felt.' And Jim said, 'I don't want to talk.' But the father said, 'We *have* to talk. My God, all this time we hadn't talked. Now don't turn me away.' And Jim said, 'But I'm busy, I'm busy. I can't talk.' The father said, 'What are you busy about?' And Jim was going to say, 'I'm busy dying,' and drop dead. I thought what could be more enigmatic than that, to die on your parents and not tell them why."

"The actual tragedies of life," Cocteau wrote in *Les Enfants Terribles*, "bear no relation to one's preconceived ideas. One is always bewildered by their simplicity . . . the element of the bizarre in them."

Among Jimmy's close friends and those who worked with him, the reaction to his death was shock and a sense of the inevitable. It was something monstrous, yet expected.

In New York, Lee Strasberg took the news of Jimmy's death without emotion. Only later did he let himself feel what it meant: "I saw Jimmy Dean in *Giant* the other night, and I must say that . . . [he weeps] You see, that's what I was afraid of . . . [a long pause] . . . I cried. I hadn't cried when I heard of his death; Jack Garefein called me from Hollywood the night it happened, and I didn't cry. It somehow was what I expected . . . As soon as you reach a certain place, there it goes, the drunkenness and the rest of it, as if, now that you've really made it, something happens which is just terrifying. I don't know what to do. You can tell somebody, 'Go to a psychiatrist,' or 'Go here' or 'Go there,' but in the meantime there is the waste."

Others reacted at first with stunned incomprehension and grief. At Warners, George Stevens and some of the cast were watching rushes from *Giant*. Jimmy was on the screen when the call came from the guard house. "Stevens answered the phone and, God, I'd thought his son had died," Carroll Baker told Steffi Skolsky later. Elizabeth Taylor, who'd become very good friends with Jimmy, collapsed and was in a state of shock for days.

Dennis Hopper claims that Jimmy knew he was going to die. "He came over and said goodbye to me. He'd gone to a monastery for a three-day retreat and came back wearing a suit and tie. He asked me if

I'd ever read a story by Mark Twain called 'The Stranger.'"

Barbara Glenn got a phone call from Martin Landau, and before he could even tell her, she knew what he was going to say.

"I couldn't say how much I anticipated his death," Barbara said, "but he knew that was the way I felt. I don't think on that particular day he set out to commit suicide. I never expected him to get on his bike and say, 'I'm never coming back.' But I knew it was imminent. I knew some day he was never coming back. Sure, that day it was an accident. Just like any other day it would have been an accident."

One of the more bizarre aspects of Jimmy's death is that he died in a cosmetic state of premature old age. His hair had been shaved back from his forehead for his role in *Giant*. It's almost as if his identification with the aging Jett Rink had been so total that it had actually brought him to the end of his life.

Odd words surround Jimmy's life: his schoolteacher India Nose, his first mentor, James DeWeerd; Jim STARK is an anagram for Cal TRASK. Jackie Curtis has pointed out in the names of his aunt and uncle words of buried advice: MARK US WIN SLOW, OR TENSE.

"Little Bastard" on the way to Salinas. The last photograph of Jimmy.

The strangest of all names was the last, the one he collided with: TURN UP SEED.

Among mystics and primitives, speed, "fast traveling" and "magic flight" also bestow the power to become invisible and transcend the earthly dimension. In his love of speed, Jimmy had literally become invisible, and Donald Turnupseed was the first person not to see him.

In *Rites and Symbols of Initiation*, Mircea Eliade wrote, "The desire for absolute freedom . . . the desire to break the bonds that keep him tied to earth and to free him from his limitations, is one of man's essential nostalgias. The break from plane to plane effected by flight signifies an act of transcendence . . . it proves one has transcended the human condition, has risen above it, by transmuting it through an excess of spirituality . . . the longing to see the human body after the manner of a spirit."

The faster and further you go, the harder it is to stop when you come to the edge. Jimmy had been working so hard and winning so long, it seemed he would never go over. His fantasies had become reality, and that hoary old specter Jimmy had so relentlessly pursued finally came to take him away. The gap between the White Bear and the stars closed on the road to Salinas, where Jimmy's first mythic film had begun, as he disappeared in a silver car on a grey road at dusk.

Ride! Ride like the devil; ride for your
life, man! Stick spur in your pony's flank,
and press hard and press long; lean low over
your saddle bow–speak quick, sharp words of
encouragement and command to your beast, and
ride for your life! for behind you, like the
waves of a mad sea, are ten thousand frightened
steers, and you are scarce the length of
your horse ahead of them . . .

–from C. C. Post, *Ten Years a Cowboy*

CHAPTER THIRTEEN

Lone Star State
May–September 1955

Jimmy as Jett Rink;
working with Liz Taylor and Rock Hudson;
conflicts with George Stevens;
what Jimmy had planned for his future.

J immy Dean grew up on legends of the Old West: Zane Grey, Lone Ranger radio serials, Cisco Kid comics. From Fairmount, the West seemed like a child's paradise, where cowboys lived a perpetual adventure in a pre-adult world.

At a costume party for his seventh birthday, Jimmy was dressed in furry chaps, cowboy hat and a scarf around his neck. Photographs show him with a tiny cowboy doll and later sitting on a pony, ready to ride into the imaginary West away from civilization and conformity like Huck Finn escaping to the wilderness: "I got to light out for the territory ahead of the rest, because Aunt Sally she's going to adopt me and civilize me, and I can't stand it. I been there before."

Jimmy had always wanted to star in a western. Like the solitary Little Prince on his Asteroid B-612, the cowboy is accountable to no one; he is the forger of his own fantasies in his kingdom of sagebrush.

The cowboy is a logical extension of the character Jimmy had been developing in his first two films—the idealist who refuses the adult world, the outlaw in spite of himself, a wanderer, avenger and loner. Before his death, Jimmy had been cast as Billy the Kid in *The Left-Handed Gun*, but the closest he came to playing a Western hero was his portrayal of Jett Rink in *Giant*.

George Stevens, who directed *Giant*, also thought of the cowboy as a romantic hero, a "kind of coming together of heroic forces . . . the lone rider and the Knights of the Round Table with Sir Galahad riding out in front." Stevens had begun his career in Hollywood as a cameraman at the Hal Roach Studios, turning out three-reelers like *No Man's Law* and *Rock-a-Bye Cowboy*. In *Shane*, the movie Stevens directed just before *Giant*, he had begun to bring the new psychological and social interpretations to bear on the old legend of the West.

In *Giant*, Stevens' romanticism was tempered with a more skeptical viewpoint. He deliberately cast the film with actors who had never appeared in westerns before, and to show how far he was willing to go to avoid stereotypes, had thought of using Richard Burton for the part of Jett Rink.

Jimmy had never read Edna Ferber's novel *Giant*, but envisioned Jett Rink as the sort of Western character he'd always wanted to play. Our only indication of Jimmy's fantasies after *Rebel* is this portrayal of Jett Rink—the hero in space, a cowboy angel who penetrates the mystery of a new world.

"The story of *Giant* to me," said George Stevens, "was about people . . . people involved in a race, which is a very American thing, and though Texas takes the blame, it's an excellent opportunity to take a look at the American mind."

Of all Jimmy Dean's films, *Giant* was closest to the mainstream American fantasies on which Hollywood was built. The movie was more than a look at America through the eyes of Texas, it was a glimpse of Hollywood seen through its own tired lens—a Hollywood fallen victim to the perversions of its own dreams, to its gross delusions of grandeur. "What littleness is all this bigness hiding?" asks a character in the novel, and the movie business answered when it made an unintentional autobiography out of the book.

Quest, adventure and revenge are the main themes of traditional westerns. But *Giant* is an interminable hybrid, neither a good old western nor a social exploration of the new American West. Without the traditional "hero" as a focal point, the film ambles aimlessly through dynasties, fortunes and social upheavals. As American as it is in its panoramic sweep, in its three hours and eighteen minutes running time it is more like a Russian production of *War and Peace*.

One reason for this exhaustive all-inclusion may be Stevens' partnership with *Giant*'s author Edna Ferber, which probably prevented his taking liberties with the story. But another is Stevens' own exhaustive Biblical method of production. Like his later movie, *The Greatest Story Ever Told, Giant* is a three-ring circus in which the main attraction, James Dean, is nearly lost among ephemeral distractions.

Stevens began putting *Giant* together in 1953, but didn't actually start shooting until spring 1955. As an independent producer, he couldn't afford to buy the best seller outright; so, in an unprecedented move, he offered Ferber a share of the profits in lieu of an advance and formed a three-way partnership along with producer Henry Ginsberg. The long script was written by Fred Gill and Ivan Moffat, while Stevens and Ginsberg went about raising the $5,400,000 it took to finance the actual production.

"After three or four months of work on the script, I took it over to Jack Warner to ask if he'd back it," Stevens said. "They had absolutely nothing going at their studio. Jack read it and said, 'I'll put up a million.' We spent three million and then had a meeting with Jack, and he said, 'How much more?' I said, 'Two and a half million.' He

The space between Jimmy and George Stevens was as big as the Reata.

asked me if I could stick to my budget and I said, 'Sure.' Then he reached into his pocket and pulled out a check for two and a half million and said, 'Here, I thought that was just about what you needed.'"

The partnership paid off. *Giant* grossed seven million dollars the first year it was released and was Warner's biggest moneymaker until *My Fair Lady.* With *Giant*'s Byzantine plot and bombastic moral messages, it may be helpful to outline the story just to *locate* Jimmy in this Saragossa saga.

The movie begins with Bick Benedict (Rock Hudson) traveling by train (progress entering the wilderness) to Virginia, where he plans to buy a racing horse. In this "old world" atmosphere, he falls in love with the racehorse owner's daughter and two weeks later brings this "fine filly," Leslie (Elizabeth Taylor), and the new horse back to his huge Reata Ranch in Texas.

"Texas . . . is that a state of mind?" Leslie asks her new husband when she arrives at Reata, whose Gothic mansion rises surrealistically in the middle of three million acres of flat, dusty land. She soon realizes this is not the romantic West of legend.

Jett won't sell out to the land barons.

Liz Taylor acts as a sort of Greek chorus for the audience reaction to Texas and to land baron Benedict, who counts all his possessions in the millions. She is horrified by the grotesque parody of opulence and is outspoken when confronted by the philistine, macho world in which her husband lives, with its medieval structure of feudal millionaires and poor Mexicans.

Bick introduces Leslie to his unmarried sister, Luz (Mercedes McCambridge), who actually runs the ranch. She disapproves of Leslie, and goes so far as to show the newlyweds to separate bedrooms. A short while later, she takes out the new horse and is promptly killed in a riding accident.

Luz's will opens a Pandora's box by leaving ten acres of scrub land within the Reata Ranch to Jett Rink (James Dean), the Benedicts' surly ranch hand. The family lawyers try to dissuade Jett from accepting his inheritance, but he insists on keeping it out of sentimentality and pride.

Meanwhile, Leslie has discovered a seriously ill baby in the nearby Mexican shantytown. On her way back from nursing the child (who grows up to be Angel, played by Sal Mineo), she stops her 1924 Duesenburg at Jett's "Little Reata" ranch and he invites her in. Later, as she steps back into her car, her foot slips into the mud, and Jett notices a thick, black ooze. Based on this telltale sign, he finances a rig and starts drilling.

Just as everyone comes to think that Jett will have to sell out because he's broke, he strikes oil, becomes a millionaire, forms the Jettexas Company, builds a motel-airport complex and generally takes over the town.

Thirty years pass, and when we next see Jett he is a seedy-looking alcoholic, still living an extravagant life and driving around town in a fancy white convertible. During this time, Bick Benedict's children have grown up. Jordy (Dennis Hopper) wants to become a doctor, won't have any part of the ranch and marries a Mexican, and Luz II (Carroll Baker) wants to go to Hollywood and gets involved with Jett Rink.

At a testimonial dinner in his honor, Jett insults Jordy's wife, gets into a fight with Bick and finally collapses in a drunken stupor before the huge assembly. Everyone leaves and Jett is left mumbling incoherently to himself.

The film ends anticlimactically: Bick gets thrown in a garbage can by a racist luncheonette owner, and Angel (killed in the Korean War) is buried as the flag waves and the camera pans the faces of pathetic Tex-Mex children.

Most of *Giant*'s exterior scenes were shot on location in Marfa, Texas, where the cast and crew of two hundred fifty people lived during July and August. Marfa had no "on location" glamour. It was just as awful as it appeared in the movie, a veritable desert where it hadn't rained in five years.

"We'd get up about sun-up, 5 A.M. or so," said production manager Tom Andre, "and work all day until it got dark. It was hotter than Hades out there. Then we'd go back to the hotel, shower, have some dinner, watch the dailies, then try to get some sleep. The temperature would go down at night, but it didn't feel much cooler because it was so damn humid and we didn't have any air conditioning.

"There was only one hotel in town, the Picaña, and we had to sleep three and four to a room. The stars got to live in houses that we'd rented in town."

Stevens' biggest departure from the book was in casting Jimmy in the part of Jett Rink. The character, based on a real-life Texas wildcatter, Clem McCarthy, was a big, beefy, brash man as simple, wild and huge as his home state. Physically and temperamentally, Jimmy couldn't have been more different. Nevertheless, he went about his characterization in his usual intense way, soaking up authentic Texas types on which he could model his part. As he said in a Warner Brothers press release about the progress of the movie: "An actor should thoroughly understand the character he is portraying. There's no better way than trying to be that person in the house, away from the camera. I developed a program of understanding Jett Rink and doing the things he'd be likely to do. I didn't want any jarring notes in my characterization. Jett was a victim of his position in life. I wanted to play him sympathetically."

As soon as Jimmy got to Marfa, he got into his "shitkicker" costume of cowboy boots, Levi's, vest, denim shirt and ten gallon hat. He never changed clothes off camera or on, until the last couple of weeks of shooting when he began transforming himself into an aging Jett Rink.

As Jett, Jimmy took on a regional drawl, taught himself how to lasso and twirl a lariat, ride like a ranger, strum cowboy songs on a guitar and hunt jack rabbits with dialogue coach Bob Hinkle. His Texas patina even took on the surly pride of Ferber's original character. At dinner one night, Jane Withers, who played the girl next door, suggested he might change the shirt he'd been wearing for two weeks. He told her it was the shirt he liked to wear, and when she offered to wash it for him, he replied, "Thank you, ma'am, but I like it the way it is."

During the five weeks in Marfa, a cattle town with a population of about 3500, Jimmy was genuinely irritated when newspaper reporters and photographers picked him out from the local ranch hands. Unlike *Eden* and *Rebel, Giant* was filmed with an open set policy. There was a guard at the gate, but he was there more to hand out publicity information than to screen visitors, and sometimes there'd be as many as a thousand people watching a scene being filmed.

The press roamed the set freely, but Jimmy would only talk to them if he wasn't concentrating on his work. One woman reporter who wandered up at just the wrong moment implored, "But, *Mr. Dean*, I've come all the way from New York just to talk with you."

"And *I*, madame," Jimmy testily replied, "have come all this way just to act."

The mutual contempt Jimmy and Rock Hudson held for each other was not far from the on-camera hostility between Jett and Bick. Jimmy had little respect for Hudson's wooden acting, and Hudson resented Jimmy's sullen attitude. They had the bad luck of having to share a house. Some fifteen years later, Hudson admitted to the *Hollywood Reporter* that he didn't particularly like Jimmy Dean:

"He and I and Chill Wills lived in a rented house together for three months while we were doing "Giant" in Texas, and although we each went more or less our own way, Dean was hard to be around.

"He hated George Stevens, didn't think he was a good director, and he was always angry and full of contempt."

Dean, of course, was never groomed nor bent as a locker room personality, but Hudson still recalls that Dean "never smiled. He was sulky, and he had no manners. I'm not that concerned with manners—I'll take them where I find them—but Dean didn't have 'em.

"And he was rough to do a scene with for reasons that only an actor can appreciate. While doing a scene, in the giving and taking, he was just a taker. He would suck everything out and never give back."

Established Hollywood stars like Liz Taylor and Rock Hudson are

accustomed to being the center of attention off camera and on, and while Liz Taylor worked with Jimmy's intuitive scene-stealing, Hudson resented Jimmy's habit of upstaging him every time they acted together.

In their first scene, Jimmy plays on the personal animosity between the two men by not responding to Bick Benedict's invective. Instead, he mumbles, hangs his head, shuffles and pulls down his hat—a silent, threatening gesture that closes him off and contains his fury. Strasberg saw the implicit menace in this simple device as an indication of Jimmy's ability to create the physical language of the character: "Rock Hudson comes over and leans on the car, and Jimmy just watched and then he pulled that hat down. Well, that wasn't just acting. You see every actor doing it now, at any odd moment, pulling his hat down if he doesn't know what to do. Now it's become a style. But there was nothing loose about it, nothing casual, when Jim did it. Inside, he was saying, 'Gee, that son of a bitch,' but he couldn't quite say it. So he pulled down that hat. All these things were marvelously expressive. When he did that 'I'll be seein' ya,' with his hand, there was a threat and a promise."

Stevens claimed that he was satisfied with Jimmy's portrayal of Jett Rink, but remembered that Jimmy clearly wasn't satisfied with the part.

"He was too good for it," said Stevens. "Anybody could have played that part." But Jimmy is not so much miscast in *Giant* as he is misused. Like the elaborate sets, the great herds of longhorn and the mansion with its doll-house facade, Jett Rink is just another piece of furniture in this multimillion-dollar yarn.

Giant is meant to be a story about transition and social change. Jett Rink precipitates these changes while the Benedict family is shown trying to absorb them. "The *Giant* film is about change," said director George Stevens, "and the point is people *don't* change—after maturity anyway. Most of all, *Giant* is about what parents expect of their children, and in the end you realize what you expect from your children is most likely what you are not going to get."

Jett Rink is meant to be the catalyst in this transition. In his monograph on George Stevens, Donald Richie wrote, "We see in Jett Rink the little boy in *Shane* grown up, and *Giant* is seen through Jett's eyes the way *Shane* is seen through Brandon de Wilde's." But *Giant* is not clearly seen from Jett's point of view, because Jimmy was never permitted to focus or develop the personal dimensions he wanted in the part. Stevens tried to keep Jimmy under his autocratic control. He wanted him to be on time, merely act his lines, relate to the other actors—in short, to be just like the rest of the "professionals."

Jimmy followed Stevens' direction, but still managed to supply the unexpected. "Rock Hudson, Elizabeth Taylor, Mercedes McCambridge, Chill Wills . . ." wrote a reviewer in *The Nation*, "these are people who will neither astonish nor disappoint. They do what they are told and make up in experience for what they lack in imagination. For excitement, Stevens added James Dean and, as always, Dean supplied it."

Stevens recognized Jimmy's universal appeal—"Jimmy was youth and had the free faculty of youth to belong anywhere"—but he failed to utilize all the skills Jimmy brought to the part. In fact, he rejected them. Jimmy felt he knew what motivated Jett Rink and wanted to incorporate these insights into a set of personal mannerisms for the part. But the improvisations he suggested to Stevens were either turned down or cut during the final edit of the movie.

"One of my favorite scenes never made it into the movie," Dennis Hopper said. "Luz has left ten acres of land to Jett. Bick and the lawyers call him in, and Jett figures since Luz was his only ally on the ranch, they're gonna get rid of him—so he comes in with the attitude, 'You can't fire me, I quit!' But they're saying, 'C'mon in, baby, we *love* you!' And the scene plays something like this:

"The lawyers start to talk about Luz and how nice she was, and he says, yes, she always treated me well—and then they tell him, well, she left you this little shit-piece of land, so we're gonna do you a real big favor and give you five hundred, no, one thousand dollars for it!

"And he won't sell. He won't sell the land back. Now, what you see in the movie, he gets up, then it cuts to Hudson's face, then it cuts to Jimmy at the door, he tips his hat and leaves, okay?

"In between that, man, is probably the most beautiful moment that's ever been put on film. Cause he gets up and looks around at all these lawyers and powerful guys, and now *he's* a landowner too, *he's* one of them. He looks around like maybe they're gonna give him a cigar, or he wants to shake their hands . . . so he takes his bottle out of his back pocket and wants to give them a drink. There are no lines, it's just behavior, as he walks from one guy to the next until he ends up at the door. He realizes what's happening so he puts the bottle away, and when he tips his hat, it's with a 'see you fuckers later.'

"Now there were millions of these kinds of things in the film, and that's basically what the fight between Stevens and Jimmy was about. Jimmy wanted to act it out *fully*."

Jimmy felt that what he had developed from the depth of his personal understanding of Jett Rink was being sabotaged, and he fought diligently to preserve the integrity of his characterization. Though Stevens disagreed with his interpretations, he basically liked Jimmy and tried to understand what drove him: "I'd get so mad at him, and he'd stand there, blinking behind his glasses after having been guilty of some bit of preposterous behavior, and revealing by his very cast of defiance that he felt some sense of unworthiness. Yet the very next second the glasses would come off, a smile flashes and his whole being is transformed. You were disturbed by him. Now you are dedicated to him."

Stevens is known for his elaborate productions, and *Giant* was no exception. A Christmas tree was acquired in the middle of August from the Sequoia National Forest, and transportation alone cost five hundred dollars. Two snakes (never used) were captured on a three-day safari, and some forty-one hundred head of cattle were used as extras. Jimmy displayed his frustration amid this extravagance in characteristically prankish ways. "Once I got ready to shoot an outdoor sequence," Stevens said, "and I saw a red convertible parked in the middle of a herd of cattle. I didn't have to be told, I knew it was Jimmy."

Jimmy was also nervous. For the first time, he was "the runt in a litter of professionals," as Mercedes McCambridge said about him. One of the most evocative and personal moments on the set occurred while filming a scene between Jimmy and Liz Taylor. He was so aware of her status as a star that he just couldn't loosen up and do the scene.

"He was doing this scene with Elizabeth Taylor," Dennis Hopper recalled, "the scene where he has the rifle over his shoulder and he's going to ask her in for tea. He just got the land. That's the first scene he had with Liz Taylor. At that time, there wasn't anybody who didn't think she was queen of the movies, and Jimmy was really fuckin' nervous.

"They did take after take, and it just wasn't going right. He was really getting fucked up. Really nervous. Suddenly he walked away from the set toward the football field where all those people were standing. He wasn't relating to them or anything. He just walked over, he stood there, unzipped his pants, pulled out his cock and took a piss. Then he put his cock back, zipped up his pants, walked back to the set and said, 'Okay, shoot.' And they did the scene in one take.

"On the way back from location, I said, 'Jimmy, I've seen you do some way out things before, but what was *that?*'

"'I was nervous,' he said. 'I'm a Method actor. I work through my senses. If you're nervous, your senses can't reach your subconscious and that's that—you just can't work. So I figured if I could piss in front of those two thousand people, man, and I could be cool, I figured if I could do that, I could get in front of that camera and do just anything, anything at all.'"

When this scene opens, Leslie is on her way back to Reata from the Mexican shantytown. Looking down from the windmill he uses to pump water, Jett sees her and fires a shot in the air. She stops the car, and he invites her in for "tea." Jett's cabin is like a play house, and there is a fairy-tale loneliness about his excitement at having such a

Jett's playhouse, like the single rooms Jimmy called home.

beautiful lady come to visit. His attempts at domesticity, the flower pots on the window ledge and the adolescent discomfort he tries to cure with several secret belts from his flask are all aspects of the real Jimmy. The shack itself, with a copy of *How to Speak Masterful English* lying on the table, is not unlike all those single rooms Jimmy had called home: the Iroquois Hotel, his tiny apartment on Sixty-eighth Street, the dressing room on the Warner lot and his loftlike house in Sherman Oaks.

The scene is charged with sexual undercurrents. Jimmy and Liz react to each other, and we want something to happen between these two charismatic superstars. But their relationship is never developed. Stevens thought of Jett Rink as a "threat" in the movie, essentially a sexual threat. But the implications are never carried through, and as a result, Jett's conflict with Bick loses some of its edge.

Jett Rink takes the story of *Giant* out of the living room and into the earthiness of ranch life. As he paces off his ten little acres, relishes his barren "Little Reata" and, drenched with oil, bursts into laughter as his well finally delivers, Jimmy's instinctual communion with the earth shines through.

The central symbol in *Giant* is oil, a colossal metaphor for money and sex, a primeval power that can transform men, forcing change and eventual decomposition upon those who profit from it. Jett erects his one derrick, and as it erupts like a liquid libido, it embodies that mystery Freud called "a boiling cauldron of seething excitation."

Covered with crude black oil, Jimmy looks elemental and heroic, like a creature just arisen from some dark lagoon. It is this rich, magical element that transforms Jett into a veritable monster, a Midas who has lost his innocence and simple harmony with the earth. For every wish fulfilled there is a hidden curse, and by the time Jett achieves what the Benedicts have, he has lost his innocence. He is the little boy from *Shane* grown old, a drunken, middle-aged boor undone by a reality that he never really comprehends.

Critics of the movie have described Jimmy's cosmetic aging in *Giant* as a false note. Actually he ages more convincingly than either Rock Hudson or Liz Taylor, who show no signs of change over the thirty-year span of the movie except for their hair, which turns blue. Jimmy is most effective as the middle-aged Jett Rink in his shades and pencil-thin moustache. In a plush nightclub booth, trying pathetically to seduce Luz II, the daughter of the woman he loved, Jimmy as Jett parodies a vulgar Bel Air tycoon, a Howard Hughes / Jack Warner type, loudly holding court at Romanoff's.

In his portrayal of Jett Rink, Jimmy managed to incorporate his essential persona: the outsider trying to live in a society that does not want him even when he mimics its behavior. As one reviewer said: "A virtuoso performance by Dean, whose Jett Rink is a willful, brilliant variation on the character he made his own and died for—the baffled, tender, violent adolescent rejected by the world he rejects."

George Stevens thought of Jimmy as an adolescent who tried to infect the movie with his daydreams: "I used to feel that he was a disturbed boy, tremendously dedicated to some intangible beacon of his own, and neither he nor anyone else might ever know what it was. I used to feel this because at times when he fell quiet and thoughtful, as if inner-bidden to dream about something, an odd and unconscious sweetness would light up his countenance. At such times, and because I knew he had been motherless since early childhood and had missed a lot of the love that makes boyhood jell, I would come to believe that he was still waiting for some lost tenderness."

Twenty years later, Stevens admits that Jimmy's "inner-bidden" understanding of how to play Jett Rink should not have been so autocratically dismissed.

"Whenever I do a film, I always feel that *I* know the characters and the actor is just acquainted with them, because I have the whole script and relate to the whole thing. I had one scene with Jimmy—when the Benedicts give this big party for Leslie—and I told Jimmy, 'Go over toward her and as you pass the bar, pour yourself a big drink and drink it down. Pour yourself another one if you like.' And he said to me, 'Look, I have this flask in my pocket. Why don't I go over to the bar and get a glass and pour the stuff from my flask?' And I said, 'Forget it, Jimmy. It's *their* booze. Pour yourself a big drink of *their* stuff.'

"And I just realized a few years ago, that what Jimmy wanted to do would have been the cutest bit in the movie. His point was that it had to do with pride—he was *too proud* to take a drink from their table. Usually I think I know a character better than anyone, but what I told Jimmy Dean was damn wrong. His idea was too damn smart, and he didn't explain it to me, so I didn't get it then. But he really *knew* that character, and that's the best tribute I can pay to his talent as an actor."

The most difficult part of the movie for Jimmy was the final banquet scene. His impersonation in this scene never really worked and remains an embarrassment. It was simply too much to expect, even of a well-practiced chameleon like Jimmy.

"Jimmy could handle any scene that he had to do," said Stevens. "But when it came to the banquet scene, where he had to make that drunken speech, he asked me if we could work on it together. So every night after everyone else stopped working, we'd go into that empty auditorium and rehearse it for about an hour. We did that for seven nights before we finally shot the scene. And at that point, it was the end of the film, and it really depended on him doing that scene. After all we'd put in the picture, we couldn't get to that scene and not have him able to do it. I'd do the scene like a ham actor, making all the points, and then he'd do it. But it was entirely foreign to anything

. . . Jimmy seems to disappear before our eyes.   *A sullen giant in the Lone Star State.*

that should have been coming out of his mouth. It was a very strange scene that a lot of actors would have said just couldn't work."

In Jimmy's final appearance, the speaker introduces Jett as "an all-American boy . . . a legend in his own time . . . his face shone with a special light . . . the goals toward which he was working, planning, striving . . ." It seems an appropriate eulogy to an audience who saw the film after Jimmy's death. When the speaker stands aside to let Jett have the floor and make his speech to the cheering and whistling crowd, he is so stoned that he starts to get up, mumbles a word or two, then passes out "like a light," his face thudding into the table.

Jett seems to dissolve before our eyes, mumbling off into another world—an old man who has achieved everything he wanted, stumbling gracelessly away. In this scene, Jimmy's voice was so indistinct that the original sound track could not be used. Since Jimmy died before a new sound track could be recorded, an anonymous actor dubbed in the lines. Jimmy's last words were not even his own. He trails off into silence.

Giant took a year to cut and edit. Stevens called it "a terrific embroidery job," and as he watched the rushes, Jimmy seemed to him like a defiant spirit: "I spent six hours today with Jimmy Dean, as I have most of the days in these past two months. He is always up there on the projection-room screen in front of me, challenging me not to like any part of him in the picture. And there is no part of Jimmy I don't like, no part of him that hasn't always the attraction that goes with complete naturalness. Maybe it is the way he sidles next to someone, chin hugging his chest, then squints up out of the corner of his eye, mumbling a greeting. Or maybe the way he can run a boyish giggle right through his words or, without losing an iota of expressiveness, violate all the dramatic precepts and persistently present only his back to the camera."

Jimmy's contract after *Giant* called for nine pictures in the next six years. He'd told a reporter he didn't want "to burn myself out . . . I've made three pictures in the last two years." But although Warner Brothers had promised him the year off in 1956, it didn't look like his work would leave much time for relaxation. He had already been cast in two movies—as Billy the Kid in *The Left-Handed Gun* and as Rocky Graziano in *Somebody Up There Likes Me*.

Giant was the third and final film in which Jimmy starred, and though he was stifled in his efforts to fully realize the part, his skill was recognized by the novel's author, Edna Ferber.

"James Dean was a genius," she said. "I don't think there's another actor in the world who could have portrayed Jett as well as he did. But like most geniuses, Dean suffered from success poisoning."

Success poisoning was something she had invented for Jett Rink, a victim of vicuña overcoats and an insatiable hunger for power. Like Jett, Jimmy Dean's great energies sprang from an ingrained American dream that the absolute can be found immaculately present at the summit of material power. He, too, believed in success and his involvement in *Giant* was one of his own making. He believed in a Hollywood which was rapidly dissolving, a Hollywood which he helped to destroy.

Jimmy had also talked with Nick Ray about forming their own production company, hoping he'd learn directing and eventually go on to writing: "Acting is wonderful and immediately satisfying," he told Hedda Hopper, "but my talents lie in directing and, beyond that, my great fear is writing. That's the God. I can't apply the seat of my pants right now. I'm too youthful and silly. I must have some age. I'm in great awe of writing and fearful of it . . . but some day . . ."

Discontent with manipulative directors, Jimmy saw that by directing his own productions he could assemble all his powers into fantastic, visionary creations. At the time of his death, Jimmy and Bill Bast were writing a script for a film Jimmy wanted to make and in which he would star—a film which would supply the classic metaphor for his own mutation—*Dr. Jekyll and Mr. Hyde.*

"Change," Jimmy had written James DeWeerd from New York, "is the nature of genius." And long ago he had written in a teenage scrapbook this definition of genius from Elbert Hubbard, the traveling philosopher introduced to him by DeWeerd:

Genius is only the power of making continuous effort . . . 1. One who offends his time, his country and his relatives, hence any person who's birthday is celebrated throughout the world about one hundred years after he has been crucified, burned, ostracized or otherwise put to death. 2. One who stands at both ends of a perspective, simultaneity of sight; to be one's self plus; to be a synonym and antonym to everything. 3. The ability to act wisely without precedent—the power to do the right thing for the first time. 4. A capacity for putting off hard work.

Giant reveals only isolated flashes of Jimmy Dean. He sits against the parched landscape like an unlucky fisher king waiting for the sound of thunder in a land where wind reigns. Phrasing his words slowly, Jimmy told a writer: "Being an actor is the loneliest thing in the world. The stage is like a religion; you dedicate yourself to it and suddenly you find that you don't have time to see friends, and it's hard for them to understand. You don't see anybody. You're all alone with your concentration and your imagination and that's all you have. You're an actor."

át	sek - ƒ	em	ren - á	pui	en	ba	χeper-ná
Never	doth he fail	in	my name	that	of	Soul.	I have created

t'es - á	ḥená	Nu	em	ren-[á]	pu	en	χeperá	nuk
myself	with	Nu	in	my name		of	Kheperá;	I am

	χu	ámi	χu	gemam
a shining being,	and a dweller in	light	who hath been created

χeper:	em	neter	ḥāu	ṭua - ná
and hath come into existence from	the limbs	of the god.	I have adored

ámu	kekiu	se - áḥá - ná	áakebi	ámennu
those who are in the darkness.	I have made to stand	those who weep,	who hid

ḥrāu-sen	baḳa. - sen	ṭā - k	ná	re - á
their faces,	who had sunk down.	Give thou to me		my mouth

t'eṭu - á	ám - ƒ	sem - á	áb-á	en	unnut - ƒ
[that] I may speak	with it.	May I follow	my heart	at	its season

nebṭet	ḳerḥ	pert - sen	baiu	ṭep	ta	er	árit	merret
of fire	and night.	they come forth	the souls	upon	earth	to	do	the will of

kau - sen	per	ba	en	Áusár	Ani	merer	ka - ƒ
their kas,	cometh .	the soul	of	Osiris	Ani	[to do] the will of	his ka.

–from Wallace Budge,
The Egyptian Book of the Dead

CHAPTER FOURTEEN

Osiris Rising
1955–1974

Hollywood embalms its gods;
the reaction to Jimmy's death; growth of a cult;
the rag and bone trade; the impersonations of James Dean;
Osiris, the Egyptian god of regeneration.

F rom the Babylonian sagas of D. W. Griffith to Cecil B. De Mille's Biblical epics of the fifties, Hollywood's colossal productions have dealt with the "Matter of Egypt" and its cult of the living dead. Through the medium of film Hollywood has always embalmed its idols in light. Bogart, Gary Cooper, Gable, Theda Bara (an anagram for Arab Death), Boris Karloff and countless others live on in "the great company of the gods." As André Bazin writes in *What Is Cinema?*, Hollywood has been dedicated to the "Mummy Complex." Motion pictures are the fulfillment of mankind's essential nostalgia: the preservation of life by the representation of total illusion; an ideal, deathless world.

As a city itself, Hollywood has a curious funereal atmosphere—the suffocating heat of its deserted streets, its hieroglyphic, jewellike lights, the rows of dwellings resembling monuments prepared to house the dead, the morose columns of palms waving like a tide of feathers at an Ananda burial ceremony. Hollywood and Beverly Hills have the appearance of suspended animation. Like a necropolis on the Nile, the air is still and life passes through as if it were a timeless mirage.

It was through Hollywood that James Dean, model, hero and god of youth, became immortal and joined that great assembly of the living dead. By the time *Rebel Without a Cause* opened, the real Jimmy was gone; all that was left was the celluloid image of James Dean to illuminate and possess us with his powerful spirit.

The initial reaction to Jimmy's death—cults that spread throughout the world, the disbelief in his accident and letters to his dead body, the incorporation of his image in a thousand look-alikes —is less a manifestation of hysteria than a profound response to a psychic reality. If his spirit remained so omnipresent, how could Jimmy be dead?

A cult is a phenomenon built on collective will, a confirmation that something of significance has occurred and must be kept alive. After his death, James Dean's admirers created a community in which youth could recognize itself as a separate and vital force. From the first news of his crash, countless rites were performed to preserve the bond between this force and its inspiration.

Jim Bridges, who later directed *Paper Chase*, remembered a ceremony he and his friends enacted to reconnect with James Dean's spirit.

"I was a high school kid in Arkansas on a band tour when I first saw James Dean," said Bridges. "I saw this person on the screen and knew my life was changed. I'd never heard of Dean or Kazan before, but I knew when I walked out of that movie theater that my life was different.

"I was in college when Jimmy died. Some guy came running into the theater where we were working on scenery and started shouting, 'Hey, you all, Jimmmmmy Deyan is deyad,' and we all went to a place called the Polaram and bought lots of booze and got really plastered. We just couldn't stand it. We went down to the river and built a fire and had our own wake. I made an Academy Award out of mud and put it in the fire. Then we had a mud fight and started chanting, 'Give us a sign, give us a sign,' and we all had our shirts off. A dog barked on the side of the hill, so then we knew he was there. . . .

"We took our stage make-up and got ourselves done up for the dramas we would have liked to have seen Dean in. I was Oedipus, blood running down my face . . . I wrote all this into a play called *How Many Times Did You See 'East of Eden'?*, which I hope to make into a feature film."

The cult which began after Jimmy's death awakened and united young people in a bond of recognition, magic and fantasy. An inconsolable sense of loss was intensified by identification with Jimmy. His death became their death, and romantic fantasies about their own immortality overlapped with his.

Fans wrote Jimmy as if he were alive. Those who were certain he had succumbed to the crash looked forward to his "reincarnation," his "resurrection." The press was mystified. "The adoration and virtual canonization of the late James Dean continues to mushroom," reported Dick Williams. "It is one of the phenomena of this celebrity-worshipping era that future anthropologists may study with deep interest."

Some fans insisted that his mutilated but still living body was taken from the wreck and hidden in an institution, disfigured and perhaps half-insane. Eventually he would return again as the Jimmy Dean they knew, and the more fanatical would have been satisfied with a glimpse of him—even in his dismembered state. As one member of the James Dean Death Club told writer Lee Belser in 1956:

"We know where he is, and we've got a lookout there. They keep all the shades down, but one night we got close enough to look through a tear in the blind and we saw him sitting there swathed in bandages. He acted like he wasn't quite in his right mind."

It was obvious this young fanatic truly believed what he was saying. He even took us to one of the cult headquarters where he displayed 40 or 50 candles on a shelf that were lighted each week when the cultists gathered to play wild Wagnerian music and talk in low, exalted tones about James Dean, the nonconformist.

Fan clubs sprang up everywhere, communicating through letters, meetings, magazines and word of mouth. There were twenty-six fan clubs in Indiana alone. New York was headquarters for the largest American club: the James Dean Memory Ring, founded by a group of people who met at the movies, "people who, like Jimmy, say only a few words and then we know we know the same things."

Impromptu meetings were held at the apartment of Mrs. Teresa Brandes. After a letter in a fan magazine, however, mail began pouring in to Mrs. Brandes from as far away as Malta and Russia; so she started corresponding with fans, telling them where to write for more articles and more screenings of Jimmy's films and television work. The club made donations to charity and sent flowers to Jimmy's

grave. Mrs. Brandes faithfully tried to answer all the letters stacked in her closet, but realized there were more than anyone could respond to in a lifetime.

One activity of the Memory Ring was a James Dean look-alike party held every Saturday night. Songwriter Alan Bernstein attended these ceremonies when he was an aspiring actor. "Mrs. Brandes was a very nice, middle-aged Italian lady. Mostly young, hungry actors came. We didn't really have to look like Jimmy, but we all tried anyway. We'd eat and meet girls there, dance . . . we couldn't drink. She had a list of rules starting with 'no profanity, no jealousy, no feeding the dog, etc.'"

Looking like Jimmy became a primary obsession of the early devotees. Roy Schatt, impatient with Jimmy when he knew him in New York, became exasperated with the cult. "*Everybody* started looking like Jimmy. I had nineteen Jimmy Deans on my back after he died, all trying to have me discover them. I didn't discover Jimmy. Nonsense. For a while Steve McQueen hung around my studio, knowing I was a friend of Jimmy's. I told McQueen that he'd never make it. Was I wrong! I told Dean he was lousy and would never get anywhere. I was wrong there too. I still don't think they're good actors."

In 1956, a Pennsylvania high school student received some twenty thousand letters acknowledging him as the Official James Dean Look-alike. Impersonations of Jimmy Dean were so rampant during this period that when Frank Anthony Horton was arrested after a holdup and identified by the victim as "looking like James Dean," charges had to be dropped. In a *Mirror News* article entitled "Suspicious Cops Roust a 'Ghost'," the arresting detective admitted they might have nabbed the wrong man: "After all, there are thousands of kids who look like James Dean and they all seem to be out here. None of them are working either."

Nick Adams was one of the few people to use his acquaintance with Jimmy as a vehicle to further his own ambitions. He enthusiastically bestowed upon himself the mantle of James Dean. Wearing a red jacket and Levi's, he turned up at the premier of *The James Dean Story* in Marion, gave countless interviews for fan magazines and handed out photographs of a car he claimed he and Jimmy had assembled together.

In one story, Adams claimed, "I've got to have cops go by my house every hour and have a loaded gun to prevent my house [full of souvenirs Jimmy had 'given' him] from being ransacked." Adams went on to become "Johnny Yuma" in a television series called "The Rebel" and died in February 1968 from an overdose of drugs (paraldehyde and tranquilizers).

The movie industry tried to pursue a "business as usual" manner while the cult grew. In 1956, Jimmy was nominated as Best Actor for his performance in *East of Eden*, the first time an actor had been given this distinction posthumously in the history of the Motion Picture Academy. In 1957, Jimmy was nominated for a second "Oscar," this time as Best Actor for his performance in *Giant*. On both occasions, however, the Academy refrained from awarding a "ghost" the final prize.

Jimmy did win two posthumous awards for his performance in *Eden*. In December 1955, he won the Council of Motion Picture Organizations' first Audience Awards election for Best Performance of the Year, along with Jennifer Jones. The audience at the banquet in the Beverly Hilton Hotel stood for a moment of silence to honor his memory. And in February, Jimmy's grandparents, Charles and Emma Dean, flew to Hollywood from Fairmount (their first plane trip) to accept a gold medal presented by *Photoplay* magazine in recognition of their readers' selection of James Dean as Best Actor of 1955.

Warner Brothers was concerned about what effect Jimmy's death might have on the success of his pictures. The sudden death of a star had in the past caused unpredictable reactions: the contrived hysteria which followed Rudolph Valentino's death helped sell his unreleased films, but the deaths of Fatty Arbuckle and Jean Harlow had proved fatal at the box office.

Rumors spread that Warner Brothers participated in sensationalizing Jimmy's death by insinuating that he might still be alive. But the evidence shows that, if anything, Warners wanted to lay the whole matter to rest. The advertising and promotion had already been prepared for *Rebel* by the time Jimmy died, and was released as originally planned. Warners was uncertain how to approach the publicity for *Giant* and went so far as to consult a psychologist to avoid exploitation of the James Dean cult.

The first indication that the phenomenon was getting out of hand was evident to Warners by January 1956. In October the studio had been swamped with letters expressing an almost hysterical resentment at Jimmy's untimely death. Then followed a brief lull which the professionals assumed to be the traditional prelude to obscurity. By the end of December, however, there was a mysterious increase in mail and a change in content—the letters taking on a more spiritual overtone. In January more than three thousand letters came in, and by July the amount had risen to seven thousand per month. By the first anniversary of Jimmy's death, Warners had received over fifty thousand letters from fans all over the world.

"Most of Dean's fan mail was foreign," said Bob Frederick, who handled mail at the time. "A lot of it came from South America and was addressed directly to him—James Dean, Warner Brothers, Burbank, U.S.A. They didn't even know he was dead yet in some places of the world. They'd say how much they enjoyed his movie and could they please have a photograph. Ninety percent of the mail asked for photographs. We sent them out for a while until we were told to forward them to the James Dean Foundation in Indiana."

The response to Jimmy's death was so widespread and spontaneous that it is inconceivable such "mass hysteria" could have been generated by publicity. If anything, the publicity department at Warner Brothers was at a loss at how to discourage this unexpected love for a dead actor. The influx of mail had begun to interfere with other publicity campaigns, and Warners had to hire two independent companies just to handle the deluge.

Warner Brothers' executives certainly did not want to *intensify* the mourning for Dean. They actually feared a seige of the Burbank lot, alarmed by visions of millions of souvenir-hunters smashing mindlessly through the gates and tearing up sound stages *He* had worked on, the cafeteria *He* ate in, the props *He* used, as scraps for their devotional shrines. Even a small city such as Warner Brothers' Burbank lot could easily be dismantled in a day by such voracious appetites.

Warners replied to the accusations that they were inciting the Dean riot: "We have a big Dean picture coming up and we're naturally interested in keeping his name before the public, but we're as amazed as anyone else by what's taken place." The industry was inclined to go along with them. One publicist said, "I thought Dean was a legend, but I was wrong. He's bigger than that. He's a religion."

As fan clubs proliferated, the volume of mail increased and the cult of James Dean became an international phenomenon. A huge demand arose for photographs, articles, interviews about him, anything bearing his name. Commerical interests quickly recognized the enormous potential for exploitation. Though their grisly distortions appeared only briefly, the shabby products fanned the unmediated emotions of children, pre-adults and adults into a booming industry.

The media-dismembering and scramble for natural artifacts began the day after Jimmy died. "They cleaned out his whole place," said Joe D'Angelo, Jimmy's stand-in for *Giant*. "The vultures came and cleaned out everything." The same thing happened in the tiny apartment Jimmy maintained on West Sixty-eighth Street in New York. Bill Bast, then on the West Coast, heard that friends removed whatever personal belongings remained—books, letters, drawings, lists of phone numbers—to prevent further desecrations.

The wrecked Porsche Spyder was initially towed around to various high schools in Los Angeles as a warning to drive carefully. It was then purchased for a thousand dollars from a wrecking yard by Dr. William F. Eschrich, who used some parts from the engine in his own car, and loaned the transmission to a friend, Dr. McHenry. In October 1956, McHenry was killed during a race in the sports car powered by Jimmy's engine. Dr. Eschrich was also involved in an accident in the same race. When asked if he was superstitious, Eschrich said, "Not a bit."

Reports say the crumpled aluminum shell of the car was later put on exhibit "by a California couple" who charged twenty-five cents admission to view the wreckage and fifty cents to sit behind the wheel. Fragments of shriveled aluminum were sold as souvenirs. The precious chunks of metal were bought by fans who hoped these remnants of Jimmy would impregnate them with his essence.

The list of manufactured talismans is endless: phoney shreds of hair, photographs, buttons, bubble-gum cards, toy monkeys, paintings and switchblade knives labeled "The James Dean Special." At least six pop records were initially released: "Jimmy Dean's First Christmas in Heaven," "The Ballad of James Dean," "James Dean—the Greatest of All," "Secret Doorway" (the theme from *Rebel Without a Cause*), "Jimmy Plays the Bongos" and "His Name Was Dean" (which sold twenty-five thousand copies its first week on sale).

An assembly-line reproduction of Kenneth Kendall's bust of

Jimmy sold in a three-inch-high simulated stone version for thirty dollars; in bronze, it cost one hundred and fifty dollars. Lifelike masks made out of a substance called Miracleflesh sold for five dollars apiece at the rate of three hundred a week. Thousands of red jackets were sold for $22.75 at Mattson's, where the cast of *Rebel* had bought their wardrobe. "It was amazing in Hollywood after *Rebel* opened," said Steffi Skolsky. "You could drive past any of the high schools and all the kids would be wearing red jackets. Everybody wanted to be Jimmy Dean."

The cult of James Dean stimulated an unorthodox dabbling in a spiritualist concept of living death. People began to believe that James Dean was still among them, invisible but present. "Spiritualism revives the primitive notion according to which the dead, who are corporeal specters endowed with invisibility and ubiquity, live among the living," wrote Edgar Morin in *The Stars*. "This is why one girl cried out during the showing of *Giant*: 'Come back, Jimmy! I love you! We're waiting for you!' It is the living presence of James Dean which his fanatics will henceforth look for in his films."

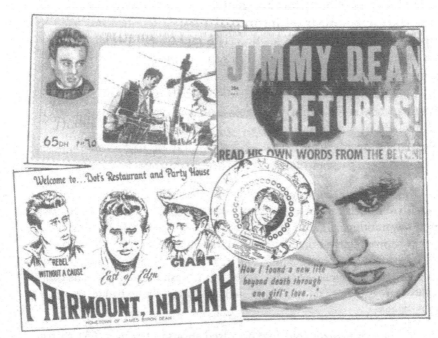

Relics of James Dean.

317

The unformed yearning to unite with Jimmy in his suspended life-and-death state took many personal forms. In poems, amateur portraits and plays, his devotees struggled to express and extend their supernatural longings. One fan wrote to Warner Brothers: "... He may be dead bodily, but please keep him alive spiritually ... To me he isn't the late James Dean and never will be. I'll see him some day, where I don't know, but I will ..."

Another sent this poem:

They tell me you are dead, yet I cannot
This night believe the unbelievable;
Your hands that moved caressing weightless things,
As beautiful as music to the soul;
Beyond the barriers of time and space
Must have their measure in Eternity.
Your guileless grace will here no more be seen;
No tears can recreate the lifeless clay;
Yet if your body but a spark retained
That love could fan to flame, my years I'd give
That you might walk the lovely earth again.

The fifties, so remote from any genuine sympathy with the spiritual, took what was initially an instinctual sense of wonder and tried to pervert it into caricature. Kids naively bought black parodies of their most intimate feelings, hoping to find clarification of a turmoil they didn't fully understand.

The worst travesty was a magazine called *Jimmy Dean Returns!* It entreats fans to "Read his own words from the Beyond–'How I found a new life beyond death through one girl's love' ..." It's a dime-store salesgirl's story of how she and Jimmy fell in love, and how he communicates to her from the dead through automatic writing:

... Your belief is like a magnet, giving me the force to be able to speak to you. If your belief ever faded, I would have to be silent again ... The crash itself was nothing. I felt no shock. No hurt. I could see myself lying there, looking down on that other person who was Jimmy Dean and yet wasn't ... I watched with amazement and wonder, and the realization gradually sank into me–this was what we called death. But it wasn't 'Death' ... The other body that lay down there was only a shell. I, the real I who had inhabited it, was still alive ...

Jimmy Dean Returns sold five hundred thousand copies. (At thirty-five cents a copy, it was fifteen to twenty cents higher than most movie magazines at the time.) It lacked taste, but played heavily on the supernatural. Neither the "author's" name (Judy Collins) nor the photograph of her in the magazine are real, compounding suspicions that this "True Confessions" type story is a deliberate fraud directed at a gullible audience only too willing to *believe* in such a transparent mockery. One writer who condemned the victims as well as the perpetrators for their mutual involvement in such spiritual hoaxes was Maurice Zolotow, who later authored a biography of Marilyn Monroe.

"To some extent, what our country will become tomorrow is determined by whom our children admire today," Zolotow said in the *Detroit Free Press,* launching an attack on Jimmy Dean. "A second-rate actor whose craze is also shocking because it is based entirely on lies and shabby nonsense . . . Why should we shed maudlin tears and slobber over the memory of such a man? What's so brave and beautiful about stepping on the gas, blowing your horn and speeding down a public highway like a maniac?"

Zolotow claims to bare these disagreeable "facts" "without any intention of condemning or judging" Jimmy, and goes on to say that Dean "made life hell for any girl who gave him her affections . . . American girls have previously idolized other motion picture stars— Valentino, John Gilbert, etcetera—but these men have a romantic flair and a genuine ability to love and respect women. Jimmy Dean was rotten all the way down the line."

Zolotow was one of the few who held Valentino in shining contrast to James Dean. Most writers fell into more simple-minded comparisons. "I want to say that not since Valentino has any actor been more idolized in death than when he was alive than the late James Dean," said Louella Parsons. News stories asked, "Is the late James Dean, who flashed with the fleeting brilliance of a shooting star across the theatrical firmament, destined to join Rudolph Valentino as an idolized screen immortal?" But despite the facile predictions, the comparison is as absurd as the early comparisons to Marlon Brando.

Valentino was a sentimental, exotic idol who catered to the lost illusions of middle-aged women, a symbol of "primitive love" who confessed to selling out and referred to himself as "Hollywood's lounge lizard." When he died at thirty-one in 1926, his funeral was attended by one hundred thousand people, many of whom were "planted" by an avaricious manager in a premeditated publicity plan to raise enough money to pay off Valentino's personal debt of $165,000.

Such comparisons to Valentino were intended to convince America that the spontaneous crowds at Jimmy's funeral and the subsequent death cult which centered around him weren't quite "genuine." But there is a huge difference. When he died, James Dean had appeared in only *one* movie, and his funeral was not held in New York City, but in Fairmount, Indiana, a rural community inaccessible by plane, bus or train.

Pilgrimages to the hometown of a movie star are almost unknown in the history of Hollywood. Yet pilgrimages to the obscure town of Fairmount, Indiana have never stopped. After Jimmy's death, literally thousands of people from all over the world found their way to the small cemetery off Jonesboro Pike, amd many stopped by the Winslows' farm after paying their respects at Jimmy's grave.

The Winslows accepted the madness which intruded on them from the outside world with a little incomprehension and a great deal of understanding considering their personal sorrow. On one weekend in November 1956, one hundred eighty-five cars parked outside their house. These visitors usually requested a chance to come in or to have something that belonged to Jimmy.

"We'd never forget for long," said Marcus, "because there'd always be somebody at the door who'd been to the cemetery to visit Jim and wanted to spend a bit of time with us. We thought it would end after a while. We thought that Jim would be left to rest quietly, but we should have known better. All his life, Jim always did the opposite of whatever we expected of him."

Letters from fans addressed to Warner Brothers and the Winslows often contained money. It was from these donations that the idea came about for the James Dean Memorial Foundation. Fans sent money for "some kind of memorial," but Marcus knew that a statue in the park or monument in the cemetery wouldn't be right: "Jimmy wouldn't have liked a statue. He'd have ducked his head and rubbed the back of his neck and said, 'Aw, not for me, Marc. That's not for me.'

"A statue would just be standing still all through the years, watching the grass turn brown in the summer and getting covered over with snow in the winter—doing nobody any harm, I guess, but doing nobody any good, either. And Jim was never one to stay still a minute, unless he way lying on the floor after dinner reading a book."

Instead, the James Dean Memorial Foundation was established on May 15, 1956 as a non-profit corporation with very specific ambitions:

1. To act as a living and perpetual memorial to James Dean.
2. To operate exclusively in the furtherance of the dramatic, musical, and literary arts and sciences.
3. To encourage and promote education in these fields by providing scholarships, fellowships, or other financial assistance.
4. To provide educational facilities and instruction in these fields.
5. To encourage achievement in these fields by the presentation of awards, cash prizes, and other tokens of recognition.
6. To promote and encourage public knowledge and support of the theatre arts and sciences.
7. To make gifts and benefactions to such organizations as shall from time to time be determined as deserving by the Board of Directors and the Board of Advisors.
8. To render needed financial assistance to any proven and deserving young professional talents as shall be determined by the two boards.

The foundation was governed by the townspeople of Fairmount, except for an executive vice-president in New York City, Kent Williams, who would act as administrator. It set up shop at 116 North Main Street in a little storefront which acted as an information center. As many as one hundred ten fans signed the book every day for the first few months. A little museum was put together with some of Jimmy's personal belongings, which were loaned by the Winslows. Volunteers helped answer the two hundred thousand letters which had poured in by the end of 1956. The foundation also sold photographs, postcards and lumpy medallions of Jimmy's profile.

For a short time, the streams of fans, the visits from celebrities, the television cameras and genuine unreality of the Memorial Foundation upset the tranquil life of Fairmount. Worship of an individual is not a virtue among Quakers, who have no saints and venerate the spirit alone. "All life is sacramental" is a favorite aphorism of the Friends. The worship of James Dean has almost always come from *outside* his hometown. A memorial service held on the first anniversary of Jimmy's death was suggested by a German fan club and some three thousand people attended. "But they were mostly from out of town," said *Fairmount News* editor Al Terhune, who helped organize the activities.

The Memorial Foundation did produce one season of summer theater. Students were put up at the homes of local people, some of them taking a brief fling at "show biz" by acting bit parts in the productions. Money dwindled, however, as rumors of mismanagement grew, and the foundation eventually went into "suspension," where it remains today.

In May of 1956, a sculpture of Jimmy's head, supposedly commissioned by Jimmy himself when he visited Kenneth Kendall's studio, was presented to Fairmount High School. A copy was placed on top of a rectangular brick column in Park Cemetery and another was given to Princeton University, which, the *Hollywood Reporter* noted, "placed the mask among the immortals of art . . . in its Lawrence Hutton Hall of Fame . . . It will share space with similar memorials to Edwin Booth, David Garrick, Beethoven, Thackeray and Keats. Dean is the youngest artist ever so honored."

The apotheosis of James Dean and the supernatural yearnings his cult inspired did not always come from outside the "Hoosier State" however. A Muncie, Indiana man named Joe Archer wrote a spiritualistic tract entitled *Here is the Real Story of My Life by James Dean as*

Memorial service in Fairmount, October 1956.

I Might Have Told it to Joe Archer. On file at the Marion Library as of November 24, 1956, it begins:

FROM SOMEWHERE BEYOND EDEN

Dear Friends on Earth:

From somewhere beyond the veil which separates the eons of eternity from the hours of time, I am writing to my living friends on earth.

No, this is impossible, and I am obliged to make contact through the medium of another mind; to a people who grope in the darkness of fiction and make believe, in the hope that some day, the light of hope will shine on them . . .

The treatise goes on about Jimmy's "average and normal boyhood" and his mother's death, but avoids any mention of Hollywood, concluding with:

Jimmie Dean and his beloved mother have gone to rest. Where the trails of time surely take every living soul. The moral to this story: Man, the masterpiece of God's creation, whether great or small, will some day enter the gate which swung ajar for Jimmie Dean . . .

Fairmount still seems uncomfortable with the ghost of Jimmy's memory shuttling about the town, an image incapable of repose. The sign that once read "James Dean Road" is gone. The little shop that housed the Memorial Foundation has become a motor vehicle agency. The "A" in James and the "B" in Byron have been gouged out of Jimmy's gravestone, but at least the stone is still there. Twin *arbor vitae* (Tree of Life) stand on either side of the stone, so tall they almost dwarf it, but were specially ordered by Charlie Dean because they'd be difficult to uproot.

The souvenir hunters who stalk the town and chip at Jimmy's gravestone are a nuisance to Fairmount, but more insidious are those who come looking for the source of his energy, who want to be just like Jimmy Dean. They confront the citizens of Fairmount with questions an oracle couldn't answer, and ask them again and again.

"The rest of the world knew him better than we did," the townsfolk say. It sometimes seems like Fairmount would like to acquit itself of the myth of James Dean, as if he were an embarrassment, a monster the town had produced and was now obliged to explain. In their silence, the townspeople become conspirators in his legend, for their bewilderment makes his achievements seem even more fantastic and fulfills one of the classic conditions of the hero: he arrives mysteriously, fully formed and apparently out of nowhere.

Adeline Nall explained the pilgrimages as a desire to "walk on the ground where Jim walked, breathe the air this child breathed. Now how about *that*? Now, when it comes to worship and that kind of thing, I don't take part in that. But there is a reverence for the land he came from."

The desire to breathe *his* air, to touch *his* earth and the pilgrimages to his point of origin are the rites accorded a hero. The pilgrims visit his shrine, his town and his home to glean some essence from his mythic life and to venerate the spirit of the place from which he came.

"Wherever a hero has been born, has wrought, or has passed back into the void, the place is marked and sanctified," said Joseph Campbell in *The Hero with a Thousand Faces*. "A temple is erected there to signify and inspire the miracle of perfect centeredness; for this is the place of the breakthrough into abundance. Someone at this point discovered eternity. The site can serve, therefore, as a support for fruitful meditation ... the shrine or altar at the center being symbolical of the Inexhaustible Point. The one who enters the temple ... and proceeds to the sanctuary is imitating the deed of the original hero."

In 1956, producer George W. George and Robert Altman began assembling *The James Dean Story*, a biographical film that provided Altman with one of his first jobs as a director. At first they wanted an actor to play Jimmy, and considered casting Robert Conrad, who later co-starred on *Hawaiian Eye* and *Wild Wild West*. At that time, Conrad was a twenty-one-year-old singer in Chicago who'd been spotted by a local public relations man and hired to pose in front of a *Giant* poster. Conrad even went to Fairmount to meet Adeline Nall to see if she thought he resembled Jimmy. Mercifully, the idea of having someone "play" Jimmy was abandoned, and the concept emerged of "James Dean playing himself" in a documentary using words, pictures, film clips and interviews.

Marlon Brando, in an interview with Truman Capote, revealed that he'd been asked to narrate the film. Brando took out a letter during their interview over dinner ". . .'from a friend of mine. He's making a documentary, the life of James Dean. He wants me to do the narration. I think I might.' He tossed the letter aside and pulled his apple pie, topped with a melting scoop of vanilla ice cream, toward him.

'Maybe not, though. I get excited about something, but it never lasts more than seven minutes. Seven minutes exactly ... But I'm really considering this Dean thing. It could be important ... Toward the end, I think he was beginning to find his own way as an actor. But this glorifying of Dean is all wrong. That's why I believe the documentary could be important. To show he wasn't a hero; show what he really was—just a lost boy trying to find himself. That ought to be done, and I'd like to do it—maybe as a kind of expiation for some of my own sins. Like making *The Wild One.*'"

Brando ultimately turned it down and Martin Gabel got the job. The narration was written by Stewart Stern, who instinctively knew better; but the producers had all the necessary permissions and when they threatened to find someone else, Stewart gave in. The result was an anecdotal, sentimental and contrived cinematic edition of what one writer called "Ralph Edwards' Memory Book." It ranged from poetic adulation to pompous insights. The worst passages combined both, as in this allusion to Jimmy as suffering shrub: "He could expose through Jim Stark the things he had to conceal as Jim Dean. But when the film was finished, Jim Stark was gone. The performance was over. The set was nothing more than a concealing leaf which covered the tree of loneliness. And after every job the tree was bare and winter returned to Jimmy."

None of Jimmy's closest friends participated in the film. Bill Bast, Bill Gunn, Barbara Glenn, Martin Landau and Elizabeth Sheridan all avoided any kind of publicity after Jimmy's death. The Winslows, Jimmy's grandparents and Bing Traster were roped into the production and are the only relief in this overloaded "tear-jerker."

The James Dean Story was advertised as "a different kind of motion picture" and boasted a new technique—the Camera Eye—which zooms in and out of still photographs and pans across them to give an illusion of movement. This was juxtaposed with film clips of Jimmy and simulated sequences: a train carrying an invisible coffin and Jimmy blaming himself for the death of his mother; a car making the fatal turn, screeching brakes and a sea gull soaring over a deserted beach.

Stewart Stern couched Jimmy's abrasive message in his own poetic vision: "He believed that the cry of the world is for tenderness between human beings—and he felt that to be tender requires more courage of a man than to be violent. Men are brave enough for war, but not brave enough for love. That's what Jimmy thought." This is hardly the core of Jimmy's message, but at the time Stewart was trying to balance the perversions of violent gangs and phoney mystics.

The James Dean Story failed miserably at the box office. Released in New York in 1957, the film was quietly withdrawn from the theater circuit by Warner Brothers (its distributor) and sold to television.

Among the articles, interviews and pseudo-bibliographies, the first full-length account of Jimmy's life by a close friend came out in 1956 when Bill Bast published a personal memoir entitled *James Dean.*

"After Jimmy died, a lot of positive things came out of it and a lot of negative things," said Bill. "Some people didn't realize what the hell they were doing, there was so much energy they had tapped into. I only did two things—I wrote a book entitled *James Dean*, and then I buried him.

"During the last week of writing the book, I had a terrible nightmare about Jimmy. It told me the book would put Jimmy to rest. In the dream, he came back and said he really wasn't dead and placed himself at my mercy. He said that I had a secret, a key and I could save him from the grave. But I *didn't* have a key, so they came to get him and dragged him out screaming and put him in a coffin and drove him away in a hearse.

"The dream was never resolved, so I went into a bad state for days. I would cry spasmodically on and off. After the emotional thing wore off, I realized I was really coming to grips with Jimmy inside myself and that in the book I *had* to do justice to him and to our relationship. So I finished it and then I let go, saying, 'I couldn't do any more to keep you alive. This is my interpretation. Now go back and be buried. *Be dead.* Because you are dead.'"

Jimmy materialized himself to other friends as they slept, leaving eerie messages. Bill Gunn had several dreams. One of the most vivid occurred when he felt on the verge of his own death.

"I was very sick with the flu," said Bill. "I had a 104-degree temperature and I was really depressed because nothing was going right. I had this lousy room—the kind with eight layers of wallpaper, all peeling—and figured what the hell, life wasn't worth living anymore. It was the middle of winter, so I opened the windows and just lay down to die.

"I fell fast asleep and had this weird dream. I was in Jimmy's room

326

on West Sixty-eighth Street, and he was sitting at his desk with his back to me. The floor seemed to be covered with a fine, white powder. I walked toward him, and he suddenly turned around and said, 'Beware of Death. He has sharp teeth,' and all this blood poured out of his mouth.

"I woke up and it was morning and I was totally cured. I had no fever, I could eat for the first time in days and I went back to work."

"It would be hard to think of a figure," said a psychiatrist interviewed in 1956 for a story on the James Dean cult, "with which the young people of today could more readily identify. In almost every way, he's a remarkably vivid and compelling symbol of the confusions and tumults experienced in adolescence and early maturity. Further-

Cover illustration by Andy Warhol for The Immortal.   *Jimmy's continuing popularity in Germany (1957).*

more, I think that there may be some pretty solid explanation for the rise in popularity after his accident.

"Teenagers, you see, long for the dignity and the sophistication that they see in older people. They want desperately to feel poised and mature. Dean's death may have given them something to satisfy that need. Just a guess, he may have given them the nourishment of a mature and sophisticated sense of tragedy."

In America, greasers, college students, transvestites and punks all identified with James Dean in the conviction that the self he projected was what they really wanted to be. Although Jimmy invented few of the attributes associated with him, he had created from his many impersonations a composite image that was universally applicable.

His inward fantastic face with its mesmerizing features became a pervasive icon, a commercial effigy to be worshipped like William Burroughs' beautiful, sinister BOY:

... The BOY turned out to be the hottest property in advertising. Enigmatic smile on the delicate young face. Just what is the BOY looking at? ... The BOY was too hot to handle. Temples were erected to the BOY and there were posters of his face seventy feet high and all the teenagers began acting like the BOY looking at you with a dreamy look lips parted over their Wheaties. They all bought BOY shirts and BOY knives running around like wolf packs ...

James Dean codified the uniform of youth, what Morin described as "the panoply of adolescence, a wardrobe in which is expressed a whole attitude toward society ... no tie, unbuttoned shirt, deliberate sloppiness, are so many ostensible signs (having the value of political badges) of a resistance against the social conventions of the world of adults ... the signs of virility, the costume of manual laborers and of artistic invention."

John Dos Passos wrote in *Midcentury*:

> There is nothing much deader than a dead motion picture
> actor,
>   and yet,
> even after James Dean had been some years dead,
> when they filed out of the close darkness and the breathedout
> air of the second and third and fourth run motion picture theatres
> where they'd been seeing James Dean's old films, they still lined up:
> the boys in the jackboots and the leather jackets, the boys in
> the skintight jeans, the boys in broad motorbike belts,
> before the mirrors in the restroom
> to look at themselves
> and see
> James Dean;
> the resentful hair
> the deep eyes floating in lonesomeness,
> the bitter beat look,
> the scorn on the lip.
>   Their pocket combs were out; they tousled up their hair
> and patted it down just so; ...

In every country of the world, James Dean became as popular an export as Coca-Cola. His image spread throughout the globe, as easy to identify with in Europe as in Asia.

Closest to Americans in language and social customs, English teenagers were the first outside the United States to emulate James Dean. Adam Faith, one of the most popular English singers of the early sixties, recalled Jimmy's instantaneous effect on him and his mates after seeing *Rebel Without a Cause.*

That affected me so much, I just felt I wanted to be James Dean. He made a cock up of it all, but somehow he just seemed to say it all. We came out of that bleeding cinema, me and my mate from school, and I remember I was wearing a Levi jacket and a pair of Levi jeans—well, they weren't Levis in those days, they were the English hackney equivalent—and I was walking along the street thinking of myself like a cowboy, and as we turned the corner to go up Birkbeck Road I said, "You know what I'm going to do? I'm going into the film business; it's the only game." And from that moment on that's all I thought about.

A man from Catford, England had his name changed to James Byron Dean, and a grand Christmas party held in his honor at a coffeehouse under the Holborn Viaduct was described with amused detachment in England's *New Statesman* by Charles Robinson, who sat among a group of uncomfortable young people drinking tea and wearing funny hats:

Then everybody played Twenty Questions about details in Jimmy's life. I had read the biography of *him* by William Bast, an intimate friend, a few days before, and therefore all set to win the Magnificent Prize. I realised how wrong I had been by question five, when we were expected to know where *he* had made a commercial for a soft drink. Throwing my paper under the chair, I turned round just in time to see a tall figure in a plum-velvet windcheater descending the stairs. It was James Byron Dean.

Mr. Dean, who comes from Catford, recently changed his name by deed poll, since he believes most sincerely that he is controlled by the spirit of the late actor. Something very remarkable has undoubtedly occurred to him, he would be the first to agree. Mr. Dean is shortly off to Fairmount, Indiana, the Birthplace, where he hopes to open a home for juvenile delinquents. About fifteen years older than his namesake, with a shock of bright yellow hair, Mr. Dean is not a person one forgets easily.

German correspondent Edmund Redschneider said about the Dean cults: "After the war everything was broken down, rotten. It was a time of consolidation among the young—a time when the old people were just glad to live. They didn't want any more responsibility. Dean showed the clash between the older and the younger generation. James Dean believed in himself. In Germany, before the war, America had always been a dream country and Hollywood had a lot to do with the creation of that image. It was rich and beautiful and who didn't like that? His biggest success in Germany was *Giant* because he represented a person who has nothing and becomes something and this was the dream of everyone at the time."

In Italy, writers speculated on "Why James Dean Is Still Alive" after having made only two films, *Burning Youth* (*Rebel*) and *The Valley of Eden* (*East of Eden*). They were convinced it was a mechanical "star-raising" device:

The publicity machine has taken advantage of the 8000 letters a month addressed to the dead actor with the most untasteful bad taste. The infatuation for James Dean is the direct result of a grave state of anguish that exists among the adolescents in America and elsewhere; the letters are not directed as strongly towards the actor as to the personalities he portrayed . . .

The publicity agents didn't have to wrack their brains for the James Dean campaign. The 8000 letters provide all the elements necessary; by reading them the different psychological aspects of this collective neurosis can be seen . . . The content of the letters filled with sadness served to inspire the stamp of publicity . . . Newspapers are founded upon sensations and scandals, when not directly on blackmailing. Actors, actresses and ambitious persons who don't stop at anything to sell copies and procure personal publicity. These hateful forms of activities are maybe only a small part of the campaigns launched by large producers, but the studios are not unhappy over the fact that they manage to tickle a certain mentality that the services of propaganda don't love to woo, and that is, after all, a major part of the mentality of cinema spectators.

France awarded Jimmy with the Crystal Star for the year's Best Foreign Actor in *East of Eden* and *Rebel*. The same rumors circulated abroad that he hadn't died, but was suffering from shock in an institution, as Jimmy rose to the top of French popularity polls. *CineMonde*, the French version of *Photoplay*, dedicated every September issue to him for four years after his death.

"The students showed up with black arm bands when they heard Jimmy had died," said a woman who grew up in a small Greek town. "And when the teachers found out there hadn't been a death in the family, we had to take the bands off until school was out, but then we put them on again. Young people wrote poems to him, went to see all his movies. There was a platonic love, but they all worshipped him. In Greece he was like a god, like Apollo. You know how romantic we are."

In Iran, James Dean became a symbol for anything that was new, modern, American and flashy. A popular expression on the streets of Tehran for anyone who was dressed in the latest fashion was: "Hey, there goes James Dean."

In a land where ancient cults still flourish, the *New York Times* reported yet another exotic Dean cult in their "Culture Notes":

Word last week from *The New York Times'* correspondent in Jakarta, Indonesia, was that a group of teen-aged worshippers of the late James Dean has turned up, of all places, in Bandung, scene of the Afro-Asian conference in 1955. The Javanese boys and girls, it was reported from the remote mountain city, which is about 100 miles from Jakarta, strolled through the streets in "blue jeans and red jackets" in sartorial tribute to the movie star, several of whose films have been shown in Indonesia.

Conservative Indonesians frown at the idea of girls wearing anything but the traditional "kain" (sarong) and "kekbaya" (a kind of blouse). This hasn't stopped the Dean admirers, though. They'll continue to wear their American-type togs and they also plan to hold regular meetings at which, the report said, "Jimmy" will be "commemorated and idolized."

By their very nature movies foster belief in the supernatural. Materializing on the boundary of reality and fantasy, their stars communicate with us from another dimension like insubstantial spirits. Through the medium of film, ". . . we were now to see the characters no longer among the objects, but as if these had become transparent through them," writes Bazin. "I mean by this that without our noticing, the world has moved from meaning to analogy, then from analogy to identification with the supernatural."

Almost twenty years after his death, identification with James Dean has been assimilated into our culture and our being. He is no longer a conscious model, but he remains innately present. The pieces of his body have been absorbed by his followers and his message taken into our bloodstream. Like Osiris, Egyptian god of fertility and regeneration, the seed of James Dean, as his friend Bill Gunn said, is at the root of the culture of the sixties and seventies.

"I think it was the beginning of more than people realized," said Bill. "I think the reaction to Jimmy led young people right on into the sixties. It pushed right through to that. It wasn't just having a friend suddenly not existing anymore. This person they wrote about after he died took everybody on a trip. 'Cause none of *us* died. We were too young to die. And it wasn't racing that killed Jimmy. Some idiot did. Mr. Turnupseed. I took that word apart you know—*Turn-up-seed*. And of course, Jimmy was the seed."

The imaginary tends to become real. What was once only possible in films and songs has become part of our lives since the fifties. Movies and music are the secret inspirations of the Teen Dream. These initial disordered and complex signals told us where we were and what we might be, and we incorporated them through our collective involvement into a way of life.

It's no accident that rock 'n' roll and James Dean entered the national consciousness at the same time. America had fulfilled its Fat Dream after the long struggle for material progress from the Depression through World War II. The affluent society of the fifties produced a reactionary subculture. Adolescents rejected the repressive conspiracy of conformity and denial on which the material utopia of their parents was built by living out their fantasies through movie stars and rock music. Able to assert their independence for the first time, they created a new vision where language is song, work is play, fantasy is reality and the childhood wishes of violence, sensuality and freedom begin to seem possible.

James Dean and rock 'n' roll expressed a changing state of mind their audiences did not completely understand, but intuitively embraced. In the degenerate labyrinth of the fifties, there seemed to be no exits, no other vehicle for unleashing these pent-up energies. The seeds germinated until the next generation could make the maze transparent and find its way out.

As different as they were in temperament, Jimmy and Elvis Presley recognized they were operating on the same plane. Jimmy's taste in music ran to African chants, classical symphonies and Bartok, but he dug Elvis and other rock 'n' roll singers. According to Nick Ray, Presley idolized Jimmy: "I was sitting in the cafeteria at MGM one day, and Elvis Presley came over. He knew I was a friend of Jimmy's and had directed *Rebel*, so he got down on his knees before me and began to recite whole passages of dialogue from the script. Elvis must have seen *Rebel* a dozen times by then and remembered every one of Jimmy's lines . . ."

The Beatles, the Rolling Stones and other English groups began to refine rock 'n' roll in the sixties, making it more palatable to the middle class. Just as Jimmy had modified Brando's proletarian hero, they created a personal style of defiance and humor influenced by Jimmy the same way their music was influenced by rhythm and blues.

Bob Dylan consciously emulated Jimmy. On the cover of his album *The Freewheelin' Bob Dylan,* he reproduced the existential slouch and cultivated an image of the loner / dreamer adrift on the grimy streets of New York. And in "American Pie," Don McLean's synthetic song / history of the sixties, Dylan is depicted as the jester singing for King Elvis and Queen Joan Baez "in the coat he borrowed from James Dean."

By the early seventies, James Dean had emerged as a primary folk hero of rock culture. He appears in a line from Lou Reed's "Walk on the Wild Side"–*"Jackie Curtis thought he was James Dean for a day"*–and again in Loudon Wainwright's "School Days." Garland Jeffries wrote a song that reads in part:

Hey James Dean
You're just a teenage dream
But the older folks too
They're tryin' to be like you

In his 1974 hit, "Rock On," David Essex fused rock and James Dean in an anthem to the movement Jimmy had begun:

Hey, did you rock and roll–rock on
oh my soul
hey, didya boogey too–rock on

Hey, shout, summertime blues
jump up and down in your blue suede shoes
hey, did you rock and roll–rock on

And where do we go from here?
which is the way that's clear?
still lookin' for that blue jean baby queen
prettiest girl I've ever seen
see her shake on the movie screen
Jimmy Dean–James Dean

Rock on–Jimmy Dean
Rock on . . .

Within a year of his death, the cult of James Dean had acquired the nature of a religious phenomenon. His life's course from bright expectancy to violent end is the stuff of all heroes and especially the mark of gods of youth.

Occult periodicals and academic studies made the inevitable comparisons with Christ, Adonis, Tammuz and Osiris. An article entitled "American Fascinations" appeared in *To-morrow* magazine, a psychic journal of the fifties. The author, Martin Ebon, cited the funerary inscription of Akhenaton, the freakish sun king of ancient Egypt (thought by Velikovsky to be the original Oedipus), and compared the wailings of Jimmy's distraught followers to the pathetic cries of Nefertiti, who longed to be reunited with her dead brother: "I long to breathe in the sweet breath of your mouth. I long to hear your voice, the wind that will restore life to my limbs. Hold out to me your hands in which your spirit dwells so that I may have the power to receive it and live in it."

In "James Dean or the Quest of the God of Springtime," Raymond de Becker, a French writer interested in the archetypes of Hollywood, introduced his mythological study of Jimmy with a funerary chant from Goethe's *Faust*:

> Alas! born for an earthly paradise
> From a proud race and with shining powers
> But tragically you became your own victim
> When you took up violent revolt
> Against tradition and conformity.
> You forced yourself towards a sublime end
> But you yourself could not attain it . . .

On the mythic nature of James Dean, de Becker wrote:

By abandoning themselves through a pure misunderstanding to violence, speed, drugs, Rock 'n' Roll, and wild sexual experimentation, teenagers look for God. But this god is closer to Dionysius, Wotan, Attis and Antinous than Christ. James Dean died at twenty-four, and as with the murder of Adonis, the sacrifice of Mithra, and the suicide of Antinous, he could not have lived on without destroying the myth on which his cult is founded. Undoubtedly the same psychological structures are recreated throughout history on different levels and adapted to different forms; it is the archetypal solution for an age of confusion. Gods who die young possess the universal power to express the themes of adolescence; at the crossroads of life they are signs of the future. The god of American youth surges up from the depths of the earth; in the delirium of a sullen energy he offers himself up to immortality. He is a dark god crying out, with a craving for power and resurrection. He is not an ascetic and scarcely a martyr; he is the Divine Dancer, and by his death he brings on the spring once more.

Movies are our primary form of mythology, and the fantasies they project form the matter of our personal myths. In the unconscious sphere, reality and inner images are often indistinguishable. Fantasy nourishes us with truer, less contaminated images than those of the day-to-day world. James Dean's audiences *participated* in what they saw represented so vividly on screen. Through photographs, fetishes and supernatural belief, they identified collectively with his mythic presence. These talismans were "so many exterior means for living the life of the stars from within," as Morin wrote. "It is the misery of need, the mean and anonymous life that wants to enlarge itself to the dimensions of life in the movies. The imaginary life of the screen is the product of this genuine need: the star is its projection."

Through his art and transformations, Jimmy projected himself out of his body and into the idealized image of James Dean. This art of metamorphosis is also attributed to the Egyptian god of the dead, Osiris. In the Egyptian *Book of the Dead,* Osiris transforms himself into any shape he wishes—a hawk, a lotus, a crocodile—through the magical power of Khepera, the self-created scarab god of essence and change, whose name can be translated as "becoming" or "evolution." Prematurely sealed in a coffin by his treacherous brother, Set, young King Osiris was subsequently torn to pieces and the parts of his body scattered to fertilize future generations of crops, trees and men. These fragments were then ritually reassembled with spells and ministrations by Isis (his sister and wife) and their followers in a ceremony that was repeated by the worshippers of Osiris for over five thousand years.

Osiris proclaimed each of his godly parts as derived from another deity: "My hair is the hair of Nu; my eyes are the eyes of Hathor; my neck is the neck of the divine goddess Isis." Jimmy, too, is a composite of "dieties" who went before: the slouch of Brando, the wounds of Montgomery Clift, the rural cadence of Gary Cooper, the radiance of Greta Garbo. His spirit animates this incorporation of where he'd come from and everything that passed through him.

This acquisition of former powers gives Jimmy Dean a supreme ability which is described in the Egyptian *Book of the Dead* as "the power of man to transform himself into any form he pleaseth." The projected spirit of this changing form is called the *ka,* which everyone possesses. As an actor, Jimmy depended on his ability to project the changing fantasies of his own creation, and, through motion pictures, the power of this *ka* was magnified enormously.

uāb - k	*uāb ka-k*	*uāb ba - k*	*uāb seχem - k*
Thou art pure,	thy *ka* is pure,	thy soul is pure,	thy form is pure.

"Man has always projected his desires and his fears in images," says Morin in his book about the movie star. "He has always projected in his own image–his double–his need to transcend himself in life and death. This double is the repository of latent magical powers; every double is a virtual god."

As Jimmy transformed himself through his *ka,* his followers would merge into this idealized image in their desire to possess and assume the strength of an angry god. A generation of embryonic Deans gravitated around his image and tried to assume his form. Jimmy's followers immersed themselves in his *ka* and became him. "He is I and I am he," they might say, in the words of the mummy to Osiris. The god is buried in us; he knows the future and waits for us there.

The cult of Osiris, as with the cult of James Dean, is a community built around a totem. Its aim is the collective identification with that power in a new society whose principal value is change. Jimmy parallels the archetype of the beautiful young god dismembered in sacrifice to generate new seasons, the spirit of transforming power whose presence makes the world grow from his body. James Dean's fans revived his body, as did the worshippers of Osiris.

"Dear Jimmy," wrote a fan in words nearly identical with "opening the mouth of Osiris" in the Egyptian *Book of the Dead,* "We love your expressive lips kissing like no one else's, or half-open searching for air as if the world smothered you; or twisted bitterly, or in the heart-rending smile that should have come more often."

The extent to which Jimmy's image penetrated all levels of correspondence can be seen in the diversity of those who identified with him—from the typical to the demonic. An actor named Tom Pittman, deliberately crashed his car against a tree in a carnal union with his dead idol, and two girls in Germany committed suicide on the anniversary of his death, leaving a note to their parents that "this was the anniversary of the day Jimmy died and life was intolerable without him."

Kenneth Anger dedicated his occult masterpiece of adolescent violence, *Scorpio Rising*, to Jimmy: "Dedicated to Jack Parsons, Victor Childe, Jim Powers, James Dean, T. E. Lawrence, the society of spartans, the Hell's Angels, and all overgrown boys who will follow the whistle of Love's Brother."

In his book *Hollywood Babylone,* a Mesopotamian phantasmagoria of gossip and intrigue, Anger attributes to Jimmy a sort of masochistic transcendence through suffering in his account of Jimmy as a tacky Saint Sebastian, a Human Ashtray who had cigarettes instead of arrows plunged into his body.

These are manifestations of the dark side of the image Jimmy projected. Like Osiris, James Dean was linked with Lucifer as both a god of youth and rebellion, king of the dead and god of light, of whom the alchemist Fulcanelli wrote, "from obscure chaos makes light ooze after having reassembled it, and this light created out of revolt shines henceforth . . . as a star."

James Dean fulfills so many mythic attributes, it's only natural that his death should have inspired a devotional cult. Traditional religions had become corporate and secularized, failing to supply the sacramental means or ecstasy of an expanding consciousness. In James Dean his followers found their own personal sacrament, a god in their own inner image of themselves. The spirit located itself in the last place conventional wisdom would look—at the summit of commercial fantasy and entertainment, the movies.

Movies are a form of magic with their projection of "a thin, insubstantial human image, its nature a sort of vapour, film or shadow." Its animated current can penetrate and divert our energy. We become what we behold and what we choose to behold. It is through our eyes that we have taken Jimmy into ourselves, and he remains there magically present like Osiris, god of regeneration.

The Mutant King

*"Try and catch me. You might think I have
to come down from up here, don't you?
I hate all earthlings."*

From the myth of his life and the reality of his movies, Jimmy created a dangerous fusion of himself and the celluloid spirits he conjured up. His sudden death only magnified the power and mystery of his enigmatic creature—James Dean.

Like Gatsby, James Dean "sprang from his Platonic conception of himself" and in this form carried his incorruptible dream through the movies and into our lives. All of his films, either by coincidence or act of God, parallel his own life and by some even greater mystery tell the story of America from ecstatic Eden to crumbling corporate Giant. James Dean is the archetypal American hero whose life is a series of modern parables: the innocence of evil (*East of Eden*), the wrath of outraged innocence (*Rebel Without a Cause*) and the betrayal of that innocence (*Giant*).

What happened to Jimmy became a record of what was happening to America. In his life and in his movie characters, he paralleled a Pilgrim's Progress through America from farm to city to the fulfillment of the dream of success. From Fairmount, Jimmy set off on his quest in the blankness of innocence. His adventures and painful adaptations speak eloquently of our condition. His life illuminates our own lives since he was curious enough to experiment with himself and sensitive enough to leave a clear print of his journey.

Jimmy invented James Dean with the intuition and patient determination of the Wright Brothers and Thomas Edison, embodying in his creature all the contradictions of the American dream—a figure of sensuality and repression, fantasy and craft, organic yet manufactured, boy and star. James Dean is a refinement of America's secret ideal of itself: the adolescent dreamer, a solitary figure and symbolic agent for change. In Jimmy's personality are all the schizophrenic elements of a nation founded on both the old and the new, romanticism and puritanism, a dream of a spiritual utopia and a material El Dorado. The spirit of the New World imprinted its double nature on Jimmy as it had on all the civilizations of the Americas. This New World needed creatures who could adapt continuously to discovery and change. The New Age would be populated by mutants.

D. H. Lawrence understood the evolution of America as the emergence of a new being who casts off the accumulated layers of the past: "This is the true myth of America. She starts old, old, wrinkled and writhing in an old skin. And there is a gradual sloughing off of the old skin towards a new youth."

In the gradual unswathing of America's hidden face, only those who could embody its original spirit would become the instrument of this vision. By the middle of the twentieth century, however, the dream had become static. The Depression and two World Wars had bred an oppressive anxiety for security. The country was driven to reach its industrial apex and the Fat Dream had come true. At precisely this point, James Dean appeared as Cal Trask as Jim Stark as Jett Rink, the inevitable Cain in America's Garden of Eden—the destroyer of illusion, the destructive adolescent, the violent agent of change and herald of a new era.

Jimmy's star ascended at a moment in American history when our original ideals had been so mislaid that a literal reading of the Constitution could be taken as treason. In the Eisenhower fifties, our country suffered symptoms not unlike those which had caused the original pilgrims to venture West and provoked the American colonists to rebel against an indifferent tyrant. Ironically, the disease created its own remedy. The new affluence had spread to one of the invisible societies within America's homogeneous identity—its adolescents. Within the framework of the decaying organism, this large group was given a new economic power which allowed it to create its own culture. Like the beginning of *A Clockwork Orange*, the middle class had moved to the moon and inadvertently left the country to its children. Unnoticed by adults, they began to shape themselves, their attitudes and their separate world, spending their own money on clothes, records and movies which would proliferate in the fifties and, by the sixties, generate a current that would short-circuit the entire adult system.

Until they started to acquire economic power, adolescents had not existed in the real world and were considered to be merely at an awkward stage of advanced childhood. This invisible state was further aggravated by the absence of heroes with whom they could identify. The idols of their parents were lifeless symbols of the status quo. James Dean gave adolescents a face, *his* face, and with this communal image they could define and defend themselves. Adolescence embodies the original fantasy of America as a child of innocence with new-found freedom and powers. It was by giving this fantasy a face that James Dean reasserted the original vision, cut adolescents loose from the family and gave them a weapon to effect change: Childhood armed.

"The mobility of his (James Dean's) expression translates admirably the double nature of the adolescent face," said Edgar Morin in *The Stars*, "still hesitating between childhood's melancholy and the mask of the adult. The photogenic quality of this face, even more than that of Marlon Brando, is rich with all the indetermination of an ageless age, alternating scowls with astonishment, disarmed candor and playfulness with sudden hardness, resolution and rigor with collapse . . . The face of James Dean is an ever changing landscape in which can be discerned the contradictions, uncertainties and enthusiasms of the adolescent soul."

For a species to survive the hazards of a changing society the mutant must arise to make the transition from the old organism to the new. In the evolution of America this has always meant going back to the beginning. Our catalysts are always radicals and rebels who want to tear out the degenerate plant and begin again at the roots. How badly such a catalyst was needed in the fifties can be gauged by Jimmy's immediate acceptance.

Teenagers were the first to recognize this beautiful monster, this creature of a new species: James Dean, the mutant king. He appealed to them through the desperate and infectious condition of the mutant: *I need creatures who resemble me!*

He became a psychological center around which adolescence organized itself into a community, a sort of group soul. "Even intelligent and practical youth can be glad to have the larger framework of mythologies and ideologies predicting the course of the universe or the historical trend," said Erik Erikson. "Thus 'true' ideologies are verified by history—for if they can inspire youth, youth will make the predicted history come more than true."

A mutant is a freak, a sport of nature who must play two roles at once. He must be part of the old and play out the new. His success depends upon his performance and on that performance depends the future of the new species. As they adapt and transform into new creatures, mutants usually destroy themselves at an early stage. Jimmy Dean, who fought all the old hang-ups while showing us the future, was torn apart and erased in the process. In his attempt to embody the myth of total life, Jimmy confused himself with the world so often that a friend once said, "You'd think they were a simultaneous equation." In this impossible quest, like the hero of folklore, Jimmy sacrificed himself and encountered death.

This was the fulfillment of Jimmy's mission and his innermost wish. "I think there's only one true form of greatness for man," Jimmy said to James De Weerd, "if a man can bridge the gap between life and death. I mean if he can live on after he's died, then maybe he was a great man ... to me the only success, the only greatness, is immortality."

Jimmy's inner vision was so absolute he willingly sacrificed himself for its fulfillment. He longed to exist in the state of a divine Narcissus as a star. Only mirrors, photographs and movies can capture the true nature of these bodies of light. Jimmy collided with his own star, smashed the mirror and left us only the reflection. It is the fatal attraction heroes have for their own self-generated life—a worship of themselves which, like Cain's sacrifice, is a form of blasphemy, an image in the image of God.

In their narcissism stars tend to become interchangeable, as if the same presence radiates from all their features. Jackie Curtis said, "The young Gary Cooper looked in the mirror and saw Greta Garbo. Greta Garbo looked in the mirror and saw James Dean." But unlike the masks of Cooper or Garbo, Jimmy's face is iridescent and multifaceted. His star is both a beacon and symbol of transition, a mysterious emanation that persists long after its source has been destroyed.

Mutant derives its meaning from the same root as myth, and James

Dean became a myth through his mutations, a mystery we will never completely comprehend. "It's the secret that's never told that gives Jimmy the most extraordinary suspense," said Stewart Stern. "Even in death the secrets are still being withheld; the mystery of James Dean isn't over. It's the core of his excitement: what he did show and what he *refused* to show but indicated he might."

James Dean's death completed his invention. The mutant form he had unleashed would never be compromised. We are left with the myth of James Dean, a figure of light some twenty millimeters across on a strip of celluloid.

Bibliography

Numbers in parentheses give pages on which entries are cited in the text.

BOOKS

Allen, Steve. *Mark It and Strike It*. New York: Hill McFadden, 1976.

Anger, Kenneth. *Hollywood Babylone*. Paris: J. F. Pauverte, 1959. (150,337)

Astor, Mary. *A Life on Film*. New York: Delacorte Press, 1971. (108)

Backus, Jim. *Rocks on the Roof*. New York: G.P. Putnam's Sons, 1958. (3)

Barthes, Roland. *The Eiffel Tower*. New York: Hill and Wang, 1979.

Bast, William. *James Dean: A Biography*. New York: Ballantine Books, 1956. (38, 68–70, 71, 75, 88, 92, 127–8, 136, 138, 268–9, 326)

Bazin, André. *What is Cinema?* Vols. 1 and 2. Berkeley and Los Angeles: University of California Press, 1971. (309, 331)

de Becker, Raymond. *De Tom Mix à James Dean*. Paris: Librarie Anthème Fayard, 1959. (334–5)

Black, Matthew and Rowley, H. H. (eds.), *Peake's Commentary on the Bible*. London and New York: Thomas Nelson & Sons, 1962.

Blum, Daniel. *Pictorial History of Television*. Philadelphia and New York: Chilton Co., 1959.

Bockris, Victor. *With William Burroughs: A Report from the Bunker*. New York: Seaver Books, 1981.

Brough, James and Hedda Hopper. *The Whole Truth and Nothing But*. Garden City, N.Y.: Doubleday & Co., 1963. (8; 19, 20, 33–4, 72, 186, 268, 307)

Budge, E. A. Wallace. *The Egyptian Book of the Dead*. New York: Dover Publications, 1967. (xiii, 308, 335–6)

Burroughs, William S. *The Wild Boys*. New York: Grove Press, 1971. (328)

Campbell, Joseph. *The Hero with a Thousand Faces*. Cleveland: The World Publishing Co., 1949. (324)

Carey, Gary, *Brando!* New York: Pocket Books, 1973.

Carpozi, George, Jr. *That's Hollywood* Vol. 1. New York: Hill McFadden, 1962.

344

Céline, Louis-Ferdinand. *Guignol's Band*. New York: New Directions Books, 1954. (184)

Ciment, Michael. *Kazan on Kazan*. New York: The Viking Press, 1974.

Cole, Toby. *Acting: A Handbook of the Stanislavsky Method*. New York: Bonanza Books, 1971.

Corley, Edwin, *Farewell, My Slightly Tarnished Hero*. New York: Dodd, Mead & Co., 1971. (150)

Dalton, David. *James Dean: The Mutant King*. San Francisco: Straight Arrow Books, 1974.

Dickens, Charles. *The Pickwick Papers*. New York: Continental Press, 18–? (51)

Dos Passos, John. *Mid-Century*. Boston: Houghton Mifflin Co., 1960. (328)

Ellis, Royston. *Rebel*. London: Consul Books, 1962.

Erikson, Erik H, *Identity: Youth and Crisis*. New York: W. W. Norton & Co., 1968. (341–2)

Ferber, Edna. *Giant*. New York: Doubleday & Co., 1952.

Fox-Sheinwold, Patricia. *Too Young To Die*. New York: Bell Publishing, 1979.

Gide, André. *The Immoralist*. New York: Alfred A. Knopf, 1930.

Gilmore, John. *The Real James Dean*. New York: Pyramid Books, 1975.

Goetz, Augustus and Ruth. *The Immoralist: A Play*. New York: Dramatists Play Service, 1962. (144–5)

Goldman, Albert. *Elvis*. New York: McGraw-Hill, 1981.

Gow, Gordon. *Hollywood in the Fifties*. The International Film Guide Series. New York: A.S. Barnes & Co., 1971.

Hannah, David. *Hollywood Confidential*. New York: Leisure, 1976.

Hart, Jeffrey. *When the Going Was Good*. New York: Crown, 1982.

Heard, Gerald. *Pain, Sex, and Time*. New York: Harper & Brothers Publishers, 1939. (263)

Herndon, Venable. *James Dean: A Short Life*. New York: Doubleday & Co., 1974.

Hethmon, Robert H. *Strasberg at the Actors Studio: Tape Recorded Sessions*. New York: Viking Press, 1965. (287)

Howlett, John. *James Dean: A Biography*. London: Plexus; New York: Fireside/Simon & Schuster, 1975.

Hubbard, Elbert. *The Note Book of Elbert Hubbard*. New York: William H. Wise & Co., 1927. (104, 307)

Hyams, Joe. *Mislaid in Hollywood*. New York: Peter H. Wyden, 1973. (187, 199, 201)

Kael, Pauline. *I Lost It at the Movies*. Toronto: Little, Brown & Co., 1954. (180–1)

Kelley, Kitty. *Elizabeth Taylor: The Last Star*. New York: Simon & Schuster, 1981.

Kinder, Chuck. *The Silver Ghost*. New York: Harcourt Brace & Jovanovich, 1979.

Lawrence, D. H. *Studies in Classic American Literature*. New York: T. Seltzer, 1923. (28,340)

Lewis, R. W. B. *The American Adam*. Chicago: The University of Chicago Press, 1955. (55)

Lindner, Robert M. *Rebel Without a Cause*. New York: Grove Press, 1944. (223)

Lorca, Federico García. *Poet in New York*. New York: Grove Press, Inc., 1955.

Lynd, Helen Merrell and Robert S. *Middletown: A Study in Contemporary American Culture*. New York: Harcourt, Brace & Co., 1930.

McGrew, W. H. *Interesting Episodes in the Early History of Marion and Grant County, Indiana*. Grant County Historical Society, 1966. (14–5)

McLuhan, Marshall. *The Medium is the Message*. New York: Random House, 1967. (93–4)

Malone, Michael. *Heroes of Eros*. New York: E. P. Dutton, 1979.

Marinetti, Ron. *The James Dean Story*. New York: Pinnacle Books, 1975.

Mellen, Joan. *The Big Bad Wolves*. New York: Pantheon, 1977.

Minahan, John. *9/30/55*. New York: Avon, 1977.

Morin, Edgar. *The Stars*. New York: Grove Press, 1960. (317, 328, 335–6, 341)

Parish, James Robert. *Actors' Television Credits, 1950–1972*. Metuchen, N.J.: Scarecrow Press, 1973. (98–100)

Richie, Donald. *George Stevens: An American Romantic*. New York: The Museum of Modern Art, 1970. (299)

Riley, James Whitcomb. *The Complete Biographical Works of James Whitcob Riley*. Indianapolis: Bobbs-Merrill, Inc., 1913. (283)

Riley, James Whitcomb. *Joyful Poems for Children*. Indianapolis: Bobbs-Merrill, 1941.

Ross, Walter. *The Immortal*. New York: Simon & Schuster, 1958. (23,150)

de Saint Exupéry, Antoine. *The Little Prince*. New York: Harcourt, Brace & Co., 1943.

Schatt, Roy. *James Dean: A Portrait*. New York: Delilah Books, 1982.

Schilder, Paul. *The Image and Appearance of the Human Body*. New York: International Universities Press, Inc., 1950. (80, 118, 337)

Shulman, Arthur and Youman, Roger. *The Television Years*. New York: Popular Library, 1973.

Shulman, Irving. *Children of the Dark*. (Novelization of *Rebel Without a Cause*.) New York: Henry Holt, 1956.

Stanislavsky, Konstatin. *An Actor Prepares*. New York: Theatre Arts Books, 1936.

Stanislavsky, Konstatin. *My Life in Art*. New York: Viking Press, 1948. (80, 93)

Steinbeck, John. *America and Americans*. New York: Viking Press, 1966. (161–2)

Steinbeck, John. *East of Eden*. New York: Viking Press, 1952.

Steinbeck, John. *Journey of a Novel (The East of Eden Letters)*. New York: Viking Press, 1969.

Stock, Dennis. *Portrait of a Young Man*. Tokyo: Kukto Kawa Shoten, 1956.

Stock, Dennis. *James Dean Revisited*. New York and London: Penguin Books, 1978.

Suares, Carlo. *The Cipher of Genesis*. Berkeley: Shambala Publications, 1970. (183)

Tanners, Louise. *Here Today*. New York: Delta, 1959.

Tarkington, Booth. *Penrod*. Garden City, N.Y.: Doubleday, Page, 1914. (30–2)

Tashman, George. *I Love You Clark Gable . . . etc*. [Foreword by Natalie Wood.] Richmond, Calif.: Brombocher, 1976.

Taylor, Liz. *An Informal Memoir*. New York: Harper & Row, 1965.

Thomas, Bob. *Marlon: Portrait of the Rebel as an Artist*. New York: Random House, 1973.

Thomas, T. T. *I, James Dean*. New York: Popular Library, 1957. (8)

Truchaud, François. *Nicholas Ray*. Paris: Classiques du Cinema, 1965.

Twain, Mark. *The Adventures of Huckleberry Finn*. Indianapolis: Bobbs-Merrill, 1913. (291)

Villiers, Marceau. *James Dean*. Paris: Anthologie du Cinema, L'Avant Scene du Cinema, 1966.

Wilder, Thornton. *Our Town: A Play in Three Acts*. New York: Coward, McCann, 1938. (17, 27)

Williams, William Carlos. *The American Grain*. New York: New Directions Books, 1925.

Winters, Shelley. *Shelley Also Known as Shirley*. New York: William Morrow & Co., 1980.

The Films of James Dean. London: B. C. W. Publishing, 1974.

The First American Teenager: James Dean. Tokyo: 1980.

James Dean Catalogue. Tokyo: 1980.

James Dean ou le mal de vivre. Paris: Pierre Horay, 1957.

The James Dean Story. Paris: Rene Chateau, 30 September 1975.

La vida apasionate de James Dean. Madrid: Figuras De Toy, 1979.

ARTICLES

Adams, Nick. "Jimmy's Happiest Moments." *Modern Screen*, October 1956.

Agan, Patrick. "James Dean: The Rebel Who Wouldn't Die." *Hollywood Studio Magazine*, August 1982.

Alpert, H. "It's Dean, Dean, Dean." *Saturday Review*, 13 October 1956.

Anderson, Lindsay. *New Statesman*, 12 January 1957. (304)

Angeli, Pier. "James Dean's Ghost Wrecked My Two Marriages." *National Enquirer*, September 1968. (196, 198)

Archer, Eugene. "Generation Without a Cause." *Film Culture*, no. 1, 1956.

Archer, Joe. "Here Is the Real Story of My Life—by James Dean, as I Might Have Told It to Joe Archer." Original manuscript on file at Marion, Indiana Public Library, dated 24 November 1956. (322–3)

Aros, Andrew. "Yearbook Reviewed." *Journal of Popular Film*, no. 1, 1975.

Astrachan, S. "New Lost Generation." *New Republic*, 4 February 1957. (285–6)

Baker, B. "James Dean." *Film Dope*, April 1976.

Bast, William. "There was a Boy." *Photoplay*, November 1956.

Bean, R. "Dean: Ten Years After." *Films and Filming*, October 1965.

Beinedet, Yvette. "Contact." *American Photographer*, November 1982.

Belser, Lee. "James Dean's Fans Still Write to Him." *Los Angeles Mirror*, 30 September 1960. (311)

Brandes, T. J. "Fan Interview." *New Yorker*, 2 August 1969.

Brock, A. "My Experiences as an Agent: Brando and Dean." *Classic Film Collector*, Summer 1975.

Calende, John. "Vampira and the Ghost of James Dean: Interview with Maila Nurmi." *Interview*, October 1975.

Capen, Jeanne Balch. "The Strange Revival of James Dean." *Indianapolis Star Magazine*, July 1956.

Capote, Truman. "Brando by Capote." *The New Yorker*, November 1957. (194–5, 324–5)

Chouraqui, Monique. "James Dean Aura Toujours 20 Ans." *20 Ans*, December 1980.

Clemens, Harry. "The Romance Jimmy Dean Couldn't Kill." *Uncensored*, March 1957.

Cole, C. "The Dean Myth." *Films & Filming*, January 1957.

Coleman, A. D. "Review of Dennis Stock's Photographs," *Village Voice*, 25 May 1972.

Conn, Earl. "James Dean . . . Fairmount Guard." *Indianapolis Star*, 22 February 1959. (48–51)

Connolly, Mike. "Jimmy Dean's Last Message." *Modern Screen*, January 1957.

Conroy, Frank. "America in a Trance." *Esquire*, June 1983.

Cook, Jim. "Jimmy Dean Is Not Dead." *Motion Picture*, May 1956.

Cotton, J. Von. "La Fascinante reincarnation des grandes stars disparus." *Ciné Review*, 23 April 1981.

Crowther, Bosley. "The 'East of Eden' of Elia Kazan Has That, But Not Much More." *The New York Times*, 20 March 1955. (177)

Crowther, Bosley. "Rebel Without a Cause." *The New York Times*, 27 October 1955. (284)

Crowther, Bosley. "The Screen: 'East of Eden' Has Debut." *The New York Times*, 10 March 1955. (178)

Crumpacker, Samuel. "James Dean Retrospective." *Santa Monica City College Yearbook*, 1973. (62).

Dalton, David. "The Making of a Celluloid Rebel." *Rolling Stone*, 20 June, 1974.

Dangaard, Colin. "A Mine Giant Who Cried for Love." *National Star*, 18 September 1974. (28)

Dean, Emma Woolen. "The Boy I Loved." *Photoplay*, March 1956. (4, 5, 6, 21, 41–2, 54, 213, 216–7)

Dent, Alan. "Delinquents All." *Illustrated London News*, 4 January 1956. (239)

Denton, Charles. "James Dean Legend May Swell to Make Him Valentino of Present Generation." *INS*, 4 March 1956. (319)

Dixon, Daniel. "Darling Jimmy Dean." *Pageant*, October 1956. (315, 327)

Dos Passos, John. "Death of James Dean." *Esquire*, October 1973. (157)

Dudar, Helen. "The Legend of Jimmy Dean." *New York Post*, 19 August 1956.

Ebon, Martin. "American Fascinations." *To-morrow*, December 1956. (334)

Flattery, Paul. "Adam Faith: Ex-Pop Idol a TV Star." *Rolling Stone*, 15 March 1973. (329)

Funk, Arville L. "The First Big Train Robbery." *Outdoor Indiana*, July-August 1972. (19)

Goodman, Ezra. "Delirium Over Dead Star." *Life*, 24 September 1956.

Halzenad, Chris. "James Dean and Ferment in the Fifties." *After Dark*, February 1976.

Hamilton, Elroy. "Forty Isn't Old for a Legend." *Chicago Sun Times*, 24 January 1971.

Hanson, Kitty. "Jimmy Dean: They Won't Let Him R.I.P." *New York Daily News*, 28 September 1956.

Harrison, Carroll. "James Dean Planning to Go On Racing Kick When 'Giant' Ends." *Los Angeles Herald-Examiner*, 16 September 1955. (27)

Hatley, Guy. "At the Movies." *The New York Times*, 8 October 1976.

Haun, Harry. "James Dean." *New York Sunday News*, 28 September 1980.

Heffernan, Harold. "The Cult That Won't Quit." *Detroit Free Press*, 31 August 1956.

Hendrickson, Paul. "The Legend That Won't Go Away." *Philadelphia Enquirer*, 22 July 1973. (25)

Hill, Ken. "Hill-Side Views." *Marion Chronicle*, 13 August, 1970. (48–51)

Holmes, John Clellan. "The Philosophy of the Beats." *Esquire*, June 1983.

Honor, E. "Hollywood Tragedies." *Cosmopolitan*, October 1956.

Hopper, Hedda. "Young Men of Hollywood. *Coronet*, July 1955.

Hunt, E.H. "To James Dean." *Photoplay*, July 1956.

Hyams, Joe. "James Dean." *Redbook*, September 1956. (38, 44–5, 274–5)

Hyams, Joe. "When James Dean Lost Pier Angeli to Vic Damone." *National Enquirer*, 4 November 1973.

Jahr, Cliff. "James Dean was Maybe Dylan and Garbo Too." *Village Voice*, 6 October, 1975.

Kazan, Elia. "Interview with Elia Kazan." *Cahiers du Cinéma*, March 1967. (162, 172)

Kazan, Elia. "Interview with Elia Kazan." *American Film*, March 1976.

Kendall, Robert. "James Dean Collecting is Now Worldwide." *Saturday Review*, August 1982.

————. "A World of James Dean Memorabilia." *Hollywood Studio Magazine*, December 1982.

Knight, Arthur. "Celluloid Monument." *Saturday Review*, 3 August, 1957.

————. "Saturday Review Goes to the Movies." *Saturday Review*, November 1955. (283)

Lalonde, Gaby. "Perche 'James Dean E' Ancora Vivo." *Cinema Nuovo*, March 1957. (330)

Lambert, Gavin. "Rebels and Causes." *Twentieth Century*, March 1956.

Lardinois, J. M. "Etude: James Dean ou la trilogie du rebelle sans cause." *Apec: Revue Belge du Cinema* vol. 13, 1975.

Lewis, Grover. "Paul Newman: Portrait of the Artist at 47." *Rolling Stone*, 5 July 1973. (155, 178)

Loehr, David. "James Dean: A Photographic Reflection." *Topman*, 29 September 1980.

Loynd, Ray. "Some Unsentimental Memories of James Dean by Rock Hudson." *Hollywood Reporter*, 9 August 1968. (297)

McCarthy, Jim. "It's Me, Jimmy." *Modern Screen*, December 1956. (52, 77–8, 148)

Marlowe, Derek. "Soliloquy on James Dean's Forty-Fifth Birthday." *New York*, 8 November, 1976.

Martin, Jack. "Cult Gathering at Grave of Movie Idol James Dean." *New York Post*, 22 September 1982.

Maslin, J. "Clift, Brando and Dean at Regency." *New York Times*, 26 May 1978.

Mellor, William. "James Dean." *Picturegoer*, 29 December 1956.

Meltsir, Aljean. "James Dean—His Life and Loves." *Motion Picture*, September 1956. (5–6, 37, 39, 63, 281, 342)

Meltsir, Aljean. "Life after Death." *Photoplay*, September 1963.

Miller, Edwin. "An Actor in Search of Himself." *Seventeen*, October 1955. (72, 194, 262–3, 306–7)

Mitgang, Herbert. "The Strange James Dean Death Cult." *Coronet*, November 1956.

Montice, G. "James Dean vit toujours." *Ane Revue*, 22 May 1975.

Morin, Edgar. "The Case of James Dean." *Evergreen Review*, Summer 1958.

Mosby, Aline. "James Dean Still Idolized." *Hollywood Citizen News*, May 1956.

Nash, Richard N. "See the Jaguar." *Theatre Arts*, August 1953. (131–2)

Nelson, Lori. "The Dean I've Dated." *Motion Picture*, September 1955.

Nolan, William. "His Love Destroyed Him." *Modern Screen*, February 1957.

Nurmi, Maila. "The Ghost of James Dean." *Borderline*, January 1964.

O'Brien, Glenn. "Interview with Elia Kazan." *Interview*, March 1972. (153, 163, 167, 172, 179, 180, 188)

O'Dowd, Brian. "James Dean Tribute." *Hollywood Studio Magazine*, May 1982.

————. "James Dean's Memorial in Chalome." *Saturday Review*, August 1982.

O'Shea, Arthur. "How a Dead Actor Was Exploited." *Detroit Free Press*, 4 November 1956. (319–20)

Olson, Nancy and R. Winer. "Satan's Own Child." *New York Post*, 26 December, 1979.

Owen, Jean. "An Unforgettable Day with Jimmy Dean." *Movieland*, February 1957. (60–2)

Parsons, Louella. "Louella Parsons in Hollywood." *Modern Screen*, March 1955; August 1956. (185, 319)

Parsons, Tony. "James Dean: Take This God and Bury It." *New Musical Express*, 16 May 1981.

Peapon, G. "The James Dean Jinx: On the Stage." *Film Illustrated*, November 1977.

Peterson, Iver. "Young Drawn to James Dean 25 Years After." *The New York Times*, October 1980.

Ray, Nick. "Portrait de l'acteur en jeune homme: James Dean." *Cahiers du Cinéma*, December 1956.

————. "Story into Script." *Sight and Sound*, Fall 1956. (222, 225–6)

Rees, Bob. "A World of James Dean Memorabilia." *Hollywood Studio Magazine*, October 1982.

Richards, May Hines. "BARS!" *Senior Approved Selections* no. 21, National Women's Christian Temperance Union, Evanston, Ill. (34)

Ringgold, Gene. "James Dean." *Screen Facts* no. 8, 1964.

————. "A James Dean Album." *Nostalgia Illustrated*, November 1974.

————. "James Dean: His Life and Legend." [Includes a list of TV and radio performances.] *Screen Legends*, May 1965.

Robinson, Charles. "Their Great Original." *The New Statesman*, December 1957. (329)

Rochlen, Kendis (Kandid Kendis). "Dean Wants Isolation." *Los Angeles Mirror-News*, 29 March 1955. (192)

———. "The Sad and the Glad." *Los Angeles Mirror-News*, 2 November 1954. (197–8)

Roth, Sanford. "The Assignment I'll Never Forget: James Dean." *Popular Photography*, July 1962. (277, 279, 281)

Roth, Sanford. "The Late James Dean." *Colliers*, 25 November, 1955. (136)

Schaeffer, Sam. "James Dean: Ghost Rider of Polono Pass." *Whisper*, December 1957.

Scheuer, Philip K. "Jimmy Dean Says He Isn't Flattered by Being Labeled 'Another Brando.'" *Los Angeles Times*, 7 November, 1954. (179, 183)

Scullin, George. "James Dean: The Legend and the Facts." *Look*, October 1956. (8)

Shafer, Jack. "What Jimmy Dean Believed." *Modern Screen*, October 1957. (134)

Shales, Tom. "TV Film on James Dean: Tries to Ignore the Myth." *Washington Post*, February 1976.

Shaw, B. "Dead 25 Years: James Dean is Given Touching Hometown Tribute by Nostalgic Fans." *People*, 13 October, 1980.

Sheridan, Elizabeth. "In Memory of Jimmy." *Photoplay*, October 1957.

Siclier, Jacques. "James Dean as Patron Saint of the Rebels Without a Cause." *Présence du Cinéma*, April 1962.

Simsolo, Noel. "Nicholas Ray." *La Revue du Cinéma*, July 1970.

Skolsky, Sidney. "Demon Dean." *Photoplay*, July 1955. (193)

Stevens, George. "Interview with George Stevens." *Cahiers du Cinéma*, April 1960.

———. "A Tenderness Lost." *Modern Screen*, January 1956. (304, 306)

Stock, Dennis. "Moody New Star." *Life*, March 1955.

Sullivan, Dennis and Wayne Jones, "Rebel Without a Cause." *Nostalgia World*, March 1979.

Tanner, L. "Best Years of Their Lives: Condensation of *Here Today*." *Coronet*, March 1960.

———. "Here Today . . ." *Bark Digest*, 14 August, 1960.

Taylor, T. "His Name was Dean." *Cue*, 29 September 1956.

Thompson, Howard. "Another Dean Hits the Big League." *The New York Times*, 13 March 1955. (174–6)

Thompson, K. "1956: Year of Dean's Triumph." *Film Illustrated*, November 1977.

Truffaut, François. "Feu de James Dean." *Arts*, September 1956. (286)

Tsyl, Robert Wayne. "Continuity and Evolution in a Public Symbol: An Investigation into the Creation and Communication of the Image of James Dean in Mid-Century America." Ph.D. dissertation, University of Michigan, 1983.

Tweedale, Tony. "The Legend of James Dean." *Photoplay*, June 1972.

Vallance, T. "James Dean Soundtracks." *Focus On Film*, Winter 1976.

Weales, G. "Movies: The Crazy Mixed Up Kids Take Over." *Reporter*, 13 December 1956.

White, Christine. "James Dean: Prelude to a Legend." *International Press Bulletin* no. 5, 1966. (84–5, 89–91, 209, 217)

Williams, Dick. "Continued Worship of Dean Assumes Macabre Aspect." *Los Angeles Mirror-News*, 6 August 1956. (311)

———. "Elia Kazan Decries the James Dean Myth." *Los Angeles Mirror-News*, 25 April 1957. (92)

Williams, Joy. "Rebel Without a Cause." *Esquire*, October 1982.

Wills, Beverly. "I Almost Married Jimmy Dean." *Modern Screen*, March 1957. (70–1, 73–5)

Wilmington, Mike. "James Dean: An Appreciation. *High Times*, April 1981.

Winslow, Marcus, as told to Aljean Meltsir. "You Can Make Jimmy Dean Live Forever." *Motion Picture*, November 1956. (320–1)

Winters, Shelley. "The Loneliest Years of My Life." *Seventeen*, Summer 1962.

Wood, Natalie. "You Haven't Heard the Half About Jimmy Dean." *Photoplay*, October 1955. (204–7)

Worth, Frank. "Don't Print That Photo." *Sixteen*, November 1957. (193–4)

Wutherich, Rolf. "The Last Story About Jimmy." *Modern Screen*, October 1955.

———. "Death Drive." *Modern Screen*, October 1957. (179–81, 275–6)

York, Cal. "Inside Stuff." *Photoplay*, November 1954; October 1955. (178, 195)

Zavatsky, W. "Epitaph for a Rebel: Reflections in the Life and Death of James Dean." *Rolling Stone*, 16 October 1980.

Zinsser, William. "East of Eden." *New York Herald Tribune*, 10 March 1955. (177)

———. "Rebel Without a Cause." *New York Herald Tribune*, 27 October 1955. (283)

Zolotow, Maurice. "Are Dean Fans 'Buying' Phony Idol?" *Detroit Fress Press*, 28 October 1956. (319)

"Avere vent'anni non e' sufficiente per essere felici." *Ciao Amici* (Italian), 11 December 1965.

"The Boy Who Followed Jimmy Dean to Death." *Movie Stars*, March 1959.

"Cause Or Causes Unknown." *Inside Hollywood* no. 2, 1956.

"Come Back to the Five and Dime." *The New York Times*, 14 November, 1982.

"Culture Notes." *The New York Times*, September, 1957. (331)

"Dean Cult." *Time*, November 1956.

"Dean of the One-Shotters." *Time*, March 1956.

"Death of Star James Dean in Crash Stuns Hollywood." *New York Post*, 2 October 1955. (281)

"Did James Dean Commit Suicide?" *Inside*, May 1956.

"Entire Script 'Eden.'" *Literary Cavalcade*, October 1975.

"A Giant Tribute for the Rebel James Dean." *New York Post*, 1 October, 1980.

"Good Country Boy." *Time*, July 1957.

"Goodbye, Jimmy: Letters." *Modern Screen*, March 1956. (318, 336)

"Gringo with Guts." *Modern Screen*, March 1958.

"Hollywood's Unhappy Stories." *Movie Mirror*, December 1962.

"I'm Dying to Meet You." *TV Magazine*, November 1964.

"In Death, James Dean a Hero to French." *Variety*, 11 July 1956.

"James Dean." *Variety*, 5 January 1966. (232)

"James Dean: An Assessment Ten Years After." *Films and Filming*, October 1965.

"James Dean Did Not Die in Fatal Car Crash Auto Accident. Paralysed and Mutilated He's Hidden in a Sanatorium." *Enquirer*, 1973.

"James Dean Honored at Farewell Party." *Fairmount News*, 15 June 1949. (54–5)

"James Dean Joins Theatre Group." *Fairmount News*, 27 June, 1949. (60)

"The James Dean Story." *Screenplay*, April 1965.

"The James Dean Story: A Legend Revisited." *Dig*, August 1962.

"James Dean Takes Part in TV Show." *Fairmount News*, December 1954. (101)

"James Dean Theater School Goes Broke. Shrine to New Star Now a Furniture Store." *Indianapolis News*.

"James Dean: White Hope of Hollywood Cinema." *Film Studio* no. 38, 1963.

"James Dean's Black Madonna." *Whisper*, February 1956. (191)

"James Dean's Strange Legacy." *Movie Life*, July 1956.

"James Dean e il mito dell'adolescente sinistro." *Cinema Nuovo*, November-December 1958.

"Jimmy Dean Legend is Still Fresh." *UPI*, 29 September 1960.

"Jimmy Dean Returns." *Movie Teen Illustrated*, Fall 1957.

"Jimmy Mania: Dean & Bond." *Variety*, 27 October 1965. (336–7)

"Jimmy's Happiest Moments." *Modern Screen*, October 1956.

"Jinx Trails Dean's Car." *Los Angeles Mirror-News*, 24 October 1956. (316)

"Letter to the Editor." *Whisper*, April 1956.

"A Living Memorial to James Dean." *Indianapolis Star Magazine*, 9 December 1956.

"Lone Wolf." *Modern Screen*, August 1955.

"Moody New Star." *Life*, 7 March, 1955.

"Notre Copain James Dean par Johnny Hallyday." *CinéMonde*, May 1962.

"Painting the Spirit of the Past with Biographical Sketch." *American Artist*, March 1971.

"Portrait of a Funeral." *The New York Times*, 7 October 1957.

"Princeton Honors Dean." *Hollywood Reporter*, 1 March 1956. (322)

"Quick Rise of an Early Riser." *Life*, 7 October 1957.

"Reappraisal of James Dean." *Film Kritik*, July 1964.

"Rebel and Giant Too." *Star Movie* vol. 1, no. 2.

"Rebel Without a Cause." *Screen Stories*, July 1956.

"Rebel Without Certificate Problems." *Films Illustrated*, June 1976.

"The Saga of Jimmy Dean." *Movie Life Yearbook*, 1957.

"Sand, Sweat, and Stevens." *Movie Screen Yearbook*, 1955.

"School for Actors Will Honor James Dean." *New York Herald Tribune*, May 1957.

"The Six Unsolved Mysteries of Jimmy's Death." *Movie Stars Parade*, October 1958.

"Star that Won't Dim." *Newsweek*, 18 July, 1956.

Suspicious Cops Nab a 'Ghost.'" *Los Angeles Mirror-News*, 30 November 1956. (313)

"Talk of the Town." *The New Yorker*, 2 August 1969. (311–3)

"The Unlighted Road: The Jimmy Dean Festival." *Screen Stories*, September 1956.

"Le vrai James Dean." *Photo*, January 1981.

"Warren: Le Regard de James Dean." *CineMonde*, May 1962.

"Why They Still Worship James Dean." *Tempo*, November 1956. (162)

"Your Chance to Vote: Should Elvis Presley Play Jimmy Dean on the Screen?" *Movie Stars Parade*, October 1956.

"Your James Dean Memorial Medallion." *Modern Screen*, October 1956.

SPECIAL-ISSUE MAGAZINES

Fairmount News—Special Issue, October 1955. (81)

James Dean Album. New York: Ideal Publishing, 1956.

James Dean Anniversary Book. New York: Dell Publishing Co., 1956. (228, 247–8, 266–7, 274, 306)

James Dean Returns! Read His Own Words From the Beyond. New York: Rave Publishing, 1956. (318–9)

The Real James Dean Story vol. 1, no. 1. New York: Fawcett Publications, 1956.

Hollywood Yearbook, 1957

Dig Tribute Issue. August 1962

Screen Legends Tribute Magazine vol. 1, no. 1, May 1965.
Photoplay Special Edition. 1967.
James Dean: Rebell, Idol, Legende. German Tribute Magazine 1980.
Avant Scène du Cinéma Tribute Issue. Includes: Truman Capote, Nick Ray, George Stevens, François Truffaut. December 1966.

INCIDENTAL FILM REVIEWS

America, 5 November 1955. (284)
Fairmount News, 7 April, 1955. (177)
Library Journal, 1 March, 1955. (177)
The Nation, 3 December, 1955. (285)
The Nation, 20 October, 1956. (300)
Newsweek, 7 November, 1955 (284)
Time, 21 March 1955. (177, 183)

PORTFOLIOS OF PHOTOGRAPHS

Dennis Stock. 10 prints in an edition of 125 copies. New York, Ron Cayen Inc., 1981.

Roy Schatt. 10 prints in an edition of 150 copies. New York, Peter Rose Inc, 1983.

CALENDARS

Sanford Roth: *The James Dean Calendar*. New York, The Pomegranate Press, 1982.

Roy Schatt: *James Dean*. New York, Ruggles De La Tour Inc., 1984.

Discography

The link between James Dean and rock 'n' roll is inherent, but did you know he'd written a song since he's been gone? This item appeared in Howard Smith's "Scenes" in the *Village Voice*:

James Dean's only rock 'n' roll song has never been recorded. According to Robert Bowden of New Jersey, who says he wrote the music to the song that contains Dean's lyrics, it happened this way:

A composer of 25 rock 'n' roll songs from the 1950s, Bowden was a big fan of the late film star back then.

In 1954, he began a correspondence with the actor, which ended with a suggestion that they collaborate on a song. Later that year, he says, Dean sent him a sheet of lyrics entitled "Will You Miss Me Tonight." Bowden wrote a tune to his words and sent it off to Hollywood, where Dean was working on *Rebel Without a Cause*. Bowden mentioned he was a member of BMI, so I called the performance association. His pop career checked out, but BMI told me that "Will You Miss Me Tonight" was only listed under Bowden's name; I asked the composer about it.

"James Dean didn't belong to BMI," he said. "The song is copyrighted in Washington with both our names and half the royalties go to Dean's estate."

"I never saw him in person," says Bowden. "But I think he'd like it if I could get it recorded. I think a lot of people miss him."

Allusions to James Dean in sixties rock include: Lou Reed's "Walk on the Wild Side," Loudon Wainwright's "School Days," Bruce Springsteen's "Cadillac Ranch," Mott the Hoople's "All the Young Dudes," and Don McLean's "American Pie," not to mention entire cuts such as Phil Ochs's "James Dean of Indiana," David Essex's "Rock On," and the Eagles' "James Dean."

Steve Yeager has compiled the following discography of James Dean tribute records from the fifties, the best of which will be included on a compilation album to be issued in the next year as a two-record set.

JAMES DEAN RECORDS—45 RPM

NAME	ARTIST	TIME	LABEL
JAMIE BOY (Joe Shapiro-Lou Stillman) B/W	KAY STARR	2:07	RCA VICTOR 47-6864 Rush Music Co
A LITTLE LONELINESS	——	2:24	BMI
DEANIE BOY (T. Dean) B/W	TOMMY DEANS ORCHESTRA	2:30	VEE-JAY 54-216 Conrad Music
EVENTIME	JOE BUCKNER	2:30	BMI
THEME FROM *EAST OF EDEN* (Leonard Rosenman) B/W	VICTOR YOUNG	3:12	Decca 9-29523
THE WORLD IS MINE	——	3:09	
THEME FROM *EAST OF EDEN* (Leonard Rosenman) B/W	DICK JACOBS AND HIS ORCHESTRA	2:27	Coral 9-61692
THE SEVEN WONDERS OF THE WORLD	——	3:01	
SECRET DOORWAY (Theme from *Rebel Without A Cause*) (Rosenman-Discant) B/W	SHIRLEY HARMAR ORCHESTRA & CHORUS BY LEROY HOLMES	3:22	M-G-M K12121
PLEASE HURRY HOME	——	3:10	

NAME	ARTIST	TIME	LABEL
GIANT (Dimitri Tiomkin- Paul Francis Webster) B/W	JACK PLEIS AND HIS CHORUS AND ORCHESTRA	2:56	Decca 9-30055
LONESOME WITHOUT YOU	——	2:48	
GIANT (Dimitri Tiomkin- Paul Francis Webster) B/W	LES BAXTER HIS ORCHESTRA & CHORUS	2:05	Capital F3526 ASCAP
*THERE'S NEVER BEEN ANYONE ELSE BUT YOU (Love Theme from *Giant*)	——	2:31	
GIANT (Dimitri Tiomkin- Paul Francis Webster) B/W	ART MOONEY AND HIS ORCHESTRA & CHORUS	2:10 2:12	M-G-M K12320
ROCK AND ROCK TUMBLEWEED	——		
JAMES DEAN (Larry Coleman) B/W	JIMMY WAKELY AND GEORGE CATES ORCHESTRA & CHORUS	2:41	Coral 9-61722
*JIMMY, JIMMY (Ben Weisman-Aaron Schroeder)	——	2:12	
HIS NAME WAS DEAN (Eddie Stuart) B/W	JIMMY WAKELY AND GEORGE CATES ORCHESTRA & CHORUS	2:32	Coral 9-61706
*GIANT (Dimitri Tiomkin-Paul Francis Webster)	——	2:47	
HIS NAME WAS DEAN (Eddie Stuart)	NATHAN RUSSELL ORCHESTRA & VOCAL UNDER THE DIRECTION OF RAY ELLIS	2:11	Forest 45-FB-448 Scope Music, Inc.
B/W I WALK IN THE FUTURE	——	2:35	BMI

NAME	ARTIST	TIME	LABEL
THE BALLAD OF JAMES DEAN (Jack Hammer) B/W	DICK JACOBS AND HIS CHORUS	2:47	Coral 9-61705
*A BOY NAMED JIMMY DEAN (Stanley Clayton-Ruth Roberts–Bill Katz)	——	2:31	
THE BALLAD OF JAMES DEAN (Jack Hammer) B/W THE JAPANESE FAREWELL SONG	THE FOUR TUNES ——	2:12	Jubilee 45-5255 Goday Music BMI
JAMES DEAN'S FIRST CHRISTMAS IN HEAVEN	RED RIVER DAVE	2:41	TNT Dave McEnery Music A.S.C.A.P.
MESSAGE FROM JAMES DEAN (Danger, Danger, Danger) (E. Deane-H. Stride) B/W TRAIL'S END	BILL HAYES ORCHESTRA CONDUCTED BY ARCHIE BLEYER	1:52 2:35	Cadence 1301 Larry Taylor Music ASCAP
THE JAMES DEAN LOVE SONG (Springsong) B/W	RED RIVER DAVE	3:01	T.N.T. 9006 Dave McEnery A.S.C.A.P.
*JAMES DEAN (The Greatest of All) (Dave McEnery)	RED RIVER DAVE	3:08	

JAMES DEAN ALBUM EP NO. 1

| JAMES DEAN DECK OF CARDS
(Dave McEnery)
JIMMY DEAN IS NOT DEAD
(Dave McEnery) | RED RIVER DAVE

RED RIVER DAVE | 3:01

3:12 | T.N.T.
Dave McEnery
Music
A.S.C.A.P. |

EP NO. 2

| *HYMN FOR JAMES DEAN
(Dave McEnery)
HOME IN INDIANA, JAMES DEAN | RED RIVER DAVE WITH CAROLYN | 3:02

3:13 | T.N.T.
Dave McEnery
Music
A.S.C.A.P. |

NAME	ARTIST	TIME	LABEL
JAMES DEAN'S MESSAGE TO TEENAGERS (Buckley meets Jimmy at Jazz City) B/W SPEAK FOR YOURSELF JOHN (Hip version for John Alden & Priscilla)	As told by "LORD" RICHARD BUCKLEY ——		HIP RECORDS HI 302-1
LET ME BE LOVED (Theme from *The James Dean Story*) (Livingston-Evans) B/W LOVE ME FOREVER	EDIE GORME ARRANGED & CONDUCTED BY DON COSTA TRUMPET SOLO BY BERNIE GLOW ——	2:45	A.B.C. Paramount 45-9863 Livingston-Evans Music Co. ASCAP
LET ME BE LOVED (Jay Livingston-Ray Evans) (Theme from *The James Dean Story*) B/W FANTASTICALLY FOOLISH	TOMMY SANDS ——	2:27	Capital 45-16865 Livingston-Evans Music Co. ASCAP
LET ME BE LOVED (Livingston-Evans) (Main theme from *The James Dean Story*) B/W CALL OF THE WEST	MANTOVANI AND HIS ORCHESTRA TRUMPET SOLO BY STAN NEWSOME	2:39	London 45-1761 Livingston-Evans Music Co. ASCAP
THE BALLAD OF JAMES DEAN (Jack Hammer) B/W MORE PRECIOUS THAN GOLD	DYLAN TODD WITH JOE REISMAN AND HIS ORCHESTRA ——	2:42	RCA Victor

NAME	ARTIST	TIME	LABEL
GIANT From (George Stevens Prod. *Giant*-presented by Warner Bros. Pict. PF. Webster Tiomkin B/W	RAY HEINDORF AND THE WARNER BROS. ORCHESTRA		Columbia 4-40761
*THERE'S NEVER BEEN ANYONE ELSE BUT YOU From George Stevens Prod. *Giant* presented by Warner Bros. Pict. P.F. Webster- Tiomkin	——		
TRIBUTE TO JAMES DEAN THEME FROM *EAST OF* *EDEN* (Warner Bros. Pict. *East of* *Eden*) (Rosenman) B/W	ART MOONEY AND HIS ORCHESTRA		M-G-M K12312
*THEME FROM *REBEL* *WITHOUT A CAUSE* (Warner Bros. Pict. *Rebel* *Without A Cause*) (Rosenman)	——		
TRIBUTE TO JAMES DEAN THEME FROM *EAST OF* *EDEN* (From the soundtrack of the Warner Bros. Pict. *East of* *Eden*—Rosenman) B/W	RAY HEINDORF AND THE WARNER BROS. ORCHESTRA	1:48	Columbia 4-40754
*THEME FROM *REBEL* *WITHOUT A CAUSE* (From the soundtrack of the Warner Bros. Pict. *Rebel* *Without A Cause*-Rosenman)	——	2:36	

NAME	ARTIST	TIME	LABEL

MUSIC FROM MOTION PICTURES
STARRING JAMES DEAN

1) GIANT	ART MOONEY		M-G-M
(From George Stevens *Giant*	AND HIS		EP-X1342
for Warner Bros.)	ORCHESTRA AND		
(Tiomkin-Webster)	CHORUS		
2) THEME FROM *EAST*	-----		
OF EDEN			
(From Warner Bros. Film			
East of Eden) (Rosenman)			
3) THEME FROM *REBEL*	-----		
WITHOUT A CAUSE			
(From Warner Bros. Film			
Rebel Without A Cause)			
4) THERE'S NEVER	-----		
BEEN ANYONE ELSE			
BUT YOU			
(From George Stevens *Giant*			
for Warner Bros.)			
(Tiomkin-Webster)			

JAMES DEAN ON CONGO DRUMS IN AN
AD-LIB JAM SESSION—BOB ROMEO
ON FLUTE

DEAN'S LAMENT	JAMES DEAN, BOB		Romeo
(B. Romeo-H. Prujan)	ROMEO		Records
			C100
			ASCAP

B/W			
JUNGLE RHYTHM	JAMES DEAN, BOB		
(B. Romeo-I. Lane)	ROMEO, DUKE		
	MITCHELL		

GIANT SOUND TRACK			Capitol
Warner Bros. Presents			Album
Dimitri Tiomkin's			EDM-773
Music From the Soundtrack			
of the George Stevens'			4- 45RPM *set*
Production *Giant*			

JAMES DEAN ALBUMS 33⅓ RPM

A TRIBUTE TO JAMES DEAN
Music from *GIANT, EAST OF EDEN, REBEL WITHOUT A CAUSE*
Played by Ray Heindorf and The Warner Bros. Orchestra
Columbia CL 940

A TRIBUTE TO JAMES DEAN
Selections from The Warner Bros. Pictures *EAST OF EDEN, REBEL WITHOUT A CAUSE,*
GIANT
Conducted by Leonard Rosenman
Imperial LP 9021

MUSIC JAMES DEAN LIVED BY
Side 1
1) The Story of James Dean
2) East of Eden
3) I'll Close My Eyes
4) Misunderstood
5) Give Me A Moment
6) Dream Lover

Side 2
1) Giant
2) There's Never Been Anyone Else But You
3) Rebel Without A Cause
4) Masquerade
5) Love Story
6) We Could Make Such Beautiful Music Together

Unique LP-109, Diamond-True HiFi Sound
A subsidiary of RKO Teleradio Pictures, Inc.

GIANT
Warner Bros. Presents Dimitri Tiomkin's Music
from the soundtrack of the George Stevens' Production
Capitol W773, High Fidelity Recordings also available in
Capitol Duophonic for Stereo Phonographs only DW773

THE JAMES DEAN STORY
A Different Kind of Motion Picture
Music from the Motion Picture Soundtrack
Composed and Conducted by Leith Stevens
Theme "Let Me Be Loved" by Jay Livingston and Ray Evans
Capitol W 881

9/30/55
Music from the Original Motion Picture Soundtrack
Music Composed and Conducted by Leonard Rosenman
MCA Records 2313

JAMES DEAN
Original Soundtrack Excerpts, Dialog and Music
from James Dean's Three Greatest Performances
East of Eden, Rebel Without A Cause, Giant
Warner Bros. Records

JAMES DEAN
Stars in Two of His Very Greatest Dramas!
Diary of a Young Fool and *The Dimly Lit Highway*
Movie God Records MSRIP-3000

THE JAMES DEAN STORY
Music From *East of Eden, Rebel Without A Cause, Giant*
Interviews with Friends of James Dean
Narrated by Steve Allen
Coral Records

*indicates flip side is also a song about James Dean

Index

This page intentionally left blank

Picture Credits

United Press International, 6; Courtesy Warner Bros., 33, 116 (right), 155, 164, 168, 170, 173, 181, 197, 224, 238, 245, 253, 259 (right), 305; Dennis Stock / Magnum, 10, 25 (left), 44, 176, 205, 211, 212, 214, 216, 218–219; Barbara Malarek, 16, 18, 25 (right), 35; Courtesy Adeline Nall, 40, 43, 46, 49, 50; Courtesy Santa Monica City College Archives, 61; Courtesy *The James Dean Story,* 64 (top); Courtesy Universal Pictures, 64 (bottom); Courtesy Father Peyton's TV Theater, 66; from a cartoon biography, *The Tragedy and Triumph of Jimmy Dean,* 86; *Pictorial Parade,* 89; Courtesy United Artists, 102, 103, 116 (left); Roy Schatt, 107, 109, 111, 123, 139; Courtesy Bill Gunn, 113; Joseph Abeles, viii, 121, 132; Courtesy Barbara Glenn, 146, 338; Courtesy *Rave* magazine, 147; Courtesy Museum of Modern Art / Film Stills Archive, 167, 256, 294, 302; Earl Leaf, 189; Courtesy *Whisper* magazine, 191; Globe Photos, 200; Courtesy Bev Long Dorff, 229; The Bettmann Archive, 235, 271; *Photoworld,* 259 (left); Dick Miller / Globe Photos, 269; Sanford Roth, 276, 288, 298, 327 (right), 343; Courtesy The Academy of Motion Picture Arts and Sciences, 293; *Chicago Tribune,* 312; *Marion Chronicle-Tribune,* 322; Courtesy Andy Warhol, 327 (left); Montage by Ray Johnson, 351.